THE
AMERICAN MUSICAL
LANDSCAPE

ƐꞰ
ꞓꝹ

The Ernest Bloch Professorship
of Music and the Ernest Bloch Lectures
were established at the University of California
in 1962 in order to bring distinguished figures
in music to the Berkeley campus from time to time.
Made possible by the Jacob and Rosa Stern
Musical Fund, the professorship was founded
in memory of Ernest Bloch (1880–1959),
Professor of Music at Berkeley
from 1940 to 1959.

THE ERNEST BLOCH PROFESSORS

1964 RALPH KIRKPATRICK
1965 WINTON DEAN
1966 ROGER SESSIONS
1968 GERALD ABRAHAM
1971 LEONARD B. MEYER
1972 EDWARD T. CONE
1975 DONALD JAY GROUT
1976 CHARLES ROSEN
1977 ALAN TYSON
1980 WILLIAM P. MALM
1981 ANDREW PORTER
1982 TON DE LEEUW
1983 JAMES HAAR
1985 RICHARD CRAWFORD
1986 JOHN BLACKING
1987 GUNTHER SCHULLER
1988 GEORGE PERLE
1989 LÁZLÓ SOMFAI
1993 SUSAN MCCLARY
1994 WYE J. ALLANBROOK
1995 JONATHAN HARVEY
1997 LYDIA GOEHR

The American Musical Landscape

The Business of Musicianship
from Billings to Gershwin

Updated Edition with a New Preface

RICHARD CRAWFORD

University
of California Press
Berkeley, Los Angeles, London

University of California Press
Berkeley and Los Angeles, California

University of California Press, Ltd.
London, England

First Paperback Printing 2000

Library of Congress Cataloging-in-Publication Data

Crawford, Richard, 1935–
    The American musical landscape / Richard Crawford.
        p.   cm. — (Ernest Bloch lectures)
    Includes bibliographical references and index.
    ISBN 0-520-22482-5 (alk. paper)
    1. Music—United States—History and criticism.   I. Title.
II. Series.
ML200.C68   1993   92-11237
780'.973—dc20

Printed in the United States of America

09   08   07   06   05   04   03   02   01   00
      10   9   8   7   6   5   4   3   2   1

The paper used in this publication meets the minimum
requirements of ANSI/NISO Z39.48-1992 (R 1997)
(*Permanence of Paper*). ♾

To my mother
and to the memory of
my father

CONTENTS

PREFACE TO THE PAPERBACK EDITION

The driving force behind *The American Musical Landscape,* conceived as a series of lectures in 1985 and published in somewhat expanded form (1993), was a desire to affirm the richness of American music as a field for historical study. More or less neglected by musicology at the time of my own graduate training (1959–61), the study of music in the United States began to blossom in the years leading up to the nation's bicentennial anniversary in 1976. Thanks in part to the bicentennial boost, by the mid-1980s, when I was invited to the University of California, Berkeley, campus as Ernest Bloch lecturer, a certain scholarly momentum had taken hold. The Sonneck Society for American Music was almost a decade old, the American Musicological Society had formed a Committee on the Publication of American Music, *The New Grove Dictionary of American Music* (1986) was nearing completion, and the number of graduate students making U.S. music their specialty was on the rise. American musicology, never closely in touch with American music making, seemed to be awakening to homegrown musical endeavor.

As one whose research on American music had begun in 1961, I recognized that the Bloch Lectures gave me a rare opportunity to speak on behalf of my field—a job that would call for both connecting and debunking. First and foremost, I hoped to show that American music studies linked up with issues worthy of any musicologist's attention. At the same time, while avoiding polemics, I wanted to undermine the basis of musicology's past indifference: the assumption that, musically speaking, the United States was a land where tradition, history, and musical quality ran thin.

Today, six years after the book was published (and nearly a decade

and a half after the lectures were delivered), I would judge its success
to be mixed. Let's start with the pluses. Having decided to devote the
final section to success stories—to chapters on an eighteenth- , a nine-
teenth- , and a twentieth-century composer who "reached a broad audience in his own century" and to one noteworthy piece of music—I
could hardly have done better than to choose Duke Ellington as my
twentieth-century example (chap. 6). At the time I made that choice I
was just starting to understand the scope of Ellington's achievement as
an artist. (George Gershwin was the only other figure I seriously considered.) As things turned out, Ellington's long life, vast output, adroit
career management, and unusual approach to composition, as well as
his race, offered a challenge that taught me more, I think, than if
Gershwin had served as my twentieth-century figure. Indeed, as Ellington's centennial year (1999) nears its end, his music, thanks in large
part to record reissues and the rise of jazz repertory ensembles, enjoys
a substantial presence among both performers and listeners. He is now
perceived not only as a key jazz figure (bandleader, pianist, arranger,
songwriter), an outstanding black musician, and an American original,
but a significant twentieth-century composer.[1]

Another plus, I believe, is the book's engagement with historiography. Whether or not it has so far had much influence on others, the
chance to read, critique, and interpret past general histories of music
in America has turned out to be a transforming event in my own scholarly course. Historians' treatment of the same event will obviously vary
with their outlook. But if one starts with the reality that classical composers, for all their prestige, have played only a marginal role in shaping this nation's musical life, the range of possible outlooks widens.
When I drafted the 1985 lecture that became chapter 1, I had no
thought of becoming a general historian of American music myself.
While refining that chapter's ideas over the next few years, however, I
found myself imagining how other authors might tackle the job. By
1993, when I accepted a commission to write a general history of music
in the United States, I had come to understand that performance and
American history, not composition and inherited categories of musical
style, held the key to our musical development. The roots of that outlook, which stands behind *America's Musical Life: A History* lie in my own
encounter with historiography.

Rereading the chapter on Gershwin's "I Got Rhythm," I now see it
as testimony that performance is the straw that stirs the drink in Ameri-

can music. (Gershwin, a songwriter by trade, was fond of telling interviewers that he wrote concert works like *Rhapsody in Blue,* and an opera like *Porgy and Bess,* because they might win a permanence that popular songs could never achieve. In defiance of his forecast, "I Got Rhythm" is just one of many Gershwin songs that survive today in performance.) Yet the original impulse behind chapter 7 was bibliographical, not historiographical. From the early 1980s into the early 1990s, I was interested in looking at musical genres through "core repertories": groups of compositions whose popularity could be documented objectively— that is, through bibliographical counting. While I would prefer to report otherwise, only in retrospect have I recognized the link between that approach and the realms of performance and historiography.

Here perhaps it will be useful to back up for a moment to the early 1960s and my doctoral dissertation on the Connecticut psalmodist Andrew Law (1749–1821), whose publishing schemes had baffled earlier scholars but whose personal papers turned up in the late 1950s, allowing most of the puzzles to be solved. Wrestling with those problems convinced me that establishing a solid bibliographical foundation for the work of America's first indigenous composers would be a worthwhile thing to do. And from 1969 through the latter 1980s, with substantial help from the research of Allen Perdue Britton and Irving Lowens, that is where I spent much of my energy as a scholar.[2] As part of that project I indexed all the music in all the tunebooks and determined, among other things, a core repertory of the tunes most often printed in those books.[3] The inspiration behind the whole endeavor was Oscar G. Sonneck's dictum, repeated often by Lowens, that "bibliography is the backbone of history" (see p. 25). Sonneck, the first person to tackle early American music as a full-fledged research scholar, counseled that only after reconstructing the bibliographical record could a music historian take the true measure of any older tradition. His bibliographical zeal and interest in musical topography fueled my engagement with America's deep musical past. Studying old tunebooks introduced me to a world that, while artistically remote, triggered the scholarly imagination. (Why was this turning out to be such an absorbing exercise?) The bibliographic work of those years complemented the foundation laid by others for a history of early American music that—though I myself for many years felt pulled in that direction—remains unwritten.

Chapter 4, on William Billings, comes out of those bibliographical investigations. Indeed, the part that I think may hold the most promise for further study is the attempt to figure out why—musical attractiveness aside—other compilers borrowed certain pieces from Billings and not others (see, e.g., pp. 138–39 and 144–47). So far, however, the Billings chapter seems not to have triggered much response. (As well as the widely-publicized Ellington and Gershwin [1998] centennial years, the 1990s saw the 250th anniversary of Billings's birth come and go in 1996 without much of a stir.) The indebtedness of the Gershwin chapter to a similar approach may be less obvious, but it is there. After studying multiple recordings of "I Got Rhythm" and its offspring, I turned my attention to other jazz favorites, eventually arriving at a core repertory of ninety-seven numbers that jazz musicians recorded most often during the given time period.[4] Intended at first to provide context for one Gershwin song, that enterprise turned into an attempt to connect specific pieces of music to a basic concept whose details were usually left vague: the concept of the jazz "standard." (One useful aspect of the jazz standards project lay in documenting the different musical genres—ragtime, blues, Tin Pan Alley songs, Broadway show tunes, instrumental originals—that fed into the list of compositions that earlier jazz musicians knew and performed repeatedly.) The Gershwin chapter, which is just one of the many tune biographies that deserve to be written, extended bibliographical chronicling to include discography. I learned much from writing it—a tribute to the collaborative chemistry that invites singers and players to create performance traditions around individual songs and dance numbers.

The life and music of George Frederick Root, the subject of chapter 5, have interested me since the mid-1970s, when I conducted public performances of his cantata *The Haymakers* (Part II). Though that work was written in 1855 for unsophisticated singers, I had the pleasure on several occasions to see groups of American college students warm to the task of singing it. Root's Civil War songs are still remembered, and his autobiography, *The Story of a Musical Life* (1891), is full of common sense and musical insight. Of all nineteenth-century American composers, the one who fit my criteria best was Stephen Foster. But Foster's music had already been the subject of a major study by William Austin (1975) and insightful treatment by such scholars as Charles Hamm and H. Wiley Hitchcock, not to mention a fully researched biography by John Tasker Howard. I chose Root as my nineteenth-century figure because he succeeded handily at what he tried to do as a musician, gracefully coped with success, and had received far less attention than Foster.

Root, who spent his composing life feeding the public's appetite for "elementary" pieces of music, had some astute things to say about musical categories (see esp. pp. 154–56 and 180ff., and the backnotes on pp. *309–10*). Yet *The American Musical Landscape*, while approaching this slippery, often contentious subject from more than one direction, ends up ducking a direct confrontation, neither endorsing any of the standard classification schemes nor proposing one of its own. In the years I worked on the book, feeling no need to account for the entire sweep of American musical activity, I critiqued other scholars' schemes but never quite moved beyond them. Not until later, when forced to tackle the issue of musical categories head on, did I discover a comprehensive scheme that seemed to work. It is interesting now to reread chapters 2 and 3 of *The American Musical Landscape*, noting which elements of the categorical outline I have adopted are found there and which ones are missing.

Here is how the Introduction to *America's Musical Life: A History* addresses the subject of categories:

> A historian grappling with the whole of American music cannot avoid encountering generic differences in the way that music has been created, performed, and transmitted—differences that explain why such terms as "classical," "popular," and "folk music" are part of the common vocabulary. While using familiar labels for these categorical varieties, however, I have linked them not to an aesthetic hierarchy but to something more concrete and practical: the degree of authority wielded by musical notation.

Readers of *The American Musical Landscape* will find the root of this last idea in chapter 2, pp. 58–65, where the tie between notation and economic opportunity is also made. They will also find a categorical distinction between "composers' music," for works whose notation embodies the authority of the composer, and "performers' music," for works whose notation is intended as an outline to be shaped by performers as they see fit (p. 65). Having distinguished between composers' music and performers' music in an earlier article, "American

Music and Its Two Written Traditions" (1984), I now revisited the issue without criticizing particular classical performers, as the article did, for taking popular-song notation as prescriptive. Yet I still did not see how composers' music and performers' music fit into a broader context in which unwritten music and recording played key roles.

An invitation in the early 1990s to contribute an article on music to *The Encyclopedia of the United States in the Twentieth Century,* edited by Stanley I. Kutler (1996), brought me closer to the outlook I was seeking. The assignment called for a perspective that would encompass the whole, at least from 1900 to the present. Sensing that general readers might find the categories of composers' music and performers' music too technical, I turned to chapter 3 of *The American Musical Landscape.* There musical classifications such as classical and popular, cultivated and vernacular, and serious and light music are discussed from the standpoint of performers' attitudes, which I summarize as leaning either toward "authenticity" or "accessibility" (pp. 85–88). Maintaining the emphasis on performance, I proposed in the new article that the United States, historically speaking, has been both an Old World colony and a New World democracy; and I argued that music in twentieth-century America had unfolded as an interplay not between two attitudes or musical levels but rather among three independent yet related "spheres": the colonial, the democratic, and the traditional, each emphasizing a different ideal or goal.

That model was in my mind in 1993 when I began work on the general history. But the categories (spheres) had obviously arisen in response to changing historical conditions and could not serve as a framework from the start. Moreover, during the course of writing my historical narrative, I cooled off on the idea of new labels. Thus the Introduction to *America's Musical Life: A History* calls the first category the "classical sphere," "ruled by the written directives of composers . . . a realm where works aspire to transcendence: to outliving the time and place of their creation." And it adds that the second category, "ruled by performers who shape composers' scores to fit the occasion, is the popular sphere, a realm where works aspire to accessibility: to acceptance by the target audience." Moreover, "with written compositions split into two categories, music that circulates orally may then be considered a third: the traditional (or folk) sphere, often linked with particular customs and ways of life. Tending to preserve each culture's linguistic and musical practices, the traditional sphere is ruled by a belief in continuity."

Chapter 12 of *America's Musical Life: A History* describes how a music publishing trade, beginning in the late 1780s, took shape during the next half-century around a market centered on amateur performers and home music making. Here the issue of categories enters my story for the first time. And the book thereafter

> offers an account of three spheres of musical activity, coexisting and sometimes interacting in a nonhierarchical continuum of time and space. The labels are not always crucial to the story: classical, popular, and folk examples are all described here simply as music. Yet the notion of categorical difference is built into the consciousness of Americans. And because the three spheres have been seen as hierarchically ordered (from high to low), the crossing of boundaries—as in George Gershwin's borrowing of jazz for concert hall works or the Beatles' use of a string quartet in the recording studio—has often carried a jolt of surprise and excitement. Moreover, as recordings have turned performances into permanent works, the classical sphere has lost its monopoly on the ideal of transcendence.[5]

The effect of technological change, and especially that of recorded performances, is taken up in chapter 3 of *The American Musical Landscape* (pp. 90–93), where the economics of jazz performance is also discussed in some detail (pp. 93–102). And pages 102–7 describe the possibility of categorical shift. They show that some music originating in the popular sphere and aspiring to accessibility has outlived the circumstances of its origin and begun to partake of authenticity—a value overlapping to a large extent with what I now call transcendence, the classical sphere's primary ideal.

Focusing on economics, notation, and performance, then, chapters 2 and 3 suggest the possibility of a categorical map that moves away from a highbrow/lowbrow hierarchy. Yet they fail to describe a real alternative. In retrospect, the lack of one makes this part of the book feel incomplete to me, though when it was published, my thinking had not gone beyond the point of raising questions that might in the future help clarify the issue.

These reflections aside, the strongest memories evoked by my own rereading of the book are musical: coming to appreciate more the surefooted artistry behind Billings's and Root's unpretentious vocal music; following and comparing dozens of improvisers as they negotiated Gershwin's "rhythm changes"; trying to figure out what Ellington was doing in the first few choruses of "Diminuendo in Blue" and feeling, when I finally did, that I had moved a bit closer to grasping what made this complex artist tick. More than any other scholarly project that I have tackled before or since, the Bloch Lectures conferred the freedom to define one's turf and to set one's own terms for performing on it. And I believe that some of the chapters (esp. 1, 6, and 7) benefit from having been delivered often as oral presentations. Working on *The American Musical Landscape* was a highly satisfying experience. I am delighted that this paperback printing will make the book more widely available.

NOTES TO THE PREFACE TO THE PAPERBACK EDITION

1. In 1985, when the Bloch Lectures were given, Ellington's music, apart from the popular songs he wrote, existed chiefly on phonograph records made by his orchestra (see p. 209). But in the years since, the growing availability of scores and parts has allowed others to play the music. In 1999, I heard two live all-Ellington concerts that, though in different ways, I found artistically wonderful: on March 12, in Fort Worth, Texas, by the University of North Texas jazz ensemble, directed by David Joyner; and on April 23, in Ann Arbor, Michigan, by the Lincoln Center Jazz Ensemble, directed by Wynton Marsalis.

2. The result was published as Allen Perdue Britton, Irving Lowens, and Richard Crawford, *American Sacred Music Imprints, 1698-1810: A Bibliography* (Worcester Mass.: American Antiquarian Society, 1990).

3. See Richard Crawford, ed., *The Core Repertory of Early American Psalmody*, vols. xi–xii in Recent Researches in American Music (Madison: A–R Editions, 1984). Nicholas Temperley's monumental *Hymn Tune Index*, 4 vols. (Oxford: Oxford University Press, 1998), carries the work of ordering much further, covering all published strophic hymnody in English from the 1560s through 1820.

4. See Richard Crawford and Jeffrey Magee, *Jazz Standards on Record, 1900–1942: A Core Repertory* (Chicago: Center for Black Music Research, 1992).

5. Richard Crawford, *America's Musical Life: A History* (New York: Norton, 2000), introduction.

PREFACE

This book comes out of a search for a better understanding of the conditions within which, since the eighteenth century, Americans have made music. Shortly after beginning work in the field early in the 1960s, I realized that key issues in my academic training—style criticism, genre studies, and the detailed analysis of musical scores, for example— matched poorly with the American music I was studying. Other approaches needed to be found. But what were they? Answers were slow to come. And they have taken shape only gradually, in the course of research on many different American topics.[1]

The American Musical Landscape seeks to identify big questions about American music that contain some of the smaller ones. It moves from the general to the specific: two complementary framing parts followed by a third devoted to case studies. Part I (chap. 1), inspired by the question "How have Americans understood American music?", traces the history of the writing of American music history. Part II (chaps. 2 and 3) outlines the key role of money in shaping this country's musical development and responds to the question "How have Americans supported the making of music?" It surveys the history of several musical professions in the United States, noting where patronage—the giving of money for music-making—has supplemented the marketplace. Part III offers four success stories: a chapter on each of three composers who reached a broad audience in his own century and another on one American composition. "William Billings (1746–1800) and American Psalmody" (chap. 4) looks for evidence about how the music of eighteenth-century New England's premier sacred composer circulated. "George Frederick Root (1820–95) and American Vocal Music" (chap.

5) provides a glimpse of a leading nineteenth-century teacher and song-writer and the marketplace in which he worked. "Duke Ellington (1899–1974) and His Orchestra" (chap. 6) examines certain aspects of a re-markable twentieth-century American composer's artistry. Finally, chapter 7, "George Gershwin's 'I Got Rhythm' (1930)," takes one piece of American music—a Broadway show song—and traces its unusual "bi-ography" in performance.

The view of American music history set forth here reflects several assumptions. It's a viewpoint that tries to take Old World musical prac-tices (especially European) into account, that encompasses both "cul-tivated" and "vernacular" traditions,[2] that looks beyond composers to the contributions of performers, that distrusts music history written free of economic considerations, and that holds the United States to have enjoyed a vital, distinctive musical life for more than two centuries.

My own experience has led to the not very original conclusion that historical observers see and hear what they are looking and listening for. *The American Musical Landscape* is not a nationalistic polemic. But it is written out of a belief that, to borrow a phrase from Ralph Ellison, in the field of music we Americans have tended to be "victims of various inadequate conceptions of ourselves."[3] While recognizing that our dem-ocratic legacy has led to a unique musical life, musicologists have not always known what to make of that life, much less measure or relate American achievements to Western music-making patterns that have shaped the field's outlook. *The American Musical Landscape* is one schol-ar's attempt to define and illuminate a few such achievements.

The manuscript was drafted in the winter of 1985. Chapters 1–2 and 4–7 were delivered, in somewhat different form, as a series of public lectures at the University of California at Berkeley (February–April 1985). Chapter 2 was expanded in the winter of 1990; chapter 3 was written in the spring and summer of 1990; and everything was revised again in the spring and summer of 1991. Parts of chapters 1, 2, and 3 have been given several times as public lectures, as have chapters 6 and 7, the latter two illustrated with recorded musical examples.

For the invitation to deliver these lectures as Ernest Bloch Professor at the University of California at Berkeley I have the Berkeley Music Department to thank. Bonnie C. Wade was Department Chair during my visit, and she could not have been more generous with wise counsel and moral support. Joseph Kerman, Anthony Newcomb, Philip Brett, Michael Keller, and Lawrence Levine all offered kindnesses that enhanced my stay on the Berkeley campus, and I benefited greatly from the chance to exchange ideas with Olly Wilson. Among students I worked with there, Marnie Dilling deserves special mention for her reviews of the lectures in *Cum notis variorum.*

John Spitzer, a former colleague at the University of Michigan, read the whole manuscript in its first draft and gave me excellent advice and support. I'm also grateful to H. Wiley Hitchcock for the encouragement he offered after an early reading. Among friends and colleagues who have seen individual chapters, I wish to acknowledge Mark Tucker, the late Martin Williams, Karl Kroeger, Michael Broyles, James Dapogny, David Brackett, and Nym Cooke, whose careful reading of chapter 4 tightened and improved it. A fellowship at the University of Michigan's Institute for the Humanities in 1989–90 allowed me to revise and expand Part II (chaps. 2 and 3). To James A. Winn, Director of the Institute, go special thanks for his role in creating an exemplary scholarly environment. Among colleagues there, Fatma Müge Göçek, June Howard, and Louise K. Stein all helped to steer me in productive directions. As part of my duties at the Institute, I also taught a seminar whose members (including Karen Ahlquist, Karen Harrod, Todd Levin, James Manheim, and Timothy Taylor) provided helpful feedback.

PART I
HISTORIES

· 1 ·

Cosmopolitan and Provincial: American Musical Historiography

Historical writing is judged on quality of information and authority of interpretation. Other scholars are its ultimate judges, for worth is measured by its usefulness to them. Quality of information depends upon accuracy and thoroughness. (Are the facts true? Are the sources comprehensive? Is the documentation complete?) But the quality of a study's information can be hard to judge apart from the author's interpretive perspective. As time passes, the past enlarges and, like the road already traveled, takes on new aspects. Facts about the past do not change. But as one's vantage point moves, the meanings of facts often change with it. New interpretive perspectives appear, sometimes strongly reacting against earlier ones. Such shifts can carry the temptation to dismiss earlier work, as if a perspective that one no longer accepts taints even the facts its author has brought to light. Fresh insights are sure to follow a break with past perspectives. But if such a break is allowed to relegate older histories to oblivion, it works against the building of a tradition of historical study.

A scholarly field forms a tradition of historical study when earlier writers on the same subject are recognized as predecessors, when their work is studied closely, when the questions they raise are identified, discussed, and debated, and when their findings are assimilated. A tradition of historical study progresses, in the sense in which E. H. Carr has defined historical progress, by transmitting the knowledge and experience of one generation of scholars to the next.[1] Entry into a musicological field with a tradition thus depends upon mastering a core of scholarly writings, which themselves deal with a certain musical repertory and are centered on fundamental issues, subject to changing interpretations and approaches.

Within American music, one can find a few fields in which such a tradition has formed. The music of Charles Ives is one. In Ives studies, and a few others as well, bibliographical and editorial foundations have been laid, biographical investigations undertaken, local inquiries launched, and style-based books and articles written. In such fields, an agenda has been set and a process of distillation begun. Scholars have mapped the terrain, data are more known than unknown, major issues have been defined, and interpretive refinements are proceeding apace.[2]

No such tradition has formed for historical studies in American music as a whole. Since 1955, Gilbert Chase, Wilfrid Mellers, H. Wiley Hitchcock, and Charles Hamm, four respected scholars, have each written a history of American music from earlier times to the present. Chase's, Hitchcock's, and Hamm's books were published for the American college textbook market, while Mellers's was brought out by a trade publisher.[3] As a group, the four books are most remarkable for having so little to do with each other, either in approach or in territory covered. Hamm's work, the most recent of the four, contains the following statement: "Though I have dealt with a wider range of music than is found in any earlier histories of music in the United States, much has been left out. In fact, one could easily write another book, perhaps of equal length, dealing with the music I have chosen to exclude. Perhaps I will undertake such a book myself one day."[4] Hamm's words suggest that historians of American music have yet to agree what the history of American music *is;* the four books I've mentioned bear out this suggestion.

Chase's book is comprehensive by the lights of its time, and it is written with the conviction and documentary command of a seminal work. Chase breaks sharply with earlier histories by devoting more than half his book to folk and popular music, which he claims as our chief source of musical vitality.[5] Mellers praises Chase's work as "admirable" and then proceeds to go his own way, saying little about folk music or the years before 1900. He distinguishes elements in American music that are "genuine and meaningful" from those that are not,[6] and he concentrates on music that shows twentieth-century American composers coping successfully with a commercial environment—with special emphasis on composers and players in the jazz tradition. Hitchcock, who wrote the slimmest volume of the four, acknowledges the influence of Chase's work on his own, but his account includes folk music only peripherally.[7] His division of the nineteenth century into two streams—the "cultivated" and the "vernacular" traditions—has been widely borrowed. But not by Hamm, who deals with his predecessors in a respectful footnote, then strikes out on an entirely new path, concentrating on music brought to the New World from Europe and Africa and changed in its subsequent history here. Folk and popular musics fill a large proportion of his book, as they do Chase's. But unlike Chase, Hamm cares most about reception—about the music that has won the widest audience; and he flaunts folkloric values by claiming "contaminated" music as America's "most characteristic and dynamic" musical product.[8]

These contrasts may be pursued a bit more through glimpses of further details. Chase violates chronology by ending his book with a chapter on Charles Ives, for him the culminating figure in American music, because, "first and alone among American composers," Ives "was able to discern and to utilize the truly idiosyncratic and germinal elements of our folk and popular music."[9] With Ives identified as the Messiah, one tends to notice in the earlier parts of Chase's text prophecies of his eventual coming. Mellers's scholarly apparatus—a bibliography of books running barely to a page and a discography of more than fifty pages—shows that he approached the subject with open ears if with somewhat closed mind. Hitchcock balances his coverage between eras, genres, and approaches and preaches the gospel that American musical history is coherent. (He lacks the curmudgeonly streak of Chase and Mellers; if anything on the American music scene makes Hitchcock mad, the reader doesn't find out about it.) Hamm begins by announcing that several new record series are the most significant recent developments in American musical research. And his book reflects his own encounters as a listener with an unusually wide range of American musics.

These incongruities reflect the different backgrounds and interests of our four authors and the differing sponsorships under which their books appeared.[10] But more than that, they reflect the absence in America of a canon of musical masterworks and composers—the kind of canon on which European musical historiography centers.[11] One might guess that our historians' freedom to define their subject is a recent phenomenon—part of the general social reorientation that followed World

War II. But in fact, that freedom (or lack of continuity) goes back much further. It is present from the beginning of the writing of American music history. And it reflects the strain of randomness that, over nearly a century and a half of serious study, has run through histories of American music. If one thinks of pluralism as an American trait, perhaps it is especially fitting that such disparate figures as Hood, Ritter, Mathews, Elson, Howard, Chase, and Mellers have written histories of American music. For in background, outlook, taste, and training, it is hard to imagine a more various crew of historians undertaking the same mission. That that mission, even now, remains something of a pioneering endeavor—a trip whose route and destination are up to the traveler—testifies to the field's schismatic legacy. At the same time, it invites reflection on that legacy and the benefits of historiographical study.

Our historians and works, however various, do hold certain things in common. All take Europe as a starting point. Indeed, no fact about the writing of American music history is more characteristic than the looming presence of Europe. Scholars of music are trained and acculturated to think of European music history as their norm. Whether as provider, exploiter, or authority figure, whether in the foreground or background, Europe is the powerful "other" in the story that Chase, Mellers, Hitchcock, and Hamm tell. All agree that the U.S.A. is a European colony—an outpost of European settlement on a faraway continent. All focus chiefly on musical practices created in the Old World (whether Europe or Africa) and extended to the New. All concentrate, to one degree or another, on the *process* of extension, and especially on how Old World practices have been accepted, altered, or ignored. Finally, all have described the extension of Old World practices to the New in value-laden terms; colonialism, whether in politics, economics, or music, is a hard topic to treat from the cool, objective posture that scholars are trained to strike.

As for discontinuities, from the bird's-eye vantage point of today, the histories fall into two groups, depending upon their response to the issue of colonialism. It was on this point, in fact, that Chase broke decisively with the historical perspective of his predecessors. The issue can be drawn clearly by referring to the eighteenth century, a time when American musical life was comparatively simple. A musicologist studying the American scene before 1800 soon recognizes the existence of two sharply contrasting musical ways of life. One was carried on by musicians who took their direction from creative and intellectual centers abroad; the other involved those who resisted, or reinterpreted, or, most likely, failed to receive messages from such centers. The first group worked to extend Old World hegemony; the second, seldom conscious of more than the outlines of Old World practices, found their own ways of making music within the general run of their daily lives. The first group was small, urban, and professional, led by immigrants. The second group, larger by far, lacked intellectual focus, though most members hailed from American villages and the countryside.[12]

Here is the kind of dichotomy with which a historian can work and play. Though it is surely too black and white to account for all musicians in colonial America, it does define tendencies inescapable then and still present today. By doing so, it fixes a point of view from which American musical life as a whole can be studied. Once the two polar opposites are labeled—we'll call the first cosmopolitan and the second provincial— we have a typology that, if the labels are separated from connotations of approval or disapproval, can help to order our view of the past.

Like American musicians of the eighteenth century, historians of American music have tended to line up in two camps. The cosmopolitan school, which dominates the historiographical outlook through John Tasker Howard (and World War II), has been inclined to find European hegemony inevitable, or healthy, or both. The provincial outlook, which informs histories of New England psalmody written in the 1840s and 1850s and resurfaces in parts of Arthur Farwell and W. Dermot Darby's volume of 1915, came to full fruition only in the 1950s. Chase and Hamm have been its chief spokesmen. Rejecting Europe as a musical model for America, its advocates have concentrated on the deeds of musicians who seem to have done the same, finding value chiefly in divergence from European practices. For the cosmopolitan school, technical mastery and the acceptance of European forms and aesthetic principles are signs of musical vitality. For the provincial school, these traits are less highly prized than originality, experimentation, eclecticism, and an absence of self-consciousness.

In shaping their accounts to fit a particular point of view, historians of American music have merely borrowed a trick of the trade available to any writer seeking to order a large stock of information. Henry James gave an eloquent description of this technique shortly after the death in August 1891 of James Russell Lowell, his mentor, teacher, and friend.

7

James observed that after a man dies those who knew him "find his image strangely simplified and summarized." He continued:

> The hand of death, in passing over it, has smoothed the folds, made it more typical and general. The figure retained by the memory is compressed and intensified; accidents have dropped away from it and shades have ceased to count; it stands, sharply, for a few estimated and cherished things, rather than, nebulously, for a swarm of possibilities. We cut the silhouette, in a word, out of the confusion of life, we save and fix the outline, and it is with his eye on this profiled distinction that the [writer] speaks.[13]

James was writing here about biography, but his words apply to the writing of history, too. For, once their research has uncovered the human achievements of the past, historians explore all available ways of revealing them: summarizing, intensifying, and casting certain events into relief in part by deemphasizing, even omitting others—by "cut[ting] the silhouette . . . out of the confusion of life." If we accept James's description as relevant to history, we are reminding ourselves that, every bit as much as an act of compilation, the writing of history is an act of clarification, compression, and surgery.

James's image of cutting a silhouette from the disorder of life is especially apt. In the first place, a silhouette fuses data and perspective into one image, which is the way they appear in written history. In the second, just as a silhouette requires a deft gesture of the artist's hand to catch the likeness, historical writing depends upon the writer's skill in holding many facts and ideas simultaneously in the mind and catching from among them precisely those that clarify—first for the writer, then for the reader—the outline and texture of the matter at hand.

The image of a field whose polarities are "cosmopolitan" and "provincial" is precisely the kind of silhouette that James described. It has served American music historians well, helping them both to order their information and to judge the music with which they have dealt. But it's important to remember that the image comes from historians' own beliefs, values, and experiences. Historical "silhouettes," formed from facts seen and heard, are summoned by the historian's own habits of seeing and hearing. Who historians are, the background and training they bring to their task, the motives behind their studies, the stake they hold in the outcome—all of these things shape the history they write.

Although the first comprehensive history of American music was a product of the 1880s, two books of narrower scope set the stage for it. Their early dates and their consistent use by later historians gives them pride of place as fundamental works of American music history. And so it is with Hood and Gould, pioneer historians of American psalmody, that our survey begins.

George Hood (1807–82) was born in Topsfield, Massachusetts. "Early in life," according to a contemporary, "he began teaching as a profession, and, in turn, was teacher of a public school, of church music, of a ladies' seminary, and finally became minister of the Gospel."[14] After his ordination as a Presbyterian clergyman (1848), Hood's involvement with music decreased. But for a decade beginning in the mid-1830s— from about the time he attended a Boston singing convention led by Lowell Mason and George J. Webb (1835)—he was occupied with the history he published in 1846.[15]

Hood wrote as a pious Christian in search of the origins of New England psalmody, the musical tradition in which he himself was a participant. He harbored no illusions about the place of musical artistry in the environment he described. "We know that our music was mean," he admitted. But by gathering the past "carefully up," he hoped to "set it with the future, that the contrast may appear the more bright and beautiful."[16] It was not Hood's style to ridicule earlier practices, however sharply they contrasted with those of the present. Like other New Englanders of his time, who, in writing the histories of their families and their communities, honored and venerated their forefathers, Hood came to admire New England's sacred music pioneers. For him, the figures meriting the deepest respect were the Reverends John Cotton, Thomas Symmes, Cotton Mather, and other clergymen who led the reforms of sacred music in the seventeenth and early eighteenth centuries. "Never was a discussion in this country conducted by better men, or men of better minds," wrote Hood.[17] While promising to carry his account "to the beginning of the present century," Hood focused on earlier times, when sacred music was a matter of deep concern to these redoubtable men. Thus, Hood's history is about the implanting of English psalmody in the colonies, the Regular Singing controversy, and the founding of singing schools and choirs.

Having chosen an antiquarian subject, Hood discovered how elusive historical documents could be. "The matter has been gathered by much labor, time and expense from different parts of the Union, and frequently in very small portions. The labor has been almost incredible. To show something of its difficulty, there are six consecutive lines that were unfinished more than one year." But once the documents were in hand, he determined "to give the facts as he found them."[18] He did so chiefly by letting the original authors tell their own stories. Of Hood's first 150 pages, two-thirds are direct quotations from seventeenth- and eighteenth-century writers. Several more pages are devoted to a chronological listing of American sacred tunebooks, based on his own collection and that of Lowell Mason. Hood proposed that this list be completed by others and that the books themselves be collected and deposited in the Massachusetts Historical Society. "In the future," he explained, they will "tell the history of the past, far more impressively than the page of history."[19]

Here, in a nutshell, is Hood's historiographical philosophy. For him, documents were primary, historical opinion and interpretation secondary. Hood's appreciation of the value of historical documents is distinctly modern. It explains why, while other nineteenth-century histories of American music lie neglected on library shelves, Hood's *History of Music in New England* has provided the foundation for all later accounts. Hood's struggle to find accurate information on the remote past took on the character of a passionate quest, at one point provoking the following outburst: "When we see the devastation that is almost universally made, with old books, papers, and records, valuable for their historic information, by brutes in human form, what language is harsh enough to denounce such impious destruction?"[20]

It's hard to imagine such thoughts crossing the mind of Nathaniel D. Gould (1781–1864), whose history followed Hood's by seven years.[21] Although Gould, like Hood, restricted his account to psalmody, he shared neither Hood's love for research nor his fascination with origins. Gould's story picks up where Hood's left off: with the career of William Billings, who for Gould exemplifies the "dark age" (1770–1805) when psalmody in America began to be carried on largely free of religious control.[22] Its main subject, however, and its method are more autobiographical and practical than historical. Gould's last eight chapters concentrate on the singing school since 1800. As teacher of some 115 singing schools and "not less than *fifty thousand*" scholars, Gould could look back over half a century in the field—he was seventy-two years old when his book appeared—and see himself not as "a mere compiler, but a busy actor in the scenes he has described."[23]

Born in Bedford, Massachusetts, Gould opened his first singing school in 1799 and from that time followed the teacher's trade, chiefly in New Hampshire and Massachusetts.[24] His authority as a historian varied with his chronicle's proximity to his own experience. After an erratic sprint through Billings's American predecessors, he announced: "We now leave the traditional history of church music, and enter a field where, for the last fifty years or more, we are enabled, from experience, observation and information, to vouch for the facts we relate."[25] There follows a participant's account of the workings of the New England singing school during the late eighteenth and early nineteenth centuries. Gould wrote in the belief that "unless accomplished by some one soon, the history must forever remain a mere matter of hearsay."[26] He evoked vividly the world of early American choral singers and their eccentricities. These were the conditions we teachers faced in those backward days, Gould told his readers, and I know because I was there.

Gould's underlying theme was that sacred music, a powerful aid to religious devotion when sung to God's glory, was vulnerable to corruption for profane ends. In Gould's account, human nature seems perpetually at odds with the proper employment of sacred music. To gain musical skill as a performer of psalmody is to be tempted to forget its sacred purpose. Tippling teachers, status-seeking singers, choristers who sleep through sermons, viol players who tune at distracting length, parishioners who criticize the choir's singing: These are the characters in Gould's tale for whom psalmody had become human display drained of sacred content. American sacred music-making achieved its true purpose, Gould believed, only when carried on under the scrutiny and control of religious leaders.

Gould's theme was a familiar one in the Calvinist tradition. Yet his account is no jeremiad. He took a bemused pleasure in his countrymen's musical superstitions, as in his tale of the congregation in which erstwhile foes of instruments in church were won over when told that the sounds accompanying their Sunday morning psalm singing were those of the "Godly Viol."[27] The relish with which Gould cataloged the "improprieties" of American choral singers seems rooted not in a reformer's zeal to condemn but a patriarch's inclination to temper judgment with humane understanding.

That a wide gulf separates Frédéric Louis Ritter (1834–91) from his predecessors is clear to even the most casual observer. That gulf may be measured by time (three decades elapsed between Gould's work and Ritter's *Music in America*),[28] by scope (Ritter's work encompasses the whole of significant music-making in America as he saw it), and by the author's outlook. For it was Ritter, writing as a scholar grounded in a knowledge of European music history, who introduced the cosmopolitan perspective. At a time when New Englanders were still debating whether the Bible authorized them "to sing or read the psalms in the church," Ritter reminded his readers, Bach and Handel had already begun "to fashion their immortal strains." And while "the child Mozart was astonishing the European musical world as a performer and a composer," on this side of the Atlantic the likes of Lyon, Flagg, and Bayley, borrowing from "the weak and often insipid strains of a Tansur, Williams, [or] others of that stamp," were compiling their rudimentary tunebooks.[29] Ritter brought to his work the experience of a historian who had already written a two-volume *History of Music* (1870–74). Moreover, on the very same date that Ritter's *Music in America* was published, a companion volume, *Music in England,* also appeared. "When I determined to write the history of musical development in the United States," he explained, "I found, that in order to enable my readers to understand the peculiar beginnings and first growth of that development, an insight into the history of musical culture in England was desirable. I therefore concluded to introduce the history of music in America, by that of the immediately preceding period in England."[30]

If Hood had written to reconstruct the record of a forgotten age and Gould to preserve hallowed memories, Ritter stated a more complex agenda:

> [to present] a faithful mirror of past music life in the United States, to accentuate that which is in accord with a true art spirit, ... to expose ... that which is puerile, hollow, pretentious, fictitious, and a great hindrance to progress; to give their justly

merited due to those musicians who, by means of great exertions in the interests of higher musical culture among the American people deserve the grateful remembrance of the present . . . generation; to dispel, as far as possible, the errors and false views still entertained in Europe regarding musical affairs in America.[31]

These words introduce an account of American music history deeply imbued with cosmopolitan values. Ritter was a native Alsatian, trained musically in Europe, who arrived in this country in 1856, directed choruses and orchestras in Cincinnati and New York, who composed vigorously throughout his life, and who served as professor of music at Vassar College from 1867 until his death in 1891.

For Ritter, the reformed Calvinists of England and America were religious zealots who stifled music's development as either an independent art or a characteristic folk expression. Ritter treated the Puritan attitude with undisguised scorn. He found it the chief source of a religious climate that, in his judgment, lay like a wet blanket over American musical life. Even in the nineteenth century, he wrote, America was full of "church-people"—people "opposed to all aesthetic tendencies that cannot be rendered absolutely subordinate to ecclesiastical power."[32] That state of mind, Ritter believed, robbed Americans of all incentive to develop their musicianship beyond an elementary level. Ritter's acid comments on nineteenth-century psalmody provide a succinct measure of the distance between the cosmopolitan and provincial outlooks of his day:

In the time of Hastings, Mason, [and] Gould, the New-England psalm-tune teacher thought, on the whole, little of the professional musician, who was not able to quote the Bible on each and every occasion, and who could not lead a revival meeting. The professional musician, on the other hand, thought little of the psalm-tune teacher, who, in general, could not play, sing or compose.[33]

Ritter's European birth, his forthright antiprovincialism, and his often sarcastic pen have combined to give him a terrible reputation. It has become almost obligatory for writers on American music, if they mention Ritter's name, to take a shot at him.[34] If historians worked by deduction, one could infer from Ritter's values that, borrowing from

Hood and Gould, he would polish off the early years of American music in short order and then move on to greener pastures. He doesn't. Instead, he devotes almost a quarter of his book to the eighteenth century, basing his own account on Hood (whom he admired) and Gould (whom he didn't) and on his own research in primary sources from the period, some of which he acquired for his own library.[35] Ritter's reputation might serve as a cautionary note to the foreign-born critic of America's music. He is remembered as an ardent Columbiaphobe and a prejudiced man, even though his evaluations of American musical practices are presented and documented as those of a reputable historical craftsman, working from research and personal observation.[36]

Ritter's history focuses chiefly upon two processes in nineteenth-century American musical life. In the foreground is the implantation of cultivated European music in America. (What European musicians traveled, performed, or settled here? What European music did Americans hear and perform, and in what circumstances?) More in the background is a second process: that of Americans struggling to free themselves from the legacy of musical Puritanism. (What institutions offered American singers and players the chance to widen their technical and aesthetic horizons beyond the requirements of the simplest church and instructional music?) Ritter describes the two streams of American musical development separately. In doing so, he concentrates all the interpretive precision he can muster upon these questions, which, for him, were the central ones of American music history. Both his questions and his answers show that he understood the complexity of his subject. Ritter had worked long and widely enough as a musician in America to appreciate the achievements of musicians who had come before him, even as he took them to task for their outlook. Ritter's work has sometimes been read as an ideological tract. But his treatment of the battle between cosmopolitan and provincial forces is also an account emanating directly from his own practical experience as a music-maker.

Six years after Ritter's history was published, *A Hundred Years of Music in America. An Account of Musical Effort in America during the Past Century . . .* , (etc., etc.) appeared in print.[37] Here was a book whose size and comprehensive scope seemed to promise the whole story. The introduction predicted: "We are confident that no reader will rise from a careful examination of this book unimpressed by the richness of the material here presented."[38] The richness turns out to be biographical.

The book is first and foremost a gallery, its text recording the lives of some 500 musicians, supplementing the "two hundred and forty portraits" (i.e., photographs) of the men and women whose likenesses stare with unrelieved dignity from its pages. "None of the sciences, arts and industries," the reader is told,

> compare with music in the extent, universality, directness or beauty of the beneficence with which it dowers the human family. . . . Yet what other has been so neglected in that kind of honor which places its representative men in enduring eminence upon fame's immortal scroll? . . . The priests of music . . . are alone left to the transient and evanescent reward of passing praise. To what more eloquent task can type . . . be placed, than to that of rescuing these from ingratitude and forgetfulness, and giving them, both for the present and for posterity, enduring place and honor?[39]

A Hundred Years is based on information gathered from the subjects themselves "or their immediate representatives . . . at immense expense of trouble and patience."[40] The early chapters, drawn from Hood, Ritter, and other secondary sources, are written as historical narrative. But once the time of Lowell Mason is reached, most chapters turn into successions of brief biographies, dwelling upon the positive achievements of their subjects, introduced and connected with narrative explanation. The progress of music education, for example, is shown by two whopping chapters, filling some 200 pages with accounts of the lives of music teachers. The book's tone is hagiographical. One imagines, in fact, that data were extracted from these priests and priestesses of music with a promise to accentuate the positive. Nevertheless, the book shows a common sense awareness of the process of colonization from a perspective different from Ritter's.[41] Topics seldom covered in histories are broached here: the importance of publicity in musical life, the different values that separate the pianist's world from that of the singer, or American singers' difficulties with English (attributed "in part" to foreign training "and in part to their own mistaken ideals of . . . singing of the highest class").[42]

Although no author claimed *A Hundred Years,* it was the brainchild of W. S. B. Mathews (1837–1912). A native New Englander and a pianist,

Mathews lived in Chicago for most of his mature life, working as a teacher, journalist, and critic. *A Hundred Years* describes him "as a music educator, in the widest sense of the term," explaining: "his higher vocation is that of an intermediary between purely musical ideas and purely literary ideas, in which sphere he has been the means of conveying to literary life something of the impression that music makes upon those who understand it intimately."[43] This characterization suggests how Mathews's book can best be read: as the work of a facilitator, a man who understood and recognized the many different levels and lingoes of his subject, who combined the pride of a provincial enthusiast with the experience of a cosmopolitan critic, and who could communicate with a broad readership. Mathews's work is most valuable as a compendium of firsthand data about American musical life in the second half of the nineteenth century, compiled by a man who experienced, understood, and sympathized with an unusually wide range of it.

The early years of the twentieth century saw the publication of three new histories of American music (1904–15), each commissioned to fill a niche in a larger series of books.[44] In contrast to the histories of Ritter and Mathews, all are works more of compilation and summary than of original research. While varied in approach and content, all seem rooted in a wish to illuminate and assess the present-day scene. All attempt comprehensiveness. All seek, with the help of a growing secondary literature, to cover earlier periods. Nevertheless, the authors all show more interest in describing the present state of American music-making than in trying to discover how it got that way. In all three histories, the reader is shown a musical culture whose potential outweighs its achievements. Louis C. Elson, in comparing American and European musical life, expresses hope for the future but finds his own country's musical training misdirected: too much emphasis on solo performance, too little on ensembles and music appreciation, and the whole carried on too hastily for students to digest.[45] W. L. Hubbard warns that, although American musicians are overcoming geographical isolation and "the utilitarian spirit always in evidence in young nations," the United States would become "a true home of art" only when it produced a composer of "genius."[46] Arthur Farwell (writing in the book coedited by W. Dermot Darby), interpreting musical life as a reflection of "national ideals," sees the present as a time when "the many are striving to obtain [what] has been the exclusive possession of the few." That process, he predicts, will soon transform the art of music as practiced on American shores.[47]

Elson's, Hubbard's, and Farwell and Darby's histories were all written by experienced writers who were inexperienced historians. In an age where reliable musical information could be hard to come by, these men worked to supply it and hence to meet a public need. But they were no explorers of the mysteries of the past. Elson (1848–1920), a Bostonian born and bred, worked there all his life, chiefly as a music critic for the *Daily Advertiser* and a teacher of music history and theory at the New England Conservatory.[48] Elson's interest in folk music and patriotic song had also helped to inspire his *National Music of America and Its Sources* (Boston, 1900). Among the others involved in this historiographical flurry, composer Arthur Farwell (1872–1952) seems to have held the highest personal stake in telling the story of American musical life. In four cross-country trips (1903–7), he had presented lecture recitals on contemporary American music and experienced musical conditions in the United States firsthand.[49] Less is known about the other two authors, and nothing about their interest in American music. William Lines Hubbard (1867–1951) worked off and on from 1891 to 1907 as music critic and editor of the *Chicago Tribune*—he was also dramatic editor (1902–7)—while teaching singing and living in Europe from 1893 to 1898.[50] W. Dermot Darby (1885–1947), Farwell's coeditor, was a native of Ireland. Trained in England and New York, Darby served as secretary of the Modern Music Society in New York in 1916 and helped to edit *The Art of Music* (1914–17) but has left no further mark on the written record.[51]

Elson's *The History of American Music* is the closest thing to a coffee-table book that the field has yet produced and, if later editions signal success, the most successful before Howard's *Our American Music*.[52] Printed on thick, glossy paper, bound so that it will lie open, supplied "with twelve full-page photogravures [the first one of the author himself] and one hundred and two illustrations in the text,"[53] it is a handsome volume by any measure, and especially so when compared with its modestly produced predecessors. (At nearly three pounds, it weighs in at about the level of a volume of *The New Grove*.) Elson's work owed its sumptuous format to the circumstances of its issue. As part of a series edited by John C. Van Dyke, a critic, professor of the history of art at Rutgers College, and a president of the National Institute of Arts and Letters, it was designed to sit on the shelf next to such companion volumes as Lorado Taft's *The History of American Sculpture* and Samuel Isham's *The History of American Painting.*

Earlier historians of American music had begun their books by announcing why they were writing them and what they hoped to show. In Elson's history, however, the only prefatory statement was the general editor's. "This series of books brings together for the first time the materials for a history of American art," Van Dyke announced.

> The present volumes begin with colonial times, and carry the record down to the year 1904. They are intended to cover the graphic, the plastic, the illustrative, the architectural, the musical, and the dramatic arts, and to recite the results in each department historically and critically. That the opinions ventured should be authoritative, the preparation of each volume has been placed in the hands of an expert,—one who practices the craft whereof he writes.[54]

Of Elson's history, Van Dyke notes: "Many of the events here narrated occurred but yesterday or are happening to-day, and hence have little perspective for the historian." In *The History of American Music,* he adds, "the widely scattered facts have been brought together and arranged sequentially that they might tell their own story and point their own conclusion." Elson's history shows every sign of having been written to specifications set by its editor.

Though it covers different ground, Elson's *The History of American Music* shares with Mathews's a topical organization. It begins with the New England Puritans and proceeds to the middle of the nineteenth century, tracing the founding and progress of performing institutions—choral societies, orchestras, opera troupes—and the building of concert halls. At this point, it goes off in a new direction. First, by introducing chapters on American "folk music" (ten pages on American Indians, one and a half on black Americans, and five on Stephen Foster) and patriotic music (e.g., "The Star-Spangled Banner," "The Battle Hymn of the Republic"), it steps outside a chronological framework. Then, in a sequence of seven chapters, it reviews American composers' contributions to the major genres of art music, concentrating almost entirely on living composers. The final chapters return to a topical approach, treating, in turn, American women in music, American writing about music, and music education. But with nearly half of the book devoted to them, the central role in Elson's *History of American Music* is occupied by composers of the present and recent past and their music.[55]

Elson documents the historical sections of his history and identifies sources in a bibliography. (He's the first historian of American music to include one.) Mathews's history is mentioned in the bibliography but remains untapped in the text. Ritter comes in for more attention. For Elson, Ritter was a "profound musician" who "in the domain of music literature" was "as important a figure as any in America after Dwight and Thayer."[56] Of Ritter's history of music in America, however, Elson writes:

> Dr. Ritter approached his subject with little sympathy. . . . Our national music did not appeal to him deeply, and of the American composers he had not a word to say. . . . Dr. Ritter, however much he labored for us, worked from without, not from within; he was among us, but not of us. He could not realize what a group of good American composers was growing up around him.[57]

The *History of American Music* that appeared in W. L. Hubbard's The American History and Encyclopedia of Music (1908–10) carries on its title page only Hubbard's own name as volume "editor," which means that he wrote the chapters whose author is unnamed.[58] Hubbard's *History* has a shape all its own. It begins with chapters by two leading American musicians: George W. Chadwick on living American composers (chiefly Bostonians)[59] and Frank Damrosch on public school music.[60] Then it takes up American music outside the concert hall: "Music of North American Indians," "Negro Music and Negro Minstrelsy," "Popular Music," and "Patriotic and National Music." By the time the New England Puritans appear on the scene (p. 138), their position as musical founding fathers is seriously weakened. In earlier histories, the past is the foundation of the present. But Hubbard's organization undermines the past as a shaping force, clearing the way for the subject he seems most eager to discuss: the United States as a musical democracy.[61]

The distinctiveness of Hubbard's work lies not in the survey of "the aesthetic side" of American music that occupies numbers seven through twelve of its fourteen unnumbered chapters but in its discussion of a widening range of American people's music. Hubbard deals respectfully even with genres absent from earlier histories, including college songs (pp. 88–89), gospel hymns (pp. 89–90), songs of Tin Pan Alley (pp. 83–87), the Broadway stage (pp. 97–99), and the American wind band (pp. 285–87). Hubbard is not known to have written elsewhere on American music, either before or after his history appeared. Nor, like Elson, did he state his historiographical philosophy or describe his book's purposes. On the strength of what he wrote, however, Hubbard may be judged a musician with broad tastes and a man who saw American music whole in a way very different from those who wrote its history before him.[62]

Music in America, the third pre-World War I history, bears the marks of a collaborative enterprise even more openly than its immediate predecessors. Arthur Farwell contributed the introduction and two chapters on living composers. His coeditor, W. Dermot Darby, wrote the nine chapters that carry the historical chronicle from the Puritans to the late nineteenth century. And specialist collaborators were brought in for the rest.[63] Like Hubbard's *History, Music in America,* embedded in a multivolume set, seems to have made little impact on American music historiography, except for its introduction, which some decades later helped to inspire Chase's fresh approach.

Farwell wrote his introduction as a composer involved in American musical life and deeply concerned with its character. Farwell's concern ran in two complementary streams. As founder of the Wa-Wan Press (1901–12), he was an early leader of the movement toward American musical nationalism. As a critic for *Musical America* (1909–13) and supervisor of New York City's municipal concerts (1901–13), he was also active in an effort to bring Americans into contact with music. In choosing Farwell to contribute to *Music in America,* series editor-in-chief Daniel Gregory Mason had selected a man who believed, first, that American composers should seek to address as large a public as possible and, second, that the public, when given a chance to hear good music in the right surroundings, would prefer it over bad.

"Prophecy, not history, is the most truly important concern of music in America," Farwell began his introduction. "What a new world, with new processes and new ideals, will do with the tractable and still unformed art of music; what will arise from the contact of this art with our unprecedented democracy—these are the questions of deepest import in our musical life in the United States."[64] The key issue of music in America, in other words, was not its past but its future.

Farwell imagined the history of American music as a three-stage process: "appreciation, creation, and administration."[65] By appreciation, Farwell meant the New World's coming to grips with the music of the Old. Creation meant New World musicians' composition of music expressing the American nation's spirit and suited to the needs of her citizens. Administration meant the establishment of a musical life that brought American citizens into contact with the music of American composers.

Farwell believed that, in ideal conditions, appreciation would bring about creation, which would then flourish in close contact with an informed audience recruited through effective administration. But in America, conditions had not proved ideal. Too much energy was still being spent on appreciation at a time when "the evolution, broadly, of America as an appreciative nation has been fulfilled, and it can from now on find no true musical progress except as a creative nation."[66] The "creative epoch" of American musical history had begun, Farwell believed, and American composers occupied a favored position. Having benefited from rigorous German training, they had been saved from its hazards by other influences: the diverse ethnic roots of the American people, the "deluge" of modern music from non-German nations, and the unearthing of folk music "peculiar to America."[67] The true legacy of American composers, as Farwell saw it, was creative freedom: the freedom to follow or combine these strands of influence in any imaginable way.[68] That freedom had already led, in "the best of the newer work," to "a loftiness of ideals, a breadth of outlook, a definiteness of purpose, a freshness of color, a sense of the beautiful and an *esprit* which argue strongly for the future honor of American music."[69]

Yet, Farwell continued, the administration of American life had not kept pace with composers' achievements. The institutions of musical culture had concentrated almost entirely upon "the commercial exploitation of foreign artists" (i.e., performers), for the benefit of the rich.[70] Orchestra, chamber music, and opera in America had fostered "an aristocracy of musical appreciation" and a tone of "retrospective hyper-refinement" at a time when the nation's "rugged creative strength" most needed support.[71] "Aristocratic" institutions had no interest in what Farwell saw as the primary musical issue of the day: the interaction between "musical art and democracy."[72] "The people of the nation," Farwell believed, had always received "cordially the work of their own composers." But the third phase of American music history, administration, could begin only when the barriers erected by "the narrow arena of the concert halls of 'culture' "[73] were breached, and "music in all of its forms" was brought "directly to the masses of the people."[74] Farwell saw activities directed to that end as a national movement: outdoor drama festivals, municipal concerts of orchestras (*not* bands), concerts given in public school halls, local music festivals, community choruses, low-priced symphony concerts, community pageants, and the growing popularity of the phonograph and player piano.[75] Each, in his view, was a blow struck for musical democracy.

Three-quarters of a century after the fact, Farwell's introduction still carries the force of an original vision—especially his claim that in the United States "the musical needs of the American people" were opposed, rather than served, by "the standards of the centres of conventional and fashionable musical culture."[76] Yet the introduction had little impact upon *Music in America,* the book that followed it. Even the book's table of contents exposes the loose fit between it and Farwell's introduction. Its three-part division, like his, begins with "appreciation." But that section emphasizes the eighteenth century, while Farwell carries appreciation almost to the end of the nineteenth. Farwell's second stage, "creation," occupies the third section and longest part of *Music in America,* encompassing folk music, popular music, and composers in the concert-hall tradition from the 1850s to 1915. Farwell's third stage, "administration," is missing entirely from the book, whose second section, called "organization," deals with institutions, concert life, and music education. As the disparity might suggest, *Music in America* cannot be read as an illustration of Farwell's thesis, as Ritter's history was of his introduction or, later, Chase's was to be of his. Rather, the book is cobbled together from Darby's historical chronicle (Chaps. 1–9), Farwell's portrait of the compositional present—which *does* reflect his prophetic introduction—and additional chapters written by collaborators with compatible views.[77]

If Hood and Gould were the first generation of American musical historians, Ritter and Mathews were the second, and Elson, Hubbard, Farwell, and Darby the third. What is most striking about these books, despite the elements they share, is each author's freedom—imperative, perhaps—to define his territory. Rather than taking their predecessors' works as a starting point, each saw American music in his own way and considered its history as revolving around a different set of issues and sources. Ritter's process of colonization, Mathews's homage to the burgeoning ranks of American professional musicians, Elson's interest in American composers, Hubbard's acceptance of musical democracy in vernacular styles, Farwell's faith that creative eclecticism and the mass audience would intersect on American shores—none of these central notions overlaps much with the others. In each historian's response to his predecessors lies the pattern we have observed in more recent histories of American music. Earlier histories are consulted for reference, are evaluated, if at all, in only the most general terms, and receive no exegesis. Mathews, Elson, Hubbard, and Farwell, for example, clearly find Ritter's perspective too narrowly cosmopolitan, but none of them really take on the issue. For all of these men, the historian's task is to set a suitable agenda and carry it through, not to debate the premises of other histories. Thus, the writing of American music history was established and carried out in an atmosphere almost entirely free of intellectual debate or even exchange.

One more thing needs to be emphasized about second- and third-generation histories. They were written by men who in one way or another were deeply involved in American musical culture and in fact made their living by serving the needs of some branch of it other than historical study. It is no disrespect to Ritter's, or Mathews's, or Elson's, or Hubbard's, or Farwell's achievements to think of them not as historians in the modern-day sense of the word but as historically minded musicians grappling with the complexity of lives devoted to the pursuit of some musical, rather than scholarly, end. It is precisely their involvement with the musical culture of their time and place that gives energy and immediacy to their historiographical vision.[78]

We now come to the point where some might say that the historiography of American music really begins: to the career of Oscar G. Sonneck (1873–1928). While his predecessors have faded into antiquarian obscurity, Sonneck remains a redoubtable figure: as the man who made a major research collection of the Library of Congress's Music Division, the founding editor of *The Musical Quarterly,* the compiler of many useful bibliographical aids, the inventor of the Library of Congress classification system for music, and the patron saint of the Sonneck

23

Society for American Music. Much has been written and said about Sonneck in recent years. His works are widely quoted. Everybody agrees that Sonneck was wonderful.[79] (Praising Sonneck is as much a ritual in our field as abusing Ritter.) And yet his place in the historiography of American music is not quite as clear as might be imagined.

Sonneck was born in 1873 in New Jersey, and his mother took him at the age of two to Germany, shortly after his father's death. He grew up in Frankfurt-am-Main, attended the universities of Heidelberg and Munich, and explored his capacities as a composer. Around 1900 he returned to the United States and began research on music in eighteenth-century America. In 1902, shortly before his twenty-ninth birthday, he was appointed chief of the Library of Congress's Music Division;[80] in 1917, he resigned that post to join G. Schirmer music publishers in New York as director of publications. There he remained until his death in 1928.

Sonneck's work began to be published directly on the heels of Elson's history, which, by the way, Sonneck called "clever" in 1905 and "fresh and smooth-flowing" in 1909.[81] But it breathed the air of a new planet and a new generation. Whether or not his German university education was responsible, Sonneck was the first to look into the abyss of American musical history and to recognize, define, and illustrate a real historiographical philosophy for music in the United States. He is thought of chiefly, and properly, as a builder: a man who filled an open landscape with soundly constructed, useful monuments. But he was also a destroyer of historiographical illusion. Sonneck's work and writings dismiss as pure fiction the idea that "authoritative" music history can be written from available evidence. Ritter, Elson, et al. had been guided through their histories by Jamesian silhouettes, reflecting their own musical involvement and their different shades of cosmopolitanism. Sonneck cut loose from such devices. In his own researches, he chose to be guided by his scholar's persona, that of the bibliographer who searches for the truth about the musical past in the accumulation of scores and documents that lie, mostly forgotten, on library and archival shelves.

Sonneck's own publications do not include a history of American music. Indeed, his chief scholarly works are either detailed treatments of narrower topics or exhortations for more such work to be done, pronto.[82] Sonneck was the great cheerleader of American music historiography, if one can call such pessimistic pronouncements as the following cheerleading. In 1905, writing for the Bibliographical Society of America, he confessed:

> It is only with a keen sense of humiliation that I, as an American writer on the musical life of America, lead you for a moment into this "darkest Africa." What I mean is simply this: we do not even possess a bibliography of books and articles on the music history of our country. . . . Yet we continue to write histories of music in America, though we know, or at least should know, that bibliography is the backbone of history.[83]

By 1909 Sonneck was plugging local music history as the eventual key to a general history:

> Little has been done toward a thorough and accurate description of the music histories of the more important cities, especially those in the West. That job is much too vast for it to be undertaken by any single individual who might set himself up as a history-writing authority on the entire country—although useful and well-meaning attempts in that direction have been made. Only when objective local histories have come into being can the methodically schooled universal historian hope to render an accurate account of all that has passed.[84]

In the same year, in an address to the International Musicological Society's Vienna Congress, he spelled out some of the dimensions of what he called "musical topography" (*Länderkunde*) while lamenting the scantiness of available research on American musical life. He noted, for example, that one could not find much of anything written on "church music, chamber music, orchestral music, choral music, opera, music in our colleges, the music trades, the manufacture of instruments, the music-publishing industry, musical societies and organizations, municipal and government interest in and subvention of music, [or] folk music."[85]

As these quotations suggest, Sonneck, like Ritter, believed that American composers had played only a small role in shaping their country's musical life. For him, the true history of American music was not to be found in the realm of composition and style development but rather in an investigation of the country's musical topography and how

25

it grew. No such interpretation was possible, he believed, until the historical record of musical life in specific locales had been reconstructed in detail.

What is Sonneck's legacy to American musical historiography? If, as I said at the beginning, historians are judged on information and interpretation, then Sonneck succeeded spectacularly on the first front and more qualifiedly on the second. In less than fifteen years, while doing many other things as well, he wrote and published five accurate, fully documented books—books upon which virtually all historians of American music have since drawn—on eighteenth-century American secular music, a subject whose very existence earlier historians had ignored. As for his interpretive perspective, Sonneck's work preaches that historians *must* study the founding and development of American musical life, regardless of the artistic value they find in the music of American composers. In its most elementary form, Sonneck's credo was that the history of American music should be approached "in the proper spirit and from the proper angle: from that of *research for the sake of research,* unaffected by forethought esthetic or mercenary."[86] That belief stemmed from, and helped to feed, his fierce dedication to historical documents. By concentrating upon a remote past, which he approached by using all available materials—newspapers, periodicals, letters, diaries, printed and manuscript music—he worked to reconstruct the circumstances in which his subjects made their music, and hence he discovered a context in which their achievements could be appreciated. If we keep Henry James's earlier comments in mind while comparing Sonneck's work with that of his predecessors, perhaps we could say that Sonneck made it his business to restore the wrinkles to the folds that time had smoothed, to overload outlines until they collapsed under the weight of new evidence, to make holograms of silhouettes.[87]

For all he accomplished, Sonneck's legacy to American musical historiography lacks two things. It lacks any clear demonstration of how his detailed reconstructions of eighteenth-century musical life might be incorporated into general accounts of American music history. And it lacks any hint of the role that music itself, including the issue of musical style and its evolution, might play in such histories. Sonneck, we must remember, was not merely an archivist but a musician who once had aspired to be a composer—a man who cared deeply about music and whose musical judgments lay at the heart of his profession after he went to work for G. Schirmer. However, his own thoroughly cosmopolitan musical taste seems to have been so firmly rooted in the concert hall of his day that it simply did not come into play in his writings about his scholarly specialty.

Between Sonneck and Chase one more general history was written: the 700-page *Our American Music,* first published in 1931, by the journalist, lecturer, and later librarian, John Tasker Howard (1890–1964).[88] "This book is an account of the music that has been written in America," Howard wrote at the outset, "not a history of musical activities, except, of course, where we must have some idea of the conditions that have produced the composers of each era."[89] Active himself as a composer of songs and piano character pieces, Howard had also written widely on contemporary American composers, and he followed *Our American Music* with *Our Contemporary Composers* (1941) and *This Modern Music* (1942). With 60 percent of his book devoted to the years between 1860 and 1931, his commitment to American composers of the present and recent past was manifest. (In its concentration upon American composers, Howard's book comes closer to Elson's and Farwell and Darby's than to the others.)

Howard's work also reflects some of the preachments of Sonneck, to whom he paid tribute in his introduction. His twenty-five pages of classified bibliography were the longest list of writings about American music published to that time, and their later updates remain among the longest published anywhere.[90] Though in a less systematic way, he picked up where Sonneck had left off in 1800 and concentrated his historical digging upon the nineteenth century's first half—an age that, in Sonneck's view, called out more urgently for research than any other.[91] His investigations uncovered documents in the family papers of living relatives of Francis Hopkinson, James and John Hill Hewitt, Oliver Shaw, Lowell and William Mason, and more recent composers, including MacDowell, Parker, Paine, and Ethelbert Nevin.

Howard's perspective blends contradictory elements: a cosmopolitan musical taste coupled with an ideological commitment to the American composer and a determination to be comprehensive; an author's persona of tolerant broad-mindedness coupled with an undisguised distaste for musical expression he considered coarse; a belief that, although American composers' music had been unfairly neglected, it must be judged by the same standards as European art music. Taken together with the absence of technical discussion—like all of its predecessors, the book carries no musical examples—the tensions among these conflicting needs and beliefs have the effect of separating Howard somewhat from his subject matter. In contrast to Ritter and Mathews, who wrote, so to speak, "from the belly of the beast," and Sonneck, whose labors to steep himself in a remote past give his work a trenchant force, Howard emerges as a kind of urbane, indefatigable president of the American music fan club. For all of the admirable scope and reliability of his data, and for all his literary skill, Howard's book carries the lesser authority of a work written to gather and display knowledge rather than the greater authority of one written from the author's compulsion to find out for himself.

I should like to quote a passage from Howard that shows how the absence of a tradition of scholarly study allows fundamental issues to get plowed under. Having recognized that, after the American Revolution, immigrant musicians from England came to this country and "took largely into their own hands the management and performance of our musical affairs," Howard finds it "difficult, if not impossible, to . . . determine intelligently whether our musical life was eventually the gainer or the loser" from this development.

> Would our Billingses, our Hopkinsons, and Lyons have sowed the seeds of a truly national school of music, which would have gained in background and in craftsmanship, if its growth had been uninterrupted by the coming of skilled, thoroughly trained musicians whose knowledge and talents paled the glories of our native composers? Or would the crude yet native spark of creative genius have become sterile on virgin soil, where there was not the opportunity for exchange of ideas in a cultured environment?[92]

Howard's question is not asked with quite the precision one might wish. In fact, information in his own book shows that the composers he mentions were not the pure "nationalists" the question implies. Hopkinson's compositions, he notes elsewhere, "show the influence of the contemporary English style,"[93] and Billings "probably copied the forms of contemporary English church musicians."[94] The way Howard has asked the question suggests that if the foreign invasion had not occurred, Old

World influence already present in the music of these earliest American composers might somehow have been gradually turned off, like a faucet.

These reservations aside, however, the thrust of Howard's query goes to the heart of a fundamental question. Some later writers with a provincial perspective have decried the foreign influence of which Howard speaks.[95] And yet, was there, within the various provincial practices that existed early in our music history, the potential for technical development, apart from direct European influences, that might have led American music in a different direction? Was provincial psalmody, as Ritter assumed, a dead end because of the incuriosity about technique and craft that its religious outlook imposed? Did any provincial indigenous practices evolve perceptibly *without* contact with European music? Apart from their obvious effectiveness as quoted material in provincial (or "nationalist") contexts, what's the evidence that techniques of Native American music, or African-American, or Anglo-American folk, or of provincial American composers from Billings to Foster to Sankey to Joplin, could be applied successfully to music for the concert hall?[96] To pursue Howard's question seriously would be to confront head-on the issue of cosmopolitanism versus provincialism. Is the issue, as Ritter believed, chiefly one of artistic seriousness and technical command? Or is it, as Chase seemed to suggest, more social and ideological, with American musicians embracing cosmopolitanism because of their audiences' "aesthetic immaturity?"[97]

In Howard's *Our American Music,* the question is allowed to hang as an unaddressed speculation, functioning as a narrative device rather than a matter that kept the author awake nights. Sixty years later, it's still hanging, for more recent authors, with their own questions, schedules, and agendas, have still not taken it on. Here is such stuff as traditions are *not* made of.

Howard's book, however, played an important role as a catalyst. For, as we return to Chase and the historical present, we find Chase at pains to disassociate himself from the historiographical tradition of Ritter, Elson, and especially Howard. *America's Music* (1955), as noted earlier, marks the ascendency of the provincial perspective over the cosmopolitan. Howard's spirit of broad-minded toleration, for Chase, leans too much in the direction of genteel respectability.[98] "My own approach to America's music is not at all respectable—my bête noire is the genteel tradition," writes Chase, who turns the subject of American music history on its head by proclaiming as "the most important phase" of America's music that music most "different from European music."[99] Chase claims as predecessors such specialists as Sonneck, Waldo Selden Pratt, and George Pullen Jackson, who had explored "virtually unknown tracts of America's musical history,"[100] and Charles Seeger, whom Chase quotes as having written that the New World's "main musical concern has been with folk and popular music."[101]

In reviewing the past, we may have noticed a tendency on the part of some historians to see themselves as spokesmen for losing (or lost) causes, advocates for the historically disenfranchised. What seemed most fragile and needful of protection to Howard, writing in the late 1920s, was the impulse of American composers to transplant music as a creative fine art, maintaining an Old World standard of aesthetic integrity in a New World setting. For Howard, Americans' ignorance of what American composers had accomplished in the European tradition was a form of cultural impoverishment that *Our American Music* was designed to remedy. But when we move across our historiographical Great Divide to Chase, we encounter a very different situation.[102] As noted, Chase wrote his history in the 1940s and early 1950s as a counterstatement to Howard. Inspired by Seeger, Chase believed he had discovered the wellsprings of American musical distinctiveness among people low in the social order. Spirituals (black and white), the music of blackface minstrelsy, Anglo-American fiddle music and folk songs, shape-note hymnody, songs of American Indian nations, ragtime, blues, early jazz— all genres whose musical worth Howard could not quite bring himself to endorse—were for Chase the heart of American musical achievement. In short, Chase wrote to claim a place in American music history for these unwritten or informal kinds of music-making. Americans risked cultural impoverishment, he believed, if they failed to recognize the worth and, yes, the beauty of these musics. Where Howard had found "cultivated" fine-art music fragile and needful of his advocacy, Chase wrote to plead the case for plain Americans who, in the course of their daily lives, and drawing on the modest resources at their disposal, had succeeded in making and maintaining musics rich in human substance, if often rough and unpolished in manner.[103]

To encounter Charles Hamm's view of American vernacular music is to cross another divide and to enter a world as different from Chase's as Chase's was from Howard's.[104] What makes Hamm's work startling is that *his* protective instincts as a historian are called into play not by the obscure, forgotten figures from the musical past who play so large a role in Howard's and Chase's accounts (and those of all other historians as well) but by the most famous American musicians: composers and performers of the music that Americans have most loved and paid money for but whose popular success has made historians view them with distrust. To borrow terms from economics, we might say that, while Howard and Chase concentrate on the supply side—on the makers of the music and what they made and how—Hamm takes his cue from the demand side—from the preferences of singers, players, listeners, and other users of the music.

The economic analogy is appropriate here. For Hamm's unabashed acceptance of the music marketplace as a fact of American musical life— as a possible touchstone, even, of musical significance—leads us to recognize a fundamental assumption in earlier histories. Before Hamm, historians comfortably assumed that music whose chief aim was profit, success, or immediate impact upon the mass market was somehow not an integral part of the history of music. Or let's put the assumption this way: music tailored to the dictates of the mass market, which is governed by financial profit, is marked by traits of musical substance and structure (melody, rhythm, harmony, sound) that separate it from music that deserves scholarly study. Or, to put it even more tendentiously, the circumstances of commercial music's origins have, by definition, corrupted and debased it so that it stands outside the purview of serious scholars of the art. According to this assumption, the corrupting forces are evanescence and money. The commercial world's obsession with immediate popularity contradicts the academic world's belief that the power to endure beyond the moment is a truer measure of artistic worth. As for money, it is thought to corrupt by its plenitude, for in the world of commercial vernaculars, money exists in vast, undreamed-of quantities. Where commercial values reign, true artistic values flee. Musical artistry, in other words, cannot stand up to the commercial demands of the marketplace, where the shoddy drives out the good. Therefore, artistic quality must be sought in other genres uncorrupted by commerce.

I've put this assumption in terms that are probably more absolute than present-day musicologists would publicly endorse. But surely something like this belief lies behind earlier histories of American music and continues to be held today, even though it's been almost a decade since Hamm, in *Music in the New World,* invited Tin Pan Alley, country music, rhythm and blues, gospel, and rock 'n' roll into the mainstream of our music history. It's surely significant, too, that Chase, champion of "the vernacular" that we acknowledge him to be, in his first edition chose vernacular genres that either never had been or were no longer forces in the marketplace. In contrast, Tin Pan Alley, Broadway, and Hollywood, all major commercial venues of the 1940s and early 1950s, when Chase was writing, are conspicuous by their low profile in, or absence from, his account.

Now it's time for a few reflections on our survey. The first is that the provincial perspective adopted in recent histories proves the firm establishment of cosmopolitan values in American musical life. In the time of Ritter and Elson, music in the cultivated tradition was still struggling for a secure foothold. As its champions, many earlier historians were men who battled daily against provincial closed-mindedness. In the recent climate of historiographical opinion, their apparent empathy for the genteel stands out. That empathy has sometimes led us to see them as doctrinaire supporters of Europeanized taste when in fact they were advocates of a more diverse American musical life. By the time Chase wrote, the cultivated tradition's place in the United States could be taken for granted. A network of prestigious institutions—orchestras, opera troupes, schools, conservatories, radio stations, recording companies, publishers—had grown up in support of it. At the same time, the mass distribution of commercial popular music had helped drive older vernacular traditions to remote places of refuge. Steeped in cosmopolitan values, Chase and Company could afford to explore beyond them, discovering freshness and a kind of artistry in the very sounds and attitudes against which Ritter spent a lifetime struggling. The writing of history being a thoroughly cosmopolitan pursuit, there could be no provincial perspective among historians apart from a cosmopolitan academic establishment. Put another way, many of us love the idea of that primitive cabin in the woods—as a place to take vacations.

A second point is that American historians' tendency to plunge in, excluding older histories from their research, has been wasteful. It's not that earlier historians have been ignored. Rather, they have been reduced to the role of bit players—figures who stand for something, often the ignorance of the past—handy to use as a jumping-off point or to borrow a fact or quotation from but ultimately not worth reading. Little is expected of them. Because their perspectives are thought to be out of date, their contributions have been inferred rather than investigated. The independent spirit that has encouraged historians to hold their predecessors at arm's length has inspired some brilliant results. It has also blocked the development of a scholarly tradition in the field.[105]

What effects has European colonization had upon musicians working in America? What are the provincial elements in the music of American provincial traditions? At what points have provincial traditions absorbed cosmopolitan influences without losing their essential character? How does one balance an account of music history between pieces of music and musical topography? Why study music that gives little aesthetic pleasure to present-day ears? How does a historian deal with music created with commercial gain openly in mind? What role might style criticism play in American historical writing? How should historians deal with the phenomenon of popularity? Is it their job, in a society where certified masterpieces are few, to try to create a canon of such works and organize a history around it?[106] These are fundamental questions in American music history. Every one of them is posed, directly or by implication, on the pages of the works we have been discussing. And each is the kind of question with which a tradition of historical study is perpetually engaged. That none have been addressed at any length by general historians, the very people presumably best qualified to discuss them, dramatizes the need to establish such a tradition.

A tradition of historical study would encompass issues brought to the surface by Hood's excavations, Gould's reminiscences, Ritter's prickly disapproval of his adopted land's tastes, Mathews's faith in American musical progress, Farwell's democratic vision, and Elson's and Howard's nationalistic cosmopolitanism. It would grapple with the challenges posed by Sonneck's love of archival evidence. It would explore and debate the premises behind the shift to a provincial perspective in the middle of our own century. And it would hold Chase, Mellers, Hitchcock, and Hamm to account for their emphases and omissions.

But if several generations of dedicated, able general historians have failed to create a tradition—if one has not already evolved of its own accord—is it possible that American music is somehow resistant to such an enterprise? I don't believe so. What has been missing, I think, is an ingredient well within present scholars' capacity to supply. That ingredient is historiography. As this chapter is intended to show, for more than a century historians of American music have been making valuable statements about this country's musical life. Even today, in the midst of a burgeoning academic interest in the subject, these statements remain isolated from each other—like chemical elements lacking a catalyst—chiefly because no one has taken stock of them as a single body of work. Their authors have been too busy with their own visions of American music to bother much about other people's. Indeed, except for a few articles by Robert Stevenson over the past two decades, the history of American music history has hardly been touched.[107] As a result, scholarship in American music has gone forward without ever having claimed its historiographical legacy.

To suggest the potential stored in that legacy, let's take one more look at the four most recent histories. As we have seen, Chase could rightfully claim *America's Music* (1955) as a counterstatement because of its unprecedented emphasis on "folk and popular music."[108] And Chase's successors have all supported three propositions advanced there: (1) that writers of American music history should explore and dramatize differences between this country and Europe; (2) that one big difference lies in the relative positions of formal and informal music on the two continents; and (3) that America's chief contribution to the world's music lies in our informal genres, our so-called musical vernaculars, to use Hitchcock's word.

Basic to all three premises is the notion that American music has developed in separate binary streams: popular/classical, or light/serious, or informal/formal, or functional/artistic. In a signal contribution to the field, Hitchcock has characterized the Great Divide as a split between "vernacular" and "cultivated" musical traditions. He describes the vernacular as "music not approached self-consciously but simply grown into as one grows into one's vernacular tongue, music understood and appreciated simply for its utilitarian or entertainment value," and the cultivated tradition as "a body of music that America had to cultivate consciously, music faintly exotic, to be approached with some effort, and to be appreciated for its edification—its moral, spiritual, or aesthetic values."[109] These definitions give Hitchcock's terms a flexibility missing from other familiar pairs. The others assert, or at least imply, *properties of* music; Hitchcock's suggest *attitudes toward* it. The difference between properties and attitudes is crucial to the writing of music history. Where properties of works are the issue, one has the sense that the way a work is composed dictates the way it will be performed and received: What is important about a piece of music is what the composer puts into it. Where attitudes are also considered, however, performance and reception gain in historical significance. A historiographical model that assumes the composer as determining agent leads to a history of composers and their works (i.e., Howard's *Our American Music*). But a model in which performance and reception are also studied invites an account in which the *use* of musical works, including the spirit in which they are performed, may be as important as their original properties.

Though neither he nor his successors have said it in so many words, Chase followed the second model. As he wrote in 1955, his list of admired American musical genres endorses "folk and popular music"—or, as Hitchcock put it, "the vernacular tradition"—over music composed for the concert hall. But that endorsement led Chase to a historiographical stance more complex and interesting than he ever acknowledged. With public fanfare, Chase overturned the aesthetic hierarchy upon which earlier histories had been based. But at the same time, he tacitly restored something that Howard had ceremoniously discarded: Ritter's and Sonneck's belief that American music history had been shaped more by performance than by composition. From the time of the publication of *America's Music*, Chase's claim has been understood as a dramatic reordering of musical values. Less obvious, however—indeed, perhaps invisible outside a historiographical perspective—has been that claim's challenge to the notion that composers are the inevitable first agents of music history. Chase's list of seminal kinds of American music makes that point on its own: spirituals, blackface minstrelsy, Anglo-American fiddle music and folk songs, shape-note hymnody, songs of American Indian nations, ragtime, blues, early jazz. More than compositional types, these are genres that depend upon ways of performing music. All involve performance styles that take over, recast, and assimilate the compositions their practitioners sing and play.

Thus, from a historiographical point of view, Chase's work reconciles the new with the old. While staking out a fresh perspective tailored to the peculiar shape of American music-making and a postwar view of American culture, he also reaffirms the insight of earlier historians that a composer-centered history can tell only part of the story. Chase and his successors, we now recognize, have been responding, each in his own way, to challenges posed by unwritten and informal American music-making. Perhaps the next generation of American historians will take up the covert side of their approach, considering performance as a complementary, sometimes dominant force and following that part of the story wherever it leads.

Chase's *America's Music* carries the force of a statement written with powerful questions in mind. What would "a new world . . . do with the tractable and still unformed art of music?" Arthur Farwell asked in 1915. And what would arise from the contact of music "with our unprecedented democracy"? Chase answered these questions very differently from the way Farwell did; Mellers, Hitchcock, and Hamm have all made their own responses; and so, doubtless, will the next historians who address them. But where, in the first place, did Chase find the questions that he was to answer with a force and originality that invigorated a somewhat complacent field? He found them in an earlier general history. Here, if more is needed, is ample testimony to the worth of a barely tapped legacy.

Historiography can function as the collective memory for a field that has never set much store by memory. Its value for the task at hand is its unwillingness to allow unanswered questions asked by earlier historians to be ignored. Voices raised in the wilderness are taped and replayed in public by historiographers. The power of historiography lies in its recognition that a historian's perspective is not simply the interpretive framework within which information is delivered but an integral part of the information itself. Thus, historiography demonstrates that agreement with an earlier historian's perspective cannot be the basis for judging or using earlier work. The key, instead, is analytical appreciation: an attitude of watchful empathy that accepts what the work offers without condemning it for what it lacks. Historiography assumes that any historical account is valuable to the scholar who can read it in an attitude of analytical appreciation. By offering an analytical appreciation of earlier historians' work, historiography can help to create the chain of dependence upon which a scholarly tradition is built. And then, perhaps, the various accounts of the development of our country's musical landscape will be recognized, like the itineraries of European explorers of old, as complementary routes to understanding the experience of a New World.

PART II
ECONOMICS

· 2 ·

Professions and Patronage I:
Teaching and Composing

Iɴ ᴛʜᴇ ᴀʙsᴇɴᴄᴇ ᴏғ settings of the kind that the church, the court, and the state have traditionally provided in Europe, music in the United States has depended chiefly on the success musicians have had in finding customers and serving their needs. As Roger Sessions wrote in 1948, any serious consideration of American musical life must begin with the recognition that music in this country has been and is a "business."[1]

In one sense, Sessions's statement is a truism. *Of course* music, insofar as it depends upon the marshaling of specialists prepared for difficult tasks, is an expensive pastime, and the money has to come from somewhere. The more we study the past, the harder it is to overlook arrangements that provide for the training of artists and the commissioning, performance, circulation, and preservation of their works. Whether American or European, musicians are no different from other human beings in their need to make a living.

Yet, because Sessions has fashioned his statement to jar musical readers into recognizing an unwelcome fact of life, it's best to view it with that purpose in mind.[2] Two related premises loom behind it. One is that the European scene is different; the other is that Sessions's own kind of music operates at a disadvantage in a business climate. On the first point, Sessions's claim suggests the absence in America of prestigious institutional venues within which the creation and performance of musical works, conceived as art and *not* business, is encouraged. Readers are reminded that the realm of musical "art," which the American public is encouraged to think of as a wholly idealistic endeavor, is, for those engaged in it, an occupational calling in which musicians exchange their time and skill for money. On the second point, by restricting his discussion to music in the cultivated tradition, Sessions reveals an anomaly: The American music about which he cares the most must make its way in an environment indifferent or even hostile to it.

While Sessions's subject is music for the concert hall and opera house, his article is conceived broadly enough to take in all of American music. Rather than denouncing business, Sessions describes it. The nature of business, he reminds his readers, is to seek the highest possible return on one's investment. To that end, a business tries "to produce its goods as cheaply as possible." It also tries to encourage in customers a demand for products that are "cheapest and most convenient to produce."[3] Thus, cheap production, wide demand, and maximum profit are its prevailing values. Around these values there has been built in the United States a central marketplace—an arena centering on fierce competition for a paying audience. To compete successfully in that marketplace, musicians must follow the practices of an enterprise ruled by business. They must, in other words, produce musical commodities: goods or products suited to marketplace exchange.[4]

It is as obvious today as it was four decades ago that pure business values are foreign to the milieu in which Sessions and his compatriots understand themselves to be working. For there, works of art are privileged in and of themselves, often without reference to their exchange value. As makers of these works, composers stand at the top of a hierarchy: composer, performer, listener. Rather than catering to public taste, they seek to lead it, in the name of ideals they see as traditional and artistic—including "the prestige of sheer quality."[5] In essence, they practice art for art's sake. And they do so by making musical statements that, drawing from the full range of techniques available, seek to reflect the modern world as masterpieces of the past reflected the spirit of theirs. For Sessions, such music offers "new experience"; its makers must not shrink from placing stern demands "upon performers and listeners alike." In "an economy of scarcity," however, such "problematic" contemporary music cannot be expected to flourish.[6]

Sessions's claim that music in America is first and foremost a business makes an excellent jumping-off point for a broader inquiry. It's a strong statement from a respected source. Its application to the whole of American music—some branches of which embrace business values as unreservedly as Sessions and his compatriots reject them—can be an illuminating exercise. For example, cheap production, wide demand, and maximum profit may promote conformity, but the pursuit of such commercial goals has not cramped the diversity of American musical life. The careers of Sessions and his fellow composers testify to the flexibility possible within the larger economy of American music. The cultivated American composer's direct economic power may be modest. Yet Sessions, his compatriots, and his successors have found a way to live as musicians—to receive training, to find musical employment that involves composing, to work professionally at their calling, and to have their works performed and disseminated (i.e., published, recorded), though perhaps on a scale smaller than they wish. They have found in the larger American music business an arena for their talents and beliefs, even though those have aroused little interest in the central marketplace. They have found an economy within an economy: a realm that has also enabled them to hold to their ideals and to keep alive, in a democracy where commercial values overshadow other values, the spirit of music as an esoteric art.

It's remarkable that American composers have accomplished what they have. Their accomplishment is part of a larger story—one that considers music in the United States as an art that has grown up alongside a highly varied economic system. That system is carried forward by agents who serve the many functions necessary to the practice of music in the modern Western world.[7] All pieces of music must be created in the first place, and musical creation is the province of the *composer*. Before a composer's music can be experienced, someone must sing or play it, and that's the province of the *performer*. Composing and performing music take special skills, of course, and formal instruction in those skills is up to the *teacher*. If music is to find its way from composers to performers and, eventually, to listeners, it must be publicly performed, reproduced and distributed (i.e., published, recorded); those tasks fall to the *distributor*. As an art of sound, music relies not only on the human voice but upon musical instruments (and, in the electronic age, on mechanical playback equipment), and the *manufacturer* of such instruments is another agent of the music business. Finally, as an art form concerned with the human condition, music is an object of reflection and contemplation, and interpreting its messages in words is the province of the musical *writer*.

Each of these agents—composer, performer, teacher, distributor, manufacturer, writer—has played a role in the development of music in the Western world. Together, their efforts have created the economic structure of music-making. Yet the agents differ among themselves in background, training, and priorities, as a profession differs from a trade, a craft, or a business.[8] Sessions writes with the confidence of a true professional—a practitioner whose occupation is defined not by economic reward but by intellectual autonomy and authority.[9] According to Virgil Thomson, who wrote penetratingly on "the civil status of musicians," what separates a profession from other kinds of occupational calling are three special marks of "professional integrity": (1) "members of the profession are the final judges on any question involving technique"; (2) "professional groups operate their own educational machinery and are the only persons legally competent to attest its results"; and (3) "their professional solidarity is unique and indissoluble." Performers and music business functionaries may be brilliant or powerful or both, but they wield no authority on composers' own turf. "No executant musician," Thomson proclaims, "has the right to perform publicly an altered or reorchestrated version of a piece of music without the composer's consent." He uses an analogy from medicine to dramatize a composer's hegemony in the musical world. If a surgeon, he writes, "prefers to cut out appendices with a sterilized can-opener, no power in western society can prevent him from doing so, excepting the individual patient's refusal to be operated on at all." As for competence to judge the outcome of professional education, Thomson admits that "a certain number of prize competitions [are] still judged by orchestra conductors and concert managers." But still he insists: "Nobody but composers can attest a student's mastery of the classical techniques of musical composition or admit [another composer] to membership in any performing rights society." Finally, Thomson notes that only rarely do professionals "allow controversy to diminish their authority or their receipts." "Every profession administers a body of knowledge that is indispensable to society," he believes, "and it administers that knowledge as a monopoly."[10]

Thomson's view of musicians' occupations is functional and hierarchical. For what, precisely, do different musical agents get paid, he asks? The answers determine their places in a hierarchy that privileges intellectual autonomy and control, with composers at the top.[11] Composers make the designs upon which other agents depend. While they may work on commission—that is, collect a fee to compose a certain piece—their professional income reflects most of all their success in leasing to others the rights to perform, record, or otherwise "exploit" their music.[12] Performers "execute" the patterns made by composers and, as Thomson says, are "paid by the hour." Their work also demands a high degree of skill, which identifies them occupationally as craft practitioners. (One might add, as Thomson does not, that in vernacular music, having gained the composer's implicit or explicit assent, performers reinterpret and recompose pieces and hence assume some of the composer's function.) Teachers' occupational status is a matter of some dispute. Their calling fits the standard definition of "profession" more closely than the composer's does, for teaching is often a full-time, income-producing occupation, it requires extended practical and theoretical training as well as certification, and it espouses an ethic of service. Yet teaching—more a means to an end than an end in itself—lacks the intellectual autonomy enjoyed by other professions. For now, perhaps it will be enough to classify teaching (and writing about music, too) as part profession and part not, returning for a closer look later in the chapter.[13] As for the other agents of music, distributing music is clearly not a profession, a craft, or a trade but a business, while manufacturing musical instruments and goods involves both craft and business skills.[14]

Music-making in the United States has been shaped by professionals, trade and craft practitioners, and business people who, working alone or together, have followed the occupational callings open to them. What is crucial to note is how differently music has been financed in the United States and western Europe. In Europe, whether or not individual musicians were able to take advantage of it, financial support for artistic activity, in the form of patronage, emanated from the top of a hierarchical society whose ordering was hereditary. In America, where any social hierarchy has been unofficial, temporary, and nonhereditary, musicians have had to find their own support. In the Old World, structures dispensing artistic patronage already existed; music-making was stimulated by and flowed into them. In the New World, such structures, where there were any, were by-products, results and not causes, of musical activity. Music-making in America was able to create such structures of financial support only at points where enough money was earned or donated to perpetuate some institution with continuity—for example, a publishing firm, a conservatory, a theatrical circuit, or a symphony orchestra.

The story of American musical "economies" is complex. Each profession, craft, trade, or business has its own history, accessible chiefly through biographical study. But while the scholarly literature is rich in biographies of musicians as artists, we know much less about the field's trade practitioners and business leaders. Who were the people who had the most to do with shaping each of the American musical callings, and how do we know? What can we learn about their practice of that calling, especially from an economic point of view? What occupations did musicians pursue in the course of their lives, and how did they pursue them? By studying many individuals, will we find patterns that will lead to a better understanding of their occupations? Once occupational roles are more carefully separated and considered, what can we learn by examining their relatedness, both in the lives of individual musicians and, more generally, in the musical activity of institutions, locales, and the nation as a whole?[15]

An inquiry like the present one can do little more than to raise such questions. Nor would even detailed answers to all of them tell the full story of American musical "economies." Not all support for American music has come from earned income. At certain points in the story, patronage has appeared—patronage in the European sense, where a patron gives money to an artist for the production and/or performance of works of art. Not until well into the nineteenth century did patronage begin to contribute to American structures of musical support—structures that in Europe were traditional. And not until our own century has the state involved itself in musical support in any important way.

This chapter and the next sketch some of the ways in which musical professions and occupations have functioned in American musical life. As the normal agencies for American music-making, musical occupations offer a vantage point that, like the historiographical one of chapter 1, complements the customary view of the history of music, which is centered upon musical compositions, styles, and genres. The professions and occupations have also established the context in which patronage has appeared. As departures from the norm, examples of American musical patronage are best considered unusual events, called into play by extraordinary circumstances.

There's little ambiguity in the openly commercial grounding of many American musical transactions. But as we recognize "business" as the very turf upon which American musical life has been constituted, we see more clearly that musicians' need to make a living has been the driving force behind two centuries of American music-making. That recognition undermines confidence in a fixed border between "commercial" and "noncommercial" arenas. Moreover, as we come to appreciate the artistry of certain commercially driven American musicians—Irving Berlin is a good recent example—we are reminded that commercial motives do not necessarily overwhelm all others. The artistic legacy of unabashed commercialism may be as mixed as that of other motives that American musicians have espoused. But the reach of commercial values, however ample, has left open spaces in the American musical landscape for other values to appear. Musicians in callings remote from money and the power that it brings have shown great resourcefulness in attaching themselves to American beliefs and values that extend beyond the commercial arena and even beyond music itself. Thus, like Sessions and his compatriots, they have discovered how, within the American music business, to carry on musical activities that cannot pay for themselves.

Let's begin our survey with a statement from 1753 about the post of organist at St. Philip's Anglican Church in Charleston, South Carolina. According to the Vestry, St. Philip's organist could expect to make about £200 per year. Earnings would come from three sources:

1. pay for playing the organ, about £50 yearly, or one-fourth of the total earnings;
2. fees for "teaching the Harpsichord or Spinnet" privately, projected at "at least . . . 100 if not 150 Guineas" per year, which amounts to half, and perhaps as much as three-fourths of the total;
3. fees for performing in public concerts, which might amount to as much as "30 or 40 Guineas per Annum more" per year.

In other words, the holder of what was surely a prestigious musical post in eighteenth-century Charleston could expect to make less than half his living by fulfilling that post's official duties. Most of his income was to come from giving private lessons—from teaching music rather than playing it. As for concerts, he could expect relatively little from them, and then only if he showed "obliging Behaviour to the Gentlemen and Ladies of the place."[16]

The priorities of this document from the Colonial south reverberate through the later history of American music. Indeed, from the eighteenth century to the present, what Americans have wanted more than anything else from musicians is to be taught to sing and to play. Teaching has been the skill most widely demanded of musicians, the calling most readily available, the American musician's bread and butter, the service musicians have most often exchanged for a chance to pursue the musical passions closest to their hearts. Teaching is thus the logical starting point for our consideration of musical occupations in the United States.

In eighteenth-century America, singing masters who organized singing schools in which beginners were taught to sing sacred music outnumbered private teachers by far. Private teachers (like the Charleston organist) plied their trade chiefly in cities, where affluence and leisure time helped to form a public willing to pay for performance instruction. Singing masters worked both the city and the countryside, offering congregations and choirs in hamlets and villages the chance to improve their sung praise to the Almighty. Private lessons were one-on-one encounters; singing-school classes could reach dozens of scholars at once and cost the scholars only a modest fee.[17] A private teacher was most likely an immigrant and a professional musician, a performer on several instruments who offered other musical services for sale as well.[18] In contrast, singing masters needed to know only the standard psalm tunes and "the gamut"—the system of solmization. They were American-born, musically educated in singing schools themselves, and unlikely to make a whole career of the singing master's trade.[19] The private teacher and the singing master fit the types described in chapter 1 as cosmopolitan and provincial.

Teaching, as the Charleston document shows, could be important to a cosmopolitan performer's career. In provincial psalmody, as the only real occupational calling, it was the cornerstone of the whole enterprise. The Calvinist branch of the Protestant Reformation had assigned music to congregations—to worshipers themselves and *not* experts in the art (such as organists). By the 1720s in New England, singing schools were being founded to improve unaccompanied congregational singing. The first music published in the English-speaking colonies appeared in tunebooks compiled to serve congregations and singing schools.[20] And the first American composers, virtually all of them active as singing masters, began in the 1760s to publish their compositions in American tunebooks;[21] only in singing schools and their offshoots—meeting-house choirs and musical societies—could these composers find performers skilled enough to sing their music.[22]

Thus, in New England psalmody of the eighteenth and early nineteenth centuries, the teaching trade absorbed functions that elsewhere existed as separate occupations: the performer, the composer, and even the distributor, to the extent that singing masters were involved with the publishing and selling of tunebooks. Psalmody was a public music, of course. But because its performance, closely linked with worship, lay almost entirely with the worshipers themselves, there was no chance for performing to develop as an independent calling. While a dollar or two might change hands for the right to print this hymn tune or that one, it was an age in which authors' royalties were unknown. There is every reason to believe that profit from printed tunebooks, if there was any, went not to compilers or composers—or even to the engravers, printers, and bookbinders who produced the book—but to the publishers who assumed financial risk.[23] The chief source of income for a musician in psalmody, then, and the sole economic niche created by the widespread singing of American Calvinist congregations over nearly a century's time, was singing-school teaching.[24]

To see the life of a New England singing master like Andrew Law (1749–1821) as the exercise of a career in music is to encounter a condition of stark scarcity.[25] Law's activities and those of most of his fellow psalmodists dramatize a truth often overlooked: In most places on this continent, and for most people before the recent past, music-making has relied relatively little on cash. As an economy, early American psalmody was a subsistence enterprise. Religious zeal combined with social aspiration and musical responsiveness to attract scholars, the customers whose tuition fees funded the singing school. Drawing upon the energy and dedication of its participants, the singing school required only enough money to secure a steady supply of teachers. There is no evidence that it produced additional capital.[26] Masters who aspired to more profitable careers moved on to other trades. Andrew Law himself was an unusually energetic and strong-minded man—a born reformer with enough stamina to survive half a century of singing-mastering. Yet Law, like his contemporaries, was constrained by the acute scarcity of the economy in which he worked.

When Waldo Selden Pratt wrote, early in the twentieth century, that the authors of earlier American tunebooks "had no ambition except to serve an actual musical situation as they knew it,"[27] he must not have been thinking of Law or Andrew Adgate, two psalmodists who, in the early Federal period, harbored visions of their field as an agent of religious and musical change.[28] Pratt was right, however, about the outcome of these men's efforts. Both Law and Adgate come down through history as men who struggled bravely and vainly: Law to reform American musical taste and Adgate to fund singing schools through concert proceeds. Perhaps they failed for different reasons. But both lacked cohorts who might have aided their cause, as well as economic capital which might also have provided the means for success.[29]

While it may seem strange to equate discipleship with money, in an economy like that of early American psalmody the two had much in common. They were the only resources that might have enabled the chief agent—the musician with a vision of change, a desire not just to serve an existing situation but to alter it—to extend his influence. Discipleship, by increasing the number of spokespersons, helps to communicate the chief agent's message; money enables the chief agent to hire others to do routine tasks, leaving him free to devote more attention to extending the reach of his enterprise. So powerful is the hold of music over those who love it that many American musical enterprises have, in effect, been subsidized by the devotion of the musically inclined—by those willing to trade their energy and skill not for money but for the worthiness and pleasure of serving the cause. As it happened, Law's goal of musical reform was achieved in New England in the years 1805–10, not through his own efforts but because a coalition of religiously motivated disciples appeared in those years, steering psalmody toward a more Europeanized style.[30] This was not an economically driven reform. Rather, it resulted from the effective coordination of participants' energies. But money did play a key role two decades later in a development that profoundly reshaped the teaching trade. Because one music teacher found, first in psalmody and then in teaching itself, an economic potential far beyond anything his predecessors imagined, the course of American musical economics, and hence of American musical life, changed dramatically during the third and fourth decades of the nineteenth century.

Lowell Mason (1792–1872) has long been recognized as an important figure in American music, and for good reason. Indeed, once we understand the economic context of psalmody that Mason inherited, his use—indeed transformation—of that economy reveals him as a musician uncannily in tune with the aspirations of his public. A Massachusetts native, Mason attended singing school as a youngster, and he also learned to play several instruments.[31] In 1812 he left his home town of Medfield for Savannah, Georgia, where he was employed first in a dry goods store and then as a bank clerk. He maintained his involvement with music by leading church choirs and studying harmony and composition with Frederick L. Abel, an immigrant musician. It was also in Savannah, while still in his late twenties, that he compiled his first tunebook.

Mason's compilation was noteworthy for its content but even more for the circumstances of its publication. Much of the music he had chosen came from William Gardiner's *Sacred Melodies, from Haydn, Mozart and Beethoven* (London, 1812–15), whose appeal lay in its adaptation of melodies from great European masters like Handel, Haydn, Mozart, even Beethoven, to English hymn texts.[32] Bearing his manuscript, whose stylistic consistency and purity were unusual, Mason visited Boston in the autumn of 1821. There he approached the Handel and Haydn Society, founded in 1815 to improve musical taste through performances of sacred works by European masters.[33] The society agreed to sponsor his collection for an equal share of the profits.[34] Appearing first in 1822, *The Boston Handel and Haydn Society Collection of Church Music* was a resounding success. It went through nearly two dozen editions, and proceeds from its sales helped to support the society's activities for years to come.[35] It also earned a considerable sum for Mason—according to Pratt, $12,000 by the time the last edition appeared (1839).[36] In 1827, Lowell Mason, now thirty-five years old and thanks to his tunebook at least $2,000 richer,[37] left Savannah for Boston, where he assumed leadership of several Congregational church choirs and was elected president and conductor of the Handel and Haydn Society.[38]

So far, Mason had worked chiefly as a musical amateur: During his fifteen years in Savannah he was always employed outside music as well as in it. Nevertheless, his success there as a teacher (i.e., choirmaster) and distributor (i.e., compiler and copublisher) of music enabled him to enter the ranks of American psalmodists at a high level of income when he moved north. Not long after Mason's arrival in Boston, he detected fresh opportunities. As Pratt notes, the public school "was first establishing itself as an institution" at precisely this time.[39] Mason, who together with most psalmodists of his day felt duty-bound to "correct" the prevailing musical taste, grasped the advantages of teaching music to young children *before* their taste was formed. Earlier singing schools had welcomed teenagers and adults, but no one had ever concentrated on children. By doing precisely that—by forming a children's singing school, where receptive youngsters could learn to appreciate "good" music as they developed their skills—Mason saw a chance to strike a blow for musical improvement. Not incidentally, by extending his work beyond churchly institutions, he could also enlist new customers for his teaching and publications.

Mason refocused his energies without giving up his place in psalmody.[40] He kept one church post (organist and choirmaster at Lyman Beecher's Bowdoin Street Church, 1831–44, then at the Central Congregational Church, 1844–51) and remained active as a sacred compiler,[41] though he did resign the Handel and Haydn Society presidency.[42] Forming a singing school especially for children, he taught it free of charge and watched it grow in a few years from a class of "six or eight" to one of "five or six hundred."[43] A key to the school's success was Mason's donation of his services, made possible, at least in part, by the economic independence he had won working outside the field of music and from profits on his first tunebook. Mason's procedure was ingenious and effective. Spotting the need for a teaching service for which no niche existed, he volunteered to provide it without pay. Once he had demonstrated its worth, aided by a public performance,[44] he helped sponsors set up structures to support the new service on a paying basis. He also brought out new tunebooks aimed at his new customers.[45]

By 1832, a decade after his first sacred tunebook had appeared, Mason had embarked fully on the second phase of his musical career in Boston. A year later, in collaboration with George James Webb, Mason founded the Boston Academy of Music, centered chiefly on the teaching of music, both sacred and secular.[46] The next year, Mason began to offer teachers' classes through the academy,[47] and his *Manual of the Boston Academy of Music* (Boston, 1834; eleven more printings by 1861) was published to serve those classes.[48] In 1837, following a precedent that had served him well in the past, Mason took what has been widely considered the most historically significant step of his life: He offered free music classes in one of Boston's public schools.[49] The success of that volunteer experiment helped to establish music as a regular school subject, and it won Mason the post of superintendent of music in the Boston school system, a job he held from 1838 to 1845, when the Massachusetts State Board of Education named him to the staff of its teachers' institutes. Mason continued to teach music in the Boston schools until 1851, when he was fifty-nine years old, and he participated in the teachers' institutes until 1855.[50]

The facts of Mason's career trace a path from sacred to secular and from scarcity to abundance. Entering the subsistence economy of psalmody as the compiler of a sacred tunebook, Mason struck an agreement that brought him capital from its publication. Having earned a profit from psalmody, he could expand his range beyond it without having to depend upon new endeavors for his livelihood. Mason's first master stroke was to enlist a prestigious organization to back his debut as a tunebook compiler. Then he anticipated that vast economic gain was possible through secular education. But the crowning achievement of his later years was to target music teachers rather than music students as his chief customers. Mason's career shows a knack for assessing a rapidly changing situation while also participating in it. Hence, he was able to locate his own occupational activity in ever-widening contexts, each new stage increasing his clientele and influence. In the 1830s, without discarding the framework of psalmody, he broadened it generationally, courting hordes of future customers. Then, having made himself the first American expert on how young children learned music, he enlisted and trained as disciples the teachers of those children, supplying them not only with ideas and techniques but with publications to meet their needs in the classroom. By the 1850s, rather than "serv[ing] an actual musical situation as [he] knew it," as Pratt put it, Mason had helped to create a new one, supported by a growing trade network that he himself had invented.

Mason's erstwhile colleague George Frederick Root (1820–95) told a story about Mason that shows the latter's economic savvy at work. According to Root,[51] William Woodbridge convinced Mason that he should try to apply Pestalozzian principles to teaching vocal music. "If you will call together a class," Woodbridge promised, "I will translate and write out each lesson for you . . . as you want it, and you can try the method; it will take about twenty-four evenings." Mason agreed, and the class was assembled in "the large lecture room of Park Street Church, Boston." Root does not give the year, but it must have been early in the 1830s.[52] "Speaking to Dr. Mason once about this remarkable class," Root relates, "I asked him what those ladies and gentlem[e]n paid for that course of twenty-four lessons. 'Oh, they arranged that among themselves,' he replied. 'They decided that five dollars apiece would be about right.' 'And how many were there in the class?' He smiled as he answered: 'About five hundred.' "[53] The class, Root says, "was composed largely of prominent people of the city who were interested in musical education." If Mason could turn another man's suggestion into a more than comfortable yearly income for just twenty-four evenings of work,[54] it's clear that his earlier coup with the *Boston Handel and Haydn Society Collection of Church Music* was more than beginner's luck. Mason's was the first career that revealed American music, potentially at least, as a profit-making enterprise.[55]

The economic perspective offers a good vantage point for understanding the impact of Mason's career. In the musical environment he inherited, the pervasive issue was how music could best serve religious devotion. Giving much energy to that cause throughout his life, the devout Mason left behind a deep legacy in sacred music. But Mason's transforming insight was to recognize psalmody as part of a larger world of music, one of many worthwhile kinds of American music-making. Once he grasped that fact—once he perceived music as a realm that *contained* psalmody rather than one *contained by* religion—Mason extended his professional reach. Music-making, his insight taught him, was not only an indispensable way to enter a state of grace in worship. It was also a pleasurable human activity: a wholesome, enjoyable way to spend leisure time, and a gratifying social pastime. And a society growing more urban and middle class was beginning to find the *accessibility of musical experience* a more urgent matter than the devotional concerns of an earlier age. Teaching, Mason perceived, could be the key to accessibility. If Americans were steered toward music as youngsters—if they were shown how to sing and to read notes, and provided with simple, attractive, affordable pieces to perform—the pleasures of making music would be open to them for the rest of their lives. A musician who understood how to teach children, who could convey that understanding to other teachers, and who could supply music that beginners would enjoy singing could benefit society while at the same time finding more customers than earlier American music teachers ever dreamed of.

Mason's career points the way to certain formative patterns in American musical life. It dramatizes the significance of teaching as *the* American musical occupation. It shows how one occupational calling can provide a framework in which others can develop. And it reveals that American music, at first strictly a subsistence enterprise, was transformed into a capitalistic one by discovering a musical service or artifact for which demand is large, pricing it within many customers' reach, and keeping control over the surplus income that results.[56] The implications of the latter point have shaped the American music business in many of its manifestations since Mason's time, especially in its tireless cultivation of arenas of demand. Surely it's worth noting that, while Mason himself got rich through a shrewd use of opportunities within the teaching trade, other musical callings can be much more profitable. But if teaching offers even its successful practitioners lesser rewards than some other callings, the pervasive and continuing demand for it has given teaching considerable economic power, which has helped it to foster an immense range of American musical activity.

Changes in the teaching trade during and after Mason's time reflect new demands. Private teaching broadened its sphere considerably. On the cosmopolitan end, it grew more specialized and, as conservatories and college music departments sprang up after the Civil War, began to provide high-level training.[57] Moreover, the activities of both private teachers and singing masters grew more diversified.

The role of the private teacher, restricted in the eighteenth century mainly to the secular cosmopolitan tradition, found a new focus during the nineteenth, chiefly in response to the boom in middle-class home music-making. Chapter 5 will take up this issue in more detail. But for now, it's worth noting that with the creation of a vast repertory of songs and instrumental pieces—composed or arranged with the skills of American musical amateurs in mind, published and sold in sheet-music form, supported by the successful design and marketing of affordable pianos— the middle-class American home was turned into a center of musical performance and a prime market for the music business. The aspirations of this new set of performers were served by a new corps of private teachers.[58]

As for the singing class and the provincial singing master, both survived in their earlier forms in certain regions; the farther from the influence of urban centers, the more likely they were to continue.[59] (Washington Irving invented Ichabod Crane, a singing master, in 1819.) Mason's efforts helped to separate the singing class from its sacred origin and install it in the public school, where it has maintained a place to the present day. A roughly parallel process took place somewhat later in instrumental music. Early in this century, the instrumental ensemble, and especially the wind band, perceived as a wholesome, constructive, group enterprise for youngsters, was also embraced by the public school, creating a need for bandmasters and instrumental teachers as well as vocal ones.[60]

The sharp increase in the number of Americans seeking musical instruction widened the range of occupational skills and expectations of the musicians who taught them. At one end of the spectrum stood the Edward MacDowells and Horatio Parkers, hired in the 1890s by prestigious universities as professors chiefly because of their work as composers. At the other stood the school master or marm whose professional credentials consisted of attendance at a "normal institute," a summer residency program that trained music teachers in a few weeks' time.[61] Somewhere in between stood men like W. S. B. Mathews, the historian of American music we met in chapter 1, whose activities reveal the American music teacher in a role familiar today: the inveterate scrambler whose livelihood depends on energy, versatility, and tight scheduling. Writing in 1859, Mathews described in *Dwight's Journal of Music* his own activities—typical, he said, for a music teacher "out west."[62] In a single week, Mathews gave twenty-eight private lessons on the piano or melodeon at 50 cents each, taught three singing schools in three different towns at $1 per scholar for twelve sessions, led three choir rehearsals and two public-school music classes, and presided on

Sunday at four worship services. Mathews, it should be noted, was twenty-two years old when he fired off this dispatch. Whether or not he eventually suffered what a later age has come to call "burnout," by the time he was thirty he had settled in Chicago as a church organist, editor of a music periodical, music critic, and prolific writer on musical subjects. Teaching for Mathews, and for many other American music teachers as well, was a stepping stone, a way to maintain musical skills and to survive as a musician while remaining alert for new opportunities.

The more specialized the musical skills taught, the more expert command a teacher needs, and the more likely it is that teaching will occupy a secondary rather than a primary place in the teacher's musical aspirations. In this century, the teaching trade has broadened to encompass other specialties. Financial support, both public and private, has grown for conservatories and university music departments staffed by musicians who, while instructing student performers, conductors, composers, scholars, and teachers, are expected also to carry on their own specialties at a high level of competence. The presence of such specialist-teachers has allowed these institutions to build professional composing, performing, and writing about music into their educational programs.[63]

The link between higher education and the professions of music deserves more comment. In some academic environments, musicians who teach for a living maintain another musical profession outside the academy. Colleges and universities have also helped to bridge the gap between the professions and patronage by supporting things—compositions, performances, scholarly research and writing—that cannot survive in the marketplace.[64] Such activities are accepted not so much because society values them but because they are carried on in the name of education. They reflect public approval of the more conspicuous results of teaching, from opera performances and orchestral concerts to glee clubs and marching bands. Or, more precisely, they reflect public trust that good teaching lies behind these public successes. Many skillful musicians have found in teaching a way to buy time for their own work. Lowell Mason's career is simply one of many illustrations that, more than any other musical occupation, teaching has stretched the framework within which American musicians find employment. Since the eighteenth century, teaching has touched upon, overlapped with, infused, and in some cases subsumed other occupations for which demand has been less direct.

In some academic settings the position of teachers recalls that of musicians under European patronage: They are supported by private or public funds and given the freedom to pursue their own professional ends as long as their teaching gets done. This freedom has been won not by official decree but more gradually and indirectly: by the efforts of musicians working on two separate fronts over several generations. On the one hand, by teaching students how to sing and play and teach music themselves, colleges and universities have responded to society's direct musical needs. On the other hand, by using teaching as a way to subsidize performance, scholarship, and composition—as Roger Sessions and his compatriots have discovered—the academy has helped to create an appetite for more and more specialized instruction and a protected niche for music outside the marketplace.

I have claimed teaching as the foundation of the American music business and hence of much in American musical life; perhaps now we should look at the bedrock on which the foundation itself rests—the most fundamental musical calling of all. Composition, or musical authorship, is the act that sets Western music-making in motion. Other musical occupations depend upon it, for all music must be invented sometime by somebody. And yet, in the United States, composing can hardly be said even today to provide a real livelihood for many, as other occupations have.

From the very beginnings of musical commerce on this side of the Atlantic, there was little chance for composing to become a livelihood, not to mention a profession. In the eighteenth century, American performers, teachers, publishers, and instrument makers each had their own special concerns. But all could take it for granted that music was available in ample supply—music from the British Isles and the European continent. The needs of Old World people and institutions brought this music into being. Oral tradition and written notation circulated and preserved it. It was composed by musicians in Europe, some of whom were able to pursue composing as a substantial part of their own occupation. Americans, too, began to compose in the eighteenth century, but they did so almost entirely outside the music business.[65] Why? Chiefly because the ready supply of European music made American compositions unnecessary to the functioning of the other occupations.

Composers in America have earned money by writing music only at points where the supply of music from the Old World has failed to meet American needs.

The problem of composing as a way to make a living lies in the nature of musical notation. As the means by which composers fix, communicate, and sell their music, musical notation is indispensable to composing as a profession.[66] Yet, by preserving and circulating music in the absence of its composer, notation complicates the role of musical authorship. Once performers get hold of scores they can read, the composers of these scores become superfluous to them. While teachers, performers, publishers, and the rest find employment by acting in the present, the composer lives in a less time-bound arena; for notation brings into the present music that people wish to play or sing. Performances exist in the present, or at least they did before recordings. But the notation upon which performances depend can be supplied from other times and places. To make a living as a composer, one must therefore compete successfully not only with one's contemporaries and compatriots but also with one's predecessors from elsewhere in the world.

Since the eighteenth century, Americans have been amply supplied with music by European composers. This European legacy has been fundamental to American musicians. It has also helped to shape the working life of composers. To illustrate this point, let's look at a career that comes as close as any to marking the start of composing as a profession in the United States.

Alexander Reinagle, son of a professional trumpeter, was born in Portsmouth, England, in 1756 and established himself as a harpsichord teacher in Glasgow by 1778. Around 1784, he traveled to Hamburg, where he met C. P. E. Bach, with whom he later corresponded. The Royal Society of Musicians in London admitted him to membership the next year. In the spring of 1786 Reinagle sailed for New York and, after spending two months there, moved to Philadelphia, where he settled. Reinagle taught privately and gave concerts over the next several years. Then, early in the 1790s, he became comanager of the New Company, a Philadelphia-based theatrical troupe for which the city's famous Chestnut Street Theater was built in 1793. From his seat at the pianoforte, Reinagle presided over the music in the New Company's performances. Behind the scenes, he served as the company's chief composer until he moved to Baltimore in 1803. Reinagle died in 1809.[67]

During his early years in America, Reinagle's own compositions served him in the public performances he gave. He organized benefit concerts for himself in New York and Philadelphia, participated in other musicians' concerts, and also presented subscription concert series in both cities. His programs, which contain listings like "Sonata for Pianoforte by Mr. Reinagle," testify that he often played his own keyboard works in public. He also conducted his own overtures, played his own violin compositions, and even sang songs that he had composed.[68]

Reinagle's published music reveals his right to a special niche in the evolution of the professional composer's role in the United States. When he arrived in the New World in 1786, no such thing as an American music publisher existed. Printed music in the cosmopolitan tradition was imported from abroad; the typical domestic musical publication was the sacred tunebook, brought out by book publishers. However, by the time Reinagle assumed his theatrical duties, several American music publishing firms had entered the business. The American music publishing trade, in fact, was born in Philadelphia while Reinagle was working there as a freelance musician. Its founding and Reinagle's presence were no coincidence. For between 1787 and the beginning of 1793, sheet-music publication in this country took place only in the shop of John Aitken, a Philadelphia engraver and silversmith. Aitken issued sixteen works in those six years, chiefly songs and keyboard pieces. As Richard Wolfe has shown, all but four of the sixteen were either composed by, arranged by, or printed for Alexander Reinagle.[69]

Reinagle's compositions are not the only evidence of his involvement in the American music publishing trade from its very beginning. In a newspaper announcement soon after his arrival in New York, he advertised for pupils "in Singing, on the Harpsichord, Piano Forte, and Violin," and he added that he proposed "to supply his Friends and Scholars with the best instruments and music printed in London."[70] This suggests that he left England planning to act as a New World representative of London music merchants. Wolfe has also shown that the punches Aitken used in his shop were of English design, and he speculates that Aitken may well have acquired them through Reinagle in his role as London publishers' agent.[71]

The opening of music publishing shops in America was a key event in the establishment of composing as a profession. As suggested above, not until music was notated and put into salable form for circulation did it become a commodity that could be bought and sold. Only if the composer participated in the publication process, as Reinagle apparently did in his work with Aitken—sharing at least some part of the financial risk—or, as was more common later, struck a royalty agreement with a publisher, could he hope to profit from his labors.[72] I have said that composing in America became a profession only at points or in genres where the supply of music from the Old World failed to meet American needs. As it turned out, the American music publishing trade relied heavily on Old World music during the first half-century of its existence.[73] Yet, with an American composer actively involved from its very beginning, seemingly as a prime mover, the founding of a music publishing trade opened to musicians on this side of the Atlantic a way to participate in the music business as composers.

Reinagle's post with the New Company at the Chestnut Street Theater brought composing closer to the center of his professional life than it had been earlier. Between 1793 and his death, he supplied music for more than twenty new stage works; he also composed and arranged songs, and he wrote overtures, incidental music, and orchestral accompaniments for theatrical works by other composers. Almost all of Reinagle's theater music was later destroyed in a fire, so that side of his work is mostly inaccessible today. But the music that does survive provides a good idea of what was expected of its composers.

Music in the eighteenth-century Anglo-American theater served as a pleasant, entertaining embellishment to the story acted out on stage, much of which was carried on in speech. The ability to write graceful tunes with clear text declamation, to highlight the vocal strengths of the company's performers, to provide effective orchestral accompaniments, to know what to borrow from other composers and where to place it for strongest dramatic effect, to work quickly and efficiently under pressure, and to accept one's subordinate place in the whole enterprise—these were the traits valued in a composer in this position. All indications are that the musical tasks for which the New Company employed Reinagle were more or less routine for a composer of his skill.[74]

With Reinagle's career in mind, let's look at two examples of his music. Figure 1 is the first page of a piano sonata he composed in Philadelphia, probably between 1786 and 1794;[75] it shows his command of the keyboard idiom of eighteenth-century European masters.

FIGURE 1. Folio IV, opening page of Sonata No. 1, from Reinagle's autograph manuscript, ca. 1800 (Library of Congress ML96.R28)

EXAMPLE 1. Reinagle, "America, Commerce, and Freedom," bars 28–42 (*The Sailor's Landlady* [1794]; after H. Wiley Hitchcock, *Music in the United States* [Englewood Cliffs, N.J., 1969], 29)

Example 1 is part of a song Reinagle wrote for the ballet pantomime *The Sailor's Landlady* (1794).[76]

By almost any accepted standard of aesthetic judgment, Reinagle's sonata is a more impressive piece of music than his song. Yet the sonata never found its way into print until 1978, while there is every reason to believe that "America, Commerce, and Freedom" was published immediately after it was composed.[77] Why should a good piano sonata lie neglected while a routine song by the same composer is printed and offered for sale to the public? Because in eighteenth-century America there was a healthy market for songs and almost no market for piano sonatas. Songs were short, melodious, inexpensive, and they had words—all appealing traits to the amateur performers of the time who bought sheet music. The theatrical context of songs added to their attractiveness: One could hear a song performed onstage, buy a copy, and sing the song at home oneself. Sonatas, on the other hand, were reserved for more accomplished musicians. Mastering a sonata required skill, practice, and, most likely, lessons. Besides, players who were technically accomplished could buy music by European masters like Handel, the sons of Bach, and Haydn himself. Who needed a piano sonata by Alexander Reinagle? Reinagle's own answer remains elusive, for his four sonatas stayed in manuscript for nearly two centuries after he composed them.

In Reinagle's two compositions may be read the divided heritage of composing as a profession in the United States. Reinagle the composer with intellectual autonomy and authority appears in figure 1, Reinagle the composer with economic muscle in example 1. The gap between composing as a profession of the kind Virgil Thomson has described and composing as a livelihood is dramatized by the differences between the two pieces. In the sonata, Reinagle exercised technical command and seriousness of artistic purpose for their own sake, unconnected with economic potential. In the song, technique and constructive power yielded priority to making a tuneful surface to catch the public ear.

Having noted the professional implications of Reinagle's sonata and his song, we may consider something else about the way notation has functioned in American musical life. Here we must be careful not to speak about written music as if it were simply one thing. For there are actually two distinct kinds of written music, illustrated by Reinagle's two pieces.

The first kind, exemplified by the sonata, is what both Thomson and Jacques Attali describe as a normative musical composition. Here a composer invents a piece of music and writes down his or her instructions in enough detail that it can be played or sung precisely as the composer has conceived and imagined it. The performer, in turn, accepts the composer's score in an attitude of deference and strives to carry out the latter's instructions as closely as possible. In the second kind of written music, exemplified by Reinagle's song, things work differently. The composer's score is far less detailed. And its lack of detail is an invitation for performers to sing or play it any way they like. Some performers might want to simplify or decorate the written version. Some might prefer it in a different key. Some might accompany it with cello or guitar, or with the final keyboard section left out, or lengthened, or sing it with no accompaniment at all, or at a very fast clip or a slow one. Departures from the score like these would be unacceptable in the sonata; they would change its very nature. But in the song, they would hardly be noticed. For the score of a song like "America, Commerce, and Freedom" is understood not as a finished statement but an outline to be filled in, to be "realized," by performers in any way they choose.

In an article published some years ago, I called the first kind of written music "composers' music" and the second "performers' music."[78] I did this because I felt uneasy with the standard polarities— "classical" and "popular," or "cultivated" and "vernacular," or "serious" and "light" music—because they seemed more categorical and value-laden than a historical view of music would support.[79] With the typology of "composers' music" and "performers' music" in mind, it's clear that professionalism's different elements pulled Reinagle in opposite directions as a composer. "Performers' music" like "America, Commerce, and Freedom" offered the chance of pecuniary success but no authority over its performances. "Composers' music" like the piano sonata offered intellectual autonomy at the price of economic potential. Reinagle's two pieces reflect the structure of a divided profession: To compose either composers' or performers' music was to forfeit one of the profession's traditional perquisites, whether it be technical control or economic reward. By writing both, Alexander Reinagle managed to exercise in his compositional mind, if not embody in his music, the full range of a professional composer's opportunities and obligations.

If composing became a livelihood in America only where the supply of music from the Old World failed to meet American needs, we can see that it has been in performers' music, not composers' music, that the Old World has fallen short. American composers of performers' music—from Reinagle's "America, Commerce, and Freedom," to Stephen Foster's "Old Folks at Home," to W. C. Handy's "The St. Louis Blues," to Irving Berlin's "White Christmas," to Bob Dylan's "The Times They Are A-Changin' "—are the composers who have won a secure place in the American music business. By appealing to the tastes and adapting to the talents of many performers, the music of these men has established them as "professional" composers in an economic sense if not in the full sense of Thomson's intellectually based hierarchy.[80]

Having noted the importance of performers' music, let's look again at composers' music—at Reinagle as a writer of piano sonatas and at Sessions and company as writers of music for the concert hall—and examine its professional heritage. During the nineteenth century, as in the eighteenth, American composers' music existed mostly outside the music business. This did not discourage Americans from composing it, any more than Reinagle was stopped from composing sonatas because sonatas were unmarketable. In fact, the widespread impulse to compose is a striking feature of nineteenth-century American musical life. Scratch an organist, a pianist, even a historian, and you find a composer with a drawerful of songs, sonatas, concertos, cantatas, symphonies.[81] Little of this music was professionally motivated. But there it stands—or, rather, lies: testimony to the industriousness of its authors and of their urge to contribute their own mite to the tradition of the European masters.

The twentieth century has seen the gradual alienation of many composers of composers' music from other musical trades and occupations and from much of the concert-going audience as well. Yet alienation has not dampened the urge to compose. The writing of new composers' music goes on at what seems like a quickening pace, and all over the United States composers are hard at it, pouring their creative efforts into works that may never be heard, except in their own imaginations. This state of affairs suggests that complex, even contradictory impulses are at work. One step toward sorting them out is to distinguish between the *profession* of composer, the *role* of the composer, and the *place* of the composer, considering them as three different though complementary things.

Thomson described in 1939 how American composers make a living: "[the composer] plays in cafés and concerts. He conducts. He writes criticism. He sings in church choirs. He reads manuscripts for music publishers. He acts as musical librarian to institutions. He becomes a professor. He writes books. He lectures on the Appreciation of Music."[82] Conspicuous by its absence from the list are the words "he writes music." Perhaps the range of duties has changed a bit in the half-century since Thomson wrote. But the principle remains the same. As has been true since the time of Alexander Reinagle, the profession of composer of composers' music is only indirectly linked to a livelihood, and almost all such composers earn their keep by doing something else.

What about the *role* of composer? The question answers itself, for what nation would admit that it has no composers? Certainly we have composers: hundreds, even thousands of them. And we are knee-deep in composers' music.[83] Perhaps, as in the nineteenth century, the supply would have been assured in any case. But something new has appeared in the twentieth century: an institutional commitment to supporting the *role* of composer. This commitment is reflected by the beachhead that composers have won in the academy, the preserve gained by teaching. It is also reflected by patronage—in earlier years devoted almost entirely to supporting performers in the concert hall and opera house—which in our century has begun to be available to composers.

During and after World War I, as the reverberations from radical movements in Europe began to reach American shores, a few modernist composers, rejected by the concert establishment, managed to find patrons, as in Gertrude Vanderbilt Whitney's support of Edgard Varèse, or Harriette Miller's of Carl Ruggles, or Alma Wertheim's of Aaron Copland and Roy Harris.[84] But more typical has been the institutional patronage that began in the 1920s. In 1925, for example, Elizabeth Sprague Coolidge established at the Library of Congress an endowment for commissions, prizes, and concerts, with the funds open to European and American composers alike.[85] Beginning the same year, the John Simon Guggenheim Foundation offered the first of the year-long stipends it has since granted to North American composers.[86] Then there is the Fromm Music Foundation, established in 1952 to commission, record, and sponsor repeated performances of new works.[87] Other private agencies, such as the Ford[88] and Rockefeller Foundations,[89] have also supported and commissioned new works from living composers. As for the federal government, whose earlier support of music had been limited to the military (since the end of the eighteenth century)[90] and the depression-inspired relief measures of the WPA (1935–41),[91] it established its own program of composers' patronage in 1965 when the National Foundation on the Arts and Humanities was founded.[92] These programs, and others like them, distribute funds on a revolving basis, treating applicants' claims to patronage as more or less equal and rewarding them after they take their turn in line. The way the programs are administered testifies at once to their commitment to supporting and maintaining the *role* of composer and their democratic reluctance to favor any single composer.

If the *role* of the composer of composers' music is firm, their *place* in our musical life is small, and the shadow they cast over the American musical landscape is hard to detect. Place means presence, and in music presence means performance. In New York and a few other large cities, and on some university campuses, the composer's place is established by the chance to hear his or her music. But outside these circles, with their groups of specialist players, who, incidentally, make *their* way chiefly by other professional activity, that music is hardly heard at all, and composers exist chiefly as representatives of an honored role, their work reviewed and cataloged but not much relished.

In the field of American composers' music today, the imbalance between composers' honored role, their neglected place, and their almost nonexistent profession is striking. These different dimensions reveal our society's respect, in principle, for what composers are and what they do: talented, dedicated musicians who, as the heirs of Beethoven, maintain the legacy of past glories while also exploring new worlds of sound on society's behalf. At the same time, they reveal an indifference, perhaps even a hostility that amounts to a rejection of the experience that modern composers' music offers.

How does modern society treat something it respects but does not savor? The way we have treated most twentieth-century American composers' music: by finding a safe place for it. Composers' music by Americans—supported by various kinds of professional arrangements (including performing-rights income),[93] complemented by a modest but steady flow of patronage in the form of commissions, prizes, and fellowships—exists today in an environment like that of a laboratory. I borrow the analogy in part from Milton Babbitt, who once likened the "specialist" academic composer to the theoretical mathematician or physicist.[94] I'm also under the impression that labs, even when funded by laypeople, are run by experts, who evaluate how the lab's work is going. That's a way of pointing toward a noteworthy development among American composers of composers' music since World War II: the winning of autonomy—the right to compose essentially outside the strictures of audience esteem, or critics' approval, or the tastes and preferences of performers.

Autonomy has expressed itself in a feeling that, as Thomson suggested half a century ago, composers are perhaps the best judges of each others' works, even to the point of dispensing patronage, for the benefactions that reach composers are dispensed, at least in part, with the advice of a review of peers. Composers' music is thus composers' music both in its premise that the score controls the performance *and* in the narrowness of the world it inhabits—a world of composers and a small number of specialist-theorists who know their work. This is not to say that composers would spurn the chance to be heard and appreciated by a much larger audience. It is merely to recognize their lot. Through hard labor and the acceptance of a lofty, lonely vision of their calling, they have carved out for themselves an autonomous niche within the broader world of musical professions, occupations, and patronage. Most American composers of composers' music seek a home within that niche. Finding such a home depends chiefly on how good the composer is at addressing fellow composers. In other words, composers of composers' music today write the kind of music that they are commissioned, supported, and expected to write.

Historians concentrate on what is lasting, and in music history the score lasts long after the sounds of performance have died away and the memories of personalities and public careers have faded. That's one reason that music historians have concentrated on musical scores. We earn our methodological spurs by grouping scores for study and interpreting them as distillations of musical life—as, in effect, what matters most about a given musical culture.

Musical scores, however, can distill not only music itself but the context within which music is made—not only the musical style, the artistry, and the aesthetic achievement of composers but the impact of a musician's livelihood upon his or her music-making. As Virgil Thomson argued half a century ago, in essays called "How Composers Eat" and "Why Composers Write How: Or the Economic Determinism of Musical Style," in the United States, where music reflects the pressures of the marketplace, money and musical style are closely intermingled.[95] The scores of a forgotten composer like Alexander Reinagle may seem remote from present-day concerns. But if we can understand them as reflections and distillations of a professional environment that has shaped the particular, idiosyncratic patterns of American composition, then we can begin to recognize the continuity of our country's musical history and to see Reinagle, and Roger Sessions, and today's composers of composers' music as musicians linked in a tradition that began on this side of the Atlantic at least two centuries ago.

· 3 ·

Professions and Patronage II:
Performing

Pᴇʀꜰᴏʀᴍɪɴɢ ʜᴀs ʙᴇᴇɴ the most conspicuous American musical profession and one of the most profitable. The musicians best known to the public have been performers. But behind the limelight of public regard, it must be remembered, musical performance is a distillation: the public result of many different agents' endeavors.

In the professional realm, the public concert[1] is the emblematic event, for it is there that musical effort comes to fruition. A composer's invention, a teacher's regimen, an instrument-maker's labor, an entrepreneur's search for a forum, a critic's judgment—all, in a professional sense, revolve around the moment when performers sing or play music for the public to hear. For it's up to the performer to seize the occasion and, through artistry, technique, intellect, and personality, connect with an audience. In that connection lies the ultimate power of Western music-making. Performers risk much. But their intensely competitive profession offers rich rewards in money and fame.

Famous performers have been among the most fascinating American public figures, and few musical subjects are more ineffable than the relationship between them and their audiences. What makes a star performer? How can the "magic" of an excellent performance be described? Much has been written about performers—especially their lives and personalities—with questions like these in mind. Yet answers have remained elusive. Perhaps the reason is obvious. Because musical performance seeks connection, it is often judged less by what performers do than by how they are received. Therefore, writings that concentrate on performers without considering the audience and what it expects from them leave these questions unanswered.

To think of audiences and their reception of performers is to recognize that music is a particular kind of human interaction as well as an art. But how, in America, did audiences for music come to exist in the first place? In a country lacking the institutions that in Europe sponsored musical performance, other means of support had to be found.[2] Without opportunities to sing and play for pay, there can be no career for a performer. The creation of such opportunities is itself an occupation—the arm of musical distribution that brings performers together with audiences. Entrepreneurship is intertwined with performing so completely that neither can exist without the other. In fact, impresario, performer, and audience are bound together in a round of negotiation driven by the impresario's pursuit of economic gain. French pianist Henri Herz, who toured the United States in the 1840s, attributed to his American manager Bernard Ullman a definition of music that was obviously intended to sound cynical. In Ullman's mind, Herz wrote, music was "the art of attracting to a given auditorium, by secondary devices which often become the principal ones, the greatest possible number of curious people, so that when expenses are tallied against receipts, the latter exceed the former by the widest possible margin."[3] This definition shows little respect for either manager or audience. The latter, drawn by curiosity, cannot tell "primary" from "secondary" allurements and hence hardly deserves an artist's attention, except as a source of income. The former, knowing the audience's gullibility, seeks to exploit it for his own and the performer's advantage. The performer's artistic skill is the commodity the manager seeks to peddle. But the performer's dedication to art, Herz implies, is threatened by professional circumstances, which oblige the performer to do whatever it takes to occupy a curiosity-seeking audience, lured into a concert hall by the blandishments of a money-driven promoter. Thus, Herz's mock definition of music offers an unadorned glimpse of the performing musician's profession in the mid-nineteenth-century United States.

The first performers to appear regularly before paying audiences in America were the English men and women who sang on Colonial stages from the mid-eighteenth century on, brought to the New World by theatrical managers like Lewis Hallam, Jr.,[4] and Thomas Wignell.[5] The former arrived in the 1750s and toured North America's major cities, as well as some minor ones, presenting plays and ballad operas. By the

1790s, Boston, New York, Philadelphia, Baltimore, and Charleston all had theatrical companies in residence. Their presence established in each of these places a corps of experienced, European-trained musicians—singing actors, actresses, and orchestra players—some of whom supplemented their incomes by giving concerts (and lessons). It also made familiar the idea of public events centered on music, or at least involving it, and relying on an audience to pay for them. That audience had to be recruited, and advertising was the chief means. Newspapers carried notices of upcoming plays and concerts. Such ads proclaimed the merits of the event or, if the performers were new in town, touted their credentials. "At Mr. Hull's Assembly Room, will be performed a great *Concert* extraordinary," announced the New York *Mercury* on 16 May 1774 in a typical public invitation,[6] while in 1796 an advertisement for a concert in Charleston by "Signor Trisobio" identified him as "an Italian professor of vocal music, who had the honor to be employed three years in the Royal Chapel by the queen of Portugal and who last winter sung in London before all the royal family."[7] Advertisements ranged from the informative—*these* musicians performing *this* music at *this* time and place—to the promotional, often hinting that something extraordinary, unprecedented, or elevating awaited the customer. The public was being sold a chance to see and hear professionals practicing their craft, whether to dramatize real life on stage, to mock human pretensions through comedy, or to edify, divert, or amaze audiences with musical skill: beauty of tone, agility of technique, or an affecting delivery of melody and text. Many eighteenth-century concerts were followed by social dancing, which enlivened them for audience participants.[8]

Oscar G. Sonneck has documented how theatrical and concert life dovetailed in eighteenth-century America, with many of the same people—Alexander Reinagle, for example—involved in both. His studies also show that, from a professional standpoint, the "American" musical theater of the eighteenth century, like that of Bristol or Edinburgh, or even the West Indies, was an extension of the London stage. When Wignell and company sought new works or talent, they sailed to England to find them.[9] Carried on throughout the English-speaking world, this tradition remained Colonial, and not until well into the next century did American-born singers and players begin to find places in the American theater. Concert life, though more flexibly structured than the world of theatrical companies, followed suit. Sustained by its links with the theater, it was also similar in format and repertory. Some foreign performers toured the New World, then returned to the Old. Others settled here. But more important than questions of immigration and residency was the fact that both theater and concert stage perpetuated Old World traditions. In fact, all indications are that through the first four decades of the nineteenth century, a vast majority of professional performers in America—people who made their living chiefly by singing or playing—were foreign-born.[10]

A new situation arose in the 1840s. By that time, as egalitarian ideals and technological progress moved into synchrony, economic development in the United States was shifting into higher gear.[11] Musical activity increased too, with more and more performances taking place over an ever-widening territory.[12] With a growing appetite for public performance came new theatrical forms and the rise of new varieties of entrepreneurship. In the theater, the blackface minstrel show was born. Outside it, promoters of musical attractions (like Bernard Ullman) helped to spark the increase, as did artists and troupes who by the late 1830s had begun to tour the country in search of audiences, sometimes under a manager's direction and sometimes making their own schedules and arrangements.[13] Moreover, if not new to the 1840s, local musical societies also fostered performing careers, providing occasions where amateur and professional musicians could collaborate.[14] These developments maintain some links with the past, especially in the continuing importance of the English theater and Americans' responsiveness to foreign performers and music. But the vast increase in music's potential audience and in opportunities for American-born performers, performing American music, to make a living by singing and playing signaled the start of a new era.

Theatrical managers, as holdovers from an earlier age of entrepreneurship, continued in the 1840s to house resident companies playing English opera and other dramatic entertainments. They also hosted traveling companies.[15] By all odds, however, the most significant force to hit the American performing world in the first half of the nineteenth century was Italian opera, which, from the time of its New World debut in 1825, inspired struggles of entrepreneurship on its behalf. The story of the United States' embrace of Italian opera centers on New York City, whose elite society proved neither rich enough nor sufficiently

interested to support opera on its own. Lorenzo DaPonte, who emigrated to America in 1805 and found a post as a teacher of Italian, was
involved from the start. First, DaPonte encouraged Irish-born merchant
Dominick Lynch to bring Manuel Garcia's troupe to New York for a
season of Italian opera at the Park Theater (1825–26).[16] Several years
later, he also helped to find sponsorship for a season staged by Bolo-
gnese impresario Giovanni Montresor's company (1832–33); then he and
Lynch backed the building of a new Italian opera house, which opened
in 1833. These efforts, like the launching of a new company by res-
taurateur Ferdinand Palmo in 1844 and the collaboration of 150 wealthy
New Yorkers to give the new Astor Place Opera House its own company
in 1847,[17] all failed to win a permanent presence for opera in the city.
Not until the 1850s was success achieved. At the Academy of Music,
Bohemian-born impresario and conductor Max Maretzek devised a plan
in which the works of Rossini, Donizetti, Bellini, and Verdi, as well as
other European masters, performed in a large hall (4,600 seats) at varied
prices ($1.50 top, ranging down to 25 cents), attracted an ample base
of public support.[18]

If Italian opera proved so hard to establish in New York City, and
if after 1850 New York and New Orleans were the only American cities
with permanent resident companies,[19] by what token does opera deserve
to be called "the most significant force to hit the American performing
world in the first half of the nineteenth century"? Such a statement
may imply exaggerated respect for the prestige of an Old World genre.
But in fact, there is much evidence to support it.

Italian opera relies upon the drama inherent in the notion of stage
characters who express themselves in song. And the operatic stage
proved a potent vehicle for such expressions: larger-than-life characters,
dressed in finery and with strong, sometimes beautiful voices, pouring
out their emotions—love, rage, grief, exultation—on a grand scale, to
music suited for such displays. Opera singers earned adulation and
moved audiences by making public spectacles of themselves. Their skill
at capturing, distilling, protracting, and communicating the human passions with utter conviction was surely the ingredient that enabled opera
to cut across social and class lines, attracting a wide range of nineteenth-
century American listeners in performance.[20]

But opera also reached far beyond the operatic stage. To speak of
opera's "ingredients" is to recognize that, while being a form that unites

many varied devices in one convincing whole, it is also a bundle of elements that can be pulled apart, changed, and recombined in new settings. The programs given at New York's Olympic Theater provide a vivid example of opera's adaptability. Managed from 1839 by comedian William Mitchell, and with composer-conductor George Loder as music director—both were Englishmen—the Olympic offered light entertainment and specialized in opera burlesques for an admission of 12½ cents. Mitchell's *The Roof Scrambler*, a travesty of Bellini's *La Sonnambula*, was a particular hit there, as were later *Mrs. Normer* (1841; Bellini's *Norma*), *Sam Parr, with the Red Coarse Hair* (1841; Hérold's *Zampa, or The Red Corsair*) and *Fried Shots* (1843; Weber's *Der Freischütz*).[21] In works like these, operatic characters and plots were employed to the burlesquers' own ends, with music adapted and arranged freely from the original scores. Clearly, the titles, subjects, leading characters, and plot elements of famous operas were common cultural property. Clearly, too, famous operas supplied hit musical numbers for the sheet-music trade—numbers whose performance in stage parodies struck familiar chords with the audience.[22] With opera as a source, moreover, performers could ring changes on its themes and twist its archetypal characters—the sleepwalker of *La Sonnambula*, the madwoman of *Lucia*, the magician of *Der Freischütz*—for comic effect or social comment.[23] As a theatrical form, then, opera struggled for a toehold on American shores. But as a frame of reference and a cornucopia of song, it provided the American vernacular theater, and the musical scene in general, with a vitalizing force of great richness.

It was into an environment prepared by opera that blackface minstrelsy was received. The landmark event occurred on 6 February 1843, when Dan Emmett, Frank Brower, Dick Pelham, and Billy Whitlock, billed as "the novel, grotesque, original, and surpassingly melodious Ethiopian Band, entitled the Virginia Minstrels," staged an evening's entertainment in blackface at New York's Bowery Amphitheater. The resulting mania for similar companies, and for the new sound they brought into the theater—fiddle, banjo, bones, tambourines, and, as one advertisement put it, "other instruments of music used on the Southern Plantations"[24]—is well known. Historians have explored both the minstrel show's indigenous roots and its racial stereotyping. What has been less often noticed, however, is how minstrelsy helped to transform the world of American musical performance.[25]

Blackface minstrelsy was the first musical genre to reverse the east-to-west transatlantic flow of professional performers that had existed throughout this country's organized musical life. Until Americans discovered ways to present performing styles they themselves had invented, European dominance went unchallenged. An early example occurred in the 1830s, when black trumpeter Frank Johnson of Philadelphia featured his own band in a successful series of promenade concerts.[26] But the impact of minstrelsy, a fresh theatrical form whose sudden popularity sparked a demand for American performers, went much further. Minstrelsy called for a different kind of musician: a man who could step into the character and dialect of an "Ethiopian" stage darky and entertain an audience with comic turns and the singing and playing of popular music. A minstrel's apprenticeship involved no particular pedigree or formal training. Indeed, for some its key element was personal contact with black Americans. Philadelphia-born E. P. Christy (1815–62) spent time as a young man in New Orleans, where he later claimed to have studied the Negroes' "queer words and simple but expressive melodies."[27] Christy perfected his imitation as a traveling blackface musician and comic singer in the 1830s before founding his own troupe in Buffalo in the 1840s. T. D. Rice (1808–60), who invented "Jim Crow," the "first important American stage character rooted in black contemporary culture,"[28] based his creation on the walk, dance, dress, and song of an aging black man he encountered in Louisville in the late 1820s.[29] On the other hand, Ohioan Dan Emmett, the driving force behind the Virginia Minstrels, claimed no formative experiences with black culture. The background upon which he drew in his show-business career included a stint as a military musician at Jefferson Barracks, Missouri, and travels with a Cincinnati-based circus.[30]

Inside the theater, nineteenth-century Americans seldom formed the silent, largely passive audiences that are now expected at "cultivated" events. In fact, statements like that of a Boston citizen in 1846 could be read today as evidence of that era's uncivilized behavior. "We (the sovereigns) determine to have the worth of our money when we go to the theatre," this correspondent wrote. "We made Blangy dance her best dances twice; we made Mrs. Sequin [*sic*] repeat 'Marble Halls' . . . and tonight we are going to encore Mrs. Kean's 'I Don't Believe It' in *The Gamester*. . . . Perhaps we'll flatter Mr. Kean by making him take poison twice."[31] But the audience's decorum is less the point here than its expectations, which were those of people determined to *react* to the spectacle, responding in public interchange with stage players. The work being performed was far less important to these theater-goers than the quality of their own experience. If they liked what they saw and heard, they clamored for more; if not, they demanded an end to it. Lawrence Levine has compared the atmosphere in mid-nineteenth-century American theaters to that of a modern sports event, where audience members "are participants who can enter into the action on the field, who feel a sense of immediacy and at times even of control, who articulate their opinions and feelings vocally and unmistakably."[32] The audience, in other words, consisted not of modern "spectators" but participating "witnesses" with a firm sense of themselves as an active force in the show.[33]

By all accounts, minstrel audiences were among the most boisterous, the most insistent that performers meet the expectations that had brought them to the theater in the first place.[34] That fact should be kept in mind in weighing the achievement of E. P. Christy, who managed Christy's Minstrels and also performed as the group's interlocutor (master of ceremonies), ballad singer, and banjo player. Assembled as a six-man troupe in Buffalo in 1843, Christy's Minstrels toured upstate New York and elsewhere for several years before opening in New York City in April 1846. A critic complimented their first performances for "chaste, refined, and harmonious" singing and "very fine" instrumental music. His praise of "exquisite . . . soft touches" on the bones suggests the skill of Christy and his men at playing the crowd. For, as well as meeting audience taste for the high-spirited, stomping numbers that were minstrelsy's stock-in-trade, the Christy troupe also featured pieces that, if "exquisite" touches on the bones could be heard, must have hushed the house into rapt silence. Offering family entertainment at cheap prices (25 cents for adults, half that for children), Christy's Minstrels took up residence at New York's Mechanics' Hall for a run of more than seven years (February 1847–July 1854) and 2,792 performances—ample evidence that Christy had discovered the kind of successful formula for which popular performers search.[35]

Minstrelsy, however, was just one of many attractions for which new paying audiences emerged in the antebellum years. The rise of American vernacular forms did not diminish interest in European performers, who took their offerings deeper and deeper into the continent. Through the 1840s, a troupe headed by English basso Arthur Seguin toured North America, performing operatic favorites in English translation.[36] Beginning in the middle of that decade, a wave of European virtuoso performers traveled to the United States on concert tours, including singers Marietta Alboni, Giulia Grisi, Henriette Sontag, and Jenny Lind; violinists Alexandre Artôt, Camillo Sivori, Henry Vieuxtemps, and Ole Bull; and pianists Leopold DeMeyer, Henri Herz, and Sigismond Thalberg.[37] The appearance of the Tyrolese Rainer Family at New York's Apollo Theater in November 1839 touched off a fad for "family" singing groups specializing in folk songs and part-songs.[38] Of the many Americans who followed in their wake, the Hutchinson Family Singers from Milford, New Hampshire, made the greatest impact. Touring from 1842 until 1849, the Hutchinsons were drawn to political causes such as temperance, abolition, and universal suffrage and eventually brought songs supporting such causes into their concerts.[39] Finally, English-born ballad singers William Dempster (from 1835) and Henry Russell (from 1836) found audiences for their performances on a more intimate scale, as if inviting the audience as guests into their own parlors for an evening's entertainment.

The survival of a detailed journal kept by members of the Hutchinson Family Singers provides glimpses of that group's entrepreneurial customs. During their first tour in 1842, the family's four singing members, Asa, John, Judson, and Abigail, seem to have improvised concert arrangements as they traveled. On Friday, 29 July, for example, the Hutchinsons performed in Sandy Hill, New York, and planned an appearance for the next evening in Glens Falls. Judson Hutchinson noted on Saturday that "John & A[sa] have gone to Saratoga Springs to make preparations for a concert." But a storm broke out that afternoon, delaying the brothers' return and forcing cancelation of the Glens Falls concert. John and Asa had struck a deal in Saratoga Springs to sing three concerts there for room and board, plus one-third "of what is taken." Arriving on Monday, 1 August, the Hutchinsons found the resort town "lively," with Frank Johnson and his band in residence at a local hall. Their concerts of that evening and the next, however, were sparsely attended—"Sung last night to a house full of seats," Judson wrote—and, after dispatching Asa ahead by train to explore the situation elsewhere, they left Saratoga Springs a day early, traveling to Ballston for a concert on Wednesday night, 3 August.[40]

Things changed for the Hutchinsons toward the end of their second tour. Unexpectedly, in the spring of 1843, they found themselves no longer a struggling enterprise but a success. Their final concert in New York City (25 May) earned receipts of $130 from an audience of 600. And when they moved on to Boston, where "Jesse arranged the business," they sang to a thousand spectators at the Melodeon Theater on 2 June. "Our receipts for that Evening," Asa wrote, "were as great if not larger than any receipts before, between $180 & $200."[41] The Hutchinsons' appeal was both artistic and political. A New York critic praised their "admirable" style of singing: "simple, sweet and full of mountain melody" and with voices "all rich and clear."[42] And the next week in Boston, they appeared at an antislavery rally in Faneuil Hall with leading abolitionists like William Lloyd Garrison, Wendell Phillips, and ex-slave Frederick Douglass. "Speechifying, even of the better sort," responded one newspaper correspondent, "did less to interest, purify and subdue minds, than this irresistible Anti-Slavery music."[43] The now-famous family returned to their farm in July 1843. By fall, they were back in the New York area, where they stayed for two months, giving more than twenty concerts, including two "farewell" events at Niblo's Theater. Dale Cockrell reports that each of these performances attracted an audience of 1,200 or more, which, at 50 cents per ticket, made for revenues of more than $600 each.[44] When the Hutchinsons set out again in January 1844, they entrusted management of their concerts to brother Zephaniah Kittredge Hutchinson, who traveled with them, serving as advance agent for the next year and a half.[45] It was in keeping with the tenor of the Hutchinsons' musical career—audiences and critics received them as unspoiled, talented, morally principled amateurs, and in fact they did return in the summer to New Hampshire to farm the land—that a family member would serve as their impresario.

Of all the musical performers active in antebellum America, however, none better illustrates the potential of imaginative promotion than the visit of Swedish soprano Jenny Lind. Inspired by the notion that a concert tour of the United States could be lucrative for both him and Lind, P. T. Barnum enlisted the singer's participation, then set about creating a demand for her. Well before Lind's arrival, Barnum launched a publicity campaign based on claims about her virtuous character, the prestige of opera singing, and the susceptibility of the American audience. He struck just the right chord with the public. Lind's ship from Europe was greeted by a crowd of 30,000 when it landed in New York Harbor on 1 September 1850.[46] And when she announced that she would donate to charity her share of the receipts from her first concert, Lind's stock rose even higher.[47] Newspapers throughout the country reported her every deed and character trait. But press coverage of Lind's tour did more than work Americans into a lather to attend her concerts. It provided a framework for understanding them. The rapture with which other audiences had greeted Lind's performances was a matter of record, so each new audience brought to its experience a sense of avid expectation, mixed with the usual curiosity. Lind's concerts began with playing and singing by other performers, which prepared listeners for the great diva.[48] Her appearance, always plain and dignified, confirmed the image of unpretentious virtue that Barnum had built up around her. And her singing offered something for everyone, from fiery, virtuosic Italian arias to Swedish folk songs and even favorite songs in English like "Home, Sweet Home." Lind's simple songs gave audiences a chance to measure the sound of her singing voice and to test claims of its "purity" and "sheer beauty" against their own experience. As for operatic arias, even listeners for whom such music was unknown terrain were supplied, thanks to publicity and reviews, with a language— "sweetness and compass," "extraordinary powers," "brilliant clearness"—for discussing her artistry.[49] In organizing Lind's tour, Barnum convinced Americans in large numbers that a powerful experience lay in store for them. Then, through Lind's artistry, he met their expectations. The remarkable success of Lind's tour may be judged by the unlikelihood of Barnum's achievement. By peddling recitals of a foreign opera singer, he created not only a cultural sensation but a commercial bonanza, involving everything from concert tickets, sheet music, and pianos to Jenny Lind gloves, stoves, and cigars.[50]

The 1840s represent a watershed in the history of American musical performance. By the end of that decade most of the elements that were to endure for the next century and more were in place: a ready supply of professional performers, domestic and foreign, to carry on the concert and theatrical life that prosperity encouraged; growth in the ranks of impresarios, entrepreneurs, promoters, and institutions organizing an increasingly diverse menu of performances; and a steady increase in audiences willing to pay to be regaled, entertained, amazed, tickled, or edified by the array of performances available to them. Many things changed during the nineteenth century's second half. Americans began to win places in the ranks of concert-hall performers,[51] and after Emancipation the number of black professionals grew apace.[52] Theatrical circuits consolidated entrepreneurial endeavor in new ways.[53] But all of this activity was premised on one condition: Musical performance must pay for itself.[54] Indeed, everything discussed so far about the performing professions in America occurred in the marketplace. No development in the second half of the nineteenth century was more important to the history of music in America than the creation of a new sphere for performance.[55] And no vantage point offers a clearer perspective on that development than the career of Theodore Thomas (1835–1905), the nineteenth century's premier American conductor. For the symphony orchestra provided this development its chief national focus.

Born in Esens, East Friesland, Germany, the son of a professional musician, Thomas emigrated with his family to New York City at the age of ten.[56] In 1854, he joined the first violin section of the New York Philharmonic Society, an organization built on the model of the local musical society. Founded in 1842 with an idealistic mission in mind,[57] run by its members (who included both amateurs and professionals), and financed by membership fees and concert subscriptions,[58] the society pursued its goals within the modest resources provided by concerts, typically four per year. Thomas was an accomplished violinist, and he kept playing in public well into his thirties. But even as a very young man, he showed talent for entrepreneurial leadership.[59] In May 1862 Thomas conducted his first professional orchestral concert at New York's Irving Hall, an event for which he himself took the financial risk: booking the hall, choosing the players and the program, conducting the rehearsals, directing the advertising and ticket sales, and paying the players from the proceeds while he kept the rest.[60] Soon Thomas also began conducting the Brooklyn Philharmonic Society, formed in 1857 as a local parallel to New York's.[61] Later, he served as regular conductor of the New York Philharmonic (1877–91) and founding conductor of the Chicago Orchestra (1891–1905), and led music festivals throughout the country. But it was as impresario and conductor of the Theodore Thomas Orchestra (1865–90) that he made his deepest mark on American musical life. For during that time,

Thomas—an idealist with a payroll to meet—controlled both the artistic and economic arms of his orchestral enterprise.

To identify art and economics as separate "arms" of Thomas's activity is to recognize a conflict between them. Indeed, for Americans who have written about this country's musical life, perhaps no idea has been more basic to their understanding of it than the assumption that economic interests run counter to aesthetic ones—that the marketplace is a foe of artistic values.[62] Theodore Thomas's career tests that assumption, for without a musical marketplace, Thomas's orchestra could never have survived. The conductor's great achievement was to discover *within that marketplace* an audience for orchestral music and hence to maintain a career for himself and his men as performing musicians. In the course of his struggles, Thomas came to know his audiences' habits and tastes very well indeed. Yet, he was seldom content merely to serve them. Respecting audience taste while working persistently to change it, Thomas came to be the chief actor in a drama whose denouement was the establishment of the symphony orchestra in America.

Thomas himself grew up (in New York City) in a cultural environment dominated by German music and musicians, the German language, and German artistic values. In Thomas, that Old World legacy seems to have combined with character traits—ambition, determination, independence of mind, physical stamina, self-assurance—to create a burning sense of mission. As a conductor, he would strive to make his adopted country "musical" through the cultivation of instrumental music.[63] What the United States lacked, he believed, "was a good orchestra and plenty of concerts within reach of the people."[64] To fill that need, Thomas set about providing audiences with music-making of the best quality the marketplace would support. Three related factors shaped Thomas's pursuit of quality: how his orchestra played, what it played, and where it played.

Economic conditions affect the character of any orchestra's playing. Thomas was a taskmaster who strove for precise, polished performances; these required skilled players—mostly German immigrants—and time to rehearse them; and the best players, being most in demand, preferred situations offering the most work. Thus, to keep his orchestra together, Thomas pursued every possible opportunity for performance. His entrepreneurial sense taught him that, as one writer has put it, "there was not just one symphonic audience but a variety of them."[65] The responses of each audience, Thomas recognized, depended on the performers' ability to address it on its own terms. And that demanded in turn careful consideration of musical repertory.

"Symphonic music is the highest flower of art," Thomas once wrote,[66] testifying to his belief that the music he loved was imbued with ethical force. He looked upon Beethoven in particular "not only as a great musician but [as] an almost divine embodiment of moral virtue."[67] Performers and listeners alike, he believed, were tested and measured by the best symphonic compositions. In his autobiography Thomas explained why he discouraged the telling of risqué stories in his presence and why he never read "trashy" books or attended "trashy plays": "When I come before the public to interpret masterworks, and my soul should be inspired with noble and impressive emotions, these evil thoughts run around my mind like squirrels and spoil it all. A musician must keep his heart pure and his mind clean if he wishes to elevate, instead of debasing, his art."[68] In listening to music by Beethoven and other great composers, Thomas wrote, "faculties are called into action and appealed to other than those [the listener] ordinarily uses," absorbing attention and freeing listeners "from worldly cares." More than vocal music, whose meanings are explicit, instrumental music appeals to the listener's "imagination and intellect, and permits his own interpretation to the extent of his experience."[69] Differences in listening experience were precisely what divided Thomas's audience into segments, each requiring a repertory aimed to please while also extending the reach of its taste, in line with Thomas's goal of elevation.[70]

Thomas's pursuit of different audiences also involves the third issue of quality: the venues in which he and his men performed. Throughout its history, the Thomas Orchestra played in standard concert halls, where they existed. But beginning in 1865, it also began to make a specialty of outdoor concerts. A summer series in Central Park Garden proved especially popular with the public: 1,227 programs in an eight-year period, 1868–75, or more than 150 performances per summer on the average. At Central Park, and in the other outdoor series he conducted throughout his career, Thomas served customers a mixture of symphonic movements with overtures, dances, and lighter selections in settings where they felt relaxed and comfortable—snacking, drinking, and socializing. Such "concessions," he believed, chipped away at barriers that inexperience erected between audience and orchestra. At the same time, thanks to all that performing, the Thomas Orchestra grew artistically, outstripping all other American ensembles, with their changing personnel (including conductors) and small numbers of concerts.[71]

But however popular he may have been with New York audiences, Thomas stayed in business only by turning his orchestra into a touring ensemble.[72] In 1869 the Thomas Orchestra made the first of its many journeys over the so-called Thomas Highway of the United States and Canada, which included Maine, Georgia, New Orleans, San Francisco, and many places in between.[73] The orchestra also played up to a dozen concerts per season and more in cities like Boston and Chicago that lacked permanent orchestras of their own. Through the early 1870s, the ensemble toured widely, sometimes spending more than half the year on the road. The rigors of that life worked hardships on Thomas and his men.[74] But the results justified them.[75] Pianist Anton Rubinstein testified at the end of an 1873 tour with Thomas that in the whole world, only the orchestra of the National Conservatory of Paris was the Thomas Orchestra's equal in personnel—"but, alas, they have no Theodore Thomas to conduct them."[76]

Thomas's achievement, while heroic, was no model for the symphony orchestra's establishment in this country. Dependent for support entirely on concert receipts, the Thomas Orchestra toured from necessity, not choice. Indeed, given its size and character, a symphony orchestra is far from ideal as a touring ensemble. In Europe most orchestras were local organizations. They were tied to a particular place, financed by local resources, and they addressed local audiences. Similarly, in the wake of Thomas's tours, the American symphony orchestra began to establish itself as a civic enterprise. Orchestras were formed where money could be found to free them from dependency on the marketplace—the dependency that had forced Thomas to tour and to perform music that he would rather have left to others. Such funding hinged on convincing patrons that symphonic music was worth their support. Among the factors that channeled money to symphony orchestras, one belief was fundamental: the orchestral works of great composers ranked among the supreme achievements of humankind.[77] A community, however prosperous, whose citizens had no experience of this art could hardly aspire to cultural distinction. Hence, both civic duty and a wish to foster the expression of enlightened virtue moved wealthy Americans to join the ranks of orchestral patrons.[78]

The orchestra's elevation of composers and their music broke with the customs of earlier professional concert life, which, under the control of entrepreneurs, had tended to privilege *occasions.* By the late nineteenth century, the American symphony orchestra was privileging *works* over occasions. Under the banner *ars longa, vita brevis,* symphonic performers approached their task with fealty to the score, sparing no effort to honor the composer's artistic intent. As for the audience, its members learned to behave like respectful guests, listening in rapt attentiveness and deep concentration, alert to the work's nuances and sure of the significance of the whole endeavor.[79] Presented in that ambience, music could pack enormous power. Charles Edward Russell, an early biographer of Theodore Thomas, recalled that in 1877 the Thomas Orchestra paid a visit to the Mississippi River town where he grew up, playing works by Mendelssohn, Gounod, Saint-Saëns, Schumann, Berlioz, and Liszt. For the audience, this writer later remembered, "life was never the same afterward. . . . There had been shown to them things and potentialities they had never suspected. So then there really existed as a fact, and not as something heard of and unattainable, this world of beauty, wholly apart from everyday experiences."[80] When approached with care, American audiences found the symphony orchestra's "world of beauty" so compelling that by the early twentieth century it had won a secure niche in the nation's cultural life.

This seems like the place to pause and reflect for a moment on the shape of American music-making described by general historians of the subject. Whatever their values, as noted in chapter 1, these writers have found musical endeavor divided into two broad streams: "classical" and "popular," or "serious" and "light," or "art music" and "functional music." It has already been noted that "the cultivated tradition" and "the vernacular tradition," terms offered by Hitchcock to encompass both properties of music and attitudes toward it, seem more flexible and less hierarchical than the older categories, which may explain their growing use in recent years. On the other hand, these terms, introduced in a history that deals only with American "classical" and "popular" genres, lack comprehensiveness. They tend to come up short when faced with "folk" or "traditional" musical practices. For example, in the customs of Native American communities some music combines the supposedly "vernacular" trait of acquisition—being "grown into as one grows into one's vernacular tongue"—with the supposedly "cultivated" one of function: being approached "for its edification—its moral [and] spiritual . . . values."[81] This objection aside, Hitchcock's terms fit well into a historiographically based inquiry. By making ample room for agents other than composers, they invite an approach to history in which performance and reception are allowed to play a key role.

The attitude of deep respect toward music that Theodore Thomas fostered was a change from earlier custom—a change crucial to the founding and maintenance of the institutions that still enjoy high prestige in the "cultivated" branch of American musical life: symphony orchestras, opera companies, conservatories. The change took place chiefly in the realm of attitude. Beethoven's symphonies and Bellini's operas were performed and listened to in mid-nineteenth-century America, but seldom within the aura of respectful concentration that encouraged responses like Charles Edward Russell's to the Theodore Thomas Orchestra. It's not enough to say that Bellini's works themselves were "popular" in 1850 and "classical" in 1900, for that would overlook the huge gap in musical density between, say, *Norma* and "Oh! Susanna." The terms available to us simply don't fit the matter we're talking about unless—claiming that a "popular" attitude toward Bellini was gradually replaced by a "classical" one—we stretch these terms beyond their original intent. Created with properties of music in mind, they cannot encompass the attitudes toward music brought about by the change in performing ambience. Even Hitchcock's more flexible "vernacular" and "cultivated," while taking attitude more into account, won't quite fit the present case.

If we want to do justice to nineteenth-century American music, we need a pair of attitudinal terms to supplement our familiar repertoire-based ones. Accordingly, I propose that we call the two attitudes that have dominated the performing professions in America for the last century and a half "accessibility" and "authenticity."

Opera in mid-nineteenth-century America exemplifies accessibility. As we have seen, opera flourished in the American marketplace. It flourished as entertainment for an audience that cheered favorite performers on, abused others, and expected calls for encores to be obeyed. It flourished as music for home performers to sing and for pianists and wind bands to play. And it also flourished in the form of characters and stories that caught the popular imagination. In all of these ways opera proved accessible to American audiences. Note, however, that most Americans encountered operas not as integral works of art, faithful to the composer's score, but in altered form: as adaptations, pastiches, arrangements, translations, truncations, excerpts, and single numbers. Alteration—the tailoring of the music to suit particular audiences and circumstances—was the key to opera's accessibility. In a composer-centered history of American music, opera in the nineteenth century earns little more than a footnote. But when performance and reception are brought into that history, opera looms as a significant genre in American music.[82]

In standard schemes of classification, Bellini's *Norma* belongs with the cultivated tradition, with "Western art music," or "classical," or "serious" music. But to make it accessible to nineteenth-century American audiences, and hence to maintain their own careers, impresarios and performers changed *Norma* in ways that brought it closer to the vernacular tradition—that turned it into a kind of popular music. What I'm calling "accessibility" here is itself a statement of priorities. Accessibility seeks out the center of the marketplace. It privileges occasions over works. And it *invests ultimate authority in the present-day audience.* Performers driven by accessibility seek most of all to find and please audiences and to increase their size. From the eighteenth century to the twentieth, performers and entrepreneurs in America—sometimes working with composers, sometimes not—have been ingenious in their pursuit of accessibility, which has been an agent of new styles, institutions, and techniques of merchandising from New York's Olympic Theater, to vaudeville, to the London Symphony's *Hooked on Classics* album, to Madonna.

But to suggest that the American marketplace forces performers to embrace accessibility would be to tell only part of the story. The marketplace is more complex than that. Indeed, in the second half of the nineteenth century, there took hold in this country a new attitude among some performers, the one I'm calling "authenticity," implying the genuine article—the real thing. Authenticity arose as an ideal countering the marketplace's devotion to accessibility. Authenticity privileges works over occasions. In fact, authenticity *invests ultimate authority in works and the traditions within which they are composed.* Performers who follow the ideal of authenticity believe that musical compositions, at the time of their creation, are animated with a *certain original spirit*. A performer is duty-bound to seek that spirit, to be guided by it, to remain faithful to it. Authenticity is an oppositional stance. Its disciples seek truths behind appearances, follow ideals that may (though not necessarily) involve financial sacrifice, and often set themselves against general trends of fashion and public taste. Authenticity can be an expensive proposition. Its serious pursuit requires financing that, though still connected to the marketplace, does not depend completely upon it. The combination of idealism and sacrifice that underlies authenticity helps to explain its appeal to certain kinds of performers and patrons. In high-mindedness and rigor, authenticity is somewhat akin to religion.[83]

The beliefs pulled together here under the label of "authenticity" provided the ideological cornerstone upon which the American symphony orchestra was founded. Indeed, without such an ideal—an ideal, by the way, whose intellectual appeal could be emotionally verified by the experience of listening—it is not clear how an alternative to "accessibility" could have emerged in nineteenth-century America.[84] With the help of authenticity's powerful justification, however, sources of orchestral patronage began to open up. In 1881, banker Henry Lee Higginson founded the Boston Symphony Orchestra and ran it himself for nearly four decades, hiring and firing conductors and players (all under personal contract to him), and collecting the receipts, making up deficits out of his own pocket.[85] A different strategy worked a decade later in Chicago, when, at the behest of Charles Norman Fay, a group of fifty businessmen and civic leaders each contributed $1,000 per year for three years to a fund guaranteeing the enterprise against losses, then hired Theodore Thomas himself as the orchestra's first conductor, placing artistic matters in his hands.[86] Other cities found their own schemes.[87] But no matter how the money was raised, all these endeavors were rooted in civic pride and a belief in authenticity. If the ideal of authenticity were to be served, these patrons understood, the pursuit of accessibility must be set aside.

Recently, the ambience that Theodore Thomas and his colleagues worked hard to establish has come in for criticism as historians have found fault with some of its results. What earlier writers had hailed as progress toward artistic "maturity" has begun to reveal another side: the "sacralization" of the concert hall into a place where secular rituals take place; the building of a cultural "hierarchy" in which those rituals serve as barriers; and the fragmentation of the musical audience. All of the latter symptoms are said to reflect a snobbish elitism that has plagued the cultivated American musical scene ever since.[88] Indeed, the link between social exclusiveness and the concert hall in America is an old one. In an interview published long after music publisher Gustave Schirmer's death, his daughter confided: "Father hated what he called 'social music,' glittering occasions and society patrons," which to her represented the world relished by other musical friends and family like conductor Walter Damrosch and her uncle Rudolph Schirmer.[89] Damrosch's niece Marya Mannes's description of her Uncle Walter as "always center-stage: charming host and perfect showman" helps to explain his success with musical patrons.[90] Feeling at ease with the social occasions attached to concert-giving, Damrosch gloried in both the artistic and social environments of his musical life, avidly and easily courting the favor of those who might be able to further his career. On the other hand, German-born composer Paul Hindemith, who taught at Yale University from 1940 to 1953 and became an American citizen during that time, experienced the impact of one of sacralization's more incongruous by-products after he left the United States for Europe in the 1950s. For two years, Hindemith waited vainly for invitations to conduct American orchestras. Then, early in 1956, he had his Zurich agent seek out an American management firm headed by the well-connected Arthur M. Judson for help in securing an engagement with the Chicago Symphony Orchestra, then conducted by Fritz Reiner. Judson wrote back:

> I am afraid there will be no chance for Hindemith in Chicago since Reiner does not seem to be interested in him. However, Pittsburgh is interested in having him in the first part of January 1957 for a fee of $1,000. Would Mr. Hindemith be willing to come for that one date? Please let me know immediately so as not to hold up Pittsburgh in its plans.[91]

Hindemith took Judson's letter as a snub and was deeply offended.[92] But in the sphere of "sacralized" American concert life, a prominent concert manager, aligned in his own mind with certified artistic glory, found little reason to doubt that his prestige and power far exceeded those of an active, distinguished contemporary composer.[93]

If the nineteenth-century attitudes that inspired the ideal of "authenticity" now seem narrow, exclusive, or even pernicious, we would do well to recognize that authenticity, broadly defined, has prompted most of the musical patronage that has existed in the United States. Moreover, as the course of professional musical performance in twentieth-century America will show, authenticity has proved a far more flexible ideal than its first champions could have imagined.

Over the past century, technological change has dramatically altered the face of American musical performance. This is not to say, however, that technological change is new to our age. Even without discussing musical instruments and their manufacture, the story of performers, entrepreneurs, audiences, and their interactions could be sketched over more than two hundred years from a technological standpoint. Chapters in that story include: the founding of a domestic sheet-music trade (1780s); the changing modes of printing music (punched plates, engraving, and lithography [1780s–1830s]); the improvement of transportation—especially railroads and transatlantic steamships—and the invention of the telegraph, all making musicians' travel easier and providing speedier distribution of printed music (1840s); the appearance of the phonograph (ca. 1900) and the many later developments in recording and distributing musical sound;[94] the rise of the film industry and the changing role of music within it (1910s on); the introduction of the microphone and electronic amplifier and their effect on performing styles (1920s); the advent of radio, perhaps the most democratic form of disseminating music (late 1920s); the role of television, today's most powerful, pervasive, and expensive performance medium (1940s); and the rise of electronically synthesized sound, allowing one musician to take the place of many (1970s).

To survey such developments with performers, audiences, and entrepreneurs in mind is to glimpse the shifting ground of their interaction. It is also to recognize that changes in their roles are interrelated: for performers, the evolving function of the public appearance; for audiences, the division into more and more specialized segments; for entrepreneurs, the rise of collective and corporate sponsorship.[95] These changes all involve technology's impact upon communication—its power to capture performances and to circulate them more and more swiftly and widely.

Perhaps nothing reveals the effect of technology on the performer's profession better than the changing role of the personal appearance. Until around the turn of the century, when phonograph recordings began to circulate commercially, personal appearances were the only way for performers to reach their customers. By the 1920s, recordings were becoming big business. But they still were considered an adjunct to "live" performance: an effective means of marketing performers and increasing the fees they could claim for singing and playing in theaters and on concert stages. Technology pressed forward; recorded performances became more and more faithful facsimiles of live ones. As sound quality improved, long-playing records, magnetic tape, and compact discs offered lengthier stretches of unbroken sound. New means of access dissolved traditional links with space and time. Performances were no longer restricted to concert halls, theaters, nightclubs, and dance halls, nor did listeners have to schedule their opportunities to hear them. The social experience of being an audience member changed. Broadcast and televised performances brought music into American homes, while car radios, cassette tapes, and portable playback equipment took it wherever listeners wanted to go. If in the nineteenth century music was embedded in social experience—the experience of people gathered to make music and to listen—in our time, technology, in effect, has drawn a veil over the social circumstances of music's performance.[96] In the late twentieth century, for most Americans most of the time, music is experienced as disembodied sound.

When audiences can accept disembodied sound as a "natural" form of music, on the one hand, and, on the other, buy it in packages like soap, cigarettes, or other consumer products, the implications for musical performance are considerable. The former suggests that music is *nothing more* than sound. If that is true, then one might just as well ignore music—as if it were part of the environment—as listen to it with total absorption. Disconnected from its makers, music becomes much more widely available. Even complex and culturally remote styles grow familiar with repetition.[97] At the same time, sound alone can do no more than suggest the intensity and excitement of music-making's tactile and choreographic dimensions. As for the physical packaging of music, its impact on performers has been strong. In some branches of the music business, sound recordings (including film, television, and video) have replaced "live" performance as the most desirable and lucrative means of reaching audiences. Personal appearances have become an adjunct to *facsimiles* of personal appearances: an effective way of plugging recorded music, capitalizing on the appeal of performers known for their recordings. Entrepreneurs have moved into closer contact with industry, for the technology's cost and the distribution networks' vastness have required the investment of the corporate world. Hence, a merging of interests has taken place that could hardly have been imagined a century ago: art (music) and science (technology) are joined in connubial union, under the benevolent eye of business (the entrepreneur).

The social realm's decline as the location of professional performances has further fragmented the audience, though that trend had begun long before. Cause and effect are hard to separate here, for performers, entrepreneurs, and audiences are caught up in a technologically induced spiral of means and ends. Because "music" (i.e., certain musical performances) exists in consumer-friendly packages, it can be sold in the same way; the values of the mass market ensure that such packages contain music that will sell under these conditions; therefore, some performers tailor their music-making to market specifications; and advertising encourages audiences (consumers) to buy musical packages that meet their expectations the way other good consumer products do. To the extent that audiences participate in this process, the performers who best meet their expectations within it can reap huge financial rewards. Nineteenth-century audiences, as we have seen, were given to expressing preferences noisily and in public, interacting directly with performers and with each other. Those of the later twentieth century have not lost that chance; but they exercise their preferences most tellingly, if more privately, in the mass marketplace as buyers of recorded music.

The process described here—the movement of technologically driven business innovation into American music-making—has affected agents of "accessibility" and "authenticity" in different ways. For the former, who primarily seek audience approval and the largest market for their music, technology has been a godsend. With technology's help, any style can be widely known and any function involving musical sound efficiently fulfilled. One artist, one song, even one performance can be parlayed into huge economic gain. That possibility has turned some segments of the mass media into intensely competitive arenas where musicians clamor for the public's ear.[98] Since accessibility itself *means* the wide dissemination of performances, modern technology has proved its natural handmaiden.

For authenticity, on the other hand, technological change has proved a mixed blessing. Whatever preserves and circulates performances that would otherwise be unavailable promotes authenticity's cause. But, as I have also noted, authenticity is an oppositional movement, duty-bound to protect the original spirit of the music it chooses and therefore exclusive in its choices. Committed to works for their intrinsic worth, and trusting that informed artistic efforts on behalf of such works will not be ignored, advocates of authenticity invest with deep seriousness in the authority of their performances.[99] Those performances, however, must compete in a marketplace already flooded with more music than it can possibly absorb. The glut of available performances makes it difficult for any one performance to be heard. Therefore, performances recommended by their truth to an ideal outside the central marketplace win relatively few customers. Technological change has furthered the cause of authenticity more by preserving performances than by finding large markets for their circulation.

Recorded performances, interacting with ideas about music that stem from the notions of accessibility and authenticity, have influenced American music in ways that could scarcely have been imagined a century ago. To say that most twentieth-century American performers have ranked the pursuit of audiences (accessibility) above the search for the original spirit of works (authenticity) may at first seem just another way of talking about "popular" and "classical" music. The former, from Tin Pan Alley to rock 'n' roll, has unashamedly pursued the goal of widely accessible performances. The latter, centered on concert hall and opera house, has privileged composers and their works. Accessibility and authenticity, however, are terms about musical attitudes, not musical properties; I have introduced them as a way of exploring performance, not composition. With that in mind, jazz seems the perfect genre for testing the usefulness of these terms. Jazz is an American music whose entire history has taken place since the ideal of authenticity has been in force. Furthermore, jazz is hard to pigeonhole. It took shape in the marketplace, but relatively few jazz musicians have found a mass audience.[100] Moreover, jazz is first and foremost a performer's music whose origins lie not in composition but in particular ways of playing and singing.

Jazz, a syncopated dance music played with a particular kind of expressive freedom in pitch and sound, originated in cities where black musicians found the environment hospitable. In New Orleans, the proverbial "cradle of jazz," the new style emerged in the playing of instrumental ensembles at parades, social clubs, picnics, brothels, and wherever else people danced. Some early New Orleans jazz players made music their chief livelihood, but most were day workers who performed on the side.[101] In New York the atmosphere was more professionalized, thanks to the many jobs available in a flourishing entertainment industry. There, by the start of World War I, a pianist like New Jerseyan James P. Johnson could make a good living playing in clubs, dance halls, and at private parties;[102] or a bandleader like Southern-born James Reese Europe could make a mark by accompanying Vernon and Irene Castle, a husband-and-wife team famous for starting a national dance fad.[103]

As an economic force, jazz burst upon the entertainment world in the century's second decade, with the landmark events taking place in New York recording studios. Early in 1917, during a successful engagement at Reisenweber's restaurant, the (white, New Orleans-bred) Original Dixieland Jazz Band made the first commercial jazz recordings.[104] And in 1920, black entrepreneur Perry Bradford recorded a group of black musicians—singer Mamie Smith and a jazz ensemble—on his song "Crazy Blues," in search of a market among his own "race."[105] Both endeavors succeeded. Jazz by the ODJB and blues à la Mamie Smith proved powerful in the marketplace. Jazz ensembles proliferated, and through the 1920s more and more jazz musicians, first white, then black as well, made recordings. Tunes favored by jazz musicians were also published and sold as popular sheet music. Dance halls and nightclubs hired jazz ensembles and prospered on the excitement they kindled. Jazz performers were featured in theatrical shows, including some on Broadway.[106] American composers for the concert hall wrote music inspired by jazz; European musicians and audiences noticed and responded too.[107] A vibrant new American musical style had been born.

In the years following World War I, jazz—more than just a musical style—was taken as a symbol of the whole era. A new code of manners in urban America, consciously breaking with the past, brought to the fore new styles of dress, dance, speech, and behavior. Freedom from older inhibitions and norms became a watchword of the time—including freedom from the law, for the Volstead Act (1919), prohibiting the sale of alcoholic beverages, was widely ignored by trend setters, young and old. Jazz, whose aggressive beat invited unrestrained dancing, whose sounds often mocked conventional ways of playing, and whose spontaneous spirit took original songs and numbers as jumping-off points for fresh embellishment, seemed to embody that freedom. Thus, when F. Scott Fitzgerald dubbed a set of his short stories *Tales of the Jazz Age* (1922), the label stuck. In naming his era after jazz, a vernacular musical style from the entertainment world, Fitzgerald made two connections that were to loom large through the twentieth century: a link between cultural style and consumer products and services (e.g., clothing, hair style, music in the form of phonograph recordings) and polite society's responsiveness to cultural forms that, rather than filtering down from the top of the social spectrum, percolated up from below.

From a distance, the matter looks clear-cut: in "the jazz age," jazz was the new expression of "accessibility," the popular music that reigned supreme. A look at phonograph record sales, however, undercuts that view. According to Joel Whitburn's tabulations, between 1918 and 1929 a total of 139 different recordings reached the top position in week-by-week national sales figures. Of that number, only three would be recognized today as jazz performances: the Original Dixieland Jazz Band's "Tiger Rag" (which topped sales for two weeks in 1918), Bessie Smith's "Down Hearted Blues" (four weeks, 1923), and Red Nichols's "Ida, Sweet as Apple Cider" (three weeks, 1927). Historical consensus now identifies Louis Armstrong, Bessie Smith, Sidney Bechet, Joe "King" Oliver, Jelly Roll Morton, Earl Hines, James P. Johnson, Fletcher Henderson, and Bix Beiderbecke as the leading jazz musicians of the jazz age. Except for Smith's one success in 1923, however, none of these performers made a number-one hit recording, nor did their record sales come close to matching those of Paul Whiteman's Orchestra, or Ben Selvin's or Ted Lewis's, or the singing of Al Jolson.[108]

The authority of Whitburn's findings could be challenged from several directions. It might be argued that, because his method of measuring sales is never fully explained, his figures cannot be trusted; that record sales in the 1920s are a false index of popularity; that recordings by leading jazz musicians lacked the efficient distribution other recordings received; that a largely white corps of record buyers was slow to accept black artists. But even if all these objections are true, one fact remains undeniable: as record buyers, the jazz age public preferred "sweet" music to "hot."

The popular music that, according to Joel Whitburn's research, sold most of the records during the jazz age did in fact belong to the family of syncopated dance musics introduced in the years after World War I. The Original Dixieland Jazz Band represented its informal, unbridled side; Paul Whiteman and His Orchestra, through clever arrangements and precise, well-tuned performances, sought to control that passion without extinguishing it. By 1920, Whiteman was leading a large dance ensemble that emphasized variety. Its saxophones or violins could play a melody in the smooth, legato manner of a singer. Or its brass could give the same tune a more clipped delivery. Muted or open, a cornet might "sing" the tune or a "hot" soloist improvise on it.[109] Fundamental to Whiteman's approach, though, were a fanciful presentation of the original melody and a danceable beat. A disorienting introduction, a weird concluding tag, an unexpected chord change, a surprising transition leading to a new key, a wry decoration of the melody itself, an elaborate new response to a melodic phrase's "call," a constant procession of different tone colors—these were the earmarks of the Whiteman orchestra. They added up to an artful, elaborate, often gaudy setting of the tunes Whiteman played, almost as if to disguise their foursquareness. Through variety of sound and affect, Whiteman's performances expressed "freedom" from unvaried repetition. To the public that found them novel and stylish, they were the very essence of the new dance music called jazz.

As Whiteman was discovering the approach that captured the heart of the popular music market, other musicians—chiefly black, and working in a network of dance halls and clubs parallel to though seldom intersecting with Whiteman's—were exercising a different kind of freedom. Louis Armstrong was the leader, a musician rooted more in individual expression than in Whiteman's collective ideal. Armstrong brought to playing and singing an originality that few other musicians in history have matched. Through his cornet (later trumpet) and voice,

Armstrong "freed" himself from sounding like any other musician in the world. The warmth and strength of Armstrong's tone, his command of instrumental technique, the unique "grain" of his voice, the infectious surge of his rhythm, and the inventiveness of his melodic imagination combined to give his performances overwhelming artistic authority.[110] It was Armstrong's special gift to balance disciplined artistry with the spirit of play upon which his music's accessibility, and his own livelihood, rested. Armstrong communicated an aura of freedom so powerful that even his mistakes could be heard as evidence of his reaching for the unattainable. To know and appreciate Armstrong's music was not necessarily to disdain Whiteman's. Clearly, however, the two men were doing different things. The problem was that, by the terminology of their own day, both were playing jazz.

Enter the writer on jazz. From the time it came to public notice during World War I, jazz evoked a flood of written responses, from disapproving polemics, to journalistic puffs, to the first attempts at critical appreciation.[111] Writers found much to say about jazz, concentrating especially on personalities, the racial basis of performers' behavior, the reactions of audiences, and their own responses to what they perceived as eccentric novelty. But a few writers, recognizing jazz as something more than an entertainment fad, focused on the music—on precisely what the musicians were doing and how their music related to other music the writer knew. Jazz was widely perceived as a new kind of expression. But what kind? How was it to be understood? James Lincoln Collier credits Carl Van Vechten, Abbe Niles, and especially R. D. Darrell, all active before 1930, with writing "the best American jazz criticism of the day."[112] A lesser-known figure, dancer Roger Pryor Dodge, caught the mood of his own early experience as a jazz listener deftly when he described his state of mind in the early 1920s: "I did not know what I wanted to hear. But I was looking for it."[113]

Writing on "Jazz in the Twenties," Dodge set down vivid memories of first encounters with the music and his own impatience with others' admiration for "jazz" elements that he found inauthentic. "I was taken off my feet," he recalled, by hearing Stravinsky's *Piano Rag* at a concert by Alfred Casella on 20 February 1923. "Here, for the first time, I heard what I wanted Whiteman to do." Stravinsky's rhythms convinced Dodge that "this was the new music." In 1924, Dodge heard his "first hot jazz record," Ted Lewis's "Aunt Hagar's Blues," which he found rhythmically "much simpler" than Stravinsky but "far more real." Stravinsky "inclined me to look for nothing but startling rhythm," Dodge wrote, but "Aunt Hagar's Blues" seemed "more like 18th century music; it could grasp your attention by melodic significance and did not have to rely solely upon astounding rhythmical stunts."[114] Hearing Gershwin's *Rhapsody in Blue* at a Paul Whiteman Carnegie Hall concert in April 1924 and reading the reactions to it confirmed for Dodge that music critics had only a foggy comprehension of jazz's unique and vital traits.[115]

In the winter of 1924–25, Dodge first heard the Fletcher Henderson Orchestra at the Roseland Ballroom. He especially admired Coleman Hawkins's solo on Henderson's recording of "Strutter's Drag"—"so perfect and clearly laid out"—and Charlie Green's on "The Gouge of Armour Avenue," and he told Henderson so. Henderson's response was a shock. When Dodge asked when he had written "the hot choruses," Henderson answered, "I don't write them. . . . They're played ad lib." It had "never occurred" to Dodge from listening to records, he admitted, "that the whole vitality of jazz depended upon improvisation." Dodge also questioned Henderson about an arrangement the band had played of Gershwin's *Rhapsody in Blue* and learned that Henderson considered the music "outstanding." "It was quite a jolt to find out that solos which seemed so inventive and comparable to the great written music of other periods, were not consciously plotted and composed, but were simply played *ad lib* by players who thought that Gershwin was a great composer."[116]

Now an avid collector of records, Dodge preferred "washboard bands" to fuller orchestras, found Ted Lewis "increasingly commercial" and even Henderson sometimes too "sweet and fullthroated in his arrangements," and heard in Bessie Smith's singing "an enlargement of esthetic pleasure rarely encountered."[117] By 1927 he had begun to transcribe solos he admired and to play them "with one finger on the piano." As part of a revue produced in 1930 by Billy Rose, Dodge devised an act in which he danced to a trumpet player's performances of favorite solos Dodge had transcribed, including those on Duke Ellington's "East St. Louis Toodle-Oo" and "Black and Tan Fantasy" and Armstrong's "Potato Head Blues."[118] The success of this player's imitation of the originals, Dodge wrote, "proved to me that a sympathetic reading of hot solos from notation, even on a different instrument from the original, lost nothing of the intrinsic beauty of the melodic line. Spontaneous 'hot improvisation' need not be the sole characteristic of jazz. A good solo is always a good solo." As things worked out, Dodge was able to perform his act for an extended period to the accompaniment of trumpeter Bubber Miley, the man who had first played many of Dodge's favorite solos. "Six months dancing in front of Bubber Miley," he wrote, "was an experience, extravagant or not, that I would not care to trade."[119]

Summing up the 1920s' legacy, Dodge found the balance sheet mixed. "On the credit side," he wrote, "mark up the first appearance of actual jazz melodic fragments, the growing up of these fragments into full length solos, and the hot, though somewhat florid obligato [sic] work."[120] As Dodge saw it, the solo choruses that began to appear around 1923 were "very rhythmic," in keeping with the character of "early Negro jazz," which he considered "lusty and ribald and only accessible to the musicians themselves at uncontrolled frantic moments." For Dodge, jazz at its most authentic achieved a quality that he could describe only as "*subconscious* improvisation," a state of co-ordinated thought and action reached especially in some of Ellington's pieces "of the late twenties"—"loosely orchestrated" and representing "a sort of arranged background for improvisation."[121]

Dodge's "debit side" for jazz of the 1920s included "the symphonic jazz orchestra, the bad taste of the first major jazz work (*Rhapsody in Blue*) and the commercialization of the hot virtuosi into sweet, full toned, straight players." He coined the oxymoron "refined manhandling" to describe the impact of "increased technical facility"[122] and what he saw as the stultifying effect of "conscious orchestrators." Their legacy, he wrote, was "prolonged uninventive fortissimos and 'sweet-jazz' "—the latter perfectly "suited to sentimental dancing and the dinner hour." Even jazz musicians, Dodge thought, tended to overestimate instrumental effects. "The jazz world," he wrote, "is always seriously admiring its dull orchestrations and casually dismissing its revolutionary melodic line." Dodge concluded his article with these words: "Until the significance of jazz melody becomes engrained in the mind of the arranger (later to be called composer, we hope) we shall have to continue to go through a period of self culture, before we can expand, not simply expend, the precious material wrought out by those first ten years."[123]

Dodge's article shows that, for some listeners, authenticity swiftly became a key issue in the understanding of jazz. By the 1930s, more and more writers were finding ways to describe what performers like Ellington and Armstrong were doing. In their view, these musicians, though working in a commercial environment, could be listened to as artists. Hence, they deserved to be ranked above musicians who, like Whiteman, chose a less demanding path and reaped greater financial reward.[124] Ellington's and Armstrong's music manifested an artistic ideal reaching far beyond the requirements of the marketplace in which they and their cohorts worked. Yet, even while holding to that ideal, they kept their music accessible—full of catchy, high-spirited traits that enlivened the popular music scene.

The terms "accessibility" and "authenticity" help to define where jazz fit in the economics of performance. Beginning in the limited marketplace of African-American communities, jazz soon caught the interest of whites, and some of its traits were widely borrowed—especially note-bending, syncopation, and certain sound effects. In the 1920s, jazz inspired the national music of accessibility. Since that time, however, its more "authentic" strain, tied to the risk-taking and improvisatory fire of players like Armstrong, Miley, and Hines, has come to be recognized as a tradition in its own right.[125] That strain's leaders were masters of improvisation. Some were also composers—Morton and Ellington and, later, Monk—who caught in their compositions a spirit of possibility akin to Armstrong's, leaving room for improvising or sections in the style of improvisation. Jazz styles changed as new generations came on the scene. But traits that Armstrong and his generation introduced—especially a distinctive personal sound and an inclination to explore—have marked the jazz tradition's leaders ever since. If classical performers serve the intentions and inventions of composers, authenticity in the jazz tradition follows from the charge to make every performance unique. Like their classical counterparts, however, jazz musicians locate their aesthetic ideal outside the marketplace: not in works but in a process, not in scores but in a demanding way of performing. Jazz is the source from which some musicians—Whiteman and Glenn Miller come to mind—fashioned commercially successful formulas. Jazz is also a close relative of the blues tradition, from which rhythm and blues and rock 'n' roll have come. The latter both express freedoms of their own, especially from the mores of middle-class society that in certain periods have dominated American popular music. But jazz remains unmatched in the stringency of its "authentic" ideal.

It's hard to think of a quicker way to sketch the entrepreneurial structure of jazz than to quote *The New Grove Dictionary of Jazz*'s list of venues where the music has been performed:

> nightclubs (or clubs), cabarets, casinos and gambling clubs, restaurants, bars, cafés and coffee houses, pubs, taverns, saloons, and speakeasies; ballrooms and dance halls; cinemas, music halls, theaters, concert halls, entertainment centers, and lofts; hotels, inns, roadhouses, and brothels; cruise ships and riverboats; and parks, gardens, and lakesides.[126]

There is something remarkable about a music that can flourish in all these settings. But more than that, the list dramatizes jazz's long history as an accessible music, an adjunct to Americans' pursuit of a good time. Thus, jazz musicians have been employed by theater managers, club owners, and dance-hall operators, to whom they've been responsible for attracting customers to these places.[127] On another level, beginning in the 1920s, the best-known jazz performers, like classical and popular artists, have had personal managers.[128] And on a third level, technology has vastly aided jazz's dissemination; and dissemination involves entrepreneurship. From the 1920s on, when recording challenged then outstripped publishing as its major source of revenue, the music business changed rapidly. Each change brought new agents to the fore: in the 1920s alone, for example, first publishers, then record makers, and then film companies.[129] Entrepreneurs struggled to cope with these changes, for to maintain a position of influence through all of them took shrewdness and persistence.

One jazz age figure who succeeded was Irving Mills, described by Sanjek as "a flamboyant, fast-talking figure on the Manhattan music scene." Beginning as "a songwriter and a dance-hall singer," Mills joined his older brother Jack in founding the publishing firm of Mills Music in 1919. Within a few years, Mills, as an organizer of recording sessions, had become a key figure in the record business. Experienced, as Sanjek says, in "both race music and popular-song-and-dance bands," he was reported "to have made more recordings than all other studio supervisors combined." His work in the record studio also gave him access to new songs and pieces for the Mills catalog.[130] By 1927, Mills was manager of Duke Ellington and His Orchestra, a promising black jazz ensemble for which he had earlier secured record dates.[131] "Through connections with the bootlegging underworld," Sanjek reports, "Mills booked the Ellington band into one of Manhattan's most prestigious night spots, the Cotton Club." Here the band could take advantage of a radio broadcast hookup, which introduced Ellington's "instrumental music and popular songs, most of them with . . . lyrics by Mills . . . coast to coast."[132] According to Mercer Ellington, Mills's brilliant show-business instincts were responsible for much of the aura of prestige that surrounded the Ellington orchestra in its early years.[133] Mills continued as Ellington's manager until 1939. By that time, he had established two record labels of his own, Master and Variety. The publishing firm of Mills Music, in which Irving Mills held a 39 percent share, owned some 25,000 copyrights when it was sold in the 1960s for $7.75 million.[134] In Irving Mills's career, singing, songwriting, recording, publishing, managing, and broadcasting came together in a single process that helped make Ellington—one of the truly authentic voices in jazz—widely accessible.[135]

When Gilbert Chase wrote in 1955 that American musicians had expressed the nation's spirit best in "folk and popular music," he challenged earlier historians' assumption that this country's musical achievement could be measured without considering vernacular forms seriously. Later historians have agreed with Chase. Today, the music of the American people, not the music of American composers, is the subject of our music history. Recent histories, of course, do not ignore composers. But the important contributions of performers, together with modern recording technology, have encouraged historians to recognize that "American music" means performances as well as scores from which performances are made.

Chase's insight, as shown in chapter 1, has been influential, and the early history of jazz helps to explain why. Originating with accessibility as its goal, jazz in the hands of some performers met, then transcended, that goal. Once writers came on the scene to interpret jazz as a music *in* the marketplace but not wholly *of* it, some of the audience for jazz showed an interest in reading about the music as well as listening. Histories, criticism, and journals began to appear, identifying the best performers and performances. Discography emerged, a new scholarly form listing phonograph recordings, the "documents" that preserve the music. By the early 1940s, a canon was being created for jazz: a corps of seminal performers and recordings.[136] In short, an ideal of authenticity took shape around jazz—an ideal strongly resembling the one that, half a century earlier, had inspired new American attitudes toward European art music.

By World War II jazz writers were strongly asserting the music's artistic excellence. But their claim had little impact outside the circle in which it was made. For one thing, the claimants, rather than established critics or academics, were journalists and fans, many with little or no formal training in music. For another, the performers they praised shared little, in origins or public bearing, with other musicians whom Americans had accepted as artists. Moreover, jazz still belonged to the world of commercial entertainment; advocacy for the music carried no edifying justification.[137] Finally, few Americans in positions of cultural authority were deeply enough absorbed in *both* classical music and jazz to understand them as complementary parts of American music.

In the 1960s, the position of jazz in American musical life changed dramatically. The reasons are many, and they extend beyond the realm of music, including the civil rights movement, the wave of populism that brought vernacular expressions to the fore, the role of public protest—much of it expressed through music—in the nation's political life, historians' new interest in the lives of common people, and a general distrust of "elitism" in all its forms. Within jazz, an avant-garde developed. Jazz performers, who in the 1920s and 1930s had generally accepted their role in the entertainment business, and some of whom in the 1940s had withdrawn more self-consciously into a realm of "hip" iconoclasm, now moved closer to the intellectual world, sometimes offering elaborate explanations of their music. As jazz's economic support shrank, its cultural capital grew. For jazz was coming to be seen as a music whose devotion to authenticity made it unable to compete in the marketplace. That devotion, together with the musical skill jazz demanded, opened the door to support of the kind that classical music had been receiving for years: public and private patronage, university positions for jazz musicians, and academic programs to train jazz performers and certify them with diplomas and college degrees.[138]

In identifying and privileging the original spirit of the best jazz performances, as well as works by great composers (whether European or American), authenticity has shown itself to be a flexible idea as well as a powerful one. That flexibility has allowed it to play a key role in determining what American music historians have written about. As received from Chase, the broadened view of authenticity grants the importance of many American musical vernaculars. At the same time, it holds that, because a commitment to accessibility tends to corrupt a musical genre's integrity, the most significant American music, cultivated or vernacular, has grown up on the marketplace's edge or outside it altogether. Thus, such practices as Southern shape-note singing, Negro spirituals, and Anglo-American balladry—all performing traditions originating in the vernacular tradition, in the everyday lives of particular communities—can be considered expressions of authentic artistic significance. In different ways, these and other community-based styles have intersected with the marketplace without being absorbed by it. All three have done so in published arrangements for literate singers; balladry, over the past half-century, has inspired performers carrying forward the so-called folk revival; spirituals, which preserve what Stanley Crouch has called "the molten nobility of Negro religious emotion,"[139] are a direct ancestor of the economically potent gospel tradition. The religious roots of shape-note singing and spirituals give them an indisputably authentic grounding. As for balladry, it's understood as a branch of folklore, distilling basic human truths that modern civilization has obscured. In a musical world where technology and the marketplace can supply any conceivable performing forces and produce glossy, sumptuous sound on demand, to sing in a rough, raw voice with bare accompaniment can seem a statement of moral principle. Thus, messages of political protest have gained in authority when a Woody Guthrie, a Pete Seeger, or a Bob Dylan have delivered them as proverbial truth-telling "voices in the wilderness." As spirituals and balladry have found their own paths to marketplace accessibility, their authentic links with the past have come to be an issue for performers, writers, and entrepreneurs involved with them.[140]

Recently, the ideal of authenticity has crossed another boundary. Moving beyond styles and repertories whose origins lie outside the marketplace, its advocates have taken an interest in "original" performing styles, whatever their provenance. Alec Wilder's *American Popular Song: The Great Innovators, 1900–1950* proved a harbinger of this trend. Marking the demise of the Tin Pan Alley and Broadway song as a major creative force, Wilder's study is a musician's appreciation of the art of Kern, Berlin, Gershwin, and others, as song composers. Since Wilder's book appeared, some performers have taken up this music's cause, not so much to boost its accessibility—though it still holds a niche in the repertories of some popular and jazz performers—but to revive its original spirit. From performances that stick close to the songs' sheet-music versions (Joan Morris and William Bolcom), to arrangements harking back to days of marketplace power (Linda Ronstadt and Nelson Riddle), to revivals of whole musical shows—Gershwin's *Porgy and Bess* (1976, Houston Opera) and Kern's *Show Boat* (1986, John McGlinn) "as their composers wrote them"—performers have applied to such erstwhile "accessible" works standards of authenticity like those first offered for classical music, jazz, and noncommercial vernaculars.[141]

Thus, over the past century, authenticity has broadened its focus: from works by European composers, to jazz, to vernaculars originating outside the marketplace, to vernaculars originating inside it but no longer potent there. At the same time, however, it has consistently taken an oppositional stance against accessibility and the musical conventions that rule the present-day marketplace. As the technology of dissemination—especially recording—has been simplified and democratized, and as authenticity has embraced a widening variety of music, the marketplace has turned into an arena where supply does not have to be governed directly by demand. Patronage from foundations, academic institutions, individuals, and sometimes the business itself, for performances sanctioned by authenticity, has helped to create other sources of supply, further enriching a musical marketplace already abundant and remarkably varied. That enrichment has encouraged even more audience fragmentation. Today, if an audience exists for a certain kind of music-making, some arm of the marketplace stands ready to serve it.

Of all the recent appeals to authenticity, however, perhaps the most striking has been by advocates of rock-based music, who have succeeded in planting *inside the marketplace* an ideal that separates so-called classic performances from the rest. One symptom is the "Golden Oldies" impulse, keeping certain performances available in record stores and on the airwaves. But the ideal goes further. For rock has inspired its own intellectual tradition, complete with critics, journals, discographies, biographies, histories, and serious interpretive assessments—a tradition whose implied "other" is not European music but nonrock musics, both cultivated and vernacular. Rock is rooted, after all, in African-American rhythm and blues. Hence, it began life as a music oppositional in sound, aesthetics, and its place in the music business.[142] If early rock 'n' roll brought a playful spirit to its celebration of sex, a strongly moral tone appeared in the music from the mid-1960s on. Declaring itself against middle-class authority, morality, manners, materialism, and reliance on reason, rock took a stand for freedom, sincerity, love, youth, and an idealistic moral code rooted in these elements. Moreover, in its own way, rock sought to be edifying. It is vocal music whose meanings can be explicit, strongly political, and widely understandable. In the years when Americans fiercely debated the nation's involvement in the Vietnam War, rock helped to crystallize public sentiment, not only about the war but about changes taking place in society. For the popular music industry, a happier turn of events could hardly be imagined. As a major supplier of messages that helped to fuel a national crisis, the business grew enormously in those years, both in wealth and prestige.

Before rock advocates forged their own ideal of authenticity, accessibility and authenticity could be distinguished by the repertories upon which they focused. The wide commercial appeal of rock-based music still made it seem different in kind from music whose more limited attraction supported its claim to authenticity: symphonies, operas, jazz, blues, or folk music.[143] But when advocates found a large public willing to apply authenticity's powerful justifications to music that was still commercially potent—when audience members began to choose both the accessible "other" *and* the authentic masterwork from within the current marketplace—then that audience's incentive to explore music outside the marketplace weakened, and its musical horizons narrowed.

In 1993, rock-based musical styles—that is, popular styles with black roots that have been embraced by large nonblack audiences—have a powerful hold upon the American people and others around the globe. In my own experience, if you mention "music" to a young American person today who is not a musician, he or she is unlikely to think much beyond the family of rock-based musics of the past several decades. In other words, many Americans seeking authentic experience through music find little reason to search beyond the present-day marketplace. For there, aided by consumer culture's promotional muscle, rock musicians and advocates and present-day audiences have created a self-sufficient world, complete with its own version of authenticity, preserved and disseminated chiefly through phonograph recordings. Here we can see the marketplace's uncanny power to constitute and define even the grounds upon which its own premises are criticized.

From an economic point of view, there is no greater success story in American music than that of rock-based vernaculars. Lower-class and black in inspiration, they captured first the mass market and then much of the intelligentsia, with insistent, wide-ranging messages.[144] Blending the trappings of anarchic freedom with a certain humanistic ideology, and supplied by an efficient consumer network, they have crystallized ideas and emotions in a way that many find truthful. Rock-based vernaculars have drawn a powerful portrait of the human condition as seen from the perspective of late twentieth-century American consumer culture. Their impact on the American musical landscape in the long run will depend, I think, on how much value Americans manage to find in music that treats the human condition from other points of view.

The historian's task is not to legislate but to try to understand and describe. The story of how rock has donned the mantle of authenticity formerly reserved for music outside the central marketplace needs to be written, and not as a pro- or anti-rock polemic.[145] We already have enough of those, mostly ill-informed or confused about what the music they're criticizing is really trying to do. How has a part of American music come to be taken by so many Americans as its whole? Or, to paraphrase Carl Dahlhaus: To what questions is this notion—the notion of rock's authenticity—the answer? Now *there's* a worthy subject for musicological Americanists of the 1990s!

PART III
THREE COMPOSERS
AND A SONG

· 4 ·

William Billings (1746–1800)
and American Psalmody: A Study of
Musical Dissemination

WILLIAM BILLINGS IS COMMONLY taken as *the* American psalmodist of
the eighteenth century. Self-taught, prolific, a patriot in politics, and
blessed with original vision, both as a musician and a writer, Billings
was the most famous New England composer of his age, and his reputation has long survived him. In his own day, he and his music were
widely known and admired. When psalmodists and writers of his time
chose one man to exemplify their tradition and serve as a ready point
of reference, Billings was the natural choice. When nineteenth-century
reformers wished to recall the supposedly crude, untutored beginnings
of American music, Billings served their purposes too. More recently,
when historians of American music have chronicled the beginnings of
indigenous American composition, or when choirs have performed music of eighteenth-century New England, it is to Billings and his works
that both have been most likely to turn. Billings's compositions and
writings have won for him a secure place in American musical life and
history. He stands foremost among our musical founding fathers, long
on talent if short on polish and solemnity.

Scholars have investigated Billings's life and music more thoroughly
than those of his contemporaries, and it seems fitting that, among all
the New England psalmodists, his compositions have been chosen for
a scholarly *Gesamtausgabe*.[1] In the absence of personal papers, not much
is known, and little more is likely to be discovered, about his day-to-
day activities. But other aspects of Billings call out for further study.
More work needs to be done on his musical style, a style as abundant

in rhetorical effect as it is limited in harmonic range. Billings's harmonies tend to circle narrowly around a fixed center, rarely leading the ear into unexpected tonal regions. Yet a wide vocabulary of declamatory gesture lends distinctiveness and flair to his music. Billings loved to play with musical momentum. Especially in anthems, he often built intensity by repeating the same short phrase several times. For contrast, he might then interrupt the rhythmic flow with sustained block chords, perhaps punctuated by rests and even meter changes. On another level, Billings also varied the motion of the different voices within his four-part chorus. He confessed a particular fondness for counterpoint, holding that "there is more variety in one piece of fuging music, than in twenty pieces of plain song," by which he meant tunes set in block chords and lacking word repetition. He described "fuging music" as a kind of "musical warfare" in which different voices contended for the listener's ear.[2] Billings's "fuging" passages are themselves studies in musical momentum, with individual voice parts moving from background to foreground and back again, sometimes singing bold, arching melodic lines, but sometimes, too, sustaining or repeating notes that cut, trumpet-like, through the texture. J. Murray Barbour's 1960 study of Billings's music, steeped in a knowledge of metrics, opened up its declamatory, rhetorical character for study. Barbour recognized that Billings's genius lay less in his handling of tonal materials than in his text declamation. McKay and Crawford have pursued that insight further in more recent writings, and so has Kroeger.[3] But the subject remains ripe for further study.

Billings's place in history has earned him a symbolic importance that makes it natural to view him in dramatic terms. His priority, his personality, and his skill as a composer make Billings the early American musician easiest to admire. That a self-taught, twenty-four-year-old Yankee tanner, on the eve of the Revolution, became the first American to project a vision of New World musical artistry stands as one of the enduring images of American music history.[4] Even nineteenth-century writers who refused to take Billings seriously as a composer granted his historical significance.[5] But it is one thing to admire Billings after the fact, exploring his power as a composer and personality from our point of view, and quite another to try to fathom how he was viewed in his own time. The former depends ultimately upon musical performance and analysis—a later age's ways of understanding a composer's artistic achievement; the latter invites us to think more about how Billings's contemporaries accepted his music. Quantitatively speaking, the printed dissemination of Billings's music in the eighteenth century supports today's view of his preeminence. He wrote more than his share of eighteenth-century New England's most popular sacred compositions, including the most widely printed American anthem of the time ("An Anthem for Easter: The Lord Is Ris'n Indeed").[6] Unlike most of his contemporaries, he was known more for a body of work than for the composition of a few "hits."[7] Moreover, as we note which of his pieces were borrowed and who borrowed them, Billings emerges as a figure through whom the dissemination of sacred music in eighteenth-century New England can itself be viewed.

In a subsistence economy like the one in which Billings worked,[8] where scarcity invested with significance every choice a tunebook compiler made, dissemination itself can be seen as a kind of drama. This drama surely lacks the immediacy of our symbolic view of Billings, which shows the unabashed young Bostonian courting "Euterpe in the wilderness," to cite John Tasker Howard's metaphor,[9] or his refusing to be bound by "Rules for Composition laid down by any that went before me."[10] Within that historical narrative, it is enough to say that Billings composed and published his music, that it found its way into the hands of singers, that it was loved and performed by two generations of New Englanders, and that it was then superseded by hymnody made more for the tastes and needs of an increasingly urbanized society. In another narrative, historians have introduced a nationalistic turn by describing the early acceptance of Billings's music and its later decline as a cultural conflict. First, the argument goes, provincial approval greeted Billings, only to yield later to more cosmopolitan values.[11] For scholars these are familiar stories, generalized to a near-mythic level. The "drama" of dissemination—a drama played out in the tunebooks of Billings's age, accessible only through close bibliographical investigation—lies deeper still. "Bibliographical adventure" may seem an oxymoron, or at least not an idea to fire the imagination. Yet, just as a small section of the forest floor can encompass a microcosm in which life-and-death struggles of nature regularly take place, the world of books and compilers, of editions and variant contents, has its own tales to reveal to the observer who looks for them.

To steep oneself in the tunebooks that survive from Billings's era is to begin to sense the drama latent in the facts of their bibliographical existence. For example, composing and publishing are so basic to the history of music that a scholar may take them for granted. But in Revolutionary-era New England—where congregations made most of the organized music, church choirs were relatively few and far between, and the chance for advanced musical training barely existed—any man who composed was unusual, and even more so was one with the entrepreneurial initiative and persistence to compile a tunebook and see it through to publication. During the 1770s, new sacred tunebooks appeared in America at the rate of only slightly more than one per year.[12] The variety of aim and content in those tunebooks shows that the conventions of the later eighteenth-century American tunebook were just being formed. Each book, especially in this early period, deserves to be viewed as a response to a particular set of circumstances: theology, the compiler's artistic, pedagogical, and economic aims, his place of residence, and his circle of acquaintants, musical and otherwise. The more fully those conditions are brought to light, the better able we will be to detect eventfulness in the compilers' world.

The characteristic form of sacred music in eighteenth-century America was the psalm or hymn tune—the strophic composition to which several stanzas of a psalm or hymn could be sung. Sacred music circulated chiefly in anthologies: collections containing psalm tunes and hymn tunes and a few through-composed anthems or set-pieces. Some tunebooks contained only foreign music. Others were devoted entirely to the music of one composer. Billings himself published six tunebooks, five of which carried only his own compositions. Moreover, almost all of Billings's pieces—Karl Kroeger has located 338 compositions in all[13]— were first published in one of his own tunebooks. Thus, Billings's own publications were the preeminent force in introducing his music to the public. Only one of Billings's tunebooks, however, enjoyed commercial success: *The Singing Master's Assistant,* which appeared in four editions (1778–?1786). If Billings's music had appeared only in his own publications, it would not have circulated very widely. It was disseminated, then, chiefly through reprintings by other compilers.

Under rubrics like "selected from the best authors" or "containing the most approved tunes," most early American tunebooks were anthologies of pieces by many different composers. The compilers of these anthologies tended to describe their authorial duties, if they mentioned them at all, as exercises in personal taste. Josiah Flagg, in the introduction to *A Collection of the Best Psalm Tunes* (Boston, 1764), explained his own strategy in these words: "The Editor . . . has endeavour'd, according to the best of his Judgment, to extract the Sweets out of a Variety of fragrant Flowers: He has taken from every Author he has seen, a few Tunes, which he judges to be *the best,* and compriz'd them within the Compass of a small Pocket Volumn."[14] Flagg's words offer little in the way of clues for a student of early American tunebook compiling. If a tunebook is simply a transcript of the compiler's personal taste, it is not clear what more one could hope to learn about how its contents were chosen.

On the subject of taste: if I were a compiler, combing Billings's *The Singing Master's Assistant* for tunes to include in my own tunebook— let's call it *The Lower Peninsula Harmony*—I would surely choose Billings's SUNDAY (ex. 2) over his AMHERST (ex. 3). SUNDAY begins conventionally enough, though the tune's traversing a tenth in the first phrase is unusual (the tune is found in the tenor voice). But when Billings reaches the last line of text, at the words "I'm lost," he shifts from triple to duple time, breaks the continuous movement with rests, and repeats the key words three times, creating a vivid musical picture of the text's meaning. Compared with this striking excursion, AMHERST is a pretty tame affair, moving through its text with unmemorable dispatch. I would most likely choose SUNDAY over AMHERST for my tunebook because I find it a more distinctive, expressive piece and a more interesting one. Billings's contemporaries didn't agree. After appearing in the four editions of *The Singing Master's Assistant,* SUNDAY was never published again. AMHERST, on the other hand, was a hit; it received seventy-four printings in the four decades that followed its first appearance in 1770.[15]

This comparison between SUNDAY and AMHERST suggests that compilers of Billings's day, in "extract[ing] the Sweets" from other tunebooks and presenting the public with their idea of "the best," either had ideas of musical quality that were different from our own or that they exercised their preferences within prescriptions and boundaries of which we are no longer aware. Granting that the first may or may not be true, the second possibility offers a challenge aptly suited to the tools at hand and the data available.

Studying the dissemination of psalmody through printed anthologies involves three steps. First, we need to look at individual pieces, remaining alert for traits that may have recommended them to people of

EXAMPLE 2. William Billings, SUNDAY (Billings) (*The Singing
Master's Assistant* [1778]; after Hans Nathan, ed.,
The Complete Works of William Billings,
vol. 2 [Charlottesville, Va., 1977], 178)

(*continued*)

EXAMPLE 2 (*continued*)

EXAMPLE 3. Billings, AMHERST (Brady and Tate) (*Singing Master's Assistant* [1778]; after Nathan, ed., *Complete Works of William Billings*, vol. 2, 54)

(*continued*)

EXAMPLE 3 (*continued*)

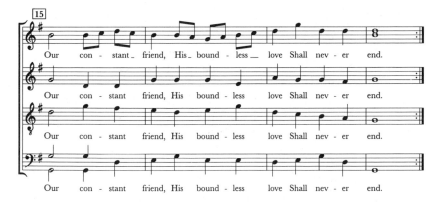

their own day. Second, we need to trace the paths of these pieces through the printed anthologies, compiling a printing history of each. And third, we need to look at anthologies themselves—to think of each anthology as a whole and then try to see how the compositions it contains *make* it a whole, or at least made it seem a whole to its compiler. By looking at individual pieces, their circulation, and the tunebooks—the "wholes" compilers created from the pieces they had to choose from— perhaps we can increase our knowledge of why compilers made the choices they did.

Early American psalmody as printed music begins in 1698, when the first sacred music in English was published in Boston, and continues to 1810, by which time American-born New England composers were beginning to be displaced by "improved" tunes with a more European stamp. During that 112-year period, 545 different issues of sacred music were printed, and they contained a total of some 7,500 compositions. Obviously, the present account can only scratch the surface of that vast repertory's dissemination. So, to narrow the focus and provide a window on the subject, I've decided to choose a single tunebook—a successful one, whose compositions circulated widely—and see what we can learn by tracing the dissemination of the music it contained. My candidate is *The Singing Master's Assistant* (Boston, 1778), Billings's greatest success.

In 1770, Billings had brought out his first tunebook, *The New-England Psalm-Singer,* which contained 127 of his own compositions. The thrill of that achievement lingered in his memory for years.

Kind Reader, no doubt you (do, or ought to) remember, that about eight years ago, I published a Book entitled, *The New-England Psalm-Singer,* &c. And truely a most masterly and inimitable Performance, I then thought it to be. Oh! how did my foolish heart throb & beat with tumultuous joy! With what impatience did I wait on the Book-Binder, while stitching the sheets and puting on the covers, with what extacy, did I snatch the yet unfinished Book out of his hands, and pressing it to my bosom, with rapturous delight, how lavish was I, in encomiums on this infant production of my own Numb-Skull?

But as Billings grew in musical experience, his pride in *The New-England Psalm-Singer* waned. By 1778, when he approached the public with his second work, he felt obliged to apologize for his first and to promise improvement:

After impartial examination, I have discovered that many of the pieces in that Book were never worth my printing, or your inspection; therefore in order to make you ample amends for my former intrusion, I have selected and corrected some of the Tunes which were most approved of in that book, and have added several new pieces which I think to be very good ones; for if I thought otherwise, I should not have presented them to you. But however, I am not so tenacious of my own opinion, as to desire you to take my word for it; but rather advise you all to purchase a Book and satisfy yourselves in that particular, and then, I make no doubt, but you will readily concur with me in this sentiment, viz. that the *Singing-Master's Assistant* is a much better Book, than the *New-England Psalm-Singer.*[16]

The public agreed with Billings's judgment of his new collection. Before the end of the next decade, *The Singing Master's Assistant* had appeared in four editions, all with the same music. Moreover, although he had fought to prevent it, his fellow compilers had given his new book the ultimate form of praise by raiding it heavily: Of the seventy-one pieces in the work, fifty-one, or nearly three-quarters, were reprinted in other tunebooks—by far the highest proportion of any collection of Billings's music.

The first step in considering how the music in Billings's tunebook circulated is to look at more of its pieces. As noted with AMHERST and

SUNDAY, *The Singing Master's Assistant* is made up entirely of unaccompanied choral music set in open score for four voices, called treble, counter, tenor, and bass, with the melody in the tenor voice. The basic musical form is the so-called plain tune, in which a stanza of metrical text is set to music without word repetition. Thus, in the plain tune, the form of the text is entirely responsible for determining the form of the music. AMHERST is a plain tune; so is BROOKFIELD (ex. 4); and so is CHESTER (ex. 5). In some pieces, Billings breaks the mold of the metrical form by repeating text, usually for expressive purposes. SUNDAY is one and MAJESTY (ex. 6) another. Moreover, MAJESTY sets two stanzas of text, introducing texture changes to striking effect. Elsewhere, I've proposed calling such pieces "tunes with extension."[17] MAJESTY, by the way, is a piece that Harriet Beecher Stowe remembered being sung in the meeting house when she was growing up in Litchfield, Connecticut.

> Whatever the trained musician might say of such a tune as old Majesty, no person of imagination or sensibility could hear it well rendered by a large choir without deep emotion. And [at the words]
>
> > On cherubim and seraphim
> > Full royally He rode,
> > And on the wings of mighty winds
> > Came flying all abroad,
>
> There went a stir and thrill through many a stern and hard nature.[18]

Psalmodists in the Anglo-American tradition formalized such elaborations in so-called fuging tunes, which contained at least one section with successive vocal entries producing text overlap. Sometimes the fuging section followed an opening section in block chords, as in MARYLAND (ex. 7). Often the fuging voices entered with some kind of imitation; MARYLAND is one of many New England fuging tunes in which the imitation is rhythmic but not melodic.

The forms described so far are strophic, with later stanzas sung to the same music as the first. Psalmodists also wrote through-composed pieces; most often these were settings of prose based on scripture. *The Singing Master's Assistant* included ten anthems, none of them reproduced here.

EXAMPLE 4. Billings, BROOKFIELD (Watts) (*Singing Master's Assistant* [1778]; after Nathan, ed., *Complete Works of William Billings*, vol. 2, 48)

(*continued*)

EXAMPLE 4 (*continued*)

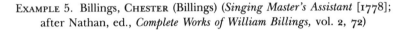

EXAMPLE 5. Billings, CHESTER (Billings) (*Singing Master's Assistant* [1778]; after Nathan, ed., *Complete Works of William Billings*, vol. 2, 72)

(*continued*)

EXAMPLE 5 (*continued*)

EXAMPLE 6. Billings, MAJESTY (Sternhold and Hopkins)
(*Singing Master's Assistant* [1778]; after Nathan, ed.,
Complete Works of William Billings, vol. 2, 203)

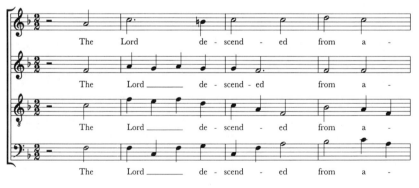

(*continued*)

EXAMPLE 6 (*continued*)

(continued)

EXAMPLE 6 (*continued*)

EXAMPLE 7. Billings, MARYLAND (Watts) (*Singing Master's Assistant* [1778]; after Nathan, ed., *Complete Works of William Billings*, vol. 2, 126)

(*continued*)

EXAMPLE 7 (*continued*)

The structures of text and musical form available to Billings provide one approach to the music in his book. There's another property of the music, however, that cuts closer to the heart of how it was most likely experienced by those who sang it. It should be remembered that, although Billings composed some pieces requiring the skill of a well-rehearsed choir, he and his brother psalmodists wrote most of all for Christians of modest vocal experience. Functionally, their compositions were extensions of congregational singing, where, as Alan Lomax once wrote, a "society" of people "call out to God together across the infinite."[19] The music, in other words, has its life in a broad context of ritual, where the singers join in declaiming sacred text, their words and voices reinforcing belief in their own hearts, but with the expectation that their singing is also being perceived by God, to whom it is ultimately addressed.

Psalmody, then, is communal sacred declamation governed by music. Because the experience of psalmody depends upon the way in which text is declaimed—on the way words flow through time, carried by the rise and fall of the vocal lines—when we consider the musical properties of pieces, declamation must be a primary concern. LEBANON (ex. 8) shows the oldest style of declamation in Anglo-American psalmody: the so-called common-tune style, whose notes of equal value move in slow-paced duple time.[20] The common-tune style harks back to Reformation times and to tunes like OLD HUNDRED, the so-called "Doxology." LEBANON also illustrates some of what Billings learned between his first book and his second. Example 8 is from *The New-England Psalm-Singer*, where the original barring, shown above the staff, ignores the placement of stressed syllables. Example 9 shows that by the time of *The Singing Master's Assistant* Billings understood that musical and metrical accents must be coordinated, and he reshaped the tune's beginning through a dactyl in the first measure.

The declamation that best fits the prevalent verse patterns of English psalmody and hymnody is iambic, alternating short notes and long, and supporting weak and strong verbal accents, as in BROOKFIELD (ex. 4). Iambic movement is usually cast in triple time. Like BROOKFIELD, many iambic tunes achieve their sense of melodic motion by dissolving whole notes into halves, or perhaps dotted quarters and eighths. The beginnings of later stanzas of BROOKFIELD fit more comfortably with Billings's music than does the underlaid one, whose first two words have their natural accent switched. A better solution for those opening words of BROOKFIELD would be a dactylic beginning: long-short-short. And indeed *The Singing Master's Assistant* has many tunes whose declamation is based on the dactyl in duple time. AMHERST (ex. 3) is a good example. Each of its six phrases begin dactylically; and all four phrases of CHESTER (ex. 5) do the same.

The style of declamation that has come to be thought of as most characteristically American in this repertory is found in MAJESTY (ex. 6). Here we have a duple-time piece in two sections, the first moving chiefly in half notes, the second shifting to syllabic declamation in quarters. MAJESTY is not a fuging tune. But in its two-part form and the aggressive text delivery of its second section, it follows the declamatory practice of many fuging tunes. Elsewhere, I've called the latter kind of motion "declamatory duple,"[21] its essence being that while the unit of

EXAMPLE 8. Billings, LEBANON OR FUNERAL HYMN (Billings) (*The New-England Psalm-Singer* [1770]; after Karl Kroeger, ed., *The Complete Works of William Billings*, vol. 1 [Charlottesville, Va., 1981], 333)

motion is the half note, one or more sections of the piece deliver text syllabically in quarter notes, producing a strong forward thrust. MARY-LAND (ex. 7) is also a declamatory duple tune.

BETHLEHEM (ex. 10) shows another declamatory approach that Billings liked. It begins in triple time, setting a full stanza of text as if it were an iambic plain tune. But then meter and texture unexpectedly change, the gentle swing of the opening giving way to the march of a duple-time fuging section as lines three and four of the text are repeated.

The styles of declamation shown here are fundamental expressive resources of the tradition of psalmody in which Billings worked. Once

EXAMPLE 9. Billings, LEBANON (Billings) (*Singing Master's Assistant* [1778]; after Nathan, ed., *Complete Works of William Billings*, vol. 2, 78)

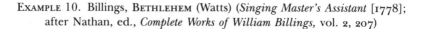

EXAMPLE 10. Billings, BETHLEHEM (Watts) (*Singing Master's Assistant* [1778]; after Nathan, ed., *Complete Works of William Billings*, vol. 2, 207)

(*continued*)

EXAMPLE 10 (*continued*)

(*continued*)

EXAMPLE 10 (*continued*)

begun, especially in a piece of strophic music that went on for many stanzas, each one established its own way of moving, which is why the breaking of the pattern, as in BETHLEHEM, or in SUNDAY, produces a sharp sense of contrast, hence of event. Billings was fond of such contrasts.

To summarize, we can say that in Billings's *The Singing Master's Assistant* both strophic settings of verse and through-composed settings of prose are found; the musical forms include plain tunes, tunes with extension, fuging tunes, and anthems; and in the settings of verse, styles of text declamation vary from the common-tune style to iambic, dactylic, declamatory duple, and mixtures thereof. These are some, though by no means all, of the traits that distinguish compositional types in early American psalmody.

Now let's find out what happened to the music in *The Singing Master's Assistant* after Billings published it. As a beginning, here's a list of the nine pieces used as examples in this chapter, with the number of printings each received in American tunebooks between 1778 and 1810.[22]

AMHERST	74	CHESTER	56	LEBANON	48
SUNDAY	4	MAJESTY	75	BETHLEHEM	42
BROOKFIELD	88	MARYLAND	60	JUDEA	4

Next, there's the question of *where* the tunes appeared in print. The geographical extent of circulation for printed sacred compositions of Billings's time may be shown by noting some of the printings outside Boston of BROOKFIELD, the tune by Billings most widely published in his own day. In 1779, BROOKFIELD appeared in a Connecticut tune-book. In the 1780s, it was picked up in northern and central Massachusetts (Newburyport, Worcester), in Philadelphia in 1788, and New York City in 1789. The next decade saw printings in Baltimore (1793), upstate New York and New Hampshire (1795), and dissemination as far south as Charleston, South Carolina (1799); by 1810 it had appeared as far west as Harrisburg, Pennsylvania.[23] A colonial New England hymn tune had won acceptance as a national favorite in the United States of the Federal era.

It was suggested earlier that tracing the circulation of each piece in Billings's tunebook would be a logical second step in our study of musical dissemination. And indeed, this work has been done. But the best way to convey its results—to do justice to both the larger question on the table and to the horde of bibliographical details on which an answer is based—is to move on to the third step: to look at the anthologies in which the tunes appear, to get a sense of their character and makeup, and then to return to the issue of dissemination with those notions in mind.

What kind of a book was *The Singing Master's Assistant* itself? First, Billings's work was intended chiefly for singing schools, as suggested by its title and shown by its front matter, which includes extensive rudiments for learners and ample advice for teachers. In addition, as table 1 shows, it was a work whose text sources ranged widely—from books like Brady and Tate's *A New Version* and Watts's *The Psalms of David Imitated* and *Hymns and Spiritual Songs*,[24] sources for several generations of English and American composers, to local poets such as Samuel Byles, Perez Morton, and even Billings himself. Furthermore, the texts Billings set in *The Singing Master's Assistant* covered a wide range of metrical patterns, from the familiar trio of common, long, and short meter to arrangements rarely encountered in psalmody of the period. Billings's book also contained ten anthems, which fill nearly half its pages. Table 1 shows that the book's settings of verse were balanced among declamatory styles. Finally, to a degree unmatched by any other American tunebook of its time, *The Singing Master's Assistant* is a personal and

TABLE 1

Texts in William Billings,
The Singing Master's Assistant (1778)

A. METERS

Metrical structure	No. compositions
CM (8.6.8.6)	20
LM (8.8.8.8)	14
SM (6.6.8.6)	8
HM (6.6.6.6.4.4.4.4)	5
PM, Ps. 50 (four 10s, two 11s)	2
PM, Ps. 149 (10.10.11.11)	2
PM, Ps. 122 (6.6.8.6.6.8)	2
PM (six 8s)	2
PM (six 11s)	1
PM (8.7.8.7.7.8)	1
PM (8.7.8.7)	1
PM (5.6.5.6.6.6.4)	1
PM (four 7s)	1
PM (11.11.11.5)	1

B. SETTINGS OF VERSE AND PROSE

61 settings of verse

10 settings of prose

C. TEXT DECLAMATION OF VERSE SETTINGS

Style of declamation	No. compositions
common-tune style	5
dactylic	11
iambic	17
declamatory duple	13
mixture	10
spondaic	4
other	1

(continued)

TABLE 1 (*continued*)

D. SOURCES OF TEXTS

Author, title	No. texts
John Arnold, *The Compleat Psalmodist*, 4th ed. (London, 1756)	1
Arthur Bedford, *The Excellency of Divine Musick* (London, [1733])[a]	1
King James Bible	9
William Billings[b]	11
Nicholas Brady and Nahum Tate, *A New Version of the Psalms of David* (London, 1696)	11
Nicholas Brady and Nahum Tate, *A New Version of the Psalms of David* (Boston, 1773), *Appendix, Containing a Number of Hymns, Taken Chiefly from Dr. Watts's Scriptural Collection*	1
Brady and Tate, *New Version*, and Watts, *Psalms*[c]	1
[Samuel Byles,] *Pious Remains of a Young Gentleman Lately Deceased* (Boston, 1764)	1
Thomas Flatman, *Poems and Songs* (London, 1674)	1
Perez Morton[d]	1
James Relly and John Relly, *Christian Hymns, Poems, and Spiritual Songs* (Burlington, N.J., 1776)	1
Thomas Sternhold and John Hopkins, *The Whole Book of Psalms* (London, 1562)	1
Isaac Watts, *Divine and Moral Songs for the Use of Children* (London, 1715)	1
Isaac Watts, *Horae Lyricae* (London, 1706)	1
Isaac Watts, *Hymns and Spiritual Songs, in Three Books* (London, 1707–9)	14
Isaac Watts, *The Psalms of David Imitated in the Language of the New Testament* (London, 1719)	11
George Whitefield, *A Collection of Hymns for Social Worship*, 13th ed. (Philadelphia, 1768)	4

E. DISSEMINATION

51 of 71 pieces reprinted in other books

---

[a] See Appendix entitled "A Specimen of Hymns for Divine Musick."

[b] On p. [3] of *The Singing Master's Assistant* (1778), Billings writes: "I have been very careful to give credit for words, and where no credit is given, the words were written by the author." That statement allows the texts to AMERICA, AURORA, BALTIMORE, BOSTON, CHESTER, COLUMBIA, INDEPENDENCE, JARGON, LEBANON, NEW HINGHAM, and SUNDAY to be identified as Billings's own.

[c] The text of STOCKBRIDGE is a composite. See Billings, *Complete Works*, 2:350.

[d] "When Jesus Wept," the text for EMMAUS, is traced to Morton in Billings, *Complete Works*, 2:347.

patriotic statement: the work of an American composer bursting with opinions, bedazzled with music as sense experience, and spiritually if not physically engaged in his country's present struggle for political independence.[25]

The Singing Master's Assistant reflects something else about the makeup of other eighteenth-century American tunebooks. In the twentieth century these anthologies, when noticed at all, are usually viewed as preservers of music. But to pass muster in the eighteenth-century marketplace, a tunebook also had to take other factors into account. Many tunebooks, though not all, sought to embrace the whole tradition of psalmody within one set of covers. They were designed to be the one book that would do it all, meeting the needs of beginners *and* experienced singers (not to mention those in between), of congregations, schools, choirs, and singing societies, by including everything from simple congregational pieces in common-tune style to anthems for choir performance on special occasions. Tunebooks of the eighteenth century also had to take certain theological guidelines into account. They had to include music in enough different text meters to cover all the psalms and hymns in the hymnals, and they had to contain sacred texts suitable for singing in both worship and recreation. The better a tunebook balanced artistic, pedagogical, and religious elements, the better its chance for success in the marketplace.[26]

A further word on texts. Not only was a tunebook expected to accommodate all the *meters* of the text in the hymnbook. Its music also had to suit the range of moods that the hymnbook expressed: minor-mode or "flat-key" tunes for sorrowful texts and major-mode tunes for triumphant ones. Thus, a tunebook needed a variety of both major- and minor-mode tunes in each of the most widely used meters; and it also needed at least one piece for each of the more unusual meters. It must be emphasized that in New England psalmody of the time, many tune–text linkings were not marriages but common-law liaisons, and printed pieces should not necessarily be considered musical-textual entities. Different texts of the same meter could be and were substituted by singers for the printed ones, according to personal choice, as with CHESTER.[27] Theologically speaking, a tune might be considered as little more than a convenient melodic formula to which any text in its meter could be sung. For example, between 1698 and 1810, the long meter tune OLD

HUNDRED was printed in America with sixteen different texts in the standard psalters and hymn books.[28]

When we think of the needs that the early American tunebook was designed to fill, and the music that was available to meet them, we can begin to get a clearer picture of how compilers made their choices. Perhaps, with all this talk of functions, texts, moods, poetic meters, styles of declamation, and religious denominations, we ought to think of the tunebook itself as a particular kind of structure—not so much a transcript of the compiler's taste (though taste surely played into it) but a formal grid divided, like an old-fashioned typesetter's case, into pigeon holes. Each pigeon hole might be considered a category of tune. And just as the typesetter needed certain numbers of each letter (more *e*'s and *s*'s than *q*'s and *x*'s), the compiler needed certain numbers of each category of tune to fill the pigeon holes of the structure he was building. Or, to try another simile, a compiler chose tunes in something of the way a baseball team selects new players. The team chooses not just the best athletes but those who are most promising at the positions it needs to fill: shortstop, catcher, or left-handed pitcher. Likewise, the tunebook compiler filled his pigeon holes according to categories of text and music. Tunes in the same category were weighed against each other: this minor-mode fuging tune in long meter or that one? This funeral anthem or that? This setting of "While shepherds watch'd their flocks by night" or that? Harking back to the earlier comparison of AMHERST and SUNDAY on the basis of my personal notion of their aesthetic appeal, we now see that it was irrelevant. AMHERST owed its circulation chiefly to its metrical structure: It is cast in the pattern 6.6.6.6.4.4.4.4, the so-called hallelujah meter, in which Psalms 136 and 148 were versified. Its competition was not SUNDAY, a long meter tune, nor any tune in common meter, long meter, short meter, or meters other than its own. AMHERST was chosen by many compilers because it best filled the hallelujah meter pigeon hole, which, if left unfilled, would leave the tunebook incomplete. A tunebook had to have at least one hallelujah meter tune or users who wished to sing the entire psalter would have to look elsewhere.[29]

Another question needs to be asked: What music was available to a compiler when he made his choices? The issue is partly one of historical chronology and partly one of law.

If William Billings had had his way, he would have controlled the circulation of his music himself. In fact, Billings was the first American composer to seek copyright protection for his compositions. In 1770 and again in 1772, he petitioned the Massachusetts legislature for exclusive right to reprint his own music; and in 1778, as *The Singing Master's Assistant* was about to appear, he sought copyright protection again. Neither petition was granted.[30] Hence, other compilers had the right to raid Billings's books freely and to reprint any of the music in them. And they did. In 1783, the Massachusetts legislature finally ruled to "secur[e] to Authors the exclusive Right and Benefit of publishing their Literary Production, for Twenty-one Years," backing up their action with fines.[31] Indeed, Billings's next work, *The Suffolk Harmony* (1786), was copyrighted and deposited in the Harvard College Library, as the law specified. But because the copyright law applied only within the State of Massachusetts, out-of-state compilers could still help themselves. Not until 1790, when the federal copyright law was passed, was there legal restraint throughout the country upon musical piracy. It was no coincidence that the circulation of pieces from *The Continental Harmony* (1794), the only one of Billings's tunebooks published after the enactment of the federal law, was by far the smallest of any of his tunebooks.[32]

It should now be obvious that the field in which a compiler made his choices was one structured by its own prescriptions and boundaries and that compiling an anthology required more than simply assembling a collection of favorite pieces. Another factor seems to have influenced compilers in the years immediately following the publication of *The Singing Master's Assistant*. Billings's tunebook appeared in a fallow period for the American tunebook trade as a whole. Wartime conditions reduced publication opportunities, and, during the entire decade of the 1770s, only twelve issues of sacred music were published, while in the 1780s more than four times that many appeared in print.[33] *The Singing Master's Assistant*, in other words, was published just before the American tunebook trade burst into full bloom. Unprotected by copyright, and full of fresh, attractive music, it was there to be raided by any other compiler.

These words about *The Singing Master's Assistant* and tunebooks in general provide a context for examining some of the collections in which music from Billings's book appeared in the decade after it was published (1779–89). All the works listed in table 2 were compiled with factors we have mentioned in mind. But the collection at the top of the list introduced another card into the deck: the issue of national origin. Andrew Law's *Select Harmony* (1779) was the first American tunebook to include English and American music in roughly equal proportion. Except for Billings's two collections, which contained only his own pieces, earlier tunebooks had been devoted either entirely or almost entirely to English music. But Law mixed an assortment of English tunes and anthems with pieces by New England composers—Oliver Brownson, Amos Bull, Abraham Wood, and others—among whom only Billings, from whom he borrowed six tunes, had been published before. Law's eclectic model and his inclusion of native-born composers were to have a powerful impact through the next decade.

Simeon Jocelin followed Law's approach to compiling in *The Chorister's Companion* (1782–83). Like Law, Jocelin balanced English and American pieces and introduced works by several new American composers, including Lewis Edson and Daniel Read. He also borrowed nineteen pieces from Billings's *The Singing Master's Assistant*. In 1783, Oliver Brownson of Simsbury brought out a tunebook emphasizing his own music and that of other Americans, though it did include a few English pieces. John Stickney's work of 1783 was the second edition of a prewar tunebook whose contents were chiefly English. Its publisher, Daniel Bayley of Newburyport, Massachusetts, was by far the most active prewar American compiler, most of his tunebooks being reissues of collections by English psalmodists. By 1784 Bayley was doing his borrowing closer to home—from Connecticut, in fact. His *Select Harmony* took the title and much of the contents of Law's earlier work, even listing Law's name on the title page. (Given the copyright situation, there was nothing illegal in this.) And Bayley's publications of 1785 and 1788 also intermixed British and American pieces. Chauncey Langdon's 1786 collection, the work of a student member of the Yale College singing society, emphasized American compositions. Law's 1786 work continued his earlier eclectic policy. All of this activity set the stage for *The Worcester Collection of Sacred Harmony*.

The Worcester Collection was the first American tunebook of the period compiled by a nonmusician: Isaiah Thomas of Worcester, Massachusetts, a professional printer who described himself as "unskilled in musick." Thomas's anthology followed the now-familiar eclectic model with its mixture of English and American pieces and its emphasis on compo-

TABLE 2

American and European Compositions
in Selected American Sacred Tunebooks, 1779–89

Year	Author, title, place	Provenance
1779	Andrew Law, *Select Harmony* (Farmington [i.e., Cheshire], Conn.)	26 American 39 non-American
1782	Andrew Law, *Select Harmony* [2d ed.] ([Cheshire, Conn.])	21 American 38 non-American
1782–83	[Simeon Jocelin,] *The Chorister's Companion* (New Haven, 1782), with *The Chorister's Companion, Part Third* (New Haven, 1782–83)	50 American 61 non-American 5 unidentified
1783	Oliver Brownson, *Select Harmony* ([Simsbury, Conn.])	52 American 17 non-American 2 unidentified
	John Stickney, *The Gentleman and Lady's Musical Companion* [2d ed.] (Newburyport)	15 American 99 non-American 2 unidentified
1784	[Daniel Bayley,] *Select Harmony, Containing . . . the Rules of Singing Chiefly by Andrew Law, A.B.* (Newburyport)	32 American 111 non-American 3 unidentified
	The Massachusetts Harmony (Boston)	17 American 67 non-American 7 unidentified
	A New Collection of Psalm Tunes Adapted to Congregational Worship ([Boston])	6 American 44 non-American 1 unidentified
1785	Daniel Bayley, *The Essex Harmony, or Musical Miscellany* (Newburyport)	13 American 27 non-American 1 unidentified
1786	[Chauncey Langdon,] *Beauties of Psalmody . . . by a Member of the Musical Society of Yale College* ([New Haven])	23 American 2 non-American 2 unidentified
	Andrew Law, *The Rudiments of Music*, 2d ed. ([Cheshire, Conn.])	23 American 17 non-American 2 unidentified
	The Worcester Collection of Sacred Harmony (Worcester)	73 American 33 non-American 2 unidentified

(*continued*)

TABLE 2 (*continued*)

Year	Author, title, place	Provenance
1787	Daniel Read, *The American Singing Book*, with *Supplement to the American Singing Book* (New Haven)	68 American 6 non-American
1788	Daniel Bayley, Sr., *The New Harmony of Zion* (Newburyport)	38 American 47 non-American 2 unidentified
	The Federal Harmony (Boston)	94 American 32 non-American 3 unidentified
	[Simeon Jocelin,] *The Chorister's Companion*, 2d ed. (New Haven)	41 American 68 non-American 1 unidentified
	Sacred Harmony or A Collection of Psalm Tunes, Ancient and Modern (Boston)	79 American 49 non-American 4 unidentified
	A Selection of Sacred Harmony (Philadelphia)	26 American 32 non-American 4 unidentified
	The Worcester Collection of Sacred Harmony, 2d ed. (Worcester)	82 American 34 non-American 2 unidentified
1789	[Andrew] Adgate and [Ishmail] Spicer, *Philadelphia Harmony* (Philadelphia)	30 American 30 non-American 1 unidentified

sitions that, by appearing in other tunebooks, had proved or were proving themselves to be favorites. Unlike its predecessors, all printed on a rolling press from engraved plates, *The Worcester Collection* was printed by letterpress, making possible larger press runs and a lower price per page.[34] Linking this new technology with an effective system of book distribution and a compiling strategy aimed toward the center of the market, *The Worcester Collection* crystallized the type of anthology that Law and Jocelin had introduced and Bayley had borrowed. Its example was widely copied, and its repertory gained especially wide circulation.[35] Thus, the music it printed received a special boost toward broad acceptance. (Nineteen of the seventy-three American compositions printed in the first edition of *The Worcester Collection* were by William Billings.)

The rest of the books in table 2 show the influence of *The Worcester Collection,* either directly or indirectly, and carry a selection of music chosen with its emphases in mind. In fact, they include many of the same pieces. Read's *Supplement* (1787), an appendix to his *The American Singing Book* (1785), which had contained only his own compositions, was chosen almost entirely from among familiar English and American favorites. Several 1788 tunebooks show other professional printers being drawn into the sacred music trade, following Thomas's example. *The Federal Harmony,* published by the Boston engraver John Norman, insisted on the superiority of its own copperplate engraving to the letterpress method; *Sacred Harmony,* compiled anonymously, mentioned *The Worcester Collection* on its title page; the *Selection of Sacred Harmony,* the first major Philadelphia tunebook since the 1760s, came from the press of newspaper publisher John M'Culloch; and Adgate and Spicer's *Philadelphia Harmony* contained a higher proportion than any work yet of that group of favorites that has been identified as the "core repertory" of early American psalmody—the 101 sacred compositions most frequently printed in America before the end of 1810.[36]

Thus, in the late 1770s and 1780s, many American compositions were printed in American anthologies, and the process of winnowing took place, accelerating after 1786. Billings's music, especially the music from his *The Singing Master's Assistant,* was right in the center of this development.

The key work in the dissemination of Billings's compositions was Jocelin's *The Chorister's Companion* (1782–83; see table 3).[37] Jocelin borrowed heavily from Billings. He picked up no fewer than nineteen pieces from *The Singing Master's Assistant* (see table 3C), and he added six more from Billings's next major tunebook, *The Psalm-Singer's Amusement* (1781), for a total of twenty-five Billings pieces in all. But these numbers only begin to tell the story of Jocelin's borrowing. Of the twenty-five compositions by Billings that were printed fifteen times or more in any American tunebook before 1811 (table 3A), nearly two-thirds (sixteen of the twenty-five) appeared in Jocelin (table 3B). Moreover, Jocelin was the first compiler after Billings to print eleven of those sixteen compositions, suggesting that if he had not picked them up, other compilers might not have either. More than any other tunebook, then, Billings's own *The Singing Master's Assistant* included, Jocelin's *The Chorister's*

TABLE 3

William Billings's Music and
Jocelin's *The Chorister's Companion* (1782–83)

A. Pre-1782 Billings pieces with 15 printings or more

AFRICA	BOSTON	MENDOM
AMERICA	BROOKFIELD	NEW HINGHAM
AMHERST	CHESTER	PARIS
Anthem: I Am the Rose of Sharon	COLUMBIA	PHILADELPHIA
	EMMAUS	RICHMOND
Anthem: I Heard a Great Voice	GOLGOTHA	STOCKBRIDGE
	LEBANON	SUFFOLK
AURORA	MAJESTY	WASHINGTON
BERLIN	MARYLAND	(*25 pieces*)
BETHLEHEM		

B. Pre-1782 Billings pieces with 15 printings or more in Jocelin

AMERICA	BROOKFIELD	PARIS
AMHERST	CHESTER	PHILADELPHIA
AURORA	COLUMBIA	STOCKBRIDGE
BERLIN	MARYLAND	WASHINGTON
BETHLEHEM	MENDOM	(*16 pieces*)
BOSTON	NEW HINGHAM	

C. Music from *SMA* in Jocelin

AMERICA	COLUMBIA	PRINCETON
AMHERST	HEBRON	SHERBURNE
AURORA	MARYLAND	STOCKBRIDGE
BETHLEHEM	NEW HINGHAM	WARREN
BOSTON	NEW NORTH	WASHINGTON
BROOKFIELD	NEW SOUTH	(*19 pieces*)
CHESTER	PHILADELPHIA	

D. Declamatory styles and meters of *SMA* tunes in Jocelin

common-tune	NEW NORTH (CM)
iambic	AMERICA (six 8s), BROOKFIELD (LM), HEBRON (SM), NEW SOUTH (SM), PRINCETON (CM), WARREN (four 7s)

(*continued*)

TABLE 3 (*continued*)

dactylic	AMHERST (HM), CHESTER (LM), COLUMBIA (HM)
declamatory duple	BOSTON (CM), MARYLAND (SM), NEW HINGHAM (SM), SHERBURNE (6.6.8.6.6.8), STOCKBRIDGE (LM), WASHINGTON (LM)
mixed	AURORA (SM), BETHLEHEM (CM), PHILADELPHIA (SM)

E. Pieces from *SMA* in *Worcester Collection* (1786)

AMERICA	CHESTER	PHILADELPHIA
AMHERST	COLUMBIA	STOCKBRIDGE
AURORA	HEBRON	WASHINGTON
BETHLEHEM	MARYLAND	*(13 pieces;*
BROOKFIELD	NEW HINGHAM	*cf. C above)*

Companion seems to have played a decisive role in determining which of Billings's pieces lived on and which were forgotten.

What, if anything, can be discovered about the reasons for Jocelin's influence upon the fate of Billings's music? The compositions he borrowed suggest some answers.

Jocelin took from Billings a group of pieces that, examined from the standpoint of meters and styles of declamation, forms a remarkably well-balanced cross-section of Anglo-American psalmody in general and of Billings's own work in particular. Among the nineteen compositions he chose from *The Singing Master's Assistant* (table 3C and D), Jocelin took only one common tune, preferring to fill that category in his own book with European favorites. But for the other categories of declamation he chose six iambic tunes, three dactylic, six declamatory duple tunes, and three mixed ones. Within these categories, he paid close attention to the variety of poetic meters. His six iambic tunes, for example, use five different text meters; further, half of them are in the major mode and half in the minor. The variety of text meters in the Billings tunes is similarly wide. With seven different meters distributed among the nineteen compositions, here was a selection of Billings pieces covering all but one meter in the entire hymnbook. Jocelin's borrowings

146

from *The Singing Master's Assistant,* in short, are by no means random, nor is it likely that simple personal preference would have produced so varied a sample. The borrowings show every sign of being systematic. They constitute in effect a tunebook within a tunebook: a microcosm of the work of Billings as a composer of metrical sacred music. Jocelin's raid may have worked against the composer's commercial interests, but it revealed a shrewd understanding of the legacy that Billings had created for his public in *The Singing Master's Assistant.*

Having noted and looked at some of the pieces Jocelin took from Billings, perhaps it's worth mentioning one he rejected. The Christmas hymn JUDEA has had a certain currency since it was edited and published in the 1940s in an octavo edition and recorded by the Robert Shaw Chorale (1952). JUDEA, however, went nowhere in Billings's own time, dropping out of print after *The Singing Master's Assistant* itself. The tune is one of a handful of spondaic pieces in the book; none of these were much reprinted.[38] Its text meter, six 11s, is nowhere to be found in the standard hymnbooks. And its character is decidedly that of a dance.[39] There is reason to think that Jocelin had JUDEA (ex. 11) in mind when, in his introduction, after praising the new style of psalm tune with "a more lively and airy turn"—a phrase certainly fitting much of Billings's music—he warned: "Altho' many improvements have been made in Church Music, yet there appears a danger of erring, by introducing, in public worship, light and trifling airs, more becoming the theatre or shepherd's pipe; a liberty . . . by no means admissible in the solemnities of Divine Service."[40] Thus, a Billings tune that has won favor in our time went unborrowed in the composer's own.

That Simeon Jocelin was a Connecticut man publishing his book in New Haven enabled him to poach on Billings's preserves in a way that a Massachusetts compiler might have hesitated to risk. Copyright, as noted above, was an issue very much in the air at this time. And Billings was not the only psalmodist to seek copyright protection. In October 1781, Andrew Law won from the Connecticut legislature control over printings of a group of some fifty pieces he had collected from various sources, both English and American, and Law was noisy in public about possible infringements of this right. The fines threatened by the Massachusetts law of 1783, and the general confusion about the whole matter that prevailed in New England, apparently help explain why Isaiah Thomas, in *The Worcester Collection* of 1786, informed his readers that

EXAMPLE 11. Billings, JUDEA (unknown) (*Singing Master's Assistant* [1778]; after Nathan, ed., *Complete Works of William Billings*, vol. 2, 52)

(*continued*)

EXAMPLE 11 (*continued*)

he had taken his Billings pieces not from the composer's own Massachusetts-published works but from Jocelin, a Connecticut source. Thus, we have it on Thomas's own authority that Jocelin was the link connecting Billings to *The Worcester Collection* (see table 3E), itself the source for so many later compilers' choices.[41]

More could be explored about the dissemination of Billings's music: about how the core of tunes that moved from *The Singing Master's Assistant* to Jocelin to *The Worcester Collection* was modified in later editions of that work; about *The Worcester Collection*'s introduction, which named and praised Billings as chief among New England composers, hence proposing his books as a field for more borrowings;[42] about the article in the Philadelphia *Columbian Magazine* in 1788 that puts Billings in the artistic company of Handel and Shakespeare and surely led to the appearance of so much of his music in the *Selection of Sacred Harmony*

of that and later years.[43] But for now we'll have to be satisfied with
having sketched the process by which Billings's pieces came to account
for nearly 20 percent of the compositions in the most successful and
influential American sacred tunebook of the decade.

This chapter has taken as its starting point Oscar G. Sonneck's maxim
that "bibliography is the backbone of history."[44] Knowing which of
Billings's pieces from *The Singing Master's Assistant* were printed, and
when and where, has provided a start toward a broader investigation
of psalmody's dissemination in print. By noting the roles sacred tunebooks were expected to play—artistic, pedagogical, theological, commercial, even nationalistic—we have recalled some of the constraints
within which their compilers made their choices and hence something
of the context within which personal preference operated. By observing
patterns of printings, we have seen that compositions can be considered
not simply as independent items circulating on their own merits but
also as members of larger clusters of pieces. Jocelin chose from Billings's
The Singing Master's Assistant a group of pieces complementing each
other so well that they formed a well-rounded, nearly complete microcosm of Billings's settings of sacred verse. Learning this, and having
retraced some of the steps by which it came about, reminds us that, in
the subsistence economy of the tunebook world, dissemination took
place in a field of resistance. New pieces appearing in the field were
accepted or rejected partly on their intrinsic qualities and partly on
their relationship to the pieces already there. Knowing something of
the nature of those relationships in the field we are studying, whatever
it may be, is a necessary step if we are to take dissemination as an issue
worthy not only of description but of analysis.

· 5 ·

George Frederick Root (1820–1895)
and American Vocal Music

GEORGE FREDERICK ROOT, a true man of the people, was, with Lowell
Mason, among the first American musicians to discover the full rewards
of reaching those people. Born on a Massachusetts farm, Root spent
his professional life chiefly in Boston, New York, and Chicago. Yet he
held fast to his rural origins. In mid-career, he moved from New York
City to the Massachusetts hamlet of North Reading, where he had grown
up. There, he later recalled, he drew inspiration from "the thoughts
that came amid the pleasant scenes that surrounded me," just as, a few
years later, the Illinois plains—his "first sight of the West"—again stirred
his creative impulse.[1] When Root began his musical career, most Americans lived in small towns or on farms. As he told the story, his professional success was that of a "country boy" who loved the rural landscape
and never lost his kinship with those who dwelt in it.[2]

Root was a prolific musician and author whose publications leave a
detailed record of his activities.[3] But the key to his character and achievement lies in the autobiography published when he was seventy-one.
According to its preface, this work was inspired by a family gathering
on the fiftieth anniversary of the day he left home to seek his fortune
in Boston (1 October 1888). The autobiography, cheerful and straightforward in tone, proceeded from a memory sharpened by a lifetime of
recording personal observations. For Root was a diary keeper whose
day-to-day record, begun in the 1840s, perished in Chicago's Great Fire
of 1871.[4] *The Story of a Musical Life* is invaluable as an account of the
musical worlds Root helped to create and his activities within them.

Absorbing too, and equally revealing, is Root's autobiographical self-
portrait. The farm boy, he recalls, was not left to discover music on his

151

own. His father and mother were musical; he had siblings, a brother and a sister, who became professional musicians; he learned as a young-ster to play the flute and other instruments; and from early childhood, "the dream of [his] life was to be a musician."[5] (Root omits mentioning that his parents named him after Handel.)[6] On the other hand, his formal education was limited to grammar school; he never played an organ or piano until he went to Boston at eighteen; and, although he won national fame as a vocal teacher, he was not naturally gifted as a singer. "I had occasionally joined in the base of simple church tunes," he confides, "but was never encouraged by listeners to continue my performances long. They'd say, "George, you'd better [get] your flute.""[7]

Implicit in this story told on himself, and present throughout his chronicle, is Root's sense of social belonging. When he decided to move to Boston to study music, there was "great excitement" in North Reading. Root recalls that he "went around telling the good news to inter-ested and sympathizing neighbors. All met me with good words. 'Go ahead!' they said; 'we'll lend a hand on the farm, if we're needed.' "[8] Thus, Root went to Boston not as a young artist escaping a philistine environment but as a proud representative of his family and home town. Together with his own hopes, he took with him the blessings of fellow townspeople, who liked him but, like himself, harbored no illusion that he was a genius.

In the preface to *The Story of a Musical Life,* Root begs forgiveness in advance for "the apparent egotism" a reader might find in "certain sayings and events which refer to myself and my career." They are included, he explains, because "my story would not be complete without them." At first glance, this comment might have the look of false mod-esty. But in fact, Root's insistence upon his own ordinariness, his refusal to claim any special gifts or talents, is one of the chief themes of his book. The leading character in Root's autobiography is a man in tune with society, sharing its tastes and working cheerfully and effectively within the musical life of a democracy.

Root's story, then, has little connection with the struggle between good and evil in which some of his Calvinistic forebears believed them-selves engaged. But at one point, evil does put in an appearance, and that episode provides a revealing glimpse of Root's sensibility. The per-petrator was Henry Russell, "an English Jew" whose songs Root ad-mired and learned to sing and play as a young man. When Russell performed in Boston in 1839, the nineteen-year-old Root was deeply impressed.

> He had a beautiful baritone voice and great command of the keyboard—played his own accompaniments, gave his concerts entirely alone, and in a year in this country made a fortune. Songs of his, like "The Maniac" and "The Gambler's Wife," were exceedingly pathetic, and always made people cry when he sang them. He looked so pitiful and so sympathetic—"he felt every word," as his listeners would think and say.

Then Root found out that Russell's sincerity was an act. "When he retired to his dressing room," Root learned, Russell "was said to have been much amused at the grief of his weeping constituents." Root could neither accept nor forgive such cynicism. "Good taste," he declared, "requires that the singer should treat respectfully the emotion he excites."[9]

Root's condemnation of Russell brings into focus the ethical side of his own code of professional behavior. In Root's mind, to make a profession of music, whether as a teacher, a composer, or a performer, was to strike a bargain with the public. When members of that public became his customers, he felt bound to respect them and their responses to his work. Russell, by harboring contempt for his audience's sentimentality, mocked their trust in him. Root, on the other hand, refused to allow any such gap to open up between him and the people whose musical needs he served. With memories of his own modest origins and background as his guide, he held fast in private to the taste he espoused in public. Shortly before *The Story of a Musical Life* appeared, W. S. B. Mathews confirmed Root's success. Writing as if the elderly composer were a beloved uncle, Mathews called him "one of those personages who have so grown into American life . . . through his work" that when he dies "each will feel that he has in some way . . . sustained a personal loss."[10] Root's bargain with his audience struck a balance that, for a man of a different time or place, or of less genuine modesty, would have required a major exercise of vigilance and willpower.

For all the genial tone in Root's autobiography, it is by no means free of conflict. From its early pages, Root carries on an argument, not with the likes of Henry Russell but rather with an attitude widespread among musicians in the cultivated tradition. The more technically accomplished they are, Root notes, the more strongly musicians tend to identify themselves with music as an art form evolving apart from the needs and wishes of most members of society.[11] In other words, musical talent, training, and experience, as they are more and more fully developed, breed a sense of autonomy. For musicians in the United States, however, intellectual autonomy bears little or no relationship to material well-being. To believe that it can form the basis for a musical career is a dangerous illusion. *The Story of a Musical Life* cites many examples of the autonomous attitude, including Root's own encounters with it.[12] Root never argues against elaborate music, for by any measure he qualifies as a lover of the classics. Beethoven and Wagner, for him, are the two geniuses of the century, Handel's *Messiah* and Mendelssohn's *Elijah* masterworks that sustained him throughout his life.[13] But as he saw the matter, his own professional choice and that of most of his American colleagues lay between serving the art of music and serving the musical needs of his fellow citizens. Root's experience taught him that "a majority of the music-loving world" enjoyed only an "elementary" state of musical knowledge. Their love for the art, he believed, was no less genuine for its "elementary" character, nor was their taste to be despised, for "all must pass" through the same levels. Moreover, Root discovered, identifying and addressing "elementary" musical needs could be a challenging, absorbing enterprise—indeed, an honorable lifelong mission.[14] In a sentence that could make a fitting epitaph, Root wrote: "I am simply one, who, from such resources as he finds within himself, makes music for the people, having always a particular need in view."[15]

Root's musical career divides into distinct phases. During his early years in Boston (1838–44), he made himself, through diligent labor and natural gifts, into an effective teacher. He moved to New York (1844–55), and there he hit his professional stride. In his New York years, Root taught singing classes, played the organ and conducted church choirs, and began the activities that were to dominate his later life: composing; participation in conventions and "normal institutes" for the training of music teachers; and compiling collections of vocal music. There followed a move to the country—to a house his musical success enabled him to build for his family in North Reading, where he had grown up. For several years, "Willow Farm" was Root's headquarters, as he gave up singing classes and church work, devoting himself entirely to "conventions, Normal [Institutes], and authorship"—that is, composing and compiling tunebooks.[16] By 1859 the bucolic interlude had run its course. Root moved west and spent the next dozen years as a partner in Root and Cady, a Chicago music publishing house founded by his brother. Here he showed his mettle in the competitive world of the music business. The destruction of Root and Cady's physical plant by the great Chicago fire of 1871 brought this phase of Root's career to a close. From that time until his death in 1895, he stayed in Chicago, resuming his earlier round of normal institutes, compiling, and composing.

Success came quickly to Root. Within weeks of his arrival in Boston as a rank beginner, he was ordered by his first mentor, A. N. Johnson, to begin teaching an even ranker beginner. And not long after beginning the struggle to make his "large, clumsy fingers" negotiate a keyboard,[17] he was playing the final hymn in church services, apparently so the regular organist could leave to play another service. He explained his quick acceptance into professional ranks as more a matter of opportunity than talent.

> If my getting on so fast in a city like Boston seems unaccountable, I must explain again that music [in 1840] was in a very different condition then from what it is now. It was just emerging from the florid but crude melodies and the imperfect harmonies of the older time.[18] Lowell Mason had . . . just commenced what proved to be a revolution in the "plain song" of the church and of the people, and his methods of teaching the elementary principles of music were so much better . . . than anything . . . seen [before] that those who were early in the field had very great advantage. We had no competition and were sought for on every hand.[19]

From that time on, Root displayed a shrewd sense of his own gifts and a knack for choosing things he could master. His competence as a teacher is proved by his entry into the circle headed by Mason.[20] But teaching was not enough to keep the energetic Root occupied for long.

155

Early in the 1850s, at the age of thirty-one, he began to compose. Look-ing back on his musical life, he admitted in his autobiography that he had "never felt" he "had a 'call' to be a musical composer." He was drawn into composing, he said, "to supply my own wants." Only after his compositions were "successful for myself and others" did he decide to take composing seriously. "I can truly say," he wrote, that "I never dreamed of eminence as a writer of music, and never had fame for an object."[21]

Root expressed no regrets about his late entry into the domain of musical composition. "I have often been glad that I did not begin earlier to write for publication," he claimed. "By delaying I had become better equipped. I had heard a good deal of good music, and had been obliged to teach some of a high order. . . . The reservoir was, therefore, much better filled than it would have been if I had commenced when [first] urged to do so."[22] One experience that helped to fill the "reservoir" was a nine-month trip to Paris (December 1850–August 1851), where Root took lessons in piano and singing and heard many concerts. Re-turning in the fall to New York City and to his duties, which included daily singing classes given to hundreds of "young ladies of culture and refinement"[23] at two female seminaries, he felt the need "for something new" for these classes. Deciding that "a little musical play . . . made for girls and young ladies . . . [might] be useful," he "cast about for a subject. It was not difficult to find one; the whole world was open to me, for nothing of the kind had been done. I soon decided that the subject should be flowers choosing a queen, and that the little play should be called 'The Flower Queen.' "[24]

Root set out to compose, then, as a mature man, experienced in teaching and performing but without formal training as a composer.[25] He didn't need it. Finding a local poetess, Fanny Crosby, "who had a great gift for rhyming," and "a delicate and poetic imagination," he set to work.

> I generally hummed enough of a melody to give her an idea of the meter and rhythmic swing wanted. . . . The next day the poem would be ready. . . . After receiving her poems, . . . I thought out the music, perhaps while going from one lesson to another . . . and then I caught the first moment of freedom to write it out. Sometimes this was a half hour before dinner or supper,

sometimes a little while between lessons, and sometimes an hour
at night. This went on until the cantata was finished.[26]

Needing hundreds of copies of the new cantata for his students, Root
arranged for *The Flower Queen* to be printed, although he had no
thought "that it would ever be heard outside of the walls of the institutions in which I was teaching." His publishers, Mason Brothers of
New York City, decided it was worth a risk. "We'll publish it regularly,"
they told him: "others may want what you want."[27] And so they did.
The Flower Queen was published and performed, and it succeeded.
Others *did* want what Root wanted; the career of an American composer
had begun.[28]

Inspired by the melodies of Stephen Foster, Root next began writing
songs—"people's songs," as he called them. In this field, in sharp contrast to that of *The Flower Queen,* Root had many competitors. But again
he succeeded. Two of his early songs, "The Hazel Dell" (1852) and
"Rosalie, the Prairie Flower" (1855), became hits.[29] Let's look at a pair
of Root's songs from 1852, written at the beginning of his career as a
song composer. The first, a copy of a much more famous one, was a
failure. But the second was a success whose brisk sales helped to elevate
the erstwhile farm boy to the ranks of North Reading's gentry by the
time he was thirty-five.

Even if Root had not acknowledged the source of his inspiration, it
would be hard to miss the resemblance between his "The Old Folks Are
Gone" (1852) and Foster's "The Old Folks at Home" (1851). Similarity
of title and subject aside, Root's text and declamation follow Foster's
almost exactly (ex. 12a).

FOSTER: Way down upon de Swanee ribber,
Far, far away.

ROOT: Far, far in many lands I've wandered,
Sadly and lone.

Echoes of Foster's text resound in Root's even though Foster's song is
written in the dialect of the minstrel stage and Root's is not. Foster's
"There's where my heart is turning ever" becomes Root's "My heart
was ever turning southward"; Foster's "All de world am sad and dreary"
in the chorus becomes "Here I wander sad and lonely"; and Foster's

EXAMPLE 12. G. Friedrich Wurzel [George Frederick Root],
"The Old Folks Are Gone" (Root?)

(a) Bars 9–12, vocal part (New York, 1852)

Far, far in man-y lands I've wan-der'd, Sad - ly __ and lone.

(b) Bars 25–32, vocal part (New York, 1852); fermata added by original owner

Here I wan - der sad and lone - ly, In the dear old home,

Those that I lov'd so well and fond - ly, All, all the old __ folks are gone.

characteristic words "weary" and "roam" both appear in Root's song. In the second stanza, the modeling is no less obvious:

FOSTER: When I was playing wid my brudder,
Happy was I.
Oh, take me to my kind old mudder,
Dere let me live and die.

ROOT: Here's where I frolick'd with my brother,
Under the tree.
Here's where I knelt beside my mother,
From care and sorrow free.

Foster's hand-in-glove fit of words and music—which is the hand and which the glove?—marks "The Old Folks at Home" as superior to "The Old Folks Are Gone." One detail in a surviving copy of Root's song dramatizes the distance between the master and the novice at this stage in his career. On the last page, at the words "all, all the old folks are gone," an early owner of the sheet music has added a fermata, trying to ease the awkwardness of Root's climactic leap of a seventh (see ex. 12b).[30] (In contrast, the octave leaps in Foster's melodic line convey grace and ease, even inevitability.) The song's cover identifies it with E. P. Christy, who headed a leading New York minstrel troupe.[31] William

Austin has written that Root's song "was sung by Christy, but not often."[32] "The Old Folks Are Gone" is one of thousands of would-be American popular songs that were ignored by the populace.

Example 13, a song from 1852, received a much warmer response than did Root's "Old Folks" imitation. "The Hazel Dell" marked the first time Root managed a feat that he admitted always remained a mystery to him: He had composed a successful "people's song"—a song, as he put it, that "boys whistled . . . and . . . hand organs played . . . from Maine to Georgia." In Root's opinion, "no ambition for a songwriter could go higher than that."[33] How had he accomplished it? Root wasn't sure.

It is easy to write correctly a simple song, but so to use the material of which such a song must be made that it will be received and live in the hearts of the people is quite another matter. . . . It was much easier to write where the resources were greater; where I did not have to stop and say, "That interval is too difficult," or "That chord won't do."[34]

Root's description of how he wrote his Civil War songs shows that by the early 1860s he had a method for courting inspiration; but perhaps he discovered that earlier in his song-composing career. Beginning with words and phrases in mind, he relied on a technique he had developed while teaching singing classes—classes, he wrote, "that could be kept in order only by prompt and rapid movements." "I found my fourteen years of extemporizing melodies on the blackboard . . . a great advantage. Such work as I could do at all I could do quickly. There was no waiting for a melody. Such as it was it came at once, as when I stood before the blackboard in the old school days."[35] Thus, Root seems to have composed his "people's songs," within "the land of tonic, dominant, and subdominant,"[36] by fitting text to melodic phrases that sprang into his mind, as melodies always had when he improvised them for his singing classes. Once the melody had taken shape, he purged it of infelicities, removing anything that might make it too complicated to sing. As Root described it, composing songs was a direct extension of his work as a practical musician: a process of conception, virtually at the level of trained reflex, followed by reaction and retouching. Though he doesn't put it quite this way, Root writes as if, rather than

EXAMPLE 13. G. Friedrich Wurzel [George Frederick Root], "The Hazel Dell" (Crosby) (New York, 1852); after George F. Root, *The Story of a Musical Life: An Autobiography* (Cincinnati, 1891), 234

THE HAZEL DELL

(continued)

EXAMPLE 13 (*continued*)

constructing songs as a self-conscious craftsman, he *found* them, coming upon tunes, and sometimes texts as well, in his creative "reservoir." He once described Henry Clay Work (1832–84), whose songs Root and Cady also published, as "a slow, pains-taking writer, being from one to three weeks upon a song." Root admired his colleague's results. "When the work was done," he wrote, "it was like a piece of fine mosaic, especially in the fitting of words to music."[37] Yet Root's praise leaves the impression that Work's technique of writing songs differed profoundly from his own.

If Root referred to his musical imagination as the "reservoir" from which songs flowed, he says nothing in the autobiography about the reservoir's sources: the conventions that marked the boundaries of subject matter and diction within which he worked as a songwriter. According to Austin, "The Hazel Dell" belongs to the nineteenth-century Anglo-Irish-American genre of "poetic" songs—songs inspired by a parting or the passing of time and pervaded by a sense of dreamlike vagueness: a tradition in which "Oft in the Stilly Night" by Thomas Moore is linked with Foster's "Jeanie with the Light Brown Hair."[38] Charles Hamm locates "The Hazel Dell" on the fringes of blackface minstrelsy, though it lacks dialect or any hint of buffoonery, placing it with songs about departed young ladies with Scotch-snappable first names: Hanby's "Darling Nelly Gray," Foster's "Gentle Annie," Thompson's "Lilly Dale" and "Annie Lisle," Winner's "Listen to the Mocking Bird" ("I'm dreaming now of Hallie . . .").[39]

Austin is no admirer of "The Hazel Dell," comparing it unfavorably with Foster's "Lily Ray" (1850) and finding it "a hasty and mechanical imitation of Foster's style."[40] "The melody," Austin writes, "seems cramped in its octave range; it strikes its highest and lowest notes in every phrase, and treats most of the notes between them as mere decorations of the central keynote." And he goes on to call the rhythm "plodding."[41] With all respect for the opinion of this knowledgeable observer, I think the song's first four measures are enough to explain its appeal. Certainly that appeal does not lie in the harmony, whose only inventive touch lies in the bass's movement to B in bar 3. Most of all, the opening makes its mark through the flexible rhythm of its declamation: the pushing forward of the first five beats, the coming to rest on "sleeping," and the syncopated hitch with which "Nelly" sets the second half of the phrase into motion. The varied movement within each of the phrase's four bars gives a certain plasticity to its melodic curve. That, coupled with the economy of the text, which, in just eleven words, reveals a glen in the country, a dead maiden, and a grieving lover, were apparently enough to propel "The Hazel Dell" to wide acceptance. It's noteworthy that almost everything in the song has happened by the fifth bar. The rest of the text offers no narrative. It simply elaborates physical and emotional details of the melancholy scene. The music follows suit: Five of the six phrases in each of the three stanzas are sung to the opening melody. Text and music combine to produce a single mood, static as a picture hung on the wall or a quiet pool in the woods. "The Hazel Dell" suggests how much a "poetic" song's success could depend upon catching a mood in one quick, convincing gesture. Once caught, the mood is fixed and meditated upon through virtually unvaried repetition.

What made a song like "The Hazel Dell" appealing to the public who bought so many copies? According to no less an authority on public taste than the English publisher John Curwen, Root and other Americans composing in a similar vein had happened on to a unique, socially useful musical style. As Curwen wrote Root in the 1850s, "We have in England plenty of high-class music, and more than enough of the Captain Jinks kind of songs, but there is a wholesome middle-ground in regard to both words and music in which you in America greatly excel."[42] Curwen's comment suggests a split in English music between "high-class" compositions for the concert hall and opera house and comic songs, presumably of the kind that flourished in music hall performances. The "wholesome middle-ground" Root had discovered in a song like "The Hazel Dell" was both stylistic and social. Less elevated than an aria, more decorous than a comic song, "The Hazel Dell" was not, like most English and American-published songs of the time, composed for theatrical performance. Bone simple, musically and emotionally redundant, "The Hazel Dell" could easily be sung and played by inexperienced amateurs. And indeed, it was primarily for singing at home that it was composed. In one sense, it can be considered a secular counterpart to the hymn tunes Lowell Mason composed, selected, arranged, and published for the new musical customers he began to discover in the 1820s—a musical product fabricated within rigid, market-inspired conventions. But that view hardly explains why a song like "The Hazel Dell" could make an impact on many Americans.

Historians have advanced reasons for the appeal of such songs, including public naiveté, bad taste, and the absence of alternatives.[43] But such explanations are inclined to treat a song as an independent work of art—one to be judged against songs already *in* the canon, and hence definers of its "song" norm, which is believed to transcend questions of time and place. By thinking of "The Hazel Dell" as an occasion for experience in its own historical setting, however, one occupies a better position for glimpsing its expressive potential—its ability, in Root's phrase, to "live in the hearts of people." Those people, presumably, included both performers and listeners. From a singer's point of view, "The Hazel Dell" presents an emotional situation as uncomplicated as its musical challenge. The persona of the narrator, into which the song invites the singer to project himself (or herself), is lonely and grieving; but these emotions are expressed in a highly stylized way. In American "poetic" songs of this period, grief is conveyed through words, not music. Musical resources that, at least as far back as the sixteenth century in Europe, have evoked sadness and pain—minor mode, chromatic adventures in melody and harmony, shifts in tempo to reflect unstable emotions—are nowhere to be found in these "people's songs." Here, moods ranging from ecstatic joy to profound melancholy are all set in major mode (as, indeed, are almost all of Stephen Foster's songs). Songs of grief are slower in tempo and declamation than songs of joy. But except for that contrast, and perhaps the character of the piano accompaniment, the chief difference between them lies in their words.

As these remarks suggest, although American "people's songs" of the nineteenth century collectively cover a wide range of emotions, individual songs seldom do. In fact, most are free of emotional complexity. When they do express grief, as in "The Hazel Dell," they do so in a way seemingly drained of passion. Whatever the words assert about the singer's state of mind, the music conveys a clear sense of distancing from the experience, a kind of escape in which, rather than grappling with the sense of loss in the text, the music lyricizes it. Absorbing, diffusing, and generalizing the emotional sting of the laments offered up in such songs, the music has the effect of removing them from the present. Rather than passionate outbursts, they become gentle,

EXAMPLE 14. George F. Root, "Kiss Me, Mother, Kiss Your Darling!" (Lord) (New York, 1864), William L. Clements Library, University of Michigan

often dreamy reveries. While the foregoing may not explain the genesis of this brand of song in mid-nineteenth-century America, it does help to suggest its wide appeal. Coupled with a lack of musical complication, the emotional straightforwardness of the "poetic" song removed any technical or expressive barriers that might have deterred amateur performers from singing and playing these songs. If assuming a "dramatic" role, however momentarily, was part of what encouraged Americans of Root's day to take part in parlor singing as a form of expressive activity, then the role offered by "The Hazel Dell"—dignified, sensitive, wistful— could be slipped into and out of with ease.

Example 14 is offered here as a glimpse into the world of Root's customers. To look at this copy of "Kiss Me, Mother, Kiss Your Darling!" is to sense the earnest anxiety of the pianist who took the trouble to finger the introduction so carefully. We imagine the experience performing must have been for this musician: a tense journey through the intro, strewn with eighth notes and perilous jump-bass chords; relaxation when the simple boom-chuck harmonies arrive in support of the singer's entrance; rising tension as the end of the chorus approaches and the challenge of the introduction, to be played "tenderly," looms again.[44]

But the issue here is not one performer's skill or lack of it. It's the circumstances for which Root's songs were intended. "Kiss Me,

Mother," "The Old Folks Are Gone," and "The Hazel Dell" were only three drops in the ocean of songs and instrumental pieces composed or arranged in the mid-nineteenth century with American amateur performers in mind.[45] Set down in notation and sold in sheet-music form, accompanied by the piano—which by the 1840s had been redesigned and was beginning to be successfully merchandised as *the* American parlor instrument[46]—these songs mark the emergence of the middle-class American home as a center of musical performance and a prime target of the music business. In the first stage of his career, focused upon teaching classes and group performance, Root carried on, in modernized form, the tradition of the old singing school. Beginning in the 1850s, his composition of songs for home performers brought him into a new arena, perhaps the most volatile, competitive field of the American music business of that day.

Of all the things that historians have noted about Root, one that few have missed is that he used an assumed name as well as his own. The composer of "The Old Folks Are Gone" and "The Hazel Dell" is listed as G. Friedrich Wurzel. Get it? George Frederick Wurzel, the latter meaning "root" in German. It was under this German pseudonym that Root began to write and publish his solo songs. It has been suggested that Root did so in the hope that the name of a German composer might boost the sales of his music.[47] And that interpretation is surely consistent with what is known about the American musical scene in Root's day, including its strong strain of commercialism and the prestige a European pedigree carried. But if one takes the pseudonym as a comment on the structure of mid-nineteenth-century American musical life, another element comes more sharply into focus. By recognizing that when Root began to compose solo songs he began moving away from his professional home base, we can see the Root–Wurzel dodge as evidence of a contrast between musical worlds. The world of teacher-compiler George Frederick Root was one of singing classes, instructional tunebooks issued by book publishers, moral inculcation, invocations and benedictions, and choral performances whose pinnacle of aspiration lay in oratorio excerpts. The world of song-composer G. Friedrich Wurzel centered more on performance by individuals, on sheet music from *music* publishers, on parlor singing for recreation and enjoyment, and on bringing stage works—from opera to blackface minstrelsy—into the home circle. The latter's secularity and unabashed commercial orientation made it suspect to some who gravitated toward the former, devoted as it was to edification and things of the spirit. When we recall that in Paris in 1851 Root had felt compelled to refuse an invitation to the opera because his church forbade its members to attend the theater,[48] the pseudonym—whether a serious attempt to protect a respected name or a more playfully offered disguise—is not hard to understand.[49]

Beginning in 1852 and continuing for some years thereafter, Root maintained *two* personas, each with its own identity, separated not only by vocational emphases and institutional bifurcation but by musical style. Root dramatized their separateness by maintaining his career as a teacher-composer while continuing to write popular songs under a different name.[50] And this brings us to *The Haymakers*, composed in 1856 by Root, not Wurzel, the fourth cantata in the line that followed *The Flower Queen*.[51]

The Haymakers came straight out of Root's own boyhood experience. He wrote it, words and music both, in his library at Willow Farm, where, he recalled:

> by stepping to the door, I could see the very fields in which I had swung the scythe and raked the hay, and in which I had many a time hurried to get the last load into the barn before the thunder-storm should burst upon us. In fact, nearly every scene described in the cantata had its counterpart in my experience on the old farm not many years before.[52]

Calling his piece "an operatic cantata," Root published it with detailed directions for costuming and staging, even to the point of describing how to make, from walnut shells, parchment, and catgut, an imitation katydid to contradict the city-slicker, Snipkins, in one of his songs. (Snipkins: "Sweet Kate *never* loved anybody but me!" Katydid: "Katydid, Katydid, Katydid." Snipkins: "Katy didn't.")[53]

During Part I of *The Haymakers*, a crew of happy workers is assembled, mows the hayfield, then beds down for the night to the strains of a choral lullaby. Part II traces the next day's events, beginning with "Good Morning" (ex. 15), a spirited part-song in praise of the dawning of a new summer day. In its ABA form the chorus is straightforward and conventional. In texture it is not, for Root overlays the choral block

EXAMPLE 15. George F. Root, "Good Morning!" bars 1–22 (Root)
(*The Haymakers* [New York, 1857], No. 23, p. 44)

(*continued*)

EXAMPLE 15 (*continued*)

(If convenient let the voices be so chosen for these two parts, that they will answer to each other from different parts of the choir, each voice singing perhaps a measure or two, and then joining in the Chorus.)

(*continued*)

EXAMPLE 15 (*continued*)

chords with patter divided among a gaggle of solo voices. The conversational, chattering quality of the solo singers, filling the gaps in the larger chorus's sound, creates a mood of youthful effervescence that seems especially suited to light, untrained voices—presumably those of the singers for whom *The Haymakers* and other works like it were composed.

The chorus "Shrouded Is the Sun" presents the work's chief dramatic crisis. Haymakers need the cooperation of the weather. They cut the grass in sunshine and warmth. Once it's been cut, they hope the weather holds until the grass has dried into hay, been collected into bales, and safely stored in the barn. In Root's drama, the sky darkens during the gathering, and the workers rush to finish the job. Just after the barn door closes on the new crop, a fearsome storm breaks. And Root's musical treatment of it shows that by 1856 he commanded an idiom that went far beyond that of his Wurzellian "land of tonic, dominant, and subdominant" in an omnipresent major mode, with choruses in block chords and strophic repetition. Here the mode is mostly minor, as befits the subject, but with telling key changes. Opening in G minor, the chorus sings of the gathering storm, with "distant thunders" mur-

muring in the bass (bars 1–16; see ex. 16a). Then, hearing God's voice in the thunder's roar, it modulates to B-flat major as it marvels at his power. Scurrying sixteenth-note scale passages depict "the rushing, howling wind" in G minor (ex. 16b). The trees pitch violently. With the storm's full force about to break, the chorus's awe takes on a note of fear, and its harmonizing gives way to octaves (bars 51–52; ex. 16c). But suddenly, coordinating text, tonality, and texture, Root engineers an unexpected shift of mood. Instead of the chorus in full cry, a quartet of soloists, sounding as if offstage, offers a calming message in B-flat (bars 52–60; ex. 16c): "Yet fear not we. He, whom the winds obeyed, is master of the storm."

From this point on, the piece is a dialogue between the chorus—louder, more and more agitated as the storm hits with full force, and always in G minor—and the quartet: calm, collected, and in the relative major. At the sound of a mighty crash of thunder, "earth trembles with afright." Then comes the rain, "in torrents pouring down." Finally, struck by lightning, a "mighty oak is riven in twain, as 't were a quiv'ring reed." But each new episode of violent destruction gets the same response from the quartet: we need not fear, for "the tempest but obeys" the heavenly father's will. The B-flat episodes in the piece not only provide contrast; they intensify the impact of the G-minor sections. As the number ends, quartet and chorus join together for the first time, the former's message prevailing (in B-flat) as the storm loses force and dies away (ex. 16d).

In "Shrouded Is the Sun," Root shows himself able to spin out more than 120 bars of through-composed choral music packing considerable dramatic wallop. Here is the kind of piece—and there are others in the work—that moved John Sullivan Dwight, usually no fan of the Mason-Root school, to review *The Haymakers* favorably in 1859, commenting that it needed "only the addition of orchestral accompaniment to entitle it to the name of an opera."[54]

Root was not to do much more with his *Haymakers* style, which brought together elements of the reformed American hymn tune, the English glee, and the Mendelssohnian oratorio. Nor, after *Belshazzar's Feast*, a "dramatic cantata in ten scenes" (1860), was he to write another work in so rich an idiom. Instead, the events of the early 1860s brought him back to songwriting, this time with militant fervor. In the late 1850s, as convention trips took him more and more to Chicago, he had begun

EXAMPLE 16. George F. Root, "Shrouded Is the Sun" (Root)
(*The Haymakers* [New York, 1857], No. 36)

(a) Bars 1–16, p. 71

EXAMPLE 16 (*continued*)

(b) Bars 37–42, p. 72

(c) Bars 50–60, p. 73

(*continued*)

EXAMPLE 16 (*continued*)

"to play . . . at business" in his brother's publishing firm, and by the time he joined Root and Cady as a partner, he was publishing popular songs under his own name.[55] Root recalled his first years with Root and Cady as quiet ones: "We began to publish a little. First a song or two, and some instrumental pieces in sheet form. After a while we decided to venture on a book, and put in hand one that I was then working on for day-schools; but now the WAR burst upon us!" For the next ten years (1861–71) he found himself caught up in "a whirl . . . of hard and confining work."[56] Again, as in the past, he proved equal to the task that fate brought his way.

Root's description of how he "found" the melodies of his Civil War songs has already been noted. In writing their lyrics, he assumed the role of people's minstrel, seeking to capture and transmute the public's

EXAMPLE 16 (*continued*)

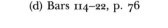

(d) Bars 114–22, p. 76

feelings. "When anything happened that could be voiced in a song, or when the heart of the Nation was moved by particular circumstances or conditions caused by the war, I wrote what I thought would then express the emotions of the soldiers or the people."[57] Root composed his war songs fully convinced of their moral and material worth in the cause. One Root and Cady advertisement called the songs "munitions of war."[58] "If I could not shoulder a musket in defense of my country," the composer later wrote, "I could serve her in this way."[59]

Root's "The Battle Cry of Freedom" reveals some of the properties that recommended it to those who sang and were stirred by it. One striking feature of this song is the comparative richness of the musical material itself, especially when compared with "The Hazel Dell." "The Battle Cry of Freedom" contains three distinctive, memorable ideas— "Yes, we'll rally round the flag," "Shouting the battle cry of Freedom" (ex. 17a), and "The Union forever" (ex. 17b)—more than the quota for people's songs in general, which could get by on just one. Since every phrase in the song is a statement or variant of one of the three, melodic energy stays at a high level throughout. Dotted rhythms on weak beats tie the three melodic phrases together; and the syncopation in the chorus on the song's highest pitch casts the word "forever" into relief, making it the song's climactic jolt. These elements are supported in the first, second, and fourth phrases by a harmonic twist that reaches beyond the "land of tonic, dominant, and subdominant." A little island of submediant follows the firm establishment of tonic; and after the D major (V of vi) in bar 5, the E-flat triad carries a nice ambiguity: possibly a deceptive cadence in G minor, but really the subdominant, restoring the B-flat tonic. When these musical details are linked with some of the resonant phrases in Root's text—each of the three main melodic ideas is set to a memorable text phrase—there is little mystery why this piece became the Union's most effective and popular martial song.[60]

Root's war songs explore the conflict from many angles. "The Battle Cry of Freedom" was written to inflame patriotic spirits at recruiting rallies.[61] "Just Before the Battle, Mother," in contrast, recounts a soldier's "thoughts of home and God" on the evening before he takes to the battlefield. Another Root favorite, "The Vacant Chair," sets the scene in the home of a soldier who's been killed in battle. ("We shall meet, but we shall miss him. There will be one vacant chair.") And "Tramp! Tramp! Tramp!" takes place in the cell of an imprisoned Union soldier as he anticipates the sound of the marching feet of his comrades, coming, he hopes, to set him free.

In "Tramp! Tramp! Tramp!" the sources that filled Root's "reservoir" of melody are not entirely mysterious (see ex. 18). The verse, from its opening gesture, to its continuation over a subdominant chord on the sixth degree, to its outright borrowing (bar 6, beat 4 to bar 7, beat 3) takes its impetus from the tune to which "The Battle Hymn of the Republic" was sung, right down to the key of B-flat, in which both were

EXAMPLE 17. George F. Root, "The Battle Cry of Freedom" (Root) (Chicago, 1862)

(a) Bars 4–8

(b) Bars 12–14

EXAMPLE 18. George F. Root, "Tramp! Tramp! Tramp!
(The Prisoner's Hope)," bars 4–20 (Root) (Chicago, 1864)

(*continued*)

EXAMPLE 18 (*continued*)

published as sheet music. As for the chorus, a story about that was told by W. S. B. Mathews in 1889. Speculating about the mysteries of popularity in song, he wrote:

> Every popular melody will be found on examination to be very much like something else, generally like a melody by an older and more capable writer. A folks song, nine times out of ten, is a degradation of type, a feebler reminiscence of something better. Very many of the melodies of Mr. Geo. F. Root are very like parts of melodies in opera.

And then came Mathews's story, a parable on the perils of musical evangelism. It seems that William Mason, distinguished pianist and son of Lowell Mason, was once

> sitting upon a hotel piazza watching some negro roustabouts unload the cargo of a steamer. As they worked they whistled or sang one melody, which seemed to him exactly like Verdi's anvil chorus [from *Il Trovatore*], until a certain point was reached. At

this point they uniformly turned aside and ended Verdi's melody improperly. Hearing this for an hour or more finally awakened a missionary spirit in the conscientious musician, and he strolled down to the wharf to give the dusky singers a lesson, and secure artistic justice to Verdi's music. But when he began to teach them the correct interpretation, he seemed to them to be spoiling their melody, which upon further investigation proved to be Geo. F. Root's "Tramp, Tramp, Tramp, the Boys are Marching."[62]

Root was fifty-one when fire destroyed his business in 1871. Financially well off, he was widely honored as he approached old age, chiefly on the strength of his war songs.[63] On a trip to England in 1886, he was astonished to find that twenty-four pages of the library catalog of the British Museum were devoted to listings of his music.[64] As noted above, London publisher John Curwen had written him as early as the 1850s to compliment him on supplying "wholesome," accessible music for which the British Isles had no equivalent.[65] From that time on, Root's cantatas and songs began to be published in London. And on his trip he met English music teachers who had "taught and conducted my music, more or less, from the beginning of their work—indeed, as one said, some of them 'had been brought up on it' before they became teachers and conductors."[66]

Root's autobiography is filled with insights about the musical traditions in which he worked. While many elements of his world no longer exist, others have endured, and none more persistently than the need for American musicians to position themselves in the marketplace. Root's own success on that score was uncanny. In line with his pragmatic philosophy, his commitment to accessibility, to serving customers' needs in the marketplace, provides the framework for Root's professional life. Beyond that, however, the marketplace becomes an ideal: not just the arena where commercial transactions take place but the forum in which democratic consensus is shaped and registered. Once Root decided to compose for the largest possible number of customers, only the sales of his compositions in printed form and their performances in public and private venues could gauge his success accurately. Thus, *The Story of a Musical Life* depicts the marketplace as a positive force—the final measure of achievement—not because it offers musicians a chance for commercial gain but because it is the incorruptible reflection of public judgment.

Root's experience taught him that the ultimate challenge of songwriting lay in outcomes beyond the composer's control. Reception, not composition, defined what he called "people's songs." As Austin has explained, Root's notion of "people's song" was "comprehensive." It encompassed many song genres: home and poetic songs, minstrel and other theatrical songs, patriotic and war songs, hymns and sacred songs, all of which had their own conventions, functions, and audiences.[67] Root enjoyed his first success as a composer, as we have seen, with *The Flower Queen*. Such pieces caught on with singing classes, providing unpretentious musical dramas well within the capacities of young, inexperienced singers. As artifacts to be sold, cantatas of this kind opened up a new niche in the marketplace, complementing the tunebooks already in general use. At the same time, works like *The Flower Queen*—"for the use of singing classes in academies," its title page noted—and *The Haymakers* remained solidly within the realm of instructional music. Published and marketed by Mason Brothers, a tunebook firm, they enriched the musical world that Root had entered when he arrived in Boston in 1838 without challenging its boundaries.

But the example of Stephen Foster showed Root that a much bigger arena lay open to the writer of solo songs. The songwriter's profession used sheet music, not tunebooks, to reach its public, and its purveyors were music publishers, not the tunebook firms who specialized in sacred and instructional music. Root composed "The Hazel Dell" under contract to the house of William Hall and Son of New York, known for effective marketing of sheet music through advertising and a wide network of selling agents. Hall boasted in 1856 that music from its presses could be had "from Maine to Oregon, the Sandwich Islands and Australia."[68] Considering, too, that song sheets were sold to individuals, not whole classes, at prices ranging from twenty to thirty-five cents—cantatas cost between sixty cents and a dollar—sheet music reached people who would never have bought tunebooks or cantatas. Root entered wholeheartedly into the songwriter's profession when success in its marketplace taught him that he had something to say to an audience more diverse than the congregations, singing pupils, and music teachers who had been his first customers. With "The Hazel Dell," "There's

Music in the Air," and especially his war songs, he achieved the ultimate goal of the popular artist: in the words of Greil Marcus, "to discover what it is that diverse people can authentically share." Novelist Raymond Chandler once noted the "vast difference between writing down to the public . . . and doing what you want to do in a form that the public has learned to accept."[69] Not a man to write down to anyone, Root made it a tenet of his professional life never to separate himself from the social order in which he lived and worked and whose taste he sought to please. From that grounding, he maintained a purity of spirit and intent that helped to fill the "reservoir" of musical imagination from which he drew his compositions.

Root's inability to explain his success as a song composer increased his respect for the marketplace. He confided: "I do not think a composer ever knows when that mysterious life . . . that power to retain their hold upon the hearts of the people . . . enters his work."[70] The story of how he composed his best-known hymn tune, "The Shining Shore," confirmed the mystery. One summer at Willow Farm, Root recalled:

> Mother, passing through the room, laid a slip from one of her religious newspapers before me, saying: "George, I think that would be good for music." I looked, and the poem began, "My days are gliding swiftly by." A simple melody sang itself along in my mind as I read, and I jotted it down, and went on with my work. . . . Later, when I took up the melody to harmonize it, it seemed so very simple and commonplace that I hesitated about setting the other parts to it. But I finally decided that it might be useful to somebody, and completed it. . . . When, in after years, this song was sung in all the churches and Sunday-schools of the land, and in every land and tongue where our missionaries were at work, and so demonstrated that it had in it that mysterious life of which I have spoken, I tried to see why it should be so, but in vain. . . . I say so much about this little song because it is a particularly good illustration of the fact that the simplest music may have vitality as well as that which is higher, and that the composer knows no more about it in one case than in the other.[71]

In short, the vitality found in a true "people's song" is revealed only by the people's acceptance of it. And acceptance is measured by the marketplace: the public tribunal to whose judgment Root learned to bow. Root launched his musical career as a teacher who, however modest his own knowledge, prospered by passing on what he knew to a public hungry for what he could give them. But the musical environment he lived in was more than a one-way street. The people, however receptive they might be to Root's teaching, also had something to teach him. For, expressing themselves as a collective entity in the musical marketplace, they could distinguish the few songs that deserved to live from the many that deserved oblivion. No one, including those who aspired to write "people's songs," could anticipate that judgment, nor could it be reduced to a formula or a theory. But neither was there any point in second guessing it.

As a teacher, then, Root gathered, structured, refined, and polished his musical knowledge, dispensing it in classes, conventions, "normals," and instructional books with efficiency and skill to a public of teachers and pupils who recognized his authority. As a song composer, in contrast, he worked quickly and spontaneously, then cast his bread upon the waters of the marketplace, hoping that he had captured something vital and enduring but fully aware that the results lay in the hands of public opinion. This dual relation to his audience—pedagogical authority and control, on the one hand, and compositional deference on the other—seems contradictory to a later age. Indeed, predecessors such as Thomas Hastings and Lowell Mason, contemporaries such as Stephen Foster, and later figures such as Theodore F. Seward and Charles K. Harris took one or the other of these stances but not both. Root and his generation seem to have been the first and last in which the two could combine in one person, suggesting an environment whose leaders understood knowledge and taste to be two different things, each with its own integrity.

Root's aspirations as a song composer affirmed his respect for the instinctive taste of the people. *The Story of a Musical Life* convinces the reader that, however he may have prospered financially from his musical strivings, Root gloried even more in his acceptance by those from whose ranks he had sprung and whose taste he shared, to his own benefit and to theirs.

· 6 ·

Duke Ellington (1899–1974)
and His Orchestra

EDWARD KENNEDY ELLINGTON once put the story of his life into two paragraphs.

> Once upon a time a beautiful young lady and a very handsome young man fell in love and got married. They were a wonderful, compatible couple, and God blessed their marriage with a fine baby boy (eight pounds, eight ounces). They loved their little boy very much. They raised him, nurtured him, coddled him, and spoiled him. They raised him in the palm of the hand and gave him everything they thought he wanted. Finally, when he was about seven or eight, they let his feet touch the ground.
>
> The first thing I did was to run out into the front yard, and then through the front gate, where I found someone who said, "Go ahead, Edward! Right over there." Once on the other side of the street, I ran into someone else who gave me the Go sign for a left-hand turn to the corner. When I got there, a voice said, "Turn right, and straight ahead. You can't miss it!" And that's the way it has always been. Every time I reached a point where I needed direction, I ran into a friendly advisor.[1]

Thus the words of a venerable black musician, an American institution by the time he published them in 1973. Ellington's words bring us into the presence of a powerful persona—a mask fashioned by an artist whose works included the public role he created for himself. "When I was a child, my mother told me I was blessed," he explained, "and I have always taken her word for it."[2] The character that Edward Ellington played in public, spoke through in interviews, and used to write his

184

autobiography was one of aristocratic confidence and grace. He was the Duke—the composer of hundreds of pieces who never seemed in a hurry; the black butler's son who talked with relaxed ease to audiences all over the world; the tough competitor in a cutthroat business who seemed unaware that he was competing at all. When Ellington lit up his famous smile and told an audience, "We love you madly," who were they to doubt him?[3]

Like many other things in Ellington's life, his persona has its roots in the central metaphor of his career: the tale of the favored child's journey. Mark Tucker's study of Ellington's beginnings in Washington, D.C., confirms his parents' key role. James ("J.E.") and Daisy Ellington, Tucker concludes, gave Edward "more than a sense of being well fed and much loved: they instilled in him a pride about who he was and what he could achieve."[4] The Ellington family's high expectations rubbed off on their son.[5] Asked late in life what had led him to begin composing "as a very young man," he replied: "The driving power was a matter of wanting to be—and to be heard—on the same level as the best."[6] Fueled by such aspiration, he set out on a lifelong quest to excel but with little technical training and no clear destination. That's where the "friendly advisors" came in. For at each crossroads, as Ellington faced a need for some new skill or a push in a new direction, he found help. Ellington's tale identifies two of the forces behind his accomplishments: competitive drive rooted in a deep hunger for personal achievement, and a gift, based on social shrewdness, for finding collaborators who could help him solve the problems he encountered.

Those who knew Ellington agree that he was a complex, enigmatic man.[7] Much the same could be said about his life's journey as a musician, for it led him to unexplored territory whose precise location remains a matter of disagreement even today, well into the second decade after his death. What did Ellington the musician really accomplish? Where did his journey take him? Clear-cut answers are hard to come by within our tradition of musicological inquiry. Just as Ellington's intense individualism and his easy sociability may seem contradictory rather than complementary impulses, it is not easy to fix his place in the world that music historians have rationalized for study.

Ellington's standing as a creator of music is one example of the problem. Gunther Schuller has called him "a major composer," indeed, perhaps "one of the half-dozen greatest masters of our time."[8] Major

185

composers, however, are usually thought of as people imbued with musical inventiveness, an instinct that appears early in life and persists thereafter; who seek and receive formal training, taking open pleasure in perfecting and exercising their craft; who work alone, courting inspiration and inventing structures of sound for performers to realize; and who "write" music, the verb implying both invention and the notation required to fix and preserve the music they create. Ellington's career contradicts these norms. He began sporadically, apparently composing his first piece at fifteen and writing songs from his mid-twenties on but concentrating on composing only after his career demanded it (he was twenty-seven at the time).[9] Except for a fairly brief period of harmony instruction from a Washington pianist and music master, Ellington was self-taught as a composer, and he showed no interest in discussing the technique of his art in public. (His resistance to more training later in life is a matter of documented fact.)[10] As for the notion of a composer working alone, significant parts of many "Ellington" pieces, especially their melodies, were contributed by other members of the ensemble.[11] Moreover, writing played only a small role in the creation of many Ellington compositions. Trumpeter Rex Stewart, who played with Ellington from 1934 to 1945, remembered the process of composition as it sometimes took place in the recording studio.

> Ellington would usually arrive late, then warm up at the piano for a quarter-hour or so. If he played fast, the band knew it was to record a stomping, roaring piece; if he played slowly, they were to record a lament. Ellington would then invariably suggest to the musicians that they make sure the piano was in tune; this in fact meant that they themselves should be.[12]

When the musicians were tuned up, Ellington might then produce the score of his new "composition," most likely written on "some scraggly pieces of manuscript paper." Stewart remembered one session at which Ellington pulled out "about one-eighth of a page on which he'd scribbled . . . some notes for the saxophones . . . but there was nothing for Johnny Hodges. Duke had the saxes run the sequence down twice, while Johnny sat nonchalantly smoking. Then Duke called to Hodges, 'Hey Rabbit, give me a long slow glissando against that progression.' " Next, Ellington urged Cootie Williams to try entering "on the second bar" of the passage with one of his patented trumpet growls. Then the leader turned to trombonist Lawrence Brown. "You are cast in the role of the sun beating down on the scene," he prompted. When that announcement brought no response, Ellington went on: "What kind of a sound do you feel that could be? You don't know? Well, try a high B-flat in a felt hat, play it legato, and sustain it for eight bars." Then, with these possible component parts in place, Ellington gave the downbeat and tried out the sound. The saxophone section played its melody, backed by the rhythm section and overlaid with Hodges's glissando, Williams's growl, and Brown's sun-warmed, muted B-flat. If the leader's guesses were on target and the men responded as he hoped, "the Ellington effect" might be invoked. "And," Stewart concluded, "that's the way things went—sometimes."[13]

On the occasion Stewart describes, Ellington composed not by drawing abstract tone combinations from his imagination but by working with his musicians so that their "tonal personalities"—their particular sound, way of playing, and inventiveness—actually helped to *create* the piece.[14] Perhaps the saxophone melody was his, perhaps not.[15] Certainly, Ellington determined the final result. But that result was the fruit of a collaborative encounter whose participants had already proved themselves unblendable individuals in Ellington's tonal coat of many colors. When trumpeter Fred Stone spent a few months in Ellington's orchestra in 1970, he was struck by the demands Ellington placed upon his musicians, far different from anything else in his experience.

> The Ellington Orchestra is the only musical outfit I know where the members are hired solely on the basis of their strength and individuality. It is the only orchestra I know where you are not required to become an exact percentage of the section you're playing with; where you are not required to match the sound of the previous member. You must function as an individual—and you are judged solely on your personal musicianship.[16]

That is what Gunther Schuller seems to have had in mind when he noted Ellington's "unique" partnership with his players, in Schuller's view "unprecedented in the history of Western music." Ellington, Schuller writes, "forged a musical style and concept which, though totally original and individual, nevertheless consistently incorporated

187

and integrated the no less original musical ideas of his players."[17] Sound was surely foremost among those ideas. Stewart's description of Ellington at work demonstrates Schuller's point. For it was *Hodges's* glissando, *Williams's* growl, *Brown's* muted B-flat that gave Ellington the elements from which, with the help of his ear and piano, he molded his compositions.[18]

The gateway to Ellington's accomplishments as a composer, the seminal moment of arrival on his artistic journey, was the discovery by 1927 of "the Ellington effect"—the unique sound that was a product of his ideas about music, the "tonal personalities" of the players he hired, and the exploration he conducted of the sound possibilities of his own instrument, the piano.[19] The Ellington effect made the orchestra easily recognizable, a big advantage in the commercial environment in which Ellington worked. But the Ellington effect was more than a distinctive sound quality. It was a carrier of emotion through which he connected with his audience.

To the question of what Ellington accomplished as a musician, one of the most obvious answers is that he managed to stay in business as leader of a working jazz orchestra for more than fifty years. Only by finding and pleasing listeners could he have achieved such longevity. In *Music Is My Mistress,* Ellington leaves little doubt of his respect for audiences. Sometimes he describes himself as their servant: "I travel from place to place by car, bus, train, plane . . . taking rhythm to the dancers, harmony to the romantic, melody to the nostalgic, gratitude to the listener."[20] Elsewhere, he notes how rhythm can bring musicians and an audience into a state of profound, if short-lived, empathy. "When your pulse and my pulse are together," he writes, "we are swinging, with ears, eyes, and every member of the body tuned in to driving a wave emotionally, compellingly, to and from the subconscious."[21] And sometimes, in his view, a knowledgeable audience can act almost like a skilled adversary who, by raising the competitive stakes, forces from the musicians the best performance they have to give.

When one is fortunate enough to have an extremely sensitive audience, and when every performer within the team on stage feels it, too, and reacts positively in coordination toward the pinnacle, and when both audience and performers are determined not to be outdone by the other, and when both have appreciation and taste to match—then it is indeed a very special moment, never to be forgotten.[22]

Comments like these reaffirm Ellington's solid grounding in society. Banking his professional fate upon the musical personalities of his sidemen, he fashioned music for a social realm in which, by connecting emotionally with dancers and listeners, the music proved its worth.

It was Ellington's ability, first, to reach new audiences and, second, to employ the Ellington effect in new and different ways that kept him moving on his long, wide-ranging, and profitable journey. Rooted solidly in African-American culture, he began early in life to make music that reached beyond his own community.[23] And from November 1926, when Irving Mills became his manager, he courted new audiences on several fronts. In the United States sixty years ago, it was rare for black jazz bands to be listed in white record catalogs, to appear in Hollywood films, to perform in Broadway shows, or to receive prestigious bookings of the kind Ellington enjoyed when he played opposite French entertainer Maurice Chevalier at New York's Fulton Theater in 1930. Moreover, no other jazz ensemble, black or white, had a leader capable of producing a steady flow of new recorded compositions, much less one who—apparently at his manager's prompting—could write a "rhapsody" filling both sides of a 78-rpm disc. Finally, it was unusual, though not unprecedented, for black American ensembles to perform in Europe. With Mills's help, Ellington accomplished all these things by 1933.[24] Perhaps Mills's motive in each case was economic. But whatever the manager's goal, these challenges also had the effect of sharpening Ellington's technical skill and enlarging the expressive resources he commanded. Each, while broadening his audience, also enhanced Ellington's growth as an artist (and the artistic growth of his men) while at the same time undermining the public's notion of the boundaries within which black musicians worked. Mills's energetic pursuit of accessibility—his desire to reach a bigger and bigger audience on its own terms—had found a perfect foil: a group of black musicians, no less eager for popular approval than he, but with a leader whose music, at its best, struck a balance among three diverse forces: his own restless inventiveness, the imagination and skill of his players, and the audience's appetite for entertaining experience.[25]

What Ellington accomplished as a composer must be considered in light of that three-way relationship. Locating the balance point was Ellington's own doing. That he was able to maintain it over so many years is a tribute not only to his musicianship but to extraordinary personal qualities. In fact, the more closely one studies Ellington's career, the more clearly one sees his "enigmatic" personal complexity as an indispensable tool in the process of weighing, balancing, and negotiating that lay behind his rise to fame. Ellington described himself as an observer by nature, a trait he attributed to artists in general.[26] As a musician, he says, he was always an avid listener.[27] As an African-American, he became a close student of artistry in all its forms and an admirer of theatrical effects.[28] As a man, though to claim it for himself would be "square," Ellington was in all things "hip"—possessor of the quality he once defined as "up-to-the-minute awareness."[29] These traits helped him create an environment in which his players' tonal personalities could flourish, even in the face of a grinding year-round performing routine, while still satisfying an attentive, critical, dancing, listening audience.[30] Ellington's resources of character and personality left even those who knew him best in awe—reedman Otto Hardwick, for example, who grew up on Washington's T Street just a block away from the house where Ellington lived, and who played with Ellington-led groups from the 1920s into the 1940s. "The amazing thing about him," Hardwick told an interviewer in the 1960s, "is that the language, the slant, everything, it's all acquired. It didn't rub off from someone else, and it wasn't a legacy, either. He went inside himself to find it."[31]

When Ellington began his professional life, the standard persona of black men in American show business was a shuffling, comic stereotype inherited from nineteenth-century blackface minstrelsy. Ellington rejected that stereotype, creating instead, surely with the help of Irving Mills, a dignified public image. In the 1920s, an African-American artist with aspirations to compose found himself in what Lawrence Gushee has called a "minefield" of ideological polarities: "first of all," Gushee writes, the polarity of "classical and popular—that is to say, enduring and ephemeral, inspirational and industrial, idealistic and functional"; second, he continues, a black composer had to deal with the polarity of "Old Europe" and "New America"; and third was the "American polarity" of black and white.[32] During the first half of this century, African-Americans created, within the field of popular dance music, a music that, if it did not demand, nevertheless invited the development of expert musicianship and intensity of musical expression.[33] This music, jazz, mediated between and among the existing polarities. Jazz, Gushee writes, was a music not for high financial profit, "yet not coopted by institutions, neither absolutely contemporary nor traditional, partly 'functional' and entertaining, partly not, and finally, neither completely black [nor white], American [nor] European."[34]

Ellington, as we have already seen, was one of the pioneers whose instinct for the delicate balance enabled him to flourish, even prosper, in the music business's "minefield." He succeeded, during the late 1920s and early 1930s, in forming and leading a successful dance orchestra, in making himself into an effective pianist, and in finding a personal voice as a composer. He accomplished these things not in seclusion but on the job, while leading his orchestra's nightly engagements. What he did was hard to do. But through his achievements, Ellington maintained an urbane, relaxed presence that concealed the difficulty of what he and his men were accomplishing.[35]

It was Billy Strayhorn, Ellington's close collaborator, who made the now-familiar observation that "Ellington plays the piano, but his real instrument is his band."[36] As leader of a band whose members, especially in earlier days, were not all schooled musicians or secure readers of music, Ellington was also a *composer* who worked in an improvisatory tradition. Of this polarity, Francis Newton has written that Ellington "solved the unbelievably difficult problem of turning a living, shifting and improvised folk-music into *composition* without losing its spontaneity."[37] Moreover, the orchestra's long engagement at the Cotton Club in Harlem, beginning in 1927, required Ellington to write not just for dancing but for the club's floor shows. Hence, he learned to work for effects and to master musical forms that reached beyond the standard conventions of dance music. Nevertheless, as Martin Williams has observed, whether writing for dance hall, nightclub, or theater, Ellington was in show business. The circumstances of his employment dictated that his music always be immediate in its impact.[38]

Sound was Ellington's primary tool for achieving that immediacy. Indeed, this sharpest of listeners, this man who sought tonal "charisma" in his players,[39] learned to distill his extreme aural sensitivity into unprecedented timbres, thereby seizing listeners' rapt attention. When he began working in the band business, Ellington recalled, "the chief req-

uisite was good personality of tone."[40] Experience in the music business
had taught him that some musicians revealed their inner selves most
deeply in their sound and that audiences knew it. Johnny Hodges's
"sultry solos," for example, were powerful because Hodges played them
"in true character, reaching into his soul for them, and automatically
reaching everybody else's soul. An audience's reaction to his first note
was as big and deep as most applause for musicians at the end of their
complete performance." But Ellington also noticed that listeners' responses to Hodges, affirmed in "grunts, oohs, and aahs," with an occasional "Yes, daddy!" thrown in, were "never too loud to prevent their
hearing the next note he played."[41]

It was this kind of response—assenting, delighted, unreserved, yet
also attentive and ready to be led—that Ellington sought to elicit through
the immediate impact of his orchestra's sounds. (Admittedly, their impact can only be conveyed by hearing them, and the description that
follows depends upon having recordings handy for listening.)[42] By all
accounts, the chief architect of the Ellington effect as it first emerged
in a piece like "East St. Louis Toodle-Oo" (ex. 19) was trumpeter James
"Bubber" Miley, who discovered that by blowing, gargling, and hum-
ming at the same time, and shaping the sound with a plunger mute, he
could "growl" through his trumpet.[43] Ellington loved this sound. For
him it was no mere technical trick but a call from Miley's heart. "He
was raised on soul and saturated and marinated in soul," Ellington wrote
of Miley. "Every note he played was soul filled with the pulse of compulsion."[44] After Miley left the band in 1929, his successors had to master
the growl, which shows up again and again in Ellington's later music.[45]

After entering Ellington's arsenal of sounds, the trumpet growl
quickly took on programmatic implications as a feature of the so-called
jungle music Ellington sometimes played to accompany the Cotton
Club's exotic floor shows.[46] But this style combined elements that could
also be used separately. In "Concerto for Cootie" (1940; ex. 20), written
to display the versatility of Charles "Cootie" Williams, the trumpet
growl, which can sound like a distorted human voice, is liberated from
the minor mode and from the jungle and used as just one of the many
timbres at Williams's command.[47] Or the minor mode and chromaticism
of jungle music could be detached from trumpet growling, as in the
minor blues, "Ko-Ko" (1940; ex. 21). The menacing sound of the beginning is built on the foundation of Harry Carney's room-filling bari-

EXAMPLE 19. Duke Ellington and Bubber Miley, "East St. Louis Toodle-Oo," bars 8–16 (29 November 1926, Vocalion 1064; composite transcription after Gunther Schuller, *Early Jazz* [New York, 1968], 327, and Mark Tucker, *Ellington: The Early Years* [Urbana, Ill., 1991], 249)

tone sax, with the trombone section responding to Carney's rhythmicized pedal point.[48] Then, Juan Tizol on valve trombone plays a repeated riff—Schuller calls his sound "leathery, slithery"—responded to by the full saxophone section.[49]

Another kind of Ellington sound is found in a large family of pieces slow in tempo, rich and often chromatic in harmony, meditative in mood, of which the most famous is "Mood Indigo." In "Dusk" (ex. 22), after Ellington's piano introduction, the theme is played by a closely voiced trio: muted trumpet with the tune, muted trombone in the middle, and clarinet on the bottom, as in "Mood Indigo." In performance, the trio surrounds the mike and plays as one. The sound's impact lies perhaps as much in the intentness of listening that underlies such a delicate blend as in the notes themselves.[50]

EXAMPLE 20. Duke Ellington, "Concerto for Cootie," bars 20–27 (15 March 1940, Victor 26598; after Ken Rattenbury, *Duke Ellington, Jazz Composer* [New Haven, 1990], 183–85)

From this brief primer of Ellington sounds, let's move to some of his and his men's effects that can only be described as astonishing, both in conception and execution. "Braggin' in Brass," featuring the band's trumpet and trombone sections, begins with scurrying passagework for muted trumpets over the harmonies of the last strain of "Tiger Rag," an Ellington favorite. Then it's time for the trombones to brag. How does Ellington show them off? Through stinging attacks and a coordination that perhaps only Brown, Tizol, and Nanton, among trombone

EXAMPLE 21. Duke Ellington, "Ko-Ko," bars 1–8 (6 March 1940, Victor 26577; after Rattenbury, *Duke Ellington*, 107–10)

EXAMPLE 22. Duke Ellington, "Dusk," bars 8–12 (28 May 1940, Victor 26677; after Gunther Schuller, *The Swing Era* [New York, 1989], 122)

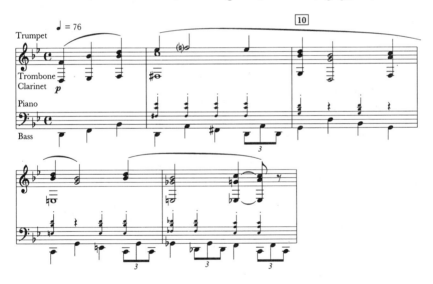

EXAMPLE 23. Duke Ellington, Henry Nemo, and Irving Mills, "Braggin' in Brass" (3 March 1938, Brunswick 8108; after Schuller, *Swing Era,* 94)

(a) Chorus 2, bars 1–2, conflating three trombone parts into one line

(b) Chorus 2, bars 1–2, showing the three trombone parts

sections, could have managed. Ellington writes a descending broken chord figure whose notes look conventional enough on paper (ex. 23a). In performance, however, it's another story, for he divides the line so that each man plays only every fourth note (ex. 23b). Given the tempo— Schuller has clocked it at ♩ = 316—and the cross-accents produced by Ellington's division of four-note groupings among three players, a lurching, spattering melodic line results—as Schuller aptly writes, a hocket, drawing from listeners a response of "disbelief."[51]

"The New Black and Tan Fantasy" (1938) contains another marvel. Its third chorus is ostensibly a trombone solo by Nanton, with Ellington playing a stream of mysterious, parallel chords in lagging quarter-note triplets behind him. Further in the background, at least at the start of the chorus, is Barney Bigard's clarinet. At the very end of the preceding chorus, Bigard has swooped up to a high concert D-flat (the "blue" third in the piece's key of B-flat), which he sustains softly, without vibrato, like a tiny beam of light. As Nanton's solo unfolds with Ellington's backing, the D-flat begins to increase in volume and, ever so slowly, to rise in pitch. By the downbeat of bar 10, Bigard's note has blossomed into a fortissimo F, a dominating dominant ringing high above the orchestra.[52]

Ellington sometimes took advantage of the freedom that introductions afforded. For there, whatever strangeness he wanted to hazard could be set forth audaciously, then jettisoned in favor of more conventional material when the main tune entered. "The Sergeant Was Shy" begins with a riff that was to be heard again in the novelty pop hit "Boogie Woogie Bugle Boy (from Company B)."[53] Ellington starts with clarinets playing that riff figure on B-flat in $\frac{4}{4}$ time. He then adds layers at four-bar intervals: trombones in what sounds like $\frac{6}{8}$ time, playing a contrasting figure on D-flat (so they introduce bitonality and polymeter); then muted trumpets enter with a clipped, military-sounding pattern in B-flat minor; and finally a clarinet trill on F. The resulting cacophony is never resolved. It's simply abandoned for a four-bar series of guitar chords, modulating from B-flat to D-flat, in which the main theme is introduced.[54]

But Ellington's music was not made to be swallowed in small doses. His mastery extended to musical form, and especially the short forms determined by the length of recordings of his day. I've chosen "Old Man Blues" (1930) to exemplify what we might call one-side form and "Diminuendo and Crescendo in Blue" (1937) for two-side form.

Bearing no relationship in its phrase structure or harmonies to the standard twelve-bar blues or its relatives, "Old Man Blues" shows Ellington's fondness for playing with musical form—for sparring with the listener through unexpected extensions, ellipses, and new melodic strains.[55] It also illustrates two other techniques that pervade Ellington's music. One is the quality of wordless singing that the plunger-mute technique produces, whether on trumpet or trombone. And this imitation of the voice, though a somewhat grotesque one bordering on the comic, leads one to hear many Ellington pieces or passages as conversations between instruments—often in the form of the call-and-response pattern that lies at the very heart of the blues. "Old Man Blues" is scored for three instrumental groups: the reed section (clarinets and saxes), the brass (trumpets and trombones), and the rhythm (piano, guitar, bass, drums). While Ellington's sections often play as units, a listener never knows when an individual voice will detach itself to comment on what other instruments are saying or singing.

197

TABLE 4
Ellington, "Old Man Blues" (1930)

Formal function[a]	Featured instrument(s)	Key
I^8	soprano saxophone	E♭
A^{30} (aaba′)	trombone and clarinet	
B^{20} (vcd)	♩ 𝄾 ♩ 𝄾 (4) saxophone section (8) trumpet section (8)	
A^{32}	brass tune (16) trombone (8) brass tune (8)	F
A^{32}	baritone saxophone and piano brass backing on bridge	
A^{30}	soprano saxophone backed by brass (16) trumpet (14)	
B^{10} (c′x)	saxophone section (6) brass (4) 𝄾 ♪ ♩ ♪ ♩ ♪ ♩ ♪	
A^{32}	brass tune with clarinet swoops (16) trombone and clarinet (8) brass tune (8)	

[a] *I* stands for intro; *A*, *B* for full thematic statements; *a, b, c, d* for parts of thematic statements; *v* for vamp; *x* for extension; and superscript numbers for the number of bars.

After its introduction, "Old Man Blues" begins with such a conversation, though perhaps it would be better to call it a series of assertions by trombonist Nanton, around which clarinetist Bigard deftly dances. To borrow a line from a well-known poet, Bigard floats like a butterfly, while Nanton stings like a bee. "Old Man Blues" teems with unexpected details (see table 4). The second strain (B), for example, comes in two bars early both times it appears. The move from E-flat to F after the second strain is more a tonal ratcheting than a modulation, and by way of parallel fifths and octaves at that. The real tune isn't introduced until the second A section (A^{32}). The trumpet solo in the fourth A section evokes a standard piece of stage business by beginning hopelessly behind the action and then catching up. And the brass section's break (x^4) just before the last A is twice as long as expected.[56]

Even though the ending of "Old Man Blues," a ritard, sounds a bit stilted, the quality of playing on this recording is sharp, disciplined, crackling with excitement, and utterly convincing as an artistic statement.[57]

Ellington is renowned as one of the first jazz composers to explore "extended" form—that is, to write pieces too long to fit on one side of a ten-inch 78-rpm recording.[58] One such piece was "Diminuendo and Crescendo in Blue" (1937).[59] When Ellington composed this piece (actually a combination of two pieces, "Diminuendo in Blue" and "Crescendo in Blue," each written for one side of a 78-rpm record), there was no form in jazz more familiar than the twelve-bar blues, with its three four-bar phrases, its characteristic harmonic progression (moving from tonic to subdominant in bar 5 and to dominant in bar 9), and the implied call-and-response built into every phrase. Ellington's achievement in "Diminuendo and Crescendo in Blue" was to use this straightforward, conventional form, on which many of the musicians in his band could have improvised effectively, as the basis for a fanciful, beautifully shaped composition in which improvisation played only a small role. Ellington made his piece, of course, to be experienced from start to finish. But to appreciate the strangeness of its beginning, perhaps we should first discuss some of the work's simpler, more straightforward sections.

The fifth chorus of "Diminuendo" (bars 53–64)—one chorus of the twelve-bar blues pattern upon which the whole composition is based—features a call-and-response pattern operating in two-bar units. The trumpets give out an abrupt, two-beat call, and the saxes respond with a four-beat answer (ex. 24a). In the jazz tradition of Ellington's day, the chorus is the basic unit. And it is axiomatic that the harmonic progression of the chorus, tended by the rhythm section, recurs through a piece as its chief organizing force. When the chorus is as short as it is here—twelve bars at a brisk tempo—changes are most likely to occur from one chorus to the next rather than within choruses. That premise holds for "Diminuendo and Crescendo in Blue." In Chorus 6, the trombone section, silent in Chorus 5, takes the lead with a new melodic figure; the saxes respond, now in unison where before they had played four-part harmony (ex. 24b). In Chorus 7, short figures are replaced by a fully harmonized tune played by the saxes while the brass sit silent (ex. 24c).

EXAMPLE 24. Duke Ellington, "Diminuendo in Blue" (20 September 1937,
Brunswick 8004; manuscript in Smithsonian Institution,
Duke Ellington Collection)

(a) Chorus 5, bars 1–4

(b) Chorus 6, bars 1–4

Sectional interplay has dominated Choruses 5–7; but the next three
choruses feature soloists. First, trombonist Nanton, master of the sub-
verbal growl, responds with hoarse mockery to the saxophone section's
calls (Chorus 8). Then baritone saxophonist Carney fits his own responses into the windows in the trombone section's clipped chordal
gestures (Chorus 9). And then Ellington himself plays a chorus that
begins high and descends to a concluding cadence (Chorus 10). Through

EXAMPLE 24 (*continued*)

(c) Chorus 7, bars 1–8

Choruses 5–10, colors have been gradually growing darker, the range moving downward, and the dynamic level decreasing. The trumpets do nothing important after Chorus 5. The key level has moved from the sharp side (G major) to the flat side (D-flat). Ellington has reached the end of the first half of his piece (and of side A of the disc on which it was first recorded). The "Diminuendo" is complete.

By now the "plot" of Ellington's "Diminuendo and Crescendo in Blue" is obvious enough, even if we have yet to discuss its beginning. Its shape is concave. Starting at peak level, intensity gradually subsides, all the way down to the pianissimo that ends the first half. Then the process is reversed. Table 5 shows a map of the "Crescendo in Blue," the piece's second half (side B). Among the striking features of its beginning is a brand new sound. Ellington's four reed players exchange their saxophones for clarinets, which they play with round, liquid fullness in the low-register unison tune that begins the "Crescendo" (ex. 25a). Behind them, the trombone section enters softly with dark, mahogany warmth. The unison tune, moreover, harks back to the lyric saxophone chorus heard in the "Diminuendo" (Chorus 7). And, as table 5 shows, its opening rhythmic motive recurs through the first three choruses of "Crescendo." One more thing sets off the beginning of the "Crescendo": Each of its first two choruses ends with a two-bar extension—Ellington's way of warning listeners away from complacent formal expectations.

TABLE 5

Ellington, "Crescendo in Blue" (1937)

Chorus no.	Bars	Lead[a]	Responses[a]	Motive
1	1–14	u clarinets	h trombones h trumpets at end	♩.♫♪♩
2	15–28	u clarinets	h trumpets and h trombones	
3	29–40	h trombones	u clarinets	
4	41–52	h trumpets	solo clarinet	
5	53–64	h clarinets	u trombones	♪♩♪♩
6	65–76	h clarinets	h trumpets	
7	77–86	h clarinets	u trombones and h trumpets	
8	87–98	h trumpets	8ve trombones	♩.♫♪♩
9	99–110	h clarinets	h trombones and trumpets	𝄾♫♫♩
10	111–22	h trumpets and trombones, with screech	u clarinets (mostly)	♪♩.𝄾♪♩
11	123–34	h clarinets and trumpets	u trombones	♩.♫♪♩
12	135–46	h trumpets and trombones, with screech	h clarinets	♩♩.𝄾♫
Tag	147–56	h ensemble		

[a] u stands for unison; h stands for harmonized

The fifth chorus of the "Crescendo" finds clarinets once more in the lead. But now they play a new, busier tune, and they are harmonized. Again, clarinets are answered by trombones, this time with a unison countermelody, which they phrase uncannily together, with the deftness of a single voice and the weight of three (ex. 25b). By Chorus 10, the orchestra is in full cry. The volume has been growing, chorus by chorus. The range has expanded, the melody rising to higher and higher registers. The brass join in on what's left of the thematic statement, now pared down to the briefest of motives (ex. 25c). In the gaps left by brass rests, clarinet responses are heard. And, as often happens toward the

EXAMPLE 25. Ellington, "Crescendo in Blue" (20 September 1937, Brunswick 8004; manuscript in Smithsonian Institution, Duke Ellington Collection)

(a) Chorus 1, bars 1–4

(b) Chorus 5, bars 1–12, trombone part

(c) Chorus 10, bars 1–3

end of Ellington's up-tempo numbers, one trumpet breaks loose from the others to fill the rest of the unclaimed space with screeching high notes. The texture has thickened; the instruments now play clusters of tones that are acidly discordant. Consonance is being overwhelmed by dissonance as the piece builds toward its conclusion.

With the full-throttle ending of Ellington's "Crescendo" in mind, let's go back and pick up the opening bars of the "Diminuendo." The music there, as expected, is loud, dense, and dissonant. But where the acrid pillars of sound with which the "Crescendo" climaxes are firmly and obviously embedded in the twelve-bar blues structure, the "Diminuendo" begins with less formal clarity. To recognize what Ellington is up to in these opening bars, it is worth recalling that in later parts of the work he follows both the standard harmonic structure and two more blues conventions as well. Ellington consistently begins the first two phrases of each twelve-bar chorus with a statement and restatement of the same melody. (The figure that begins bar 1 of a chorus also begins

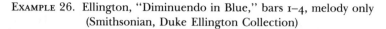

EXAMPLE 26. Ellington, "Diminuendo in Blue," bars 1–4, melody only
(Smithsonian, Duke Ellington Collection)

Saxophones unison

bar 5.) And he relies heavily on call-and-response: the instrumental
dialogue in which a statement by one voice is answered by another.
These habits are missing from the beginning of "Diminuendo." In fact,
through its first four choruses (bars 1–52), something is always out of
kilter. In Chorus 1, it's the cross-rhythmic, athematic character of the
material, coupled with a small glitch in the harmonic progression (ex.
26). Despite the theme's strident asymmetry, the blues structure could
still be heard if the tonic chord returned in bar 11. But in bar 11, instead
of rounding off the chorus, Ellington offers lurching, offbeat figures
over some kind of F chord; the expected return to tonic E-flat is post-
poned until bar 12, leaving listeners with the feeling that a bar has been
added, or at least that they've somehow lost their way.

The harmonic resolution at the end of a blues chorus usually fills
two bars (bars 11–12), typically with one bar of tonic and one of dominant, which prepares for the tonic downbeat of the next chorus. But
because the resolution at the end of Ellington's first chorus fills only
one bar, bar 13, which starts Chorus 2, doesn't sound like the beginning
that it is. Nevertheless, Chorus 2 gets under way with a call-and-response
pattern: saxes and trumpets, densely packed, with the call, and unison
trombones with the response (ex. 27). And in bar 5 of Chorus 2, the
second phrase starts with the call repeated on the subdominant. So far,
so good. In bar 6, however, instead of the active response heard in bar
2—and expected in the supposed restatement—we get from the trombones a sustained, stationary whole note. In bar 7 the call is repeated
on the tonic. If it were repeated again in bar 9, we might still hear it
within the twelve-bar blues framework, for the blues chord progression
remains intact. But instead, bar 9 delivers new, confusing offbeat figures. The original call from bar 1 sounds again in bar 11. (Bars 11–14 of
Chorus 2 repeat bars 1–4 almost exactly.) In retrospect, it's as if two
new bars have been added to the melodic voices in bars 9–10, pulling
them loose from the harmony. Or maybe bars 5–6 are the added ones.[60]

EXAMPLE 27. Ellington, "Diminuendo in Blue," Chorus 2, bars 1–6
(Smithsonian, Duke Ellington Collection)

In any event, even more than Chorus 1, the second chorus of "Diminuendo" leaves the listener disoriented, and especially so because it ends with a tag that carries the tonality from E-flat to G. Bars 27 and 28 of the piece prepare the listener for the next chorus.

On the downbeat of Chorus 3, the bass withholds the new tonic, clouding somewhat the new section's beginning. Ellington's material clouds the issue further. In a kind of role reversal, the brass call that begins the chorus *sounds* like a response—not a "melody" but a series of offbeat chords—and the sax section responds with a melodic statement more in the style of a call (ex. 28). Because the brass chords resemble the end of something more than the start, even a sharp ear

EXAMPLE 28. Ellington, "Diminuendo in Blue," Chorus 3, bars 1–8 (Smithsonian, Duke Ellington Collection)

could hear the saxes' entry with their tune (bar 3) as Chorus 3's beginning. However, when the subdominant arrives two bars later, repeating the opening brass chords, we learn belatedly that we're hearing a restatement. By bar 7, when the sax melodic response returns, the ear has regained its place in the form, only to have it dislodged in bar 8 by the entrance of the brass call—one bar early. And that call returns in bar 11, keeping the ear formally at sea until the chorus's end.[61]

In bar 41 of the "Diminuendo," Ellington finally delivers a clear-cut beginning: an arrival on the tonic, as expected, with a fresh new melodic figure beginning in the saxes on the downbeat (ex. 29). But it takes him only four bars to resume his undermining tactics. In Chorus 4's second phrase (bar 5), instead of the sax melody's restatement, a new figure is heard from the brass. The saxes answer with a response in kind, itself a restatement. Once again, however, the absence of a restatement in bar 5 contradicts the listener's expectations, so that it is not until Chorus 5, which puts the pieces of the blues puzzle together "correctly," that the blues form's conventions finally establish themselves.

EXAMPLE 29. Ellington, "Diminuendo in Blue," Chorus 4, bars 1–7
(Smithsonian, Duke Ellington Collection)

Barney Bigard once said of Ellington: "At first, just after I joined Duke . . . I used to think everything was wrong, because he wrote so weird."[62] The opening of "Diminuendo and Crescendo in Blue" illustrates that side of Ellington, showing a capacity for obfuscation and formal play far beyond what his audience expected or his vocation as a dance band leader required. "Diminuendo" is, on the one hand, another of Ellington's adventurous introductions, like "The Sergeant Was Shy" but on a larger scale. At the same time, it's a commentary on the nature of the twelve-bar blues as an instrumental form. In each of the first four choruses, the ingredients of the standard blues form are there: the chord progression, the call-and-response pattern, and the principle of statement and restatement. Yet, by changing some element in each—by delaying a harmonic arrival point, by switching the expected ordering of melodic statements or the character of calls and responses, or by adding measures—Ellington sows seeds of doubt in his listeners. Are we, in fact, hearing standard blues choruses or aren't we? We can't be sure, at least not until Chorus 5 arrives. Thus, "Diminuendo in Blue" moves from dissonance to consonance, from loud to soft, from density to spareness, from rhythmic disruption to smoothness, and from formal opaqueness to formal clarity. Once the structure is clearly established at the start of bar 53, the ear shifts its focus from form to the flow of events—changes in texture, sound, time intervals between calls and responses, melodic invention—leaving the rather frequent modulations as the only unusual feature. Beginning on a manic note of disconnection, as if Ellington were a cubist painter probing the shape of the blues structure by pulling its pieces apart, then fitting them back together in unexpected ways, the piece settles into a groove, hits a point of calm relaxation, and then reverses the process. And it is unified not only by the harmonic progression that underlies all twenty-two of its choruses but by the melodic motive that begins the "Diminuendo," that returns in the seventh chorus in the saxes as the start of a longer melody, that begins the "Crescendo" and is heard through its first three choruses, and that reappears at the beginning of both Chorus 8 and Chorus 11 of that section.

I think Ellington's "Diminuendo and Crescendo in Blue" is an artistic success by any measure.[63] The strong first impression it makes gets stronger with more listenings. Unity and variety are well balanced. The composer's melodic invention seems fully up to the task. The music communicates on the levels both of fine detail and broad gesture, and the overall shape is there not just to be discovered analytically but to be experienced through the ears and body. Within a framework of relaxed spontaneity, the performance is polished and precise. We can feel comfortable calling Ellington's "Diminuendo and Crescendo in Blue" an excellent piece of music by an American composer of first rank.

One of the more admirable values of Western culture is its respect for works of art and the customs of preservation and connoisseurship that keep masterworks available to the public. In music, the chief means of accomplishing this are familiar: making and disseminating scores, giving concerts, and recording performances. While all lovers of music can think of pieces, even repertories, they wish were more readily available through these means, a great deal *is* within our reach already. And we who are curious about music from other times and places tend to assume that the masterworks of almost any tradition will be available to us.

But for a long time, Ellington's "Diminuendo and Crescendo in Blue" escaped the musical world's preservationist net. A score? We now know that Ellington's short score and parts are preserved in the book of his now-defunct orchestra. But until the Smithsonian Institution purchased these materials and established its Ellington Collection in the late 1980s, the only access performers and scholars had to most of Ellington's music was through transcriptions of his recordings—an option open only to those with sharp ears, a profound knowledge of the style, and lots of time. (Even after a transcription was made, copyright and performance restrictions would hinder its ready circulation.) Concert performances? By whom? It's true that jazz repertory ensembles are being formed and do exist, especially (though not exclusively) in colleges and conservatories. But they need scores. Recordings? Here "Diminuendo and Crescendo in Blue" would seem to be on safe ground, since that's the form in which it was first offered to the public in 1937. "They" wouldn't let a great American piece like this get lost in the shuffle, would they?

Even here we can't be too sure. At the time this chapter was first drafted (in the winter of 1985), Ellington's 1937 recording of "Diminuendo and Crescendo in Blue" was not commercially available. (That situation has now been remedied, for this performance appears in the revised edition of the *Smithsonian Collection of Classic Jazz*.) In fact, one of my anxieties as I prepared to lecture in public on Ellington was that somehow, in recording my examples, I would erase the dubbing from the tape sent me by a friend, leaving me without access to any recording at all. The precariousness of the existence of "Diminuendo and Crescendo in Blue," and of other masterpieces in its tradition, dramatizes a key point. Ellington worked in a commercial music business where salable performances were the commodity. The fate of his music, then, and, though to a lesser extent, even now, has depended, as Gushee has written, not "on the judgment of history nor of an elite of musicians, arrangers, teachers and critics" but rather reflects "the realities of selling phonograph recordings."[64]

In Ellington's drive to be "the best"—the competitive fire that propelled his "journey" as an American professional musician—he encountered no foe more intractable or persistent than the cultural "categories" against which he spoke and wrote from the time a public forum was available to him. The reach of Ellington's ambition made his life as a competitor especially complex. As a bandleader he competed against other leaders for employment. As a composer he competed, as all composers do, against the inherent difficulty of communicating with listeners through a sounding, nonverbal medium. And as an African-American artist, he battled attitudes that judged people and art by their fancied place in a network of categorical classifications: race, formal education, cultural prestige. No better emblem of his skill as an illusionist exists than the spirit in which he waged the latter struggle. As in other things, he staked out a position on high ground—not the familiar territory of "prejudice," about which many Americans held fixed positions, but the less explicit terrain of "category," free of political taint and bearing an air of philosophical detachment. (Did any of Ellington's interviewers ask him what, exactly, he *meant* by "category"?) Then, using an often gnomic style of expression drawn from home, school, poolroom, and the Bible, he denounced categories: the human propensity to overgeneralize and underestimate, to classify rather than respond. On racial discrimination in the United States, for example, he held strong feelings. Yet, understanding that the Declaration of Independence and the U.S. Constitution embody an ideal of social equality, he embraced without hesitation his identity as an American. As a man of the theater in its broadest sense, he believed that "a statement of social protest in the theater should be made without saying it."[65] His own career undermined and overthrew cultural categories at every turn. Black musicians of Ellington's generation were not called "Duke," didn't play in Carnegie Hall, didn't compose "extended works," and didn't receive honorary degrees or invitations to be fêted at the White House. Ellington did all of those things, mindful that, in the categorical world of American culture, his personal achievements might carry reverberations that would change the way Americans thought about American music—might, perhaps, even help to ease some of the restrictions under which other African-Americans led their lives. He was certainly right about the former. For today, rather than placing in a lesser category all musicians who pursue accessibility and broad commercial acceptance, historians and critics are more likely to find the commercial framework unworthy of some of the great figures who have toiled within its limitations. (Gunther Schuller sometimes writes of Ellington this way.)[66] In such an ambience, "the realities of selling phonograph recordings" becomes a jejune detail, which indeed it may appear to be in the reordered world that Ellington helped to create.

Today we are free to declare record sales and popular acceptance dead issues and to say of Ellington, in effect, "now he belongs to the ages." But to take that position, to treat the world of popular entertainment in which he lived and excelled simply as an inhibiting force on his art, is to risk underestimating one of his primary achievements as an American artist. Living his professional life in a world devoted to ephemera—to fads, the pursuit of pleasure, and musical means (improvisation, recordings rather than scores, distribution of music by commercial hawking) geared to immediate economic gain—Ellington left an enduring legacy, both as a man and a composer. His personal achievement deserves the honor that it now is beginning to receive. It also testifies that, as noted in earlier chapters, in American music the need for "accessibility" does not always overwhelm artistry. Perhaps Ellington did spend his life overcoming artistic limitations his profession imposed on him; but in the course of that effort, by having to be concise and to create an impact or a mood immediately, he also gained needed discipline and skill that other composers might envy.[67] Rather than decrying commercial influence, we might do better to think of how Ellington turned it to his artistic advantage. Here, as elsewhere, we encounter the extraordinary blend of private and social, of independence and collaboration, that characterizes his music-making. The inner drive to be the best, coupled with the knowledge that only by creating a unique social network could he *be* the best in the way he wished, is another such instance. Thus the chapter title, "Duke Ellington and His Orchestra," like the tale of his life's journey, is intended to suggest the pull of opposing forces that somehow, in his hands, were reconciled— a kind of magnetic field in which (individual) inspiration is realized through the (collaborative) execution of musicians who, though nominally under his direction, are left firmly in control of their own "tonal personalities."

As Ellington grew older, he was invited more and more often to think of himself as transcending the world of present-day concerns in which his professional life had always been lived.[68] Here, for example, are two exchanges from the seventy-four-year-old composer's autobiography:

Q: Which of all your tunes is your favorite?

A: The next one.[69]

Q: Is there satisfaction in knowing that what you have created gives you a chance to live and be known beyond your time?

A: I have no interest in posterity.[70]

There's that Ellington persona again. Perhaps we should take his professed indifference to us no more at face value than the sunniness of his autobiography—or than the assumption that the lightheartedness of much of his music's surface and the circumstances of its creation mean that it's superficial music.[71] In the years since his death Ellington has been enshrined on the Mount Rushmore of American musical heroes. Songs like "Satin Doll" and a Broadway revue like *Sophisticated Ladies,* coupled with the vast Ellington iconography and the Ellington legend, are enough to maintain his presence before the public. But let's not be misled by that smiling presence. Behind it, Ellington and his music lie like a submerged subcontinent that is only now beginning to be seriously explored. I can think of no tougher scholarly challenge in the field of American music than such an exploration, nor, at the same time, any task that promises to shed more light on the question of what, in the broadest terms, it means to be an American composer.

· 7 ·

George Gershwin's
"I Got Rhythm" (1930)

Thanks to Ira Gershwin, we know something about the making of the song "I Got Rhythm." The year was 1930, and the Gershwin brothers were at work on the score of *Girl Crazy*, their next Broadway show. George had presented Ira with the music for the new song, leaving it to him to come up with lyrics. (Ira once wrote about his craft that since most of his lyrics "were arrived at by fitting words mosaically to music already composed, any resemblance to actual poetry, living or dead, is highly improbable.")[1] The chorus of the song George gave Ira, based on a syncopated four-note figure (ex. 30), was cast in standard thirty-two-bar AABA form with a two-bar tag.

Ira struggled with the lyric. "Filling in the seventy-three syllables of the refrain wasn't as simple as it sounds," he later recalled. "For over two weeks I kept fooling around with . . . sets of double rhymes for the trios of short two-foot lines," that is, with the rhyme scheme aaab/cccb. Here's Ira's illustration of the kinds of rhymes he first tried to write:

> Roly-Poly,
> Eating solely
> Ravioli,
> Better watch your diet or bust.
> Lunch or dinner,
> You're a sinner.
> Please get thinner.
> Losing all that fat is a must.

Yet, no matter what series of double rhymes . . . I tried, the results were not quite satisfactory; they . . . [gave a] jingly

213

EXAMPLE 30. George Gershwin, "I Got Rhythm," chorus,
melody only, bars 1–8 (*Girl Crazy* [1930])

EXAMPLE 31. George Gershwin, "I Got Rhythm" (Ira Gershwin),
chorus, melody with words, bars 1–8

Mother Goose quality to a tune which should throw its weight
around more.

Ira solved his problem only after he began to try nonrhyming lines.
"This approach felt stronger," he recalled, "and finally I arrived at the
present refrain (the rhymed verse came later), with only 'more—door'
and 'mind him—find him' [as] the rhymes. Though there is nothing
remarkable about all this, it was a bit daring for me who usually depended on rhyme insurance." Ira also explained that he did not write
"I've got rhythm" but borrowed the verb's "most colloquial form,"

> the one used for the present tense instead of "have," and the
> one going back to my childhood: e.g., "I got a toothache" didn't
> mean "I had a toothache," but only "I have" one. . . . Obviously,
> I've got nothing against "I've got" since the verse ends with
> "Look at what I've got." [But] . . . the musically less assertive
> and regularly rhymed verse seems to require the more conven-
> tional phrasing.[2]

In the finished song, Ira used the four-note figure to list life's valued
possessions (ex. 31).

Girl Crazy opened on 14 October 1930.[3] It told the story of a collection of New Yorkers and San Franciscans, transplanted to the one-horse town of Custerville, Arizona, who succeed in bringing high city life with them, including a bevy of Broadway beauties.[4] The part of "Frisco" Kate Fothergill, wife of a gambling-room manager, was given to a newcomer, the twenty-one-year-old Ethel Merman, and it was she who introduced "I Got Rhythm" to the public. Although Merman's performance was a high point in the show, she didn't record the song until much later in her career. In a spoken introduction to a commemorative recording, Merman told the story of "I Got Rhythm" and her debut as a Broadway star.

> Once upon a time, back in 1930, I stepped out on stage at the Alvin Theater in New York, got hit in the kisser with a big spotlight, and found myself in big-time show business.[5] It was in a thing called *Girl Crazy,* which boasted Ginger Rogers, Willie Howard, and the DeMarcos,[6] and a great score by George Gershwin. One of the songs I did that memorable night was "I Got Rhythm." And as I riveted the second chorus I held on to a high C like it was from Tiffany's, and the last one in the world.[7] Anyway, it was a show-stopper. It sort of launched me on my way, so I guess you can't blow the whistle on me for saying it's one of my special favorites. It goes like this. And brother, *how* it goes![8]

When Merman published her autobiography in 1955, it was called *Who Could Ask for Anything More?*

The projection and energy of Ethel Merman's performance was not the only reason "I Got Rhythm" proved a show-stopper in *Girl Crazy.* For in the Broadway theater of that day, it was customary to turn the pit orchestra loose with hot "ride-out" choruses at the ends of peppy, up-tempo numbers like this one. Among the members of the band that played at the Alvin Theater during the show's run were musicians who must have waited eagerly for such moments and made the most of them when they arrived. The band had been formed by Red Nichols, a twenty-five-year-old cornetist who had already gained a reputation in jazz circles for recordings with the group Red Nichols and His Five Pennies. It also included several others who were soon to make their mark in the world of swing: reedman Benny Goodman (age twenty-one), drummer Gene

Krupa (twenty-one), trombonist Glenn Miller (twenty-six), and trumpeter Charlie Teagarden (seventeen).[9] Because Goodman, Krupa, and Merman stayed before the public for many years, they may now be remembered as grandparently figures. It's well to recall how young and close to the beginnings of their careers they were when they first performed "I Got Rhythm"—a fresh new tune by a songwriter not much older than they were.

As noted in earlier chapters, from the time of the eighteenth century, with a composer like Alexander Reinagle, through the nineteenth, with Foster, Root, and others, and on into the early twentieth, American popular music circulated chiefly as sheet music designed for home performers. But in 1920 a printer's strike and a paper shortage caused production costs to triple,[10] and almost overnight the phonograph recording replaced sheet music as the chief means of popular music's circulation.[11] Numbers tell the story. During one seventy-five-week period beginning in 1922, a song by Irving Berlin, "Say It with Music," sold 375,000 printed copies—a healthy amount but barely a tenth as large as the 3.5 million sold by Ray Egan and Richard Whiting's "Till We Meet Again" in just a few months of 1918. Berlin's "Say It with Music" was nevertheless a hit. By what measure? By its sale during the same seventy-five weeks of 1 million records and 100,000 piano rolls.[12] In 1930, Broadway shows, with their capacity for plugging songs during long runs in New York and through traveling companies, were one of the sheet-music industry's chief moneymaking properties, with publishers investing in shows to obtain the copyrights of their songs.[13] A Broadway show like *Girl Crazy* thus aimed at success on two fronts: as an evening's entertainment for an audience in a theater and as a source of songs that could be published, recorded, and marketed individually, regardless of the show's fate.[14] Thus, as with other Broadway shows of the time, the music publishing and recording industries hovered over the beginning of *Girl Crazy* in hopes of finding new Gershwin songs they could turn into gold.[15]

And now a word about the composer.[16] The career of George Gershwin (1898–1937) as a professional musician began in 1914, when he quit school to work as a song-plugger on New York's Tin Pan Alley. In 1919, he composed his first score for a Broadway show, *La, La, Lucille,* and the song "Swanee," recorded in 1920, became his first bona fide hit.[17] In 1924 Gershwin became famous. He did so not by writing successful musicals or more hit songs but by composing and performing, with great public fanfare, in a concert organized by dance-orchestra leader Paul Whiteman, a piece recognized instantly as historic. The piece was *Rhapsody in Blue* for piano and orchestra. Premiered in New York's Aeolian Hall on 12 February, the *Rhapsody* owed much of its impact to the circumstances in which it was introduced. Whiteman's concert, billed as "An Experiment in Modern Music," had been designed to show that jazz, the new, vivacious, audience-pleasing dance music that most concert musicians and critics of the time associated with poor musicianship, could please cultivated tastes when performed in the "symphonic" arrangements that were the Whiteman band's specialty. And Gershwin's *Rhapsody*, billed as a "jazz concerto," testified that jazz-based music need not be confined to pieces of pop-tune length. With questions about the identity and destiny of American music very much in the air, with critics like Carl Van Vechten and Gilbert Seldes arguing that the American fine arts of the future would be vitalized through vernacular idioms, and with Whiteman personally inviting prominent classical musicians and New York's leading critics to the performance, the Aeolian Hall concert achieved a sense of occasion.[18] Gershwin's *Rhapsody* won the audience's approval and the critics' attention. It also won renown for its composer. No longer simply another talented American songwriter, he was now recognized as a historical figure: the man who brought "jazz" into the concert hall.

After the success of the *Rhapsody*, Gershwin's life as a composer changed. He continued to write for the musical theater, though at a somewhat slower pace.[19] But he gave more and more of his energy to concert music; and he continued to study composition, as he had since 1917, his teachers including Edward Kilenyi, Rubin Goldmark, Wallingford Riegger, Henry Cowell, and Joseph Schillinger. He managed this broadening of his musical activities and interests without sacrificing public appeal or fame. Rather than shrinking from success, Gershwin reveled in it, accepting praise calmly as no more than his due. By 1930, when he wrote *Girl Crazy*, Gershwin stood unmatched among American composers in his combination of eminence and range, not to mention the power to command resources for anything he decided to compose, *and* to attract an audience as well.[20]

"I Got Rhythm" occupied a special place in Gershwin's work. It was the song he himself singled out as best suited for embellished instrumental performance. In *George Gershwin's Song Book* (1932), which contained eighteen Gershwin songs in his own arrangements for piano, "I Got Rhythm" was one of only two songs—"Liza" was the other—for which he supplied two choruses rather than one. In its strict observance of the notated rhythm, Gershwin's arrangement pays tribute to the song's instrumental pedigree. Singers have tended to loosen the declamation to something closer to a half note and quarter note: ♩♩♩|♩♩ . The *Song Book* version, however, centers on a series of dotted quarter notes in duple time—a standard way of creating instrumental syncopation that dates at least as far back as Scott Joplin's "Maple Leaf Rag" (1899), whose second strain achieves that effect through figuration rather than accented chords.[21] In 1934, Gershwin returned to "I Got Rhythm," using it as the basis for a set of variations for piano and orchestra. This gave him something new to play along with the *Rhapsody in Blue* and the Concerto in F on a concert tour he took that year with the Leo Reisman Orchestra.[22] The work contains six character variations in which the tune appears as a hot Broadway number, a waltz, and in other guises as well, including one Gershwin called a "Chinese variation." On his radio show, he told his audience that that variation was inspired by Chinese flutes, "played out of tune, as they always are."

Now let's go back to October 1930. Within ten days of the opening of *Girl Crazy* on the 14th, three significant recordings of "I Got Rhythm" were made. On the 20th, Freddie Rich, conductor of the CBS Radio Orchestra, recorded it with a group under his own name. On the 23d, Red Nichols and His Five Pennies—all thirteen of them, and including Goodman, Krupa, Miller, and other members of the *Girl Crazy* pit band, plus vocalist Dick Robertson—made their own version. And on the 24th, one of New York's best black bands, Luis Russell and His Orchestra, recorded another version. Each can be taken to represent the beginning of a different approach to Gershwin's number: (1) "I Got Rhythm" as a *song* played and sung by popular performers; (2) "I Got Rhythm" as a *jazz standard,* a piece known and frequently played by musicians, black and white, in the jazz tradition; and (3) "I Got Rhythm" as a *musical structure,* a harmonic framework upon which jazz instrumentalists, especially blacks, have built new compositions.

Let's begin with the song. I noted Ira Gershwin's struggle to find a rhyme scheme fitting George's tune. But I said nothing about the words he finally wrote. William Austin has pointed out that the Gershwin brothers used the word "rhythm" in several of their songs. In 1918 Ira called ragtime "a rhythmic tonic for the chronic blues."[23] In 1924 he wrote: "Fascinating rhythm, it'll drive me insane";[24] in 1928, "Listen to the rhythm of my heart beat";[25] in 1930, "I Got Rhythm"; and in 1937, "Today you can see that the happiest men/All got rhythm."[26] Austin adds: "I believe the Gershwins are largely responsible for [the word] rhythm entering the vocabularies of millions of people for whom it had previously been too technical."[27] The two Gershwin songs with "rhythm" in the title are both built on syncopation. "Fascinating Rhythm" from 1924, sung by a character obsessed with an off-center rhythmic pattern, divides its first four bars, in effect, into measures of four, three, five, and four beats. As for "I Got Rhythm," of the seventeen lines in the lyrics of its chorus, thirteen are set to the same four-note figure, a rhythmic cell that hits only one of the four strong beats in the two bars it covers. For Ira Gershwin the lyricist, "rhythm" in this song was tied up with aggressive, accented, syncopated groupings of beats.

But Ira's lyrics are not really about rhythm in the way that those of "Fascinating Rhythm" are. They're an expression of general well-being. Rhythm and music are linked with "daisies in green pastures," with "starlight," "sweet dreams," and being in love. The message here is that "the best things in life are free"—incidentally the title of a hit song from the Broadway show *Good News* (1927).[28] Merman's performance was an outpouring of high spirits, saying, most of all, "I feel *wonderful!*" Her sustained "high C" through the A sections of the second chorus— we can imagine outstretched arms and a multikilowatt smile—is the opposite of a celebration of rhythmic trickiness.

As a show-stopping song and vehicle for a new and vibrant theatrical talent, "I Got Rhythm" could hardly have been more successful. But as a popular song independent of the show, its success was more modest. "I Got Rhythm" called for a kind of vocal energy that few popular singers of Gershwin's day possessed. The first "jazz" recording, made by Freddie Rich with Paul Small as vocalist six days after *Girl Crazy* opened on Broadway, follows the sheet music straightforwardly and attempts neither to match Merman's exuberant interpretation nor to bring out the snap of Gershwin's syncopation. Its emotional blandness is matched by that of a version recorded the same day by Victor Arden and Phil Ohman, a duo-piano team whose orchestras had played in the pit of many Gershwin shows. (Frank Luther sang on this recording.)[29] A 1938 performance by singer Jane Froman reinstates the full-throated, high-spirited Merman approach with the help of a Schubertian running figure in the violins.[30] There is a 1943 recording, from a film version of *Girl Crazy*, in which Judy Garland restores "rhythm" as an issue by conscientiously singing the syncopations that Gershwin wrote.[31] And when Mary Martin sang "I Got Rhythm" for a reconstruction of the show in the 1950s, the accompaniment in her second chorus was reduced to percussion, supporting the text's first line literally as well as figuratively.[32]

To these two distinctive approaches to "I Got Rhythm"—the Merman exuberance and the Garland/Martin beat—we can add another that turns the song into a novelty number in a theatrical context far removed from Custerville, Arizona. Vincent Minelli's film, *An American in Paris* (1951), weaves Gershwin's music into a story of romantic love in the City of Lights. In one scene Gene Kelly, playing a young American, conducts an English lesson on the streets of Paris for a group of French boys. Spoken dialogue leads into the song:

KELLY: *Parlez anglais à nous? Ecoutez. Je suis le professeur.*

BOYS: [general laughter]

KELLY: *Répétez après moi.* Door.

BOYS: Door! [shouted]

KELLY: Street.

BOYS: Street!

KELLY: Lady.

BOYS: Lady!

KELLY: Window.

BOYS: Window.

KELLY: *Allons maintenant. Une chanson américaine.* An American song.

BOYS: Oooo!! [exclamation of wonder and anticipation]

KELLY: *Dites-moi.* I got.

A BOY: I got!

KELLY: *Bon! Tous ensemble!*

BOYS: I got!

KELLY: *Bon.* [whistles two-bar introduction]

An antiphonal performance of the chorus of Gershwin's song follows, with students shouting and teacher singing. Armed with their newly learned English phrase, the boys respond individually to Kelly's prompting with eager cries of "I got," often delivered well before the beat. The performance is a reminder that "I Got Rhythm" is a "list song" depending more on incantatory repetition than on rhyme or verbal ingenuity.

A BOY: I got!

KELLY: . . . rhythm,

A BOY: I got!

KELLY: . . . music,

A BOY: I got!

KELLY: . . . my gal,
Who could ask for anything more?

A BOY: I got!

KELLY: . . . daisies,

A BOY: I got!

KELLY: In green pastures,

A BOY: I got!

KELLY: . . . my gal,
Who could ask for anything more?

(After singing the bridge section, which is free of "I got"s, Kelly asks: *Vous comprenez ça?*, to which one boy shoots back: *Non!*)[33] So the Gershwins' "I Got Rhythm" could be a song about aggressive joyfulness, or syncopated rhythmic drive, or teaching kids how to speak American.[34]

Now let's consider "I Got Rhythm" as a jazz standard. We've already noted that jazz performers were among those who first played Gershwin's song in public, and Red Nichols's recording shortly after the show's premiere was the first of dozens in the jazz tradition. Table 6 carries a list, taken from Brian Rust's jazz discography.[35]

In the jazz tradition, we usually speak of tunes, not songs. A jazz tune is defined first and foremost by its structure: by the pattern of

TABLE 6
Recordings of "I Got Rhythm" and Contrafacts to 1942[a]

Performer[b]	Date	Recording company
Fred Rich & Orch (v)	20 Oct 1930	Columbia
Red Nichols & Five Pennies (v)	23 Oct 1930	Brunswick
Luis Russell & Orch (v)	24 Oct 1930	Melotone
Fred Rich & Orch (v)	29 Oct 1930	Harmony, OKeh
Ethel Waters (v)	18 Nov 1930	Columbia
Cab Calloway & Orch (v)	17 Dec 1930	ARC; rej[c]
Adelaide Hall with piano (v)/ London	Oct 1931	Oriole
Louis Armstrong & Orch (v)/ Chicago	6 Nov 1931	OKeh
Billy Banks (v; medley)	13 April 1932	Victor test
Bobby Howes (v)/London	10 May 1932	Columbia
Roy Fox & Band (v)/London	19 May 1932	Decca
Blue Mountaineers (v)/London	18 June 1932	broadcast
Don Redman & Orch	30 June 1932	Brunswick
Ray Starita & Ambassadors (v)/ London	12 Aug 1932	Sterno
*New Orleans Feetwarmers (v): "Shag"	15 Sept 1932	Victor
*Joel Shaw & Orch (v): "Yeah Man"	Oct 1932	Crown
Arthur Briggs & Boys (v)/Paris	ca. June 1933	Brunswick
*The King's Jesters/Chicago: "Yeah Man"	29 July 1933	Bluebird
*Fletcher Henderson & Orch: "Yeah Man"	18 Aug 1933	Vocalion, Brunswick
Spirits of Rhythm (v)	29 Sept 1933	ARC; rej
Five Spirits of Rhythm (v)	24 Oct 1933	Brunswick
Freddy Johnson & Harlemites/ Paris	ca. Oct 1933	Brunswick
Freddy Johnson & Harlemites/ Paris	7 Dec 1933	Brunswick
Casa Loma Orch	30 Dec 1933	Brunswick
*Jimmy Lunceford & Orch: "Stomp it Off"	29 Oct 1934	Decca

(continued)

TABLE 6 (*continued*)

Performer[b]	Date	Recording company
*Chick Webb's Savoy Orch: "Don't Be That Way"	19 Nov 1934	Decca
Joe Venuti & Orch	26 Dec 1934	London (LP)
Stéphane Grappelli & Hot Four/ Paris	Oct 1935	Decca
*Nat Gonella & Georgians (v)/ London: "Yeah Man"	20 Nov 1935	Parlophone
Garnet Clark (piano)/Paris	25 Nov 1935	HMV
Fats Waller & Rhythm (v)	4 Dec 1935	HMV
*Chick Webb & Orch: "Don't Be That Way"	Feb 1936	Polydor (LP)
Red Norvo & Swing Sextette	16 March 1936	Decca
The Ballyhooligans (v)/London	2 April 1936	HMV
Joe Daniels & Hot Shots/London	15 July 1936	Parlophone
*Count Basie & Orch: "Don't Be That Way"	ca. Feb 1937	Vanguard
Jimmy Dorsey & Orch/Los Angeles	3 March 1937	Decca
Lionel Hampton & Orch[d]	26 April 1937	Victor
Benny Goodman Quartet	29 April 1937	MGM
Glenn Miller & Orch	9 June 1937	Brunswick
Count Basie & Orch	30 June 1937	Coll. Corner
Dicky Wells & Orch/Paris	7 July 1937	Swing
Valaida [Snow] (v)/London	9 July 1937	Parlophone
Chick Webb & Little Chicks	21 Sept 1937	Decca
Emilio Caceres Trio	5 Nov 1937	Victor
Scott Wood & Six Swingers (medley)/London	12 Nov 1937	Columbia
Benny Goodman Quartet	16 Jan 1938	Columbia
*Benny Goodman & Orch: "Don't Be That Way"	16 Jan 1938	Columbia
Bud Freeman Trio	17 Jan 1938	Commodore
*Lionel Hampton & Orch: "Don't Be That Way"	18 Jan 1938	Victor
*Benny Goodman & Orch: "Don't Be That Way"	16 Feb 1938	Victor

(*continued*)

TABLE 6 (*continued*)

Performer[b]	Date	Recording company
*Ozzie Nelson & Orch/ Hollywood: "Don't Be That Way"	5 March 1938	Bluebird
*Mildred Bailey & Orch (v): "Don't Be That Way"	14 March 1938	Vocalion
*Jimmy Dorsey & Orch: "Don't Be That Way"	16 March 1938	Decca
*Teddy Wilson & Orch: "Don't Be That Way"	23 March 1938	Brunswick
Larry Adler with Quintette of Hot Club of France/Paris	31 May 1938	Columbia
*Gene Krupa & Orch: "Wire Brush Stomp"	2 June 1938	Brunswick
*Johnny Hodges & Orch: "The Jeep is Jumpin' "	24 Aug 1938	Vocalion/OKeh
Louis Armstrong & Fats Waller (v)	19 Oct 1938	Palm Club
Clarence Profit Trio	15 Feb 1939	Epic
*Erskine Hawkins & Orch: "Raid the Joint"	8 April 1939	Bluebird
*Earl Hines & Orch: "Father Steps In"	12 July 1939	Bluebird
*Tommy Dorsey & Orch: "Stomp it Off"	20 July 1939	Victor
*Count Basie's Kansas City Seven: "Lester Leaps In"	5 Sept 1939	Vocalion
*Earl Hines & Orch/Chicago: "XYZ"	6 Oct 1939	Bluebird
Benny Goodman Sextet (medley)	24 Dec 1939	Vanguard
Caspar Reardon (v)	5 Feb 1940	Schirmer
Count Basie & Orch/Boston	20 Feb 1940	Coll. Corner
Fletcher Henderson & Horace Henderson's Orch (v)/Chicago	27 Feb 1940	Vocalion
*Duke Ellington & Orch/ Hollywood: "Cotton Tail (Shuckin' and Stiffin')"	4 May 1940	Victor
Sid Phillips Trio/London	6 May 1940	Parlophone
*Count Basie & Orch: "Blow Top"	31 May 1940	Epic
Max Geldray Quartet/London	26 July 1940	Decca

(*continued*)

TABLE 6 (*continued*)

Performer[b]	Date	Recording company
*Coleman Hawkins & Orch: "Chant of the Groove"[e]	summer 1940	[LP reissue]
Felix Mendelssohn & Hawaiian Serenaders/London	28 Oct 1940	Columbia
*Johnny Hodges & Orch/Chicago: "Good Queen Bess"	2 Nov 1940	Bluebird
*Duke Ellington & Orch/Fargo, N.D.: "Cotton Tail"	7 Nov 1940	Palm
*Johnny Hodges & Orch/ Hollywood: "Squatty Roo"	3 July 1941	Bluebird
Metronome All-Star Leaders	16 Jan 1942	Columbia

[a] Contrafacts—i.e., newly titled tunes with new melodies based on the harmonic structure of "I Got Rhythm"—are indicated by an asterisk; their titles are listed with the performers' names.

[b] Unless otherwise indicated, location is New York; *v* denotes inclusion of vocal.

[c] Here and elsewhere, "rej." identifies a rejected take: a recording that was not commercially issued.

[d] As "Rhythm, Rhythm."

[e] Not listed in Rust. See John Chilton, *The Song of the Hawk: The Life and Recordings of Coleman Hawkins* (Ann Arbor, Mich., 1990), 180.

repetition and contrast in its melodic phrases and the harmonic framework underlying them. Second, it is defined by its ethos: by the mood it projects and the tempo at which it is played. Only third does its melody come into play, for in the jazz tradition the melody is often little more than an entrée into the performance; after being heard, it is usually discarded for free melodic invention by the performers. The chorus of "I Got Rhythm" follows one of the most common Tin Pan Alley song forms: statement, restatement, contrast, and return, with the contrast being called the "bridge" or "release." We could diagram the form as AABA', the first three phrases filling eight bars and the fourth ten, by virtue of the two-bar extension. Gershwin's harmony is as elemental as his melody. The latter is cast in two-bar units, with the four-note syncopated cell moving up, then down, then up again, and then breaking the pattern with a cadence. The harmony supports these gestures with a parallel pattern: three I–ii[7]–V–I loops followed by a I–V–I cadence.

Or perhaps it would be better to describe Gershwin's harmonic *framework* that way, as Gunther Schuller does,[36] noting that the published song actually employs a more varied and colorful sequence of chords:

Bb Bb6 | Cm7 F7 | Bb6 Edim | Cm7 F7 |
Bb Bb6 | Cm7 F7 Ebm6 | Bb F7 | Bb C#dim F

Ira Gershwin liked George's tune's ability to "throw its weight around." The "weight" of "I Got Rhythm" as Gershwin wrote it stems partly from tempo and syncopation but perhaps even more from economy of material—from the song's avoidance of tonal complexity or variety. The song's first melodic statement (A) dwells on B-flat; its re-statement (A), in what is virtually a note-for-note repetition, does the same; the release (B) jumps to the relative minor, then wends its way back through the circle of fifths; and the return (A¹) restates the beginning, again note-for-note, softening the austerity a bit with a concluding tag. The classic simplicity of the song's harmonic design summoned jazz performers' inventiveness, both melodic and harmonic, to a degree matched by only one other structure in the history of jazz: the twelve-bar blues. But even before discussing jazz performances, it is well to recall the impression George Gershwin's music for "I Got Rhythm" made upon Ira Gershwin and Ethel Merman, two people far removed in sensibility from the world of jazz. Ira's response as a lyricist was a list of abrupt, colloquial claims ("I got . . ."); Merman found as a singer that one sustained note could replace the Gershwin brothers' first six bars, to the vast delight of the *Girl Crazy* audience. Both, in short, discovered in George's music a certain bare, even abstract quality—one that an Alec Wilder might consider as a weakness in a popular song[37] but that, within the genre of the up-tempo instrumental number, proved astoundingly able to unlock jazz musicians' inventiveness.

From the many available jazz-style performances of "I Got Rhythm," I've chosen three for brief discussion here. The first, from 1937, is played by the Glenn Miller Orchestra (ex. 32). This is Miller's band before it settled into the formulas that were to make it a huge commercial success; and since Miller had known the tune when it was brand new, his arrangement from seven years later carries special interest. If one accepts

EXAMPLE 32. George Gershwin, "I Got Rhythm," bars 1–8, played by Glenn Miller and His Orchestra (9 June 1937, Brunswick 7915)

the premise that a jazz arrangement is a commentary upon—even a kind of analysis of—the original tune, Miller's first chorus confirms his view that Gershwin's melody line leaves something to be desired. Melodic interest here lies more in the reed countermelody composed by Miller than in Gershwin's original, played staccato in the brass. Miller's recording suggests how most jazz instrumentalists performed "I Got Rhythm": as an up-tempo flag-waver, a piece consistently played fast, and hence a kind of test piece, putting the group, and especially the improvising soloist, on trial.[38] Later in Miller's arrangement is a striking effect that shows his band at the peak of its rhythmic drive. Discarding not only Gershwin's melody but his harmony too, Miller here reduces the first six bars of Gershwin's A section to virtually nothing *but* rhythm and sound. Twice the band crescendos on one note, played on alternate eighths by the brass and reed sections and sweeping listeners (or dancers) ahead like a canoe in white water.[39]

A notable recording from the mid-1940s testifies to the place of "I Got Rhythm" in the jazz repertory by that time. The scene was New York's Town Hall on the evening of 9 June 1945. The audience had gathered, but by concert time only two musicians had shown up, tenor saxophonist Don Byas and bass player Slam Stewart. What to do? Give the customers back their money and send them home? Not that night. Byas and Stewart set out on a voyage over some jazz standards, and "I Got Rhythm" was the second number they played. Their performance, up-tempo and obviously unrehearsed, confirms our sense of Gershwin's song as a vehicle for virtuosic melodic play over familiar harmonic ground. After paraphrasing Gershwin's melody (without the original two-bar extension), Byas improvised four fluent inventive choruses, stood by while Stewart soloed in his patented style of bowing the bass and singing (through clenched teeth, an octave above), then followed with four additional choruses that explored Gershwin's tune further.[40]

Also noteworthy is a recording made by pianist Art Tatum with guitar and bass accompaniment at around the same time, and at breakneck speed. Tatum is known for technical virtuosity and unmatched harmonic imagination. He is also known as a melody player—one who respected the original tune and tended to keep it within earshot even during his improvised choruses.[41] In "I Got Rhythm," however, Tatum flashes only a hint of Gershwin's melody, then gives it up completely in the second chorus. Tatum's recording, from the mid-1940s, also confirms a trend that had already begun in the 1930s in performances of "I Got Rhythm": that of embellishing the ii–V–I chord progressions in Gershwin's A sections with richer harmonies. In his last two choruses, Tatum begins each of the eight-bar A sections on an F-sharp seventh chord—enharmonically G-flat, or the flat sixth degree—and then moves downward through the circle of fifths in a succession of half notes until, at the beginning of the fifth bar, he reaches the B-flat tonic in which the piece is rooted. (The harmonic progression is: F-sharp7, B7, E7, A7, D7, G7, C7, F7, B-flat.)

Tatum's recording, which drapes Gershwin's scaffold with fresh harmonic material, brings us to the third approach performers took to "I Got Rhythm."[42] As early as 1932, with Sidney Bechet's recording of a tune he called "Shag," black jazz musicians had begun to invent new melodies on the structure of Gershwin's song, abandoning his tune entirely and renaming their versions as new compositions.[43] Fletcher Henderson's "Yeah Man" from August 1933 is another example, as is "Stomp It Off," recorded by Jimmie Lunceford in October 1934.[44] And so is Chick Webb's "Don't Be That Way," from November of the same year.[45] This tune, by the way, adds to the story of Benny Goodman's relationship with Gershwin's song, for he and Edgar Sampson are named as co-composers. The melody of "Don't Be That Way," a tune that Goodman played at his Carnegie Hall concert in January 1938, and that began the recording issued long after the event, is shown in example 33.[46]

The long list of tunes based on the chord progression of "I Got Rhythm" includes recordings by the best swing bands, such as Count Basie's "Blow Top" from 1940 and Woody Herman's "Apple Honey"

EXAMPLE 33. Edgar Sampson and Benny Goodman, "Don't Be That Way,"
bars 5–12, melody only, played by Chick Webb and His Orchestra
(19 November 1934, Decca 483)

from 1945.[47] In "Cotton Tail" (1940), Duke Ellington wrote three memorable strains to Gershwin's chords.[48] First, the lean explosive melody of the first chorus, played by saxes in unison and one muted trumpet (ex. 34a). Second, a sixteen-bar statement for the brass in which Ellington manages, without establishing a predictable pattern, to create a powerful sense of rhythmic coherence (ex. 34b). Finally, Ellington composes a thirty-two-bar melody—not Gershwin's AABA but ABCD—for the sax section in full harmony (ex. 34c).[49]

The so-called bebop revolution of the early 1940s broke decisively with the swing era in many things. But one tradition it carried on and even intensified was the practice of making new tunes on the chord progressions of older ones. Each of the most prominent black swing bands—Count Basie, Duke Ellington, Erskine Hawkins, Fletcher Henderson, Earl Hines, Jimmie Lunceford, Chick Webb, as well as groups featuring major soloists like Johnny Hodges and Lester Young—had its own version of "I Got Rhythm" as a standard vehicle for up-tempo "blowing." So too did many bebop musicians. The reasons were partly artistic, partly social, but they were also economic. Drummer Max Roach has been quoted as saying:

> Of course there are about ten million tunes written on the changes of "I Got Rhythm." . . . This wasn't pilfering. In cases where we needed substitute chords for these tunes, we had to create new melodies to fit them. If you're gonna think up a melody, you'd just as well copyright it as a new tune, and that's what we did. We never did get any suits from publishers.[50]

Few bebop musicians after World War II played "I Got Rhythm" as a jazz standard. But as a key,[51] a tempo, a structure, and an occasion for virtuosic improvisation, it was deeply engrained in the jazz repertory, even when its harmonic scheme was embellished with remote chords.

EXAMPLE 34. Duke Ellington, "Cotton Tail," played by Duke Ellington and His Orchestra (4 May 1940, Victor 26610; after Gunther Schuller, *The Swing Era* [New York, 1989], 127)

(a) Bars 1–8

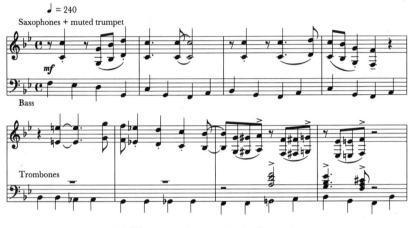

(b) Chorus 4, bars 1–16, rhythm only

(c) Chorus 5, bars 1–8, melody only

TABLE 7

Parker's Compositions on "I Got Rhythm"

Name	Recording Date[a]	Copyright Date	Copyright Entry[b]
"Red Cross"	15 Sept 1944	17 Sept 1945	EU439039
"Shaw 'Nuff"[c]	11 May 1945	11 Nov 1948	EP32267
"Thriving from a Riff"	26 Nov 1945	1 Dec 1945	EU449251
"Anthropology"[c]	March 1946	13 Aug 1948	EP29445
"Moose the Mooche"	28 March 1946	1 Nov 1946	EU51928
"Bird's Nest"	19 Feb 1947	20 April 1961	EU656872
"Chasing the Bird"	8 May 1947	20 Jan 1948	EU112914
"Dexterity"	28 Oct 1947	20 April 1961	EU65181
"Crazeology"	17 Dec 1947	21 Aug 1961	EU672281
"Constellation"	18 Sept 1948	15 Nov 1948	EU148835
"Ah-Leu-Cha"	18 Sept 1948	15 Nov 1948	EU148840
"Steeplechase"	24 Sept 1948	15 Nov 1948	EU148831
"Passport"	5 May 1949	1 June 1953	EU318785
"An Oscar For Treadwell"	6 June 1950	1956; 20 March 1967	EU431242
"Swedish Schnapps"	8 Aug 1951	26 March 1956	EU431248
"Kim"	30 Dec 1952	1956; 3 Jan 1967	EU431245
"Celerity"	none given	19 March 1958	EU517086

[a] Recording dates from Brian Priestley, *Charlie Parker*, Jazz Masters series (Tunbridge Wells, England, 1984).

[b] EU means unpublished copyright; EP means published copyright.

[c] Co-composer with Dizzy Gillespie.

And bebop musicians, like their predecessors, sought ownership in the tradition that Gershwin's show song had begun.

No one in the jazz tradition was more closely identified with the "Rhythm changes" than alto saxophonist Charlie Parker, who returned again and again to the structure of Gershwin's tune throughout his career, composing at least seventeen different pieces based upon it, many of which were picked up, played, and recorded by other jazz performers (table 7). The harmonic structure of "I Got Rhythm" won

EXAMPLE 35. Charlie Parker, "Red Cross," bars 4–12
(15 September 1944, Savoy 532)

EXAMPLE 36. Charlie Parker, "Steeplechase," bars 1–8
(September 1948, Savoy 937)

a place in Parker's imagination, much as the theme of the *Eroica* Variations or perhaps Diabelli's Waltz had in Beethoven's—though Beethoven concentrated his efforts on lengthy, integrated compositions, while Parker's "I Got Rhythm" variations are scattered widely among many performances. Following is a quick trip through Parker's *Sax-Übung,* pieced together from recordings made between 1944 and 1950.[52]

Gershwin's "Rhythm changes" inspired Parker to compose several different kinds of variations upon them. The most old-fashioned of the three employs the riff style, in which a melody is built up by repeating one brief melodic motive (ex. 35). Parker's process of abstraction here reduces the A section's harmony, except for bar 6, to a B-flat tonic chord. (In the release, however, a new riff based on Gershwin's chord changes appears.) In 1948 Parker composed a new riff for the A section, leaving the bridge free for improvisation. He called this piece "Steeplechase" (ex. 36).

The riff approach establishes a context of regular predictability as a launching pad for the improvisation that follows. But Parker's second

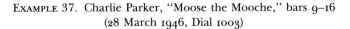

EXAMPLE 37. Charlie Parker, "Moose the Mooche," bars 9–16
(28 March 1946, Dial 1003)

EXAMPLE 38. Charlie Parker, "An Oscar For Treadwell," bars 8–16
(6 June 1950, Verve MGV800)

approach does the opposite. "Moose the Mooche," for example, is an invention for unison duet—alto sax and muted trumpet—that is rhythmically asymmetrical, broken into irregular phrases by rests in unexpected places (ex. 37). And "An Oscar for Treadwell" (ex. 38) is built in a similar way, with phrases of four beats, eight beats, fifteen beats, and five beats in its first eight bars. Its bridge is free.

Finally, Parker employed the "I Got Rhythm" chord changes to create a kind of obstacle course that only the best players could negotiate. Bassist Milt Hinton once explained how Parker, Dizzy Gillespie, and other bebop pioneers would discourage players who wanted to join their after-hours jam sessions at Minton's in Harlem during the early 1940s.

"What're y'all gonna play?" [they'd ask.] We'd say, "I Got Rhythm," and we'd start out with this new set of changes and they would be left right at the post. They would be standing

233

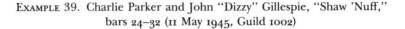

EXAMPLE 39. Charlie Parker and John "Dizzy" Gillespie, "Shaw 'Nuff,"
bars 24–32 (11 May 1945, Guild 1002)

there, and they couldn't get in because they didn't know what
changes we were using, and eventually they would put their horns
away, and we could go on and blow in peace and get our little
exercise.[53]

"Shaw 'Nuff" (ex. 39) shows this approach. Played at top speed, it also
changes harmony every two beats. Intimidation is the name of the game
here—intimidation of any neophyte with the gall to try to join such a
performance.

From Parker's heyday in the years just after World War II, many
bebop players—Thelonious Monk, Art Pepper, Miles Davis, Sonny Rollins, Sonny Stitt, Bud Powell, and Fats Navarro among them—created
their own new tunes on Gershwin's chord changes.[54] And some of these
new tunes themselves became standards. Ellington's "Cotton Tail" to-
taled more than thirty recordings in the years 1943–68, and Parker and
Gillespie's "Anthropology" logged nearly twenty more in the same period.[55] Moreover, the steady stream of "I Got Rhythm" variants that
flowed through the 1950s had the effect of updating the tune so that
when, for example, drummer Art Blakey featured the young trumpeter
Wynton Marsalis in a performance of "The Theme" in 1981, half a
century after "I Got Rhythm" first saw light of day, it did not sound
anachronistic.[56]

Gershwin's song "I Got Rhythm" is an especially good example of
what I've referred to earlier as "performers' music": music composed
and published with the expectation that performers, rather than being
bound by a composer's score, will change melody, harmony, tempo, or

EXAMPLE 40. George Gershwin, "I Got Rhythm," Chorus 2, bars 1–16, melody only, sung by Ella Fitzgerald with orchestra conducted by Nelson Riddle (1958–59, Verve VE-2-2525)

mood as they see fit, thus putting upon it the stamp of their own musical personalities.[57] "I Got Rhythm" attracted an unusually wide range of treatments from performers, flourishing in several different traditions of performance. These traditions are documented not in musical notation but in commercially produced phonograph recordings.

It seems appropriate to end this chapter with a comment on a performance that combines elements of the different traditions that made Gershwin's song their own. The singer is Ella Fitzgerald, accompanied by a sizable orchestra.[58] The presence of the verse, which is seldom sung, and a string section, helps to remind us that we're dealing, after all, with a *song* from a Broadway *show* by *Gershwin*. The introduction in the first chorus of a swinging beat and big band sound celebrates the song's pedigree as a jazz standard. But what kind of jazz standard? Ella Fitzgerald, a big band singer since 1935, knew full well the tradition of instrumental performance that lay behind "I Got Rhythm" when she made this recording in 1959. And the beginning of her second chorus (ex. 40) with sixteen bars of wordless scat-singing—clearly the musical climax of this performance[59]—can be heard as a tribute to the countless trumpeters, pianists, sax players, and guitarists, from the time of Red Nichols and Luis Russell, through Ellington, Parker, Gillespie, and beyond, for whom Gershwin's song, or his tune, or his harmonic structure, or all three, marked out a territory in which artistic capacities were tested and honed and realized—a territory in which artistic truth was to be sought and found.

NOTES

PREFACE

1. My earlier attempts include *American Studies and American Musicology: A Point of View and a Case in Point,* I.S.A.M. Monographs, no. 4 (Brooklyn, 1975); "A Historian's Introduction to Early American Music," *Proceedings of the American Antiquarian Society* 89 (1979): 261–98; and *Studying American Music,* I.S.A.M. Special Monograph (Brooklyn, 1985).

2. See H. Wiley Hitchcock, *Music in the United States,* 3d ed. (Englewood Cliffs, N.J., 1988), 53–55.

3. Ralph Ellison, *Going to the Territory* (New York, 1986), 42.

CHAPTER 1

1. Edward Hallett Carr, *What Is History?: The George Macaulay Trevelyan Lectures Delivered in the University of Cambridge, January–March 1961* (London, 1961). See chap. 5, "History as Progress."

2. The cornerstones for Ives studies were laid in the 1950s, especially by Henry Cowell and Sidney Cowell, *Charles Ives and His Music* (New York, 1955), and John Kirkpatrick, *A Temporary Mimeographed Catalogue of the Music Manuscripts and Related Materials of Charles Edward Ives 1874–1954* (New Haven, 1960). In the 1970s, as Ives's 100th anniversary was celebrated, Ives's biography was further explored. His autobiographical *Memos,* edited by John Kirkpatrick (New York, 1972) appeared, as did Vivian Perlis, *Charles Ives Remembered: An Oral History* (New Haven, 1974), Frank R. Rossiter, *Charles Ives and His America* (New York, 1975), and H. Wiley Hitchcock and Vivian Perlis, eds., *An Ives Celebration: Papers and Panels of the Charles Ives Centennial Festival-Conference* (Urbana, Ill., 1977). The Charles Ives Society was formed (1973) with the goal of bringing out authoritative editions of Ives's music. In the 1980s, J. Peter Burkholder has

revised some of the Ives legend in *Charles Ives: The Ideas behind the Music* (New Haven, 1985), and Maynard Solomon has challenged Ives's near-legendary capacity for innovation in "Charles Ives: Some Questions of Veracity," *JAMS* 40 (1987): 443–70, answered by Burkholder in "Charles Ives and His Fathers: A Response to Maynard Solomon," *Newsletter of the Institute for Studies in American Music* 18, no. 1 (1988).

3. Gilbert Chase, *America's Music: From the Pilgrims to the Present* (New York, 1955), 733 pp.; rev. ed. (New York, 1966), 759 pp.; rev. 3d ed. (Urbana, Ill., 1987), 712 pp. Wilfrid Mellers, *Music in a New Found Land: Themes and Developments in the History of American Music* (New York, 1966), 543 pp. H. Wiley Hitchcock, *Music in the United States: A Historical Introduction* (Englewood Cliffs, N.J., 1969), 270 pp.; 2d ed. (Englewood Cliffs, 1974), 286 pp.; 3d ed. (Englewood Cliffs, 1988), 365 pp. Charles Hamm, *Music in the New World* (New York, 1983), 722 pp.

To this list might also be added Daniel Kingman, *American Music: A Panorama* (New York, 1979), 577 pp.; 2d ed. (New York, 1990), 684 pp. I have not discussed Kingman's book in the text because, by the author's own description, it is not a history. Though comprehensive, it does not attempt to trace the development of American music chronologically. In the preface to the second edition, Kingman explains: "I have . . . rejected a traditional chronological-historical approach to the whole subject, and have maintained an ordering that reflects my view of American music as a number of more or less distinct but parallel streams" (xv). Kingman's six "streams" are, in the order in which he presents them: "Folk and Ethnic Musics," "Popular Sacred Music," "Three Prodigious Offspring of the Rural South" [Country Music, Blues, Rock], "Popular Secular Music," "Jazz and Its Forerunners," and "Classical Music."

Another work not discussed here is Irving L. Sablosky, *American Music* (Chicago, 1969), a volume in the Chicago History of American Civilization Series, edited by Daniel J. Boorstin. Sablosky's work is chronological, but it is also very short—just 185 pages of text, plus back matter. Written on a small scale, and by an author who seems to have had no musicological training, *American Music* is a balanced account of music in American society but hardly a major historical statement. A jacket note describes Sablosky as "a Foreign Service Officer of the United States Information Agency, where he has prepared material on American music for use overseas."

4. Hamm, *Music in the New World,* 656.

5. My foreword to Chase's *America's Music*, rev. 3d ed., gives a fuller account of his work than is possible here. There Chase is credited with being "the first general historian of the subject to recognize American music as a unique phenomenon that demanded to be studied as such" (xv).

6. Mellers, *Music in a New Found Land,* xiii. This is the only history of American music written by a historian who is not a permanent resident of the United States. Mellers writes: "While I may, as an outsider, miss many qualities, musical, psychological and social, that a native American would be aware of intuitively,

there is also a chance that, as an outsider, I may see and hear things that cannot be experienced from within the American context" (xv). Mellers acknowledges "the Mellon Trust and the University of Pittsburgh" for enabling him "to live for two academic years in the States," presumably providing the stimulus for his book.

7. Hitchcock explains in the preface to his third edition that in dealing with American vernacular secular music, as "in the Colonial era, I discuss much music now considered 'folk music'—but in its function as the *popular* music of its time." He continues: "American folk music as such is considered more broadly by Bruno Nettl and Gerard Béhague in their companion volume in the Prentice Hall History of Music Series, *Folk and Traditional Music of the Western Continents*" (x–xi).

My fuller evaluation of Hitchcock's contribution to American music studies, including his editorship, with Stanley Sadie, of *The New Grove Dictionary of American Music*, 4 vols. (London, 1986)—referred to here as *Amerigrove*—appears in *A Celebration of American Music: Words and Music in Honor of H. Wiley Hitchcock*, edited by Richard Crawford, R. Allen Lott, and Carol J. Oja (Ann Arbor, Mich., 1990), especially 6–9.

8. Hamm, *Music in the New World*, 655. Hamm writes that his *Music in the New World* was "planned to take full advantage" of New World Records' massive Recorded Anthology of American Music, "a set of 100 phonograph discs ranging over the entire 200-year history of our music since the Revolution" and issued to commemorate the United States' Bicentennial (ix–x).

9. Chase, *America's Music* (1955), 658–59. In later editions, Chase restores Ives to his rightful place in historical chronology.

10. The four men bring varied scholarly backgrounds to their work, but Chase was the most fully occupied with the study of New World music. After obtaining his B.A. degree, Chase (b. Havana, Cuba, 1906) served as a music critic in Paris (1929–35), a Latin American music specialist at the Library of Congress (1940–43), an educational music supervisor for the National Broadcasting Company (1943–47), and a U.S. foreign service officer (1951–55; 1958–60). His academic positions include stints at the University of Oklahoma (1955–57), Tulane University (1961–66), the University of Texas at Austin (1975–79), and shorter appointments elsewhere. In 1941, Chase published *The Music of Spain;* but from that time on he devoted his research and writing exclusively to music in Latin America and the United States. See *New Grove*, 4:178, and *Amerigrove* 1:409–10. Chase died in 1992. Mellers (b. 1914) read English and music at Cambridge University and studied composition in Oxford, followed by academic posts at Downing College, Cambridge (1945–48), Birmingham University (1948–59), the University of Pittsburgh (1960–63), and the University of York (1964 until his retirement). He has continued to compose while working as a scholar and teacher. Mellers's many books on topics in Western music include studies of François Couperin, the twentieth century, the Beatles, music and poetry, music and society, and Bob Dylan. See *New Grove*, 12:108. Hitchcock (b. 1923) and

Hamm (b. 1925) both hold Ph.D. degrees in historical musicology, and both have spent their working lives in academia: Hitchcock teaching at the University of Michigan (1950–61), Hunter College (1961–71), and Brooklyn College of the City University of New York (1971 to the present), and Hamm at Princeton University (1948–50; 1958), the Cincinnati Conservatory of Music (1950–57), Tulane University (1959–63), the University of Illinois (1963–76), and Dartmouth College (1976–91). Hamm was also active as a composer in his earlier years. Neither man, however, received his Ph.D. degree for American music study, and both have continued to publish in the fields in which they did their graduate work: Hitchcock in the French and Italian baroque (his dissertation was on Marc-Antoine Charpentier) and Hamm in the Renaissance (his was on Guillaume Dufay). See *New Grove*, 8:73, 601.

11. For an incisive view of the European musical canon see Joseph Kerman, "A Few Canonic Variations," *Critical Inquiry* 10 (1983): 107–25. On the modern literary canon see David A. Hollinger, "The Canon and Its Keepers: Modernism and Mid-Twentieth-Century American Intellectuals," in Hollinger, *In the American Province: Studies in the History and Historiography of Ideas* (Bloomington, Ind., 1985), 74–91.

12. See Richard Crawford, "A Historian's Introduction to Early American Music," *Proceedings of the American Antiquarian Society* 89 (1979): 281–91. See also Richard Crawford and D. W. Krummel, "Early American Music Printing and Publishing," in *Printing and Society in Early America*, edited by William J. Joyce, David D. Hall, Richard D. Brown, and John B. Hench (Worcester, Mass., 1983), 186–227.

13. Quoted from Henry James, *Literary Criticism: Essays on Literature; American Writers; English Writers* (New York, 1984), 516.

14. Simeon Pease Cheney, *The American Singing Book* (Boston, 1879; reprint, New York, 1980), 202.

15. George Hood, *A History of Music in New England: With Biographical Sketches of Reformers and Psalmists* (Boston, 1846; reprint, New York, 1970).

16. Hood, *A History*, vi.

17. Hood, *A History*, 216.

18. Hood, *A History*, iv.

19. Hood, *A History*, 169n.

20. Hood, *A History*, 51n. Hood's research went beyond printed documents, and not all of it got into his book. In his introduction, he cites Oliver Holden, Nahum Mitchell, and Edward Pierce of Brookline, Massachusetts, as sources of information, suggesting that he had conversations with these men. Holden and Mitchell both compiled sacred tunebooks, and Pierce, a clergyman, sang with Billings and told later historians about the experience. See David P. McKay and Richard Crawford, *William Billings of Boston: Eighteenth-Century Composer* (Princeton, 1975), 66, 187, 207. Hood also thanks "those persons who have so politely furnished materials for the biographical sketches of their friends" (v). Since no subject of a biographical sketch in Hood's book lived beyond the 1760s,

he must be referring here to friends of more recent New England musicians whose biographies he wrote but did not include in his book. Hood is known to have gathered data for biographical sketches of Holden, Andrew Law, Elias Mann, Lowell Mason, Daniel Read, and Timothy Swan. Early in the 1840s, he solicited letters relating to these men, and they survive in a scrapbook in the Boston Public Library. In Hood's list of New England tunebooks, on pp. 176–77, he cross-references biographical sketches of Read, Holden, Hans Gram, and Samuel Holyoke that are not printed in the book.

21. Nathaniel D. Gould, *Church Music in America, Comprising Its History and Its Peculiarities at Different Periods, with Cursory Remarks on Its Legitimate Use and Its Abuse; with Notices of the Schools, Composers, Teachers and Societies* (Boston, 1853; reprint, New York, 1972).

22. Gould, *Church Music*, iii, describes his purview as "the last eighty years." On p. iv he writes, however, that he "did not deem it advisable to commence our narrative abruptly at the period of 1770."

23. Gould, *Church Music*, 238.

24. Gould taught his first district school at sixteen, became a specialist in handwriting, and eventually published *Penmanship, or The Beauties of Writing* (Boston, 1822), which enjoyed at least four editions. He also compiled seven tunebooks, of which *National Church Harmony* (Boston, 1824–29, 7 eds.) was the most successful. See Frederick W. Coburn, "Nathaniel Duren Gould," *Dictionary of American Biography* (New York, 1928–36) 4:455.

25. Gould, *Church Music*, 39.

26. Gould, *Church Music*, iii. Gould's book was inspired by Warren Burton's *The District School as It Was. By One Who Went to It* (Boston, 1833), a nostalgic and altogether less substantial work than Gould's.

27. Gould, *Church Music*, 172.

28. Frédéric Louis Ritter, *Music in America* (New York, 1883); new ed. (New York, 1890; reprint, New York, 1970). Quotations here are from the new edition.

29. Ritter, *Music in America*, 55.

30. Frédéric Louis Ritter, *Music in England* (New York, 1883), v.

31. Ritter, *Music in America*, vii–viii.

32. Ritter, *Music in America*, 196.

33. Ritter, *Music in America*, 183.

34. Even in *Amerigrove*, which is broad-minded enough to treat Liberace with respect, Ritter earns the following barb: "Ritter's view of American music was, unfortunately, both simplistic and unsympathetic" (4:49). It should be noted that criticisms of Ritter focus not on his data but on his interpretive outlook.

35. Robert Stevenson, *Philosophies of American Music History: A Lecture Delivered in the Whittall Pavilion of the Library of Congress, January 9, 1969* (Washington, D.C., 1970), 9.

36. Ritter's evaluations are by no means all negative. For example, he considered the era of Billings one of "rich growth" for American psalmodists and "interesting" to historians. "There was original life, great impulse, and energy

about it," he added. "It was infancy in art; but it was alive, and seemed promising" (*Music in America*, 73).

37. William S. B. Mathews, assoc. ed., *A Hundred Years of Music in America. An Account of Musical Effort in America during the Past Century, Including Popular Music and Singing Schools, Church Music, Musical Conventions and Festivals, Orchestral, Operatic and Oratorio Music; Improvements in Musical Instruments; Popular and the Higher Musical Education; Creative Activity, and the Beginning of a National School of Musical Composition* (Chicago, 1889; reprint, New York, 1970).

38. Mathews, *A Hundred Years,* iv.

39. Mathews, *A Hundred Years,* 7–8.

40. Mathews, *A Hundred Years,* iii. "The material thus furnished, some of it with singular reluctance," Mathews continues, "we have carefully digested, and added to it whatever seemed necessary from the personal knowledge of the editor."

41. In fact, Ritter, identified here as an "eminent scholar and composer" (686), is one of the very few who come in for any negative comment. At one place he is claimed to have said something "with his accustomed sneer" (52).

42. Mathews, *A Hundred Years,* 169.

43. Mathews, *A Hundred Years,* 403.

44. Louis C. Elson's *The History of American Music* (New York, 1904) was commissioned for the multivolume History of American Art series, under the general editorship of art critic John C. Van Dyke. The *History of American Music* (Toledo, 1908), edited by W. L. Hubbard, was one of twelve volumes in *The American History and Encyclopedia of Music* (1908–10), of which Hubbard himself was general editor. And *Music in America* (New York, 1915), edited by Arthur Farwell and W. Dermot Darby, was one of fourteen volumes of *The Art of Music* whose editor-in-chief was Daniel Gregory Mason.

45. Elson, *History of American Music,* Chap. 18, "Qualities and Defects of American Music," 361–66.

46. Hubbard, *History of American Music,* Chap. [14], "Summary and Outlook," 345–49.

47. Arthur Farwell, "Introduction," in *Music in America,* edited by Farwell and Darby, vii–xxiii. The quotations are from vii–viii.

48. The only academic of the lot, Elson also did some composing on the side. As a writer, he produced textbooks, monographs, dictionaries, and journalistic memoirs on music. Elson's *History of American Music* was his eleventh book and, except for *The History of German Song* (Boston, 1888), the only one with a historical orientation. As noted in Richard Crawford, *The American Musicological Society 1934–1984: An Anniversary Essay, with Lists of Officers, Winners of Awards, Editors of the Journal, and Honorary and Corresponding Members* (Philadelphia, 1984), in Elson's day, the music of the concert hall was "heard, discussed, analyzed, and written about in forums accessible to music lovers—including books, articles in periodicals such as *The Atlantic, Harper's,* and *Scribner's,* and in the daily press. The most knowledgeable and active American writers about

music in those days . . . worked as critics for large metropolitan newspapers. As journalists, their work was geared to regular production and wide dissemination" (2).

49. Thomas Stoner, " 'The New Gospel of Music': Arthur Farwell's Vision of Democratic Music in America," *American Music* 9 (1991): 186. I am grateful to the author for sending me a prepublication copy.

50. Janet M. Green, *Musical Biographies*, vol. 1 of *The American History and Encyclopedia of Music*, edited by W. L. Hubbard (Toledo, [1908]), 391–92. Hubbard, a mercurial figure who in later life changed his first name to Havrah and explored the occult, lived in California from about 1920 until his death. His letterhead in 1911 describes him as "Editor in Chief, The American History and Encyclopedia of Music," "Former Musical Editor of the *Chicago Tribune*," and "author, critic, lecturer." A collection of Hubbard's personal papers is preserved in the Archives of the Peabody Institute of The Johns Hopkins University, Baltimore.

51. [Waldo Selden] Pratt, *American Music and Musicians* ([New York, 1920]), 101. According to Pratt, the Modern Music Society of New York "was formed in 1913–14 to give both choral and orchestral works by recent composers, especially Americans. Its nucleus was the Lambord Choral Society, founded in 1912 by Benjamin Lambord" (298). Richard Jackson, *United States Music: Sources of Biography and Collective Biography*, I.S.A.M. Monographs, no. 1 (Brooklyn, 1973), 16, supplies William Dermot Darby's death date.

52. Louis C. Elson, *The History of American Music* (New York, 1904); rev. ed. (New York, 1915). Edition revised to 1925 by Arthur Elson (New York, 1925). Quotations here are from the first edition.

53. Elson, *History of American Music*, title page.

54. Elson, *History of American Music*, v.

55. Elson's account of American composers includes a biography and picture, a review of works (sometimes with critical, though not technical, comments about specific compositions), and an evaluation. The composers are divided by their specialties (e.g., "The Orchestral Composers of America," "American Song-Composers"), though Paine, Chadwick, Parker, MacDowell, and Foote are honored in "American Tone-Masters," a chapter proclaiming them the leading American composers.

56. Elson, *History of American Music*, 336–37.

57. Elson, *History of American Music*, 337. Ritter says nothing about American composers in his first edition. In the second (1890), he includes a one-page, alphabetical list of

those musicians who have, as far as I am aware, endeavored to do good, meritorious work in the field of the higher branches of composition. My list comprises the names of those immigrated musicians who, by means of their talent and knowledge, have honestly helped to create an elevated musical atmosphere, and promote musical culture, as well as those who, perchance born of European parents on American soil, have greatly profited by the solid artistic labor of "those foreigners." Every honest promoter of an ideal, pure art-endeavor who has settled here is justly entitled to an honored place in the annals of the History of Music in America. (504)

58. Hubbard is also named as "editor" (i.e., author) of six of the encyclopedia's other volumes: two on opera, two more of "musical biography," a musical dictionary, and a *History of Foreign Music.*

59. On 13 September 1907, Chadwick wrote Hubbard about his article, "American Composers," which he had almost finished. "I have of course not mentioned my own share in the proceedings. But I think I may say without egotism that the whole Boston movement in composition really dates from the performance of my Rip van Winkle overture. It was the keystone of my entire success in life and brought me Horatio Parker, Arthur Whiting, F. S. Converse & Henry Hadley for pupils who went to Rheinberger from me and by my advice." In December 1879, while Chadwick was still studying in Munich, the Harvard Musical Association's orchestra performed the overture, and in 1880, the Handel and Haydn Society played it under his direction. See Victor Fell Yellin, *Chadwick: Yankee Composer* (Washington, D.C., 1990), 40, 44. Chadwick's letter then went on to ask Hubbard: "Now could not you as editor explain this in a supplementary note to my article? I know of no one who could do it better" (letter to W. L. Hubbard in The William Lines Hubbard Papers, Archives of the Peabody Institute of The Johns Hopkins University, Baltimore, Md.). Hubbard followed Chadwick's request. His signed note following the composer's article (14–15) delivers the claim in words very much like Chadwick's own, while making the composer out to be the very soul of self-effacing modesty.

60. Damrosch wrote Hubbard on 29 September 1907 about his article on "Music in the Public Schools": "I think you will find that the subject has been treated as concisely as possible considering its scope and importance." Indeed, he would have liked to provide more on the subject.

> You may, perhaps, think that I have given more space to the early history than is absolutely necessary, but I feel that the zeal, energy and clearsightedness of the early workers in this field were so wonderful that such a remarkable chapter in the history of American culture should receive the recognition it deserves. I consider the report of the school committee of Boston in 1837 [*recte*, 1836, perhaps; see 21–25] to be as clear, intelligent and comprehensive an argument in favor of music in general education as I have ever seen, and it deserves wider publicity and appreciation than it has received by its burial in the archives of Boston's School Board. (letter to W. L. Hubbard in The William Lines Hubbard Papers, Archives of the Peabody Institute of The Johns Hopkins University, Baltimore, Md.)

61. Hubbard's democratic bent comes through in his sympathetic treatment of American unwritten and informal music. In his view, American Indian music possesses "great historical value" because it preserves bits of the culture of a disappearing race (39–40). Negro music is seen to be of higher aesthetic significance. "America owes much," wrote Hubbard, "to the negro in the creation and development of its popular music, for a large part of such music is due

either directly or indirectly to negro sources" (69). Hubbard also notes that African-American influences "have had a marked effect in the production of music both of a popular and of a more pretentious character in this country" (49). As for popular music—to Hubbard, any music simple enough to be enjoyed by listeners without "special musical training" or "serious mental effort" (72)—its importance was self-evident. Although earlier historians had considered popular music unworthy of notice, except for an occasional brickbat aside, Hubbard simply stated: "Popular music always has had and always will have its place in the lives of the people" (71). Patriotic music, which Elson had made part of his historiographical turf, was seen by Hubbard in functional terms: as an agent that, by giving voice to national pride, "inspires to action" (101).

62. Neither the conception nor the data in Hubbard's account, however, have made much impact upon the writing of American music history. One searches the literature in vain for references to it. Where Elson, Mathews, and Ritter are cited with some frequency, and all are acknowledged as holding a place in the American canon of history writing, Hubbard has disappeared from view.

63. César Saerchinger wrote the chapter on "The Folk-Element in American Music," Benjamin Lambord wrote "The Classic Period of American Composition" and also "The Lighter Vein" (on popular music), and M. M. M., so far unidentified, wrote on "Musical Education in America."

64. Farwell, "Introduction," vii.

65. Farwell, "Introduction," viii.

66. Farwell, "Introduction," xi.

67. Farwell, "Introduction," xv.

68. Farwell saw modern American composers as "divided into two camps, one seeking a national individuality for American music and the other a continuation of the most recent European developments, especially those of France and post-Wagnerian Germany." Neither approach had proved dominant. "The so-called 'Nationalists' experimented to some extent with the ultra-modern technical developments, and the ultra-moderns could not refrain from some essays with primitive American themes." The result? "It was inevitable that a broad eclecticism should arise, and in this a more truly national movement stepped forth than was presented by either of the existing wings. The will for the greatest freedom, essential to the American spirit, asserted itself, and in its newest phase the nation is declaring for a complete musical independence, based upon the unrestricted assimilation and reflection of every phase of music influence, within and without" (Farwell, "Nationalists, Eclectics, and Ultra-Moderns," in *Music in America*, 407–8).

69. Farwell, "Introduction," xviii.

70. Farwell, "Introduction," xx.

71. Farwell, "Introduction," xii–xiii.

72. Farwell, "Introduction," xxi.

73. Farwell, "Introduction," xix.

74. Farwell, "Introduction," xxii.

75. Farwell, "Introduction," xxii–xxiii.

76. Farwell, "Introduction," xviii.

77. One contradiction between Farwell's faith in proletarian musical taste and the rest of the book appears at the end of Darby's chapter on opera, where he writes: "That the faculty of intelligent aesthetic appreciation is somewhat rudimentary in the average American of to-day is a fact that the unbiassed [*sic*] observer can hardly escape" (W. Dermot Darby, "Opera in the United States, Part II," in *Music in America*, 180).

78. In the 1960s, however, after musicology as a scholarly discipline had established itself in this country, Frank Ll. Harrison observed that "American musical scholarship developed in close contact with the 'official' musicological outlook of Europe, but without real involvement in the musical culture of either Europe or America." See Frank Ll. Harrison, Mantle Hood, and Claude V. Palisca, *Musicology* (Englewood Cliffs, N.J., 1963), 60.

79. William Lichtenwanger, ed., *Oscar Sonneck and American Music* (Urbana, Ill., 1983), collects articles by and about Sonneck.

80. For Sonneck's career there, see Gillian B. Anderson, "Putting the Experience of the World at the Nation's Command: Music at the Library of Congress, 1800–1917," *Journal of the American Musicological Society* 42 (1989): 108–49.

81. Quoted in Lichtenwanger, *Oscar Sonneck*, 18, 90.

82. Sonneck's books on American music, in chronological order, are: *Bibliography of Early Secular American Music* (Washington, D.C., 1905); new ed., rev. and enlarged by William Treat Upton (Washington, D.C., 1945; reprint, New York, 1964). *Francis Hopkinson, the First American Poet-Composer (1737–1791), and James Lyon, Patriot, Preacher, Psalmodist (1735–1794): Two Studies in Early American Music* (Washington, D.C., 1905; reprint, New York, 1967). *Early Concert-Life in America (1731–1800)* (Leipzig, 1907; reprint, New York, 1978). *Report on "The Star-Spangled Banner," "Hail Columbia," "America," "Yankee Doodle"* (Washington, D.C., 1909; reprint, New York, 1972). *Early Opera in America* (New York, 1915; reprint, New York, 1963). In addition, Sonneck wrote a number of articles on American music, collected in Lichtenwanger, *Oscar Sonneck*.

83. Quoted from Lichtenwanger, *Oscar Sonneck*, 29–30. The six-word aphorism ending this statement was often quoted in public addresses by Irving Lowens, founding President of the Sonneck Society for American Music.

84. Quoted from Lichtenwanger, *Oscar Sonneck*, 74.

85. Quoted from Lichtenwanger, *Oscar Sonneck*, 89.

86. Oscar G. Sonneck, "The History of Music: A Few Suggestions," in Oscar G. Sonneck, *Miscellaneous Studies in the History of Music* (New York, 1921), 334 (italics added).

87. My article, "Sonneck and American Musical Historiography," in *Essays in Musicology: A Tribute to Alvin Johnson*, edited by Lewis Lockwood and Edward Roesner (n.p., 1990), 266–83, claims Sonneck as the first historian of American

music to work from a conscious, fully developed historiographical philosophy. The article also traces Sonneck's influence on other writers. Preeminent among scholars inspired by Sonneck's belief that "bibliography is the backbone of history" was Irving Lowens (1916–83), whose bibliographically based researches in early American music began in the late 1940s. See Lowens, *Music and Musicians in Early America* (New York, 1964). See also Richard Crawford, obituary notice for Irving Lowens, *Proceedings of the American Antiquarian Society* 91 (1984): 40–44, for an assessment of Sonneck's direct influence upon Lowens. Allen P. Britton (b. 1914) began his work on early American sacred tunebooks at about the same time as Lowens. Lowens and Britton's work on early American tunebooks is brought to fruition in Allen Perdue Britton, Irving Lowens, and completed by Richard Crawford, *American Sacred Music Imprints, 1698–1810: A Bibliography* (Worcester, Mass., 1990). Gilbert Chase wrote in the first edition of *America's Music* that Sonneck, Arthur Farwell, and Charles Seeger had been his three main inspirations for that work.

It should also be recalled that Sonneck had a close colleague, Waldo Selden Pratt (1857–1939), whose work, while not including a history of American music, was carried on under the influence of a scholarly ideal akin to Sonneck's. Pratt's "On Behalf of Musicology" was the first article in the first issue of *The Musical Quarterly,* edited by Sonneck. Moreover, Pratt was editor of the *American Supplement* to *Grove's Dictionary of Music and Musicians,* 2d ed. (New York, 1920; rev. 2d ed., New York, 1928). The latter work incorporates Sonneck's historiographical precepts admirably; but, rather than a narrative history, it's written in encyclopedia format. See Richard Crawford, "Amerigrove's Pedigree: On *The New Grove Dictionary of American Music,*" *College Music Society Symposium* 27 (1987): 172–86.

In another vein, D. W. Krummel has written that, however much Sonneck has been venerated, his example has not been enthusiastically followed. Krummel describes Sonneck as a "legendary" figure, "who with Germanic thoroughness saw only one way to proceed: start at the beginning, like any good historical scholar, and expect others to be inspired or compelled by the quality of your good work to continue. Unfortunately, little has been done to continue Sonneck's good work." See Krummel, *Bibliographical Handbook of American Music* (Urbana, Ill., 1987), 7.

88. John Tasker Howard, *Our American Music: Three Hundred Years of It* (New York, 1931); rev. ed. (New York, 1939); 3d ed. (New York, 1946); 3d ed., with supplementary chapters by James Lyons (New York, 1954). *Our American Music: A Comprehensive History from 1620 to the Present,* 4th ed. (New York, 1965).

89. Howard, *Our American Music,* p. vii. Quotations here and below are from the 4th ed.

90. In the fourth edition (1965), the bibliography, "revised and brought up to date . . . by Karl Kroeger," runs to seventy-six pages.

91. In "The History of Music in America," delivered to the Music Teachers' National Association in 1916 and reprinted in Sonneck's *Miscellaneous Studies,*

he notes "the scant courtesy shown to the first half of the nineteenth century" and recommends that "some intrepid historian of uncommon constructive gifts" should "devote several years of steady comprehensive research exclusively to the earlier half-century" (339). He then offers several pages of suggestions for specific research projects (340–43).

92. Howard, *Our American Music*, 72.

93. Howard, *Our American Music*, 42.

94. Howard, *Our American Music*, 56.

95. Allen P. Britton, championing the cause of New England psalmody, wrote as early as 1949: "At this late date we can do little else than mourn the loss of our first original art music. A sacrifice upon the twin altars of good taste and correct harmony, it vanished from the knowledge of serious musicians." And Britton found the lasting impact severe: "The American people, deprived of an art music based upon a native idiom of immediate appeal to their musical sensibilities, have ever since manifested an understandable suspicion of the essential validity of all serious music" ("Theoretical Introductions in American Tune-Books to 1800," Ph.D. diss., University of Michigan, 1949, 366). Irving Lowens, writing on psalmodist Daniel Read in 1952, held foreign influence responsible for a decline in the quality of American music-making. "The crude but eloquent American product had been supplanted by second-rate English importations and insipid 'arrangements' from the classic masters. . . . In today's historical perspective, the newer music appears to have been a regression rather than an advance in popular taste, but to Read [near the end of his life], the tune-books of the supporters of 'scientific music' represented progress" ("Daniel Read's World: The Letters of an Early American Composer," *Notes* 9 [1951–52]: 243).

96. Barbara Zuck, *A History of Musical Americanism*, Studies in Musicology, no. 19 (Ann Arbor, Mich., 1980), is one of several recent studies that examine the attempts of composers for the concert hall to draw upon American musical vernaculars.

97. Chase, *America's Music*, calls psalmodist Andrew Law a " 'better music' booster" (128), labels his praise for European sacred music "snobbism" (131), and declares Law "a staunch upholder of the genteel tradition" (130). For Chase, Lowell Mason and the next generation of American psalmodists pursued a false idea of "progress" (153) for pecuniary motives (150–51). Mason especially was responsible for "thrusting" earlier New England composers "into the background, while opening the gates for a flood of colorless imitations of the 'European masters' " (160). Chase attributes the rise of "The Genteel Tradition"— the title of his chapter 9—to the "aesthetic immaturity" of "the people of the United States as a whole" during the nineteenth century (166). Quotations here and below are from the first edition.

98. As noted in my foreword to Chase's revised third edition, Howard wrote to show how well American composers had mastered European forms. He organized his book into an epic in three parts: "Euterpe in the Wilderness" (1620–

1800), "Euterpe Clears the Forest" (1800–1860), and "Euterpe Builds Her American Home" (1860–1931). The saga of American music as told by Howard lay in the struggle of the Old World muse to hack out a place for herself on American shores, triumphing over nature and poverty, indifference and ignorance. See Chase, *America's Music*, rev. 3d ed. (1987), xii–xiii.

99. Chase, *America's Music*, xvii, xix. These fighting words do not appear in the revised third edition of Chase's book.

100. Chase, *America's Music*, xi.

101. Chase, *America's Music*, xix.

102. See Richard Crawford, "Tracking Vernacular Music . . . across the Great Divide," *Music Librarianship in America*, edited by Michael Ochs, *Harvard Library Bulletin*, n.s., 2 (1991): 92–99.

103. It has been noted above that Chase believed so fervently in the truth of his historiographical image that he wrenched history out of shape to dramatize it. In devoting the last chapter of his first edition to Charles Ives, even though Ives had stopped composing more than thirty years before Chase's book appeared, Chase could treat Ives as American music's man of destiny: the amateur composer who brought together in one grand synthesis all that was most distinctive and vital in our musical past. On the one hand, Ives composed in European genres and accepted their challenge of craftsmanship and high seriousness. On the other, Ives's works drew heavily on techniques and melodic quotations borrowed from American vernaculars, including hymn tunes, patriotic and parlor songs, fiddle tunes, band music, rags—the very vernaculars that Chase had brought to the fore in his historical account. Ives's fusing of informal and formal traditions created a hybrid music that was American to the core and that also, in Chase's view, showed an artistic strength beyond anything achieved by earlier American composers working within either tradition. Chase's message was clear: The United States is a democracy, and the cultivated composers most likely to grasp the national spirit and character are those whose music, in one way or another, incorporates American vernaculars.

104. Hamm's interpretation of the central importance of popular song in American (and the world's) music was first set forward in *Yesterdays: Popular Song in America* (New York, 1979), in his articles on popular music for *New Grove* (1980) and *Amerigrove* (1986), in *Music in the New World* (1983), and elaborated in articles, speeches, and organizational activities on behalf of popular music, especially through the International Association for the Study of Popular Music (IASPM).

105. A personal experience confirms the point. Although I had worked for more than two decades in American psalmody, I never read Gould's *Church Music in America* from start to finish until I began work on this chapter. I had jumped around in it, digested certain passages, even quoted Gould from time to time in various writings. But when I finally read it all the way through, I discovered a thesis about psalmody reform that appears nowhere else and that historians, myself included, had overlooked. My statistical studies confirmed

Gould's thesis. See " 'Ancient Music' and the Europeanizing of American Psalmody, 1800–1810," in *A Celebration of American Music*, 225–55.

106. Martin Williams's *Smithsonian Collection of Classic Jazz* (1973; rev., 1987), a series of recordings, is a widely accepted effort in this direction.

107. Stevenson's writings include *Philosophies of American Music History* (Washington, D.C., 1970); "America's First Black Music Historian" [James Monroe Trotter], *Journal of the American Musicological Society* 26 (1973): 383–404; "Written Sources for Indian Music until 1882" and "English Sources for Indian Music until 1882," both in *Ethnomusicology* 17 (1973): 1–40 and 399–442; and "American Musical Scholarship: Parker to Thayer," *Nineteenth-Century Music* 1 (1977–78): 191–210. Since beginning work on this chapter in 1985, I have published a number of articles on the subject as well, most of them referred to above. See also Charles Hamm, "Some Fugitive Thoughts on the Historiography of Music," in *Essays in Musicology*, 284–91.

108. Chase, *America's Music*, xix, quotes Charles Seeger: "When the history of music in the New World is written, it will be found that the main concern has been with folk and popular music."

109. Quoted from Hitchcock, *Music in the United States* (1988), 54.

CHAPTER 2

1. Appearing in *Berkeley: A Journal of Modern Culture* (July 1948): 1–2, 7–8, reprinted in *Roger Sessions on Music: Collected Essays*, edited by Edward T. Cone (Princeton, 1979), 157. The full statement reads: "No fact regarding music in America is more obvious, more pertinent, or more all-embracing in its implications than the fact that music here is in all of its public aspects a business, and a big one." This is the first sentence of an essay called "Music in a Business Economy."

2. "There is no doubt," Sessions continues, "that this is an inevitable state of affairs. I do not regard it as a favorable one for art or for culture . . . but it is a condition which is wholly characteristic of our society, and one which exists and flourishes as a part of that society, entirely independently of the will or the intentions of individuals. I am not therefore deploring it[;] . . . we must treat it as a condition and not a temporary accident" ("Music in a Business Economy," in *Roger Sessions on Music*, 157).

3. Sessions, "Music in a Business Economy," 158–59.

4. See Jacques Attali, *Noise: The Political Economy of Music*, translated by Brian Massumi (Minneapolis, 1985), 37. When music becomes a commodity, Attali writes, it is transformed into "a means of producing money. It is sold and consumed. It is analyzed: What market does it have? How much profit does it generate? What business strategy is best for it? The music industry, with all of its derivatives (publishing, entertainment, records, musical instruments, record

players, etc.) is a major element in and precursor of the economy of leisure and the economy of signs."

5. Sessions, "Music in a Business Economy," 158–59.

6. Sessions, "Music in a Business Economy," 161–63. On 161 Sessions acknowledges that the music he writes "costs money to perform, and yields little or nothing in the sense of immediate short-range box-office returns." His analysis of the "competitive" atmosphere of the concert hall, which he finds pernicious, appears on pp. 162–63.

7. See, e.g., Howard Becker, *Art Worlds* (Berkeley, 1982), Introduction and Chap. 1, for a concise description of the sociological structure supporting the arts.

8. *Webster's New International Dictionary,* 2d ed., s.v. "trade," distinguishes among trade, craft, business, and profession. Trade, it says, "applies to any of the mechanical employments or handicrafts, except those connected with agriculture." Craft, while "often interchangeable with *trade* . . . denotes especially a trade requiring skilled workmanship; as a carpenter, bricklayer, blacksmith"; business "applies especially to occupations of a mercantile or commercial nature"; and profession "designates the more learned callings" such as "a clergyman, a lawyer, a physician, a civil engineer, a teacher."

9. Burton J. Bledstein, *The Culture of Professionalism: The Middle Class and the Development of Higher Education in America* (New York, 1976), 86–87, gives four criteria for a profession:

1. it must be a full-time occupation providing a principal source of income

2. the professional must undergo theoretical training and master an esoteric body of knowledge or skill

3. the professional must be licensed to practice by a recognized institution

4. the professional would be likely to embrace an ethic of service, so that in a conflict a client's interest takes precedence over financial profit.

In spirit, if not letter, composing meets the last three of these criteria. See n. 12 below for more on the issue of income.

10. Virgil Thomson, *The State of Music,* 2d ed., rev. (New York, 1962), 70–72. Chap. 5 is called "Life in the Big City or the Civil Status of Musicians."

11. Thomson writes: "Our western societies consider original design as something just a little bit more important than execution. Either it is paid a special fee, or it is granted a share in the profits of exploitation, or both. And although in some cases the designer is allowed, and in others obliged, to execute his own designs, his civil status as a creator is different from and superior to that of the ordinary executant workman" (*State of Music,* 69). Thomson also acknowledges that there are "rich" professions, "poor" professions, and "rich-and-poor" ones. Rich professions, which include law and medicine, operate on a fee basis and charge "what the traffic will bear." Members of poor professions, of which literature, scholarship, and musical composition are examples, "are small proprietors who live by leasing to commercial concerns the property rights in their

work." Within the rich-and-poor group—painting and sculpture are included, as well as practitioners who live "sometimes on fees, sometimes on royalties"— wide differences in financial standing exist that have little to do with technical competence (*State of Music,* 73).

12. Granting that composing provides less than a living wage for most composers, Thomson describes their working lives as a manifestation of composers' "multiple civil status." For all the "pride and intellectual authority" that musical creation brings, a composer who acts in the role of performer or teacher is at that moment behaving as a laborer, "a time-worker, a union-member, a white collar proletarian." At the same time, as an "author of published or frequently played works," a composer is "a small proprietor who leases out . . . property-rights for exploitation by commercial interests" (*State of Music,* 126–27).

Attali, concerned primarily with economics and only in passing with professional hierarchy, also views the composer as a proprietor. A composer, Attali explains, "produces a program, a mold, an abstract algorithm. The score he writes is an order described for an operator-interpreter" (*Noise,* 37). Attali describes the composer's place in the economy this way:

> Generally remunerated with a percentage of the surplus-value obtained from the sale of the commercial object (the score) and its use (the performance), he is reproduced in every copy of the score and in each performance, by virtue of the royalty laws. His remuneration is therefore a kind of *rent.* A strange situation: a category of workers has thus succeeded in preserving ownership of their labor, in avoiding the position of wage earner, in being remunerated as a rentier who dips into the surplus-value produced by wage earners who valorize their labor in the commodity cycle [e.g., performers and others]. As the creator of the program that all of the capitalist production plugs into, he belongs to a more general category of people, whom I shall call *molders.* Entertainment entrepreneurs are capitalists; workers in publishing and performers are productive workers. Composers are rentiers. (40)

13. Thomson's often disparaging comments on teachers should be read in light of his long-standing "war" on a "Germanic" attitude apparently "in control everywhere—in the orchestras, the universities, the critical posts, the publishing houses, wherever music makes money or is a power." He describes that attitude as one of pretension and self-interest, masked by solemnity and based on "an intolerable assumption, namely, its right to judge everything without appeal" (Virgil Thomson, *Virgil Thomson* [New York, 1966], quoted from Virgil Thomson, *A Virgil Thomson Reader* [Boston, 1981], 180–81). In 1939, calling teachers "trade-unionists," Thomson wrote:

> Pedagogy is not a profession like musical composition, nor even a trade like piano-playing. It has no traditions, no body of esoteric knowledge, no special skill, and no authority. . . . I don't mean to say one teacher isn't a more skillful pedagogue than another. Quite the contrary. I mean no system of pedagogy is any better than any other. The fact that there are so many systems on the market (they are as numerous in America as religions) means

that there is no tradition. If the teacher knows his subject and keeps his temper, the student can usually be depended on to get everything out of him that he can digest. (*State of Music*, 135–36).

In a further jab at pedagogues' pretensions, Thomson writes that "much as they would like to be considered an intellectual caste," teachers "are really white-collar proletarians." He explains: "Their organized activities are aimed at getting some kind of authority over school curricula and at defending their salaries and their tenure of office from the depredations of trustees and school-boards, who represent in such disputes the profit motive and the authoritarian methods of finance-capital" (136).

14. In both cases, occupationally speaking, craft practitioners (i.e., in the first case, musical performers, and, in the second, instrument makers) function as wage earners, and their labor provides money for the entrepreneur or factory owners. Thomson writes: "The organizing of musical performances is a business like fruit-vending" (*State of Music*, 67). But for Attali it is more complicated. Attali's overriding issue is "the site of the creation of money in music." His analysis, which he describes as that of Marxian political economy, asks: "What kind of musical labor produces surplus-value?" When a musician "is paid a wage by someone who employs him for his personal pleasure," no surplus-value, or capital, is created. "But if, for example, he plays a concert as the employee of someone in the entertainment business, he produces capital and creates wealth." The musician is thus the wage earner and the entrepreneur the capitalist. See Attali, *Noise*, 37–39.

15. The key question is how far economic processes might go toward illuminating musical processes. During a session entitled "Worldwide Transmutations of American Popular Music" at the Twelfth Congress of the International Musicological Society in Berkeley, California (1977), William Austin noted the difficulty of studying the "vast cultural transactions" that certain musical processes embody. Can we study such processes as a whole, he asked?

> If . . . the songs of some Eskimos are more popular than the songs of some Blackfoot Indians, or if the works of John Cage and Charles Ives are more popular than the symphonies and operas of Roger Sessions, still more popular than any of those things are, for instance, songs by Stephen Foster, Irving Berlin, Bob Dylan, and Stevie Wonder. . . . Those are very, very popular, more popular than any classical music or ethnic music. The question about this is "How are these various popular processes connected?" My personal answer so far is in thousands of ways investigated through individual biographies.

Austin's words are an apt reminder of how complex such investigation really is—especially in fields, like American musical economics, where biographical materials can be scarce and no handy "silhouettes" exist. See International Musicological Society, *Report of the Twelfth Congress, Berkeley, 1977*, edited by Daniel Heartz and Bonnie Wade (Kassel, 1981), 586–87.

16. These figures appear in a letter of 6 February 1753 from the Vestry of St. Philip's to an agent in London who was asked to recruit an organist there

(see George W. Williams, "Early Organists at St. Philip's, Charleston," *South Carolina Historical Magazine* 54 [1953]: 87).

17. Andrew Adgate's Institution for the Encouragement of Church Music, formed in Philadelphia in 1784 and supported by subscription, was one of a number of singing schools known to be free to their scholars. More usual, however, were schools for which tuition was charged. As the Reverend William Bentley wrote in his diary in 1796, solo singing, as opposed to choral singing, "has never been taught in New England as a Liberal Art, in public schools, but by private tuition" (quoted in Richard Crawford, *Andrew Law, American Psalmodist* [Evanston, Ill., 1968], 132). I have not found evidence documenting the cost of private music lessons in the eighteenth century, though it probably varied as much then as it has since. As for singing schools, in the years after the Revolutionary War, my impression is that scholars typically paid between one and two dollars per quarter (usually two meetings per week for thirteen weeks). In Salem around 1783, according to *The Diary of William Bentley, D.D., Pastor of East Church, Salem, Massachusetts,* vol. 1 (Salem, Mass., 1905), 7, a singing-school session cost each scholar one dollar, with "deficiencies to be made up from the public fund." Oscar G. Sonneck's manuscript notes record psalmodist Samuel Holyoke charging two dollars per quarter in the same city in 1796, while Louis Pichierri, *Music in New Hampshire, 1623–1800* (New York, 1960), 235, reports a singing master named [Ichabod] Johnson collecting the same fee in Portsmouth. In 1798, Andrew Law charged scholars two dollars per quarter for a Philadelphia school, plus an "equal proportion of the expenses of Wood, Room, Candles, and Doorkeeper." At the time, Law was paying $100 per quarter for the room in which he taught, high enough to complain about in a letter (Crawford, *Andrew Law,* 140). And in 1804, writing from Boston, he offered to return to Philadelphia if associates there guaranteed him "one hundred scholars for two quarters at three dollars per scholar per quarter." The latter school never materialized; perhaps Law's proposal was simply a bargaining position (178). In 1821, a friend of Law's received a letter from Bond County, Illinois, from a singing master who reported he was teaching a school of "about 45 scholars [there] at $1" (246). Two years later, in 1823, Amos Blanchard was still charging two dollars per quarter for a school he opened in Salem. See Henry M. Brooks, *Olden-Time Music: A Compilation from Newspapers and Books* (Boston, 1888; reprint, New York, 1973), 115. Available figures support the notion that urban schools cost more than rural ones. I am grateful to Nym Cooke for help in documenting the cost of singing schools and for supplying the Sonneck reference from his notes.

18. Oscar G. Sonneck, after extensive research, summed up the situation of New York's professional musicians, almost all of them immigrants, around 1800: "With their revenues from teaching, selling, copying music, with several societies and theatrical companies to engage them for their orchestras and with the salaries accruing from a participation in subscription-concerts . . . half [a]

hundred musicians . . . were able to eke out a living" (*Early Concert-Life in America* [Leipzig, 1907; reprint, New York, 1978], 223–24).

19. Allen Perdue Britton, Irving Lowens, and completed by Richard Crawford, *American Sacred Music Imprints 1698–1810: A Bibliography* (Worcester, Mass., 1990), 14–16, surveys the singing master's occupation, calling it "the only professional calling readily open to Americans who had a knack for music."

20. Britton, et al., *American Sacred Music Imprints,* 4–5.

21. Britton, et al., *American Sacred Music Imprints,* 9–10.

22. Britton, et al., *American Sacred Music Imprints,* 20–21.

23. Britton, et al., *American Sacred Music Imprints,* 26–42, analyzes the tunebook trade in sections on "publishers and publishing," "engravers and engraving," "printers and printing," and the "sellers and selling" of tunebooks. In eighteenth-century psalmody, most tunebooks were brought out by newspaper and book publishers rather than specialized music publishers.

24. In psalmody as it persisted well into the nineteenth century, performing, composing, and publishing continued as activities still existing chiefly within the teaching trade.

25. Law's letters, preserved in the William L. Clements Library at the University of Michigan, document a life of economic hardship. In December 1798, for example, Law opened a singing school in Philadelphia. Lacking enough tunebooks for his pupils, he appealed to his brother and publisher in Cheshire, Connecticut, to send the engraved plates of his *The Art of Singing* (1794) to Philadelphia for reprinting. By mid-February they still had not arrived. He complained in a letter that

> My school is coming on slowly. I have been almost sick for three weeks and unable to sing, tho I attended the school. . . . I [can] get a room, only for four evenings in a week, which is injurious to the improvement of the school; and I cannot get any except one room which, if I have it, I must take it from this time to the first of October at the rate of four hundred dollars a year. And there will be at least three [months] out of the time that I can have no school, for the people will be upon the wing [in the summer] whether there is any [yellow] fevor or not, which will make it at least 200 dollars per quarter for the room, which will take all the avails of the school. (Crawford, *Andrew Law,* 139–40)

Law's letters abound in similar laments.

26. Any substantial amount of profit made from psalmody could only have come from the publication of tunebooks. Vinson Bushnell has concluded after a study of Daniel Read's papers that, by publishing his own tunebooks, Read probably made psalmody a profitable venture. See Bushnell, "Daniel Read of New Haven (1757–1836): The Man and His Musical Activities," Ph.D. diss., Harvard University, 1979, 203–14. But Read was an exception. The only other publishers of tunebooks likely to have profited from the enterprise before the 1820s were professional printers: Isaiah Thomas, with *The Worcester Collection* (1786–1803), and Henry Ranlet, with *The Village Harmony* (1795–1821). See Britton, et al., *American Sacred Music Imprints,* 6–8, 28, 35–36.

27. [Waldo Selden] Pratt, ed., *American Music and Musicians* ([New York, 1920]), 391.

28. For comments on Adgate's ambitions, see Crawford, *Andrew Law*, 63–65. Law's aspirations as a reformer are discussed on pages 97–108, especially 97, 105–8.

29. Sonneck, *Early Concert-Life*, 103–11, describes Adgate's attempt in 1786 to pay for his school with profits from an ambitious program of subscription concerts—a dozen in one season. Early in his career, Law sought to extend his influence through younger protégés like Adgate (Crawford, *Andrew Law*, 63–69) and Thomas H. Atwill (75, 79, 200–210). When those relationships turned sour, Law tried to sell tunebooks through agents located all over the country (121–28). Finally he tried to enlist the support of Protestant denominations for his tunebooks (144–46; 190).

30. Richard Crawford, "Ancient Music and the Europeanizing of American Psalmody, 1800–1810," in *A Celebration of American Music: Words and Music in Honor of H. Wiley Hitchcock*, edited by Richard Crawford, R. Allen Lott, and Carol J. Oja (Ann Arbor, Mich., 1990), 225–55. Between 1805 and 1810, as this article shows, a social movement sparked by the belief that the sacred character of psalmody was threatened, accomplished much of what Law had been struggling to achieve for the previous dozen years. In this case, once consensus was reached on an important issue involving sacred music, social interaction proved to be an agent of change.

31. Carol A. Pemberton, *Lowell Mason: His Life and Work*, Studies in Musicology, no. 86 (Ann Arbor, Mich., 1985), 4, notes that in old age Mason referred to the clarinet as "my instrument" but that, "even as a teenager . . . he was also at ease playing the violin, cello, flute, piano, and organ."

32. Nicholas Temperley, *The Music of the English Parish Church*, vol. 1 (Cambridge, 1979), describes Gardiner's work on pages 231–32.

33. Mason wrote John Rowe Parker, editor of *The Euterpeiad*, on 20 June 1821, describing his collection as a book "containing a sufficient number of psalm and hymn tunes for . . . public worship and a small number of larger pieces for Country Choirs . . . harmonized according to the modern principles of thorough bass—and I trust every false relation, and every forbidden progression will be avoided." Mason confided to Parker his fear that the collection would "be too classical—that is—too much of Mozart, Beethoven, etc." (Pemberton, *Lowell Mason*, 32).

34. According to Pemberton, *Lowell Mason*, 35, Mason was "immediately given $500 as an advance payment."

35. Michael Broyles, *"Music of the Highest Class": Elitism and Populism in Antebellum Boston* (New Haven, Conn., 1992) contends that proceeds from the tunebook kept the Boston Handel and Haydn Society in existence during a period when financial insolvency forced many other such organizations to disband shortly after being founded. According to the secretary's minutes, Broyles writes, the society "was in serious financial trouble between 1819 and 1822." But

the treasurer's report, he continues, shows that between 1824 and 1831 profits on the tunebook "alone netted the society between $600 and $1100 per year"— half of the society's revenues and "enough to enable it to present several large concerts per year with orchestra." In a footnote, Broyles details the yearly amounts: 1824: $601.90; 1826: $964.28; 1827: $800 (estimate); 1828: $820; 1829: $1,000 (estimate); 1830: $1,000 (estimate); 1831: $1,166.67. The terms of his contract with the society called for Mason to receive like amounts in these years (167, 353).

36. Pratt, *American Music and Musicians*, 285. Arthur Lowndes Rich, *Lowell Mason: "The Father of Singing among the Children"* (Chapel Hill, N.C., 1946), 10, acknowledges that estimates of the book's total proceeds range from $10,000 to $30,000.

37. Charles C. Perkins, *History of the Handel and Haydn Society, of Boston, Massachusetts*, vol. I (Boston, 1883–93; reprint, New York, 1977), 83, writes that "at the end of five years" (1822–27) the book "had yielded the handsome profit of $4,033.32, to be divided between the contracting parties."

38. Pemberton, *Lowell Mason*, 45, reports that an offer of the society presidency helped lure Mason to Boston. In addition, he was "guaranteed $2,000 salary for musical direction in three churches during successive periods of six months each: the Hanover Street Church, the Essex Street Church, and the Park Street Church."

39. Pratt, *American Music and Musicians*, 391.

40. Broyles, *Psalmody to Symphony*, Chap. 2, argues that Mason's "historical position can be properly assessed only when his professional activities, thought, attitudes, and approach to musical issues are viewed within the context of nineteenth-century evangelicalism." Broyles believes that Mason had little interest in religion in his early years but that not long after he moved to Georgia— probably in 1813 or early 1814—he went through a life-changing conversion experience. From that time to the end of his life, Broyles believes, Mason always put religious values ahead of all others, including artistic and commercial ones (65–67).

41. Pemberton, *Lowell Mason*, 49–54. Her Appendix B, pages 223–24, lists Mason's sacred tunebooks in chronological order. From 1832 until 1854 they appear at the rate of approximately one new tunebook per year, sometimes in collaboration with others (e.g., George J. Webb, brother Timothy B. Mason). After the mid-1850s their number tapers off.

42. According to Rich, *Lowell Mason*, 12, before Mason gave up the Handel and Haydn Society presidency in 1832, "he had hoped for its support in organizing note-reading classes for children, but the society's conservative board of managers declined to sponsor them, holding that their function was to cultivate classical and not elementary music."

43. Rich, *Lowell Mason*, 14. Rich does not give the date of this school, but Mason, *An Address on Church Music* (New York, 1851), 14, recalls that Mason taught it "for six or eight years, or until it was taken up by the Boston Academy of Music, by which society it was sustained until music was introduced into the

grammar schools of the city" (quoted in Rich, *Lowell Mason,* 14). Pemberton, *Lowell Mason,* 64, reports that the school began in 1828 and grew by 1830 to 150–200 pupils. By 1832, she adds, George J. Webb had joined Mason in teaching this class.

44. For example, in Boston on 18 August 1830, the Reverend William Channing Woodbridge, an educational reformer, addressed the American Institute of Education advocating "Vocal Music as a Branch of Instruction in the Public Schools." Pemberton, *Lowell Mason,* 65–66, reports that when, as part of that event, some boys Mason had been teaching sang to illustrate the benefits of music education, "the beauty of their singing cast a spell upon the group." Writing in the *North American Review* in 1841, Samuel A. Eliot remembered the impact of Mason and Webb's first childrens' performances: "Never shall we forget the mingled emotions of wonder, delight, vanquished incredulity, and pleased hope, with which these juvenile concerts were attended. The coldest heart was touched, and glistening eyes and quivering lips attested the depth . . . of the feelings excited in the bosoms of parents and teachers. . . . A deep and lasting impression had been made on the public mind and the public heart" (quoted in Pemberton, *Lowell Mason,* 70–71).

45. *Juvenile Psalmist; or The Child's Introduction to Sacred Music* (Boston, 1829), a Sunday School tunebook, was followed by *Juvenile Lyre; or Hymns and Songs, Religious, Moral, and Cheerful . . . for the use of Primary and Common Schools* (Boston, 1831).

46. Pemberton, *Lowell Mason,* 71, adds that, though Mason was "the key figure in the academy," he "deliberately kept his name in the background." Broyles, *"Music of the Highest Class,"* 182, credits the Boston Academy of Music, especially under the leadership of Samuel A. Eliot (1798–1862), with bringing about a rapid decline in "interest in sacred vocal music . . . in favor of classical instrumental music." Within ten years of its founding in 1833, Broyles writes, the academy "became the principal purveyor of instrumental music" in Boston. With that shift in interest, he notes, Lowell Mason's influence in the academy declined.

47. Pemberton, *Lowell Mason,* 87. Twelve teachers attended the first two-day session. By 1851 the enrollment of teachers at Mason's conventions had risen to about 1,500 (89).

48. Pemberton, *Lowell Mason,* 87–88; Rich, *Lowell Mason,* 144–45, lists printings through 1861.

49. Rich, *Lowell Mason,* 23–25, and Pemberton, *Lowell Mason,* 114–17, document Mason's first year of public school teaching at the Hawes School in South Boston. Again, a new venue produced new publications. *The Juvenile Singing School,* on which Mason collaborated with George J. Webb, appeared in 1837 and was reprinted in six of the next seven years. In 1838, Mason brought out a volume to aid public school teachers: *Musical Exercises for Singing Schools, to Be Used in Connexion with the "Manual of the Boston Academy of Music, for Instruction in the Elements of Vocal Music."* See Rich, *Lowell Mason,* 148–49.

50. Pemberton, *Lowell Mason*, 118–24, traces Mason's career in the Boston public schools. Harry Eskew, in *Amerigrove* 3:187, reports his ten-year service in the teachers' institutes.

51. George Frederick Root, *The Story of a Musical Life* (Cincinnati, 1891; reprint, New York, 1973), 51–52.

52. Pemberton, *Lowell Mason*, 66–67, tells the same story, reporting that the two men were not well acquainted until the summer of 1830. According to Root, Mason put the material from these twenty-four lectures into the *Manual of the Boston Academy of Music* (1834).

53. Root, *Story*, 52.

54. Root does not report whether Woodbridge shared in the class's proceeds.

55. Mason was an active composer, performer, and writer on music. But teaching and distributing music were the keys to his economic influence and success. The years 1848–52 must have been especially profitable for him. Broyles, *"Music of the Highest Class,"* 331, quotes *List of Persons, Copartnerships, and Corporations who were Taxed Twenty-Five Dollars and Upward, in the City of Boston, in the Year 1847, Specifying the Amount of the Tax and Real and Personal Estate, conformably to an Order of the City Council* (Boston, 1848), to show that Mason's total estate in 1847 was valued at $41,000, making him "far and away the wealthiest musician in Boston." As Pemberton, *Lowell Mason*, 135–36, shows, however, four years later, in *The Rich Men of Massachusetts* (Boston, 1852), Mason's worth was set at $100,000. "His musical productions . . . are in every household," that source reported, "and this also accounts for his wealth, which would have been far greater, were his benevolence less." Pratt, *American Music and Musicians*, 391, quotes a *Journal of Education* article estimating that by September 1857, "over a million copies" of Mason's various publications had been sold. In 1869, when the Oliver Ditson Company bought the assets of the Mason Brothers publishing firm, the plates of Lowell Mason's works alone were valued at "over $100,000," according to Pemberton, *Lowell Mason*, 175. Even without a detailed profile of Mason's financial affairs, it's not hard to see how he was able to accumulate a large enough fortune to travel twice to Europe (1837, 1852–53), to purchase a large and important music library, and to engage in benefactions, such as supporting the studies and work of Alexander Wheelock Thayer. (See Pemberton, *Lowell Mason*, 179–81). Mason seems to have been the first American patron of music who made his money inside rather than outside the field.

56. Among the different musical occupations named earlier in this chapter, Mason worked as everything but a manufacturer. (His son, Henry Mason, however, with the help of a $5,000 loan from his father, established the partnership of Mason and Hamlin in 1854, eventually a successful producer of reed organs. In 1882, the firm also began making pianos. See Pemberton, *Lowell Mason*, 177.) There is no evidence that composing or writing about music brought Mason much reward. And as a choir director and church organist his career follows the standard economic pattern of the performer as wage earner. It is in his other two callings, teaching music and distributing

it, that Mason moved into arenas where he could create surplus-value, the capital described by Attali.

Publishing is a business, of course, devoted to exploiting its products through reproduction and the widest circulation possible. The materials available about Mason's life have not been researched with publishing in mind. Nevertheless, there is every reason to think that much of Mason's fortune came from sales of his publications. Mason himself was never in the publishing business. Late in his life his sons, Lowell Mason, Jr., and Daniel Gregory Mason, became partners in publishing firms—first Mason and Law (1851–53), then Mason Brothers (1853–69)—that published their father's works. There is no evidence that Lowell Mason worked personally as a part of either firm. Perhaps the spectacular success of his first publishing venture explains his lack of direct involvement in the publishing trade. If, as seems possible, Mason was able to publish later works on an economic footing like that of *The Handel and Haydn Society Collection* (not an author's royalty arrangement but something more like a publisher's cut of the proceeds), then Mason would have been in a position to reap substantial profit with little risk—ample reason to stay out of a trade that already served his interests so well.

On the matter of Mason's teaching as a capitalistic rather than a wage-earning enterprise, the evidence, while incomplete, points in that direction. As a teacher, Mason was given to launching ambitious projects that proved to be more than he could handle himself. From 1832, early in his teaching of children's classes, Mason employed George J. Webb as an assistant; and shortly after the Boston Academy of Music was founded (1833), with Mason as its "professor," Webb was named as its "associate professor" (Pemberton, *Lowell Mason*, 64, 71). At the end of 1833, Mason opened singing classes in Salem, Massachusetts, to which he traveled while keeping up his Boston commitments. Mason himself taught some of the Salem classes, but he also hired Joseph A. Keller to teach others (Pemberton, *Lowell Mason*, 79–80). And after Mason began to collect money for teaching in the Boston public schools (1838), he hired assistants to do some of the teaching for him, including Jonathan Call Woodman, James C. Johnson, George F. Root, and others, paying them out of the $120 per year that school authorities had appropriated for music instruction in each school (Pemberton, *Lowell Mason*, 117–18). By 1844–45, Pemberton writes, "Mason was teaching without assistance in six of the Boston Public Schools and supervising ten teachers in ten other schools" (121). There is reason to think that Mason did not pass on to his assistants all the money he himself was paid for this teaching—that

he hired disciples and took a cut of the proceeds their teaching produced, an act that would qualify him as an entrepreneurial capitalist of teaching. Evidence, as noted, is unclear. G. F. Root, a member of Mason's circle in the late 1830s and early 1840s, reported that Artemis N. Johnson, his first musical mentor, "proposed a partnership for five years, in which he should have two-thirds and I one-third of what we both should earn, he to have the privilege of spending one of the years in Germany, the division of profits to be the same during his absence" (Root, *Story*, 24). Perhaps Mason himself followed a similar principle: an older, well-established pedagogue, in effect, charging younger colleagues for helping set them up in the teaching trade.

At least two opponents attacked Mason for being mercenary, or overpaid, or both (see Pemberton, *Lowell Mason*, 91–92, 122). But George F. Root did not feel himself exploited. Admitting that Mason made plenty of money, Root testified that he considered Mason "the most misjudged man in this respect that I ever knew. . . . I do not believe he ever made a plan to make money, unless when investing his surplus funds. In his musical work it was . . . a clear case . . . of seeking first what was right" (Root, *Story*, 85–86).

57. Pratt, *American Music and Musicians*, 31–34, 82, surveys the development of music education after the Civil War with particular attention to conservatories and colleges. See also pages 169–74 for a detailed list, geographically arranged, of music programs in American colleges and universities. For a detailed account of one important conservatory in the late nineteenth century, see Emmanuel Rubin, "Jeannette Meyers Thurber and the National Conservatory of Music," *American Music* 8 (1990): 294–325. See also George Martin, *The Damrosch Dynasty: America's First Family of Music* (Boston, 1983), especially on Frank Damrosch's founding of the Institute of Musical Art, 226–29.

58. For empirical confirmation of this point, see Charles H. Kaufman, *Music in New Jersey, 1655–1860: A Study of Musical Activity and Musicians in New Jersey from Its First Settlement to the Civil War* (Rutherford, N.J., 1981), especially the index of music teachers and schools, 235–46. When analyzed, the data there show that almost 60 percent of the 400 music teachers known to have been active there during the entire period covered by Kaufman's book first advertised in the decade 1850–60. Of course, a wider assortment of newspapers makes data more easily available in the later years than in the earlier ones; but the evidence of increasing demand for music teachers in those years is striking.

59. Buell E. Cobb, Jr., *The Sacred Harp: A Tradition and Its Music* (Athens, Ga., 1978), 63–67, surveys the singing school in its passage from New England to the South and links it to the development of shape notation. See also *Amerigrove* 4:233–34.

60. Edward Bailey Birge, *History of Public School Music in the United States*, new and augmented ed. (Washington, D.C., [1966]), dates the beginning of the school band movement at "about 1910." See pages 186–92 for Birge's survey of the subject.

61. F. O. Jones, ed., *A Handbook of American Music and Musicians Containing Biographies of American Musicians and Histories of the Principal Musical Institutions, Firms and Societies* (Canaseraga, N.Y., 1886; reprint, New York, 1971), describes the aims of Normal Institutes of music as "primarily, the preparation of persons desiring to teach music for that profession and the improvement of teachers already in the work, and, secondarily, the advancement of musical students in general in the science of music and the cultivation of musical taste and judgment." Normal Institutes, Jones notes, generally lasted four weeks; the first was

held by George F. Root in New York City in 1852 (78). "Musical conventions," which according to Jones were devoted to "social enjoyment and musical advancement," generally lasted three or four days. Jones traced their origin to New Hampshire in 1829 (42–43).

62. By "out west," Mathews meant Illinois. Birge, *History of Public School Music,* 80–83, quotes at length from Mathews's communication.

63. The bibliography on music in American higher education is substantial. It ranges from lists and comments in Pratt, *American Music and Musicians,* 33–34, 85–86; to studies of particular institutions, like Walter Raymond Spalding, *Music at Harvard: A Historical Review of Men and Events* (New York, 1935; reprint, New York, 1977) or J. Bunker Clark, *Music at KU: A History of the University of Kansas Music Department* (Lawrence, Kansas, 1986); to inquiries into particular disciplines, like W. Oliver Strunk, "State and Resources of Musicology in the United States," *Bulletin of the American Council of Learned Societies* 19 (1932); to personal interviews like Morris Risenhoover and Robert T. Blackburn, *Artists as Professors: Conversations with Musicians, Painters, Sculptors* (Urbana, Ill., 1976); to general surveys like that by James W. Pruett in *Amerigrove* 2:17–21. No study that I have found, however, concentrates on how university teaching in music has evolved as a means of supporting and subsidizing faculty members' professional activity.

64. Occupationally speaking, many musicians who teach in American research universities carry on dual careers, of which the second is professionally oriented. Typically, such men and women belong to "professional societies," like the American Musicological Society or the Society for Ethnomusicology. These organizations are only peripherally concerned, if at all, with the livelihood of their members, many of whom hold academic teaching posts. In that sense, they don't quite fit Bledstein's definition of a profession. On the other hand, as bodies providing forums for professional work, both oral and written, and as dispensers of professional awards and prizes, they do possess intellectual autonomy and the authority to pass judgment on work done in their fields. Moreover, acceptance or rejection of work in such professional forums may affect a teacher's occupational standing in his or her own institution.

65. From James Lyon, who contributed some half a dozen compositions to his *Urania* (Philadelphia, 1761), to William Billings, whose tunebooks (1770–94) are devoted almost entirely to his own music, to a large corps of American psalmodists who began to publish their compositions in the 1780s and 1790s, American composers produced some 5,000 sacred pieces by the end of the nineteenth century's first decade. This figure is a count made from a card index I prepared while completing Britton and Lowens, *American Sacred Music Imprints.* See that work, pages 9–11, for more on early American psalmodists as composers. As noted there on pages 27–28, the tunebook business directed income toward publishers rather than authors (composers, compilers).

66. Note, e.g., Thomson's and Attali's analysis, n. 12, above.

67. Biographical information on Reinagle is taken from Robert Hopkins's article in *Amerigrove* 4:26–27.

68. Sonneck, *Early Concert-Life*, 81–87, prints the programs of Philadelphia concerts in which Reinagle performed between 1786 and 1788. They include listings for all the examples mentioned except for the overture, which appears on page 128.

69. Richard J. Wolfe, *Early American Music Engraving and Printing: A History of Music Publishing in America from 1787 to 1825 with Commentary on Earlier and Later Practices* (Urbana, Ill., 1980), 41–42.

70. Wolfe, *Early American Music Engraving*, 116.

71. Wolfe, *Early American Music Engraving*, 116–17.

72. For a description of how things worked in sacred music publishing at that time, see Britton, et al., *American Sacred Music Imprints*, 26–29.

73. Oscar G. Sonneck, *A Bibliography of Early Secular American Music (18th Century)*, new ed., rev. and enlarged by William Treat Upton (Washington, D.C., 1945; reprint, New York, 1964), and Richard J. Wolfe, *Secular Music in America 1801–1825: A Bibliography*, 3 vols. (New York, 1964), show that through the Federal era, virtually all of the music brought out by American music publishers was written by European-born composers, a few of whom immigrated to this country. The next major bibliographical source, *Complete Catalogue of Sheet Music and Musical Works Published by the Board of Music Trade of the United States of America. 1870* (n.p., 1871; reprint, New York, 1973), carries a much higher proportion of American music, reflecting the vigorous growth of secular composition on this side of the Atlantic. Nevertheless, as Dena Epstein notes in her introduction to that volume, before an international copyright agreement was reached in 1891, American publishers had a strong economic incentive to issue foreign music because no rights to print it in this country were required (vi–x).

74. Julian Mates, *The American Musical Stage before 1800* (New Brunswick, N.J., 1962), 194–207, surveys the careers of Reinagle and other immigrant composers. The basic source on this tradition and its music is Roger Fiske, *English Theatre Music in the Eighteenth Century* (London, 1973).

75. Alexander Reinagle, *The Philadelphia Sonatas,* edited by Robert Hopkins, vol. 5 of Recent Researches in American Music (Madison, Wis., 1978), [xxv]. See page xi for dating information.

76. Alexander Reinagle, "America, Commerce, and Freedom" (Philadelphia, n.d.).

77. The first edition bears no date, but the work in which it appeared was probably first performed on 3 March 1794. "America, Commerce, and Freedom" was reprinted in collections of 1813 and 1815. See Reinagle, *Philadelphia Sonatas,* xix.

78. Richard Crawford, "American Music and Its Two Written Traditions," *Fontes Artis Musicae* 31 (1984): 79–84.

79. Readers will note that although some overlap exists between "composers'

music" and "performers' music" and the other pairs of polarities, the former pair applies only to written music.

80. The talent and dedication required to write performers' music of high quality has received relatively little scholarly attention, but it looms large in the lore of the songwriting profession. Alec Wilder, *American Popular Song: The Great Innovators, 1900–1950,* edited and with an introduction by James T. Maher (New York, 1972), uses the word "professional" honorifically, applying it to masters like Arlen, Berlin, Gershwin, Kern, Porter, and Rodgers and to the tradition of craftsmanship that lies behind their songs. Irving Berlin's "ferocious appetite for work" is a leitmotif of Lawrence Bergreen, *As Thousands Cheer: The Life of Irving Berlin* (New York, 1990). In a magazine interview in 1920, Berlin's work ethic took center-stage as he denounced "mentally lazy" or "uninitiated" lyric writers for piling up images and "thereby losing simplicity" (43, 170). For Berlin, more often than not, the simplicity of a good song was the outcome of toil. More recently, V. S. Naipaul has described a meeting with songwriter Bob McDill, who enjoys "a certain fame" in Nashville circles "for going to his office every working day to write his songs." For McDill, who began his career in rhythm and blues, then moved to country music, a "professional" attitude required having "a special relationship with singers. . . . You've got to say something that the singer wants to say and can identify with," he told Naipaul. "I had to learn this mind-set. I learned this subculture, which wasn't my own. The vocabulary is very limited. You have to learn to do big things with little words" (V. S. Naipaul, *A Turn in the South* [New York, 1989], 244–45).

Charles Hamm, *Yesterdays: Popular Song in America* (New York, 1979), describes in hierarchical terms the institutional background of conflicts in vernacular songwriting since the 1950s. On one side were establishment songwriters who belonged to ASCAP (the American Society of Composers, Authors, and Publishers), the country's oldest performing rights society; on the other were those who belonged to BMI (Broadcast Music, Inc.)—"a new organization," Hamm says, "hastily formed . . . to produce music for broadcast purposes; its membership was made up of composers and lyricists who had not been invited to join ASCAP, many of them young and others who had been involved with sorts of music not favored by ASCAP songwriters and publishers" (389; see also 338–39, 376, 401–2). According to Gavin McFarlane, writing on performing right societies, "BMI's initial success was largely attributable to its open-door policy. For the first time, writers of country music, jazz, gospel, rhythm-and-blues, and other types of music that had not previously been eligible to earn performing money could share in performing rights income" (*Amerigrove* 3:504).

81. For example, Clarence Eddy (1851–1937), identified in *Amerigrove* 2:9, as "the leading organist of his time," was also described in Jones, *Handbook,* 52, as a composer of "canons, preludes and fugues, and some other organ music, all of high order." B. J. Lang (1837–1909), a pianist said in 1886 to occupy "a leading place in Boston's musical affairs" (Jones, *Handbook,* 84) and by Steven Ledbetter in *Amerigrove* (3:10) to have been "a remarkable . . . organizer" and

outstanding ensemble performer and accompanist," composed "an oratorio, *David*, as well as symphonies, overtures, piano pieces, church music, and songs" but published little of it. Frédéric Louis Ritter, Louis Charles Elson, Oscar G. Sonneck, and John Tasker Howard, all remembered as earlier historians of American music, were active as composers at different times in their lives.

82. Thomson, *State of Music*, 77.

83. Composer George B. Wilson of the University of Michigan, when asked by the author how many American composers of composers' music there are— that is, how many people in the United States write such music and consider themselves composers—replied that the figure he uses is 40,000. Wilson says he first heard that number from Gunther Schuller "in the 1970s." He notes several reasons a reliable figure remains elusive: first, the designation "composer" is amorphous; second, no umbrella organization exists to which even a majority of composers belong; and third, the music of many composers remains unpublished and hence unavailable. The American Music Center in New York, founded in 1940 "to encourage the creation, performance, publication, and distribution of American music," claimed 1,200 members in 1985, most but not all of them composers (*Amerigrove* 1:38). The American Society of University Composers in 1984 gave its membership as 900 (*Amerigrove* 1:40), presumably overlapping some with that of the American Music Center. ASCAP has more than 35,000 members; but that number includes lyricists and music publishers as well as composers of popular or "performers' " music (*Amerigrove* 1:39).

The notion that the supply of new American composers' music far exceeds the demand for it is reflected in the contents of W. McNeil Lowry, ed., *The Performing Arts and American Society* (Englewood Cliffs, N.J., 1978). This book provided background reading for "the Fifty-third American Assembly," which in 1977 "brought together at Arden House, Harriman, New York, a group of sixty-one Americans—performers, trustees, critics, directors, managers, and teachers from the worlds of ballet, modern dance, opera, theater, and symphony—to discuss *The Future of The Performing Arts*," especially in its economic dimensions (v). According to the official report, no composers were invited. But composer Roger Reynolds has told me that he attended the assembly and "was noisy."

84. Louise Varèse, *Varèse: A Looking-Glass Diary*, vol. 1, *1883–1928* (New York, 1972), shows that in 1921–22, when he was organizing the International Composers' Guild, Mrs. Whitney gave Varèse "An allowance" of $200 a month (155, 165–66, 170). She also paid the rent of a Paris apartment for Varèse and his wife during the summer of 1922 (194). Rita Mead, *Henry Cowell's New Music 1925–1936: The Society, the Music Editions, and the Recordings*, Studies in Musicology (Ann Arbor, 1981), writes that Harriette Miller, "a wealthy woman from New York," subsidized Ruggles "for years" and eventually "bestow[ed] a lifetime annuity upon him" (14–15). Aaron Copland and Vivian Perlis, *Copland: 1900 through 1942* (New York, 1984), reports Mrs. Wertheim's gift of $1,000 to Copland in 1924 (110, 112) and another of $1,800 to support Roy Harris's study

in Paris in 1926 (129). Wertheim also financed Cos Cob Press, founded in 1929, which Copland describes as "an early effort to assist young American composers to publish music that would not be taken on by established publishers" (157). See also Carol J. Oja, "Women Patrons and Crusaders for Modernist Music in New York: The 1920s," typescript, consulted in manuscript through the kindness of the author.

85. Gillian Anderson, writing on Mrs. Coolidge in *Notable American Women: The Modern Period, a Biographical Dictionary,* ed. Barbara Sicherman and Carol Hurd Green (Cambridge, Mass., 1980), 160–62, notes that the Elizabeth Sprague Coolidge Foundation at the Library of Congress, "which was to be administered by the Library's Music Division," produced "a yearly income of approximately $25,000." In addition another gift of $60,000, "later substantially increased . . . made possible the construction at the Library of the Coolidge Auditorium, a hall for chamber music." Frank Bridge and Gian Francesco Malipiero are two composers to whom Mrs. Coolidge gave long-term support in the 1920s and 1930s. Later, however, "her musical efforts were channeled through the Coolidge Foundation which, with her encouragement, supported modern music." Copland's *Appalachian Spring* (1944), choreographed by Martha Graham, was a foundation commission, as were additional new works by Bartók, Piston, Prokofiev, and Stravinsky. Pratt, *American Music and Musicians,* 130, reports all the works and many of the artists who performed at the first two Berkshire Festivals of Chamber Music (1918–19), sponsored by Mrs. Coolidge and held at her summer home in Pittsfield, Massachusetts. Reporting that a prize of $1,000 was offered "for the best chamber-work submitted" each year, Pratt notes that the winners were Tadeusz Iarecki in 1918, Ernest Bloch in 1919, and Francesco Malipiero in 1920.

86. Aaron Copland was the first recipient. He received a fellowship of $2,500 for the academic year 1925–26 and a renewal the next year (Copland and Perlis, *Copland,* 116). Other early recipients include Roger Sessions (1926, 1927), Roy Harris (1927, 1929), Robert Russell Bennett (1928, 1929), Randall Thompson (1929, 1930), and Otto Luening (1930, 1931) (John Simon Guggenheim Foundation, *Directory of Fellows 1925–1974* [New York, 1975]).

87. *Amerigrove* 2:172–73 briefly describes the foundation's goals—"to promote the composition and performance of contemporary music and restore the composer to his rightful position at the center of musical life"—and activities. The article also contains a list of composers (and works) the foundation has commissioned. See also Deena Rosenberg and Bernard Rosenberg, *The Music Makers* (New York, 1979), 378–92, for an interview with Paul Fromm, the foundation's originator.

88. The Ford Foundation, *Annual Report,* 1957 (1 October 1956–30 September 1957), 19, reports a grant of $210,000 "for a three-year experiment by the American Music Center and six American symphony orchestras in multiple regional performances of new symphonic works." The next year, ten classical singers and instrumentalists received grants-in-aid, plus the right "to name American composers to write compositions for them to perform. The foun-

dation will pay the composers' commissions plus additional rehearsal time" (*Annual Report*, 1958, 34). In 1959, the foundation appropriated $950,000 for the commissioning and performance of new American operas over the next eight years (*Annual Report*, 1959, 47–48). And the next year, a three-year grant of $302,000 was made to enable "young composers to write for and work with the musical ensembles of high-school systems." The *Annual Report*, 1960, 49, describes that program as follows:

> Conducted jointly by the Foundation and the National Music Council, the project is also intended to acquaint high-school students with contemporary music written for their specific needs and abilities, and to expand the repertory of secondary-school music throughout the United States. Under the new appropriation, the schools themselves will help finance the resident-composer project, with the ultimate aim of making it an integral part of educational and musical life of the country. By 1964, a total of about forty composers and about forty communities in the United States will have participated. In 1960, twelve composers in their twenties and thirties received stipends of $5,000 plus dependency and travel funds.

The Young Composers program was renewed for six years in 1963, this time in a grant of $1,380,000 to the Music Educators National Conference. The composers who worked in high schools during these years, as noted in annual reports, include Emma Lou Diemer, Martin Mailman, Conrad Susa, Donald Erb, Philip Glass, Salvatore Martirano, Richard Wernick, and J. Peter Schickele. See Ford Foundation, *Contemporary Music for Schools: A Catalog of Works Written by Composers Participating in the Young Composers Project, 1959–1964, Sponsored by the Ford Foundation and the National Music Council* (Washington, D.C., 1966).

89. Among its many benefactions to the creation of new music, one of the Rockefeller Foundation's most notable was a sum of $500,000 between 1953 and 1955 that allowed the Louisville Commissioning Project, first established with resources from the Greater Louisville Fund for the Arts (1948), to commission works for the Louisville [Kentucky] Orchestra. See *Amerigrove* 3:116–17, and Jeanne Belfy, *The Louisville Orchestra New Music Project: An American Experiment in the Patronage of International Contemporary Music: Selected Composers' Letters to the Louisville Orchestra.* University of Louisville Publications in Musicology, no. 2 (Louisville, 1983). In 1963, the foundation established a Cultural Development Program that announced three missions related to music: "the development of creators and performers, the dissemination of new American music, and the encouragement of critical and interpretive writings about music." See the Rockefeller Foundation, *President's Five-Year Review and Annual Report 1968* (New York, 1968), 94. Among Rockefeller-sponsored programs in the years 1963–68 was a joint project of the Atlanta Symphony Orchestra and Spelman College. According to the report (95): "Of the 15 composers whose works were read and performed, eight were Negroes, and of this group only one had ever had a composition performed by a major American orchestra. The works of four of the hitherto unknown Negro composers—T. J. Anderson, Frederick C. Tillis, George Walker, and Olly Wilson—were subsequently played by the Bal-

timore and Minneapolis orchestras, and at least one is scheduled to be repeated by the Atlanta Symphony Orchestra in its subscription series."

90. Carolyn Bryant, *And the Band Played On* (Washington, D.C., 1975), 8, notes that the United States Marine Corps Band was "officially organized in 1798." Elise K. Kirk, *Music at the White House: A History of the American Spirit* (Urbana, Ill., 1986), contains information on activities of the U.S. Marine Band as "the president's own" ensemble. (See Kirk's index, pages 453–54, for citations.)

91. See *Amerigrove* 4:567. As noted in Dick Netzer, *The Subsidized Muse: Public Support for the Arts in the United States* (Cambridge, 1978), 54, "the purpose of the program was simply to reduce the unemployment caused by the Depression." The Federal Music Project sponsored a Composers' Forum-Laboratory to encourage the composition and performance of new music. Barbara A. Zuck, *A History of Musical Americanism*, Studies in Musicology, no. 19 (Ann Arbor, Mich., 1980), 170–76, describes the Forum-Laboratory's activities.

92. See *Amerigrove* 3:325–26. Christopher Pavlakis, *The American Music Handbook* (New York, 1974), 63–68, provides a good description of the National Endowment for the Arts programs in the early 1970s, showing that little of the agency's grant money goes to composers and composition. *Amerigrove* 1:96–97 contains a list of cash prizes exceeding $500 that are available to composers.

93. *Amerigrove* 3:502–5 offers a concise introduction to "performing right societies" by Gavin McFarlane. As noted there, "in music, the most important right is the right of public performance, known as the 'performing right.' " (Others include copyright, the right to reproduce the notation in published form, and the "mechanical right," the right "to recover musical works in sound recordings.") McFarlane writes:

> It is almost always impossible for an individual copyright holder to receive royalties on more than a very small number of the performances on which they are due. Even if he could locate a few of the performances, he would not always have the means or the expertise to negotiate appropriate royalties and issue licenses. Collection for performances nationwide or overseas would be out of the question for the individual or small publishing company. Societies have therefore been set up in most countries to collect royalties for the use of copyrighted music and to distribute the revenue among the parties entitled to it." (502–3)

The two main performing-rights organizations in the United States are ASCAP (founded in 1914) and BMI (founded in 1940). The two organizations have different formulas for distributing income. See, e.g., Russell Sanjek, *American Popular Music and Its Business*, vol. 3, *From 1900 to 1984* (New York, 1988), 298–99, 403–4, et passim for detailed information on both.

94. In a famous article of 1958, originally titled "The Composer as Specialist" but published as "Who Cares If You Listen," Babbitt writes:

> The time has passed when the normally well-educated man without special preparation can understand the most advanced work in, for example, math-

ematics, philosophy, and physics. Advanced music, to the extent that it reflects the knowledge and originality of the informed composer, scarcely can be expected to appear more intelligible than these arts and sciences to the person whose musical education usually has been even less extensive than his background in other fields. (Quoted from Gilbert Chase, ed., *The American Composer Speaks: A Historical Anthology, 1770–1965* [(Baton Rouge, La.) 1966], 239)

95. Thomson, *State of Music*, Chaps. 6 and 7. Chap. 7 identifies four sources of income for a composer (whom Thomson always describes as male):

1. "non-musical jobs or earned income from non-musical sources"

2. "unearned income from all sources" ("money from home" and "other people's money," including patronage, commissions, and prizes)

3. "other men's music, or selling the by-products of his musical education" (e.g., performing, teaching, publishing, lecturing, writing)

4. "the just rewards of his labor" (e.g., royalties and performing-rights fees).

In Chap. 7, Thomson describes with gleeful irreverence the kinds of music that each income source is most likely to produce. Admitting that "art-music composers who live off their just share in the profits of the commercial exploitation of their work . . . are almost non-existent in America," Thomson pays respect to their achievement.

Of all the composing musicians, this group presents in its music the greatest variety both of subject-matter and of stylistic orientation, the only limit to such variety being what the various musical publics at any given moment will take. Even the individual members of the group show variety in their work from piece to piece. This variety is due in part to their voluntary effort to keep their public interested and to enlarge their market. (Stylistic "evolution" is good publicity nowadays.) A good part of it is due also to the variety of usages that are coverable by commercially ordered music. Theater, concert, opera, church, and war demand a variety of solutions for individual esthetic cases according to the time, the place, the subject, the number and skill of the available executants, the social class, degree of musical cultivation, and size of the putative public. Music made for no particular circumstance or public is invariably egocentric. Music made for immediate usage, especially if that usage is proposed to the composer by somebody who has an interest in the usage, is more objective and more varied. (122–23)

CHAPTER 3

1. "Concert" should be understood to include theatrical presentations that feature music (opera, operetta, musical comedy) and, secondarily, performances that are facsimiles of the concert: recordings, radio and television broadcasts, and film.

2. The longest continuing institutional support in the United States has come from churches and the military, both of which have required music to carry out their functions. A complete survey of musical performance as a profession in this country would give proper attention to both. Philip Hart, *Orpheus in the New World: The Symphony Orchestra as an American Cultural Institution* (New York, 1973), 100, notes that in the late nineteenth century, one of the issues that contributed to the formation of musicians' unions "was the performance of military bands in situations where civilian musicians felt that their employment was being jeopardized." As for American churches, for some two centuries they have supported complex music-making and musical professionalism in the name of worship. Since the nineteenth century, singers and choir directors have found paid work in churches. Many important American composers have also been organists, including George Frederick Bristow, Dudley Buck, George W. Chadwick, Arthur Foote, Charles Ives, John Knowles Paine, Horatio Parker, and, in a later generation, Virgil Thomson. F. O. Jones, ed., *A Handbook of American Music and Musicians* (Canaseraga, N.Y., 1886; reprint, New York, 1971) suggests the instrument's importance to American musical life around the time of its publication; approximately one-sixth of its 285 biographical sketches are of organists. The organ has inspired a sizable bibliography. (A helpful introductory one may be found in *Amerigrove* 3:448.) But it centers on instruments and builders and says little about players. For a brief note on organists before 1810 see Allen Perdue Britton, Irving Lowens, and completed by Richard Crawford, *American Sacred Music Imprints, 1698–1810: A Bibliography* (Worcester, Mass., 1990), 22–26. Like the military, church musicians do not perform for a paying audience. This chapter concentrates on performers who have.

3. R. Allen Lott, "Bernard Ullman: Nineteenth-Century American Impresario," in *A Celebration of American Music: Words and Music in Honor of H. Wiley Hitchcock*, edited by Richard Crawford, R. Allen Lott, and Carol J. Oja (Ann Arbor, Mich., 1990), 176.

4. Lewis Hallam, Jr. (1740–1808), came to America in 1752 with the American Company of Comedians, managed by his father. When Lewis Hallam, Sr., died in Jamaica around 1756, his widow married David Douglass, who reorganized and managed the company with her. Kenneth Silverman, *A Cultural History of the American Revolution: Painting, Music, Literature, and the Theatre in the Colonies and the United States from the Treaty of Paris to the Inauguration of George Washington, 1763–1789* (New York, 1976), notes that by 1763 the Douglass-Hallam New American Company "in effect monopolized the theater in the North American colonies" (60). In those early years, as Silverman notes, the company performed ballad operas and also other works that "demanded music, and gave employment to local musicians, professional and amateur, half a dozen of whom were needed for the theater orchestra, sometimes more" (63). By 1765, several singer-actors were performing with the company, including Miss Wainwright and Stephen Woolls, pupils of English composer Thomas Arne, and "tenor Thomas Wall, who had worked as a musician at Drury Lane and Haymarket Theaters" and

who "gave guitar lessons wherever the company played" (93). After the Revolutionary War, Lewis Hallam, Jr., and John Henry took over the New American Company. As Silverman notes, in addition to a corps of singers, in 1786 they employed "several of the recent musical emigrants, probably enlarging the theater orchestra: the French violinist Henri Capron, the German Philip Phile, and the English harpsichordist John Bentley, who later conducted the orchestra" (539). When Henry and Hallam built a new theater, Harmony Hall, in Charleston, they opened it with "a three-hour 'Grand Concert of Music in Three Acts' " including dancing and "a harpsichord performance by a 'foreign Gentleman, lately arrived in this City' " (543).

5. Thomas Wignell (ca. 1753–1803), a cousin of Hallam, joined the New American Company in 1774. When the company returned from wartime exile, Wignell was one of its leading comic stars. In 1791, he joined forces with Alexander Reinagle to form a theatrical company to occupy a new theater on Philadelphia's Chestnut Street. Wignell hired outstanding singers and players from England to perform with the new company. See n. 9, below. See also *Amerigrove* 4:524–25.

6. Oscar G. Sonneck, *Early Concert-Life in America* (Leipzig, 1907; reprint, New York, 1978), 175.

7. Sonneck, *Early Concert-Life*, 52.

8. In the Philadelphia *Pennsylvania Journal* of 8 November 1770, John Gualdo advertised that after an upcoming concert, he would "have the room put in order for a Ball, likewise there will be a genteel Refreshment laid out in the upper room for those Ladies and Gentlemen who shall chuse to Dance, or remain to see the Ball." He added: "For the Ball he has composed six new minuets, with proper cadence for dancing" (Sonneck, *Early Concert-Life,* 74).

9. Sonneck, in *Early Opera in America* (New York, 1915; reprint, New York, 1963), for example, describes the opening of Philadelphia's New Theater in Chestnut Street in 1793. Wignell, he writes, convinced "some financiers of Philadelphia that the erection of a new theater garrisoned with a company to defy comparison would pay," whereupon "a stock company" was formed with Wignell and Alexander Reinagle as managers. Wignell, Sonneck reports, then "went abroad to recruit a company" (113). He returned with Mrs. Oldmixon [*née* Miss George] "of the Haymarket Theatre and Drury Lane, who was equally famous as an oratorio singer," Miss Broadhurst, "whom Wignell captured at Covent Garden when she was barely out of her teens," plus "Mr. and Mrs. Marshall, the Warrell family, and the Darleys, who all enjoyed a good reputation in England," and Mr. and Mrs. William Francis, "popular and clever dancers and pantomimists." The company's orchestra—"probably the best yet united in this country"—was led by George Gillingham, "celebrated violinist from London," and "was largely composed of Frenchmen" (115–17).

10. Two problems make this a difficult point to document without much more biographical study. For one thing, determining what musicians of this period were able to earn a livelihood chiefly as performers in America is not easy. For

another, while we know that virtually all of the most prominent performers were foreign-born, there are many others—church organists, theater orchestra players, and bandsmen, for example—about whom we know neither birthplace nor more than the sketchiest career details. The musicians who dominated public musical life before 1840 include both immigrant professionals—James Hewitt, Benjamin Carr, George P. Jackson, S. P. Taylor, Gottlieb Graupner, George Gillingham, George J. Webb, Charles Zeuner—and performers who after extended visits returned to the Old Country, including Thomas Philipps, Charles Incledon, John Braham, the Garcia Opera troupe, Henry Russell, and Maria Caradori Allan. The former have been studied enough to show that performance was only part of their musical vocation. The latter were received with fanfare as star performers and seldom stayed more than a few years on this side of the Atlantic.

All evidence indicates that performers in theatrical companies were foreign-born. Benjamin Carr's popular ballad, "The Little Sailor Boy," was advertised on its title page in 1800 as "sung at the theatres & other public places in Philadelphia, Baltimore, New York, &c. by Messrs. J. Darley, Williamson, Miss Broadhurst, Mrs. Hodgkinson & Mrs. Oldmixon." See Oscar G. Sonneck, *A Bibliography of Early Secular American Music,* rev. by William Treat Upton (Washington, D.C., 1945; reprint, New York, 1964), 233. Thanks to Sonneck's research, we know that all of these singers had been recruited for the American stage from London. However, when we find in Richard J. Wolfe, *Secular Music in America 1801–25: A Bibliography* (New York, 1964), No. 605, that Henry Bishop's "Echo Song" was being sung "by Mrs. Burke at the theatre, Philadelphia," [1818?] or that Bishop's "popular Scotch ballad . . . Donald" (No. 601) in 1819 was sung "with great applause by Mrs. French at her vocal concerts" (57), without more research of the kind Sonneck did for earlier years, we have no way of confirming our hunch that Mrs. Burke and Mrs. French were also immigrant professional singers.

In *Amerigrove* 3:448, William Osborne notes that in the late eighteenth century "organists, nearly all of them European immigrants, began to preside" in American churches. He lists ten organists active before 1850, of whom only Samuel P. Jackson, the son of an English-born organ builder, was a native of the United States. From that evidence, one might think it fair to assume that virtually all earlier American organists were foreign-born. However, of the twenty compilers of American tunebooks before 1810 who worked as organists, only nine are known to have been immigrants. Jonathan Badger, Daniel Bayley, Jr., Peter Erben, U. K. Hill, Francis Hopkinson, and Oliver Shaw were all born in this country, and the birthplaces of Adam Arnold, William Cooper, Conrad Doll, and David Ott are unknown. If half a dozen American-born organists, if not more, were active before 1810, it seems likely that, as the population grew and prejudices against organs dissolved in some congregations, many more homegrown Americans performed as church organists. See the biographical sketches in Britton et al., *American Sacred Music.* As shown in Chapter 2, however, there is no evidence that organ playing alone formed a livelihood at that time.

One imagines that bands provided an opportunity for many American-born musicians to play in the early nineteenth century, but it seems unlikely that many at that time could have earned their living as bandsmen. Of the best-known keyed bugle virtuosi active before 1820, Richard Willis was Irish and Frank Johnson, according to Eileen Southern, hailed from Martinique or the West Indies. See Southern, *Biographical Dictionary of Afro-American and African Musicians* (Westport, Conn., 1982), 205. Thomas Dodworth, patriarch of the family that sparked New York City's band world beginning in the 1830s, was an English immigrant who arrived with two sons in 1828. The chief American-born actor in this drama was keyed bugle virtuoso Edward Kendall, a native of Newport, Rhode Island, and founder of the Boston Brass Band (1835).

11. Stuart Bruchey, *Enterprise: The Dynamic Economy of a Free People* (Cambridge, Mass., 1990), notes that "in the closing decades of the antebellum period . . . new groups rose to challenge the privileged positions of vested corporations. The note of egalitarianism is struck again and again in the political discourse of the time . . . [and one finds] hostility to the privileged corporation possessing exclusive rights entrenched in law" (208). A case decided in the U.S. Supreme Court in 1837 symbolizes the conflict between older and newer attitudes. The original investors in the Charles River Bridge, which linked Boston and Charlestown, claimed the right to collect tolls in perpetuity. The court, however, ruled that unless "granted explicitly by the corporate charter," those investors could have no "monopoly rights to income from public utilities." In Bruchey's analysis, the conflict was between an "older elite" and "the forces of change." The court came down on the side of the latter, in the name of economic development and competition (212). With such development came urbanization, a wider distribution of wealth, and an increase in leisure time, all of which helped to widen the available audience for music.

For the aristocratically minded Henry Adams, the same period brought technological progress that shattered the world into which he had been born. In a single month, he wrote in his autobiography,

> The old universe was thrown into the ash-heap and a new one created. He [Adams] and his eighteenth-century, troglodytic Boston were suddenly cut apart—separated forever . . . by the opening of the Boston and Albany Railroad; the appearance of the first Cunard steamers in the bay; and the telegraphic messages which carried from Baltimore to Washington the news that Henry Clay and James K. Polk were nominated for the Presidency. This was in May, 1844; he was six years old. (Quoted from Peter Baida, *Poor Richard's Legacy: American Business Values from Benjamin Franklin to Donald Trump* [New York, 1990], 170–71)

12. The years after 1815 saw the start of "a transportation revolution" in the United States, which by 1850 had resulted in 3,700 miles of canals and 9,000 miles of rail. See James McPherson, *Battle Cry of Freedom: The Civil War Era*

(New York, 1988), 11–12. And that made tours by performers and troupes much more feasible than they had been before. As the journals of the Hutchinson Family Singers show, however, all touring did not depend on the railroads. When, in July 1842, the Hutchinsons set out on their first tour from their native Milford, New Hampshire, they drove their own carriage. They spent most of August in the area of Albany, New York, then headed eastward into Massachusetts, giving their first concert in Boston on 15 September. By the end of the month, they were in Portsmouth, New Hampshire, and in October their itinerary took them as far north as Portland, Maine, as well. In November they were back in Boston for several more concerts. The tour ended with their return to Milford in early December. Occasionally during those months, members of the family took the train, as on 7 September 1842, when Asa wrote: "Abigail & I took the Carrs for Boston" from Lynn, Massachusetts. But, with its frequent references to boarding their team of horses, and the description of their return to Milford—their horse "was completely enveloped in the snow drifts"—the Hutchinsons' journal makes clear the manner of conveyance through the five months of their first concert tour. See Dale Cockrell, ed. and annotator, *Excelsior: Journals of the Hutchinson Family Singers, 1842–1846* (Stuyvesant, N.Y., 1989), 1–85, passim, especially 82, 89; and 388–89. References such as "we returned to Lynn by stage" (111) and "we left Boston for New York . . . in the Cars via of Wo[r]cester and Norwich. And from thence to N.Y. . . . in the Steamboat Cleopatra" (115) show that beginning with the family's second tour (May–June 1843) they relied on public transportation.

13. William Brooks, writing in *Amerigrove* 1:152, calls Jenny Lind's concerts in 1850–51, arranged by P. T. Barnum, "the first major tour in the USA to be managed by a nonperformer." Brooks adds that the tour also "marked the rise of a separate class of agents and promoters. Barnum's methods influenced popular entertainers as well as impresarios such as Max Maretzek and the Strakosch brothers; his impact on America's music industry was lasting and profound." R. Allen Lott's research, however, reveals that Leopold DeMeyer's first American tour in 1845 was managed "unobtrusively" by his brother-in-law, G. C. Reitheimer. Moreover, when Henri Herz arrived in 1846, it was with Bernard Ullman as his manager. See Lott, "Bernard Ullman," 175–76.

Jones, *Handbook*, 163, lists forty-four "famous artists" who "traveled under the management" of Max and Maurice Strakosch, including Teresa Carreño, Anna Louise Cary, Karl Formes, Louis Moreau Gottschalk, Tom Karl, Clara Louise Kellogg, Edward Mollenhauer, Christine Nilsson, Euphrosyne Parepa-Rosa, Adelina Patti, Sigismond Thalberg, and Henri Vieuxtemps.

14. Britton et al., *American Sacred Music*, 21, touches on the early history of musical societies. In bringing together local musicians for the improvement of musical life and taste, these organizations formed the model for the Boston Handel and Haydn Society, founded in 1815 and called in 1886 "the largest and most noted musical association of the United States" (Jones, *Handbook*, 18). Jones's articles on cities—especially Boston, Cincinnati, and New York—center

chiefly on musical societies active in each. Vera Brodsky Lawrence, *Strong on Music: The New York Music Scene in the Days of George Templeton Strong, 1836–1875,* vol. I, *Resonances 1836–1850* (New York, 1988), is full of information on such groups in antebellum New York City. For example, she notes the founding of the New York Sacred Music Society as a group of amateur choristers devoted to performing sacred masterworks, especially oratorios (xxxviii). And she reports that by 1836 their oratorio concerts featured as soloists "vocal luminaries from one of the theatres" (31). Here and in other cities with theaters, musical society orchestras drew on the services of local professionals.

15. Katherine K. Preston, "Travelling Opera Troupes in the United States, 1825–1860," Ph.D. diss., City University of New York, 1989, a comprehensive study, is forthcoming (1993) from the University of Illinois Press as *Opera on the Road: Traveling Opera Troupes in the United States, 1825–60.* Lawrence Levine, *Highbrow/Lowbrow: The Emergence of Cultural Hierarchy in America* (Cambridge, Mass., 1988), cites Preston's work in progress, especially on pages 88–89 and 95.

16. DaPonte assisted with Garcia's production of Mozart's *Don Giovanni,* whose libretto he had written. See *Amerigrove* 1:580.

17. According to Lawrence, *Strong on Music,* each subscriber to the Astor Place venture agreed to pay $75 per year for five years in return for seventy-five admissions to the opera house each year (454). Management of the house was leased to Antonio Sanquirico and Salvatore Patti, both singer-impresarios (457).

18. Karen Ethel Ahlquist, "Opera, Theatre, and Audience in Antebellum New York," Ph.D. diss., University of Michigan, 1991, Chap. 4. See page 313 for prices and page 312 for her analysis: "Efforts between 1847 and 1858 to find a profitable price scale eventually produced the most inclusive policy: the most expensive seats were priced high, while the cheapest cost only slightly more than at the theatres. This policy was developed as managers responded to competition and to calls for more 'democratic' prices."

19. New Orleans's operatic history can be traced back to the building of an opera house in 1792 and to performances of operas there before 1800. From 1805 such performances, under managers Jean Baptiste Fournier and Louis Tabary, seem to have been continuous. By the 1820s, John Davis's company at the Théâtre d'Orléans, stocked with singers, dancers, and orchestra players from France, was touring the northeastern part of the country; six tours between 1827 and 1833 took the company to such cities as Boston, New York, Philadelphia, and Baltimore. The opening of the lavish French Opera House in 1859, and the company assembled there by Charles Boudousquié, continued the city's strong tradition of foreign-language opera performance. See *Amerigrove* 3:341, which claims New Orleans as the first city on the North American continent to have a permanent opera company.

20. Unfamiliarity with plot, language, and the dramatic conventions of opera plus a distrust of foreign imports were deterrents for some, however. See Levine,

Highbrow, quoting Walt Whitman, who wrote in the 1840s that Americans had long enough received Europe's "tenors and her buffos, her operatic troupers and her vocalists, . . . listened to and applauded the songs made for a different state of society . . . made for royal ears . . . and it is time that such listening and receiving should cease" (94n.). Diarist Philip Hone, a former mayor of New York, had complained earlier: "We want to understand the language; we cannot endure to sit by and see the performers splitting their sides with laughter, and we not take the joke; dissolved in 'briny tears,' and we not permitted to sympathize with them; or running each other through the body, and we devoid of the means of condemning or justifying the act" (quoted from Charles Hamm, *Yesterdays: Popular Song in America* [New York, 1979], 69).

21. Lawrence, *Strong on Music,* 61, 133, 135, 218.

22. See Hamm, *Yesterdays,* Chap. 4. Hamm writes that "the music of Italian opera . . . was familiar to Americans in a wide variety of forms and at different cultural levels" (78).

23. The foreign-language opera first introduced to the northeastern United States was Italian. But French opera had played in New Orleans from even before the start of the century. German works made their appearance during the 1830s, though sometimes in Italian translations.

24. Lawrence, *Strong on Music,* 232. Hans Nathan, *Dan Emmett and the Rise of Early Negro Minstrelsy* (Norman, Okla., 1977) is the basic source on minstrelsy. See Chap. 8, 113–22, for circumstances of the Virginia Minstrels' first performance. George B. Woodridge is identified as their agent, but no details of his work on their behalf are given (see 116, 119, 138). According to Nathan, in 1839 banjo player Whitlock was being managed by P. T. Barnum (115). Whitlock later performed with Barnum's circus (*Amerigrove* 4:521).

25. Sheet-music covers reflect the change. From its establishment in America in the late 1780s, the sheet trade had emblazoned covers with the names of well-known performers identified with the pieces they published. Hamm, *Yesterdays,* 73, reprints the cover of "Once a King There Chanced to Be" by Rossini, "Sung by Mrs. Austin in the much admired new Opera of Cinderella." (Lawrence, *Strong on Music,* 40n., notes that *Cinderella* starring the English soprano Elizabeth Austin opened in New York in January 1831, so the sheet music must come from shortly after that time.) A few years later, however, the covers of Stephen Foster's early songs featured artists of another stripe. "Written for and sung by Joseph Murphy of the Sable Harmonists," read a legend on "Lou'siana Belle" (1847), and "Foster's Ethiopian Melodies as sung by the Christy & Campbell Minstrels and New Orleans Serenaders" appeared on the cover of "[Gwine to Run All Night] De Camptown Races" (1850).

26. The career of Francis Johnson (1792–1844) raises two related issues: performance style and concert format. On the first, Eileen Southern, *The Music of Black Americans,* 2d ed. (New York, 1983), reports that, as early as 1819, an observer identified Johnson as a musician with "a remarkable taste in distorting a sentimental, simple, and beautiful song, into a reel, jig, or country dance"

(108). Southern goes on to note that Johnson's surviving music, which consists only of "piano arrangements of band music or melodic skeletons . . . hardly seems extraordinary." Yet, she observes, "since Johnson competed successfully with white musical organizations for public patronage against the overwhelming odds of race discrimination, his music must have gained something in performance that is not evident in the scores" (113). As for concert format, Johnson and four of his bandsmen spent six months performing in England in the fall and winter of 1837–38. In January 1838, Londoners (and Johnson and his men) had their first chance to hear a "promenade concert." Introduced by Philippe Musard in Paris in 1833, the innovation, according to Southern, was "the concept of combining a program of light classical music with a promenade." Johnson took key ingredients of the idea back home: "the programs consisting of operatic airs and quadrilles; the use of the 'new' cornet-à-pistons and ophecleide; the arrangements to which the audience could promenade between Parts One and Two of the program; and the small admission fees." He introduced his "Concerts à la Musard" to Philadelphians during the Christmas season of 1838–39. Southern calls them "wildly successful; the press reported that thousands attended each night, and hundreds had to be turned away" (109–10).

The Hutchinson Family Singers recorded a meeting with Johnson and his men in the Pittsfield, Massachusetts, railroad depot on 1 September 1842. "The old Fellow was quite well," they noted, but then added, "Sadly he did not do so well in Albany as he Expected." Asa Hutchinson commented, "They are a *Rough* sett of Negroes" (Cockrell, *Excelsior*, 80).

27. Robert C. Toll, *Blacking Up: The Minstrel Show in Nineteenth-Century America* (New York, 1974), 46.

28. Russell Sanjek, *American Popular Music and Its Business: The First Four Hundred Years*, vol. 2, *From 1790 to 1909* (New York, 1988), 155.

29. See Sanjek, *American Popular Music*, 2:155; also *Amerigrove* 4:37–38. Rice began playing his character on stage in 1828. In the *Amerigrove* article Robert Winans has noted that, although he "is often called 'the father of American minstrelsy,' " Rice "rarely performed in minstrel shows, preferring to continue performing his songs and farces as entr'actes and afterpieces."

30. *Amerigrove* 2:47. But Nathan, *Dan Emmett*, shows that Emmett knew the "Negro" stage character well enough in 1838 or 1839 to write his first song in black stage dialect. He learned to play minstrel-style banjo in 1840–41 from a man named Ferguson, whom one circus manager described as both "the greatest card we had" and "a very ignorant person and 'nigger all over' except in color" (109–11).

31. Quoted from Toll, *Blacking Up*, 13.

32. Levine, *Highbrow*, 26.

33. Richard Sennet's word "witness" is quoted from Levine, *Highbrow*, 194. The witnessing took a variety of forms. On 10 February 1844, Asa Hutchinson of the Hutchinson Family Singers recorded in his journal that at a concert in Washington two days earlier, "the Assembly Room was full of all sorts of people.

The farmer, mechanic, clergyman, lawyers, doctors, senators, representatives, merchants and loafers. All were very quiet through the performance of every piece of music but when we closed any song they would clamor and make such noises as to shake the building to its foundation." See Cockrell, *Excelsior*, 226.

34. Toll, *Blacking Up*, 12–13.

35. According to Sanjek, *American Popular Music*, 2:174, Christy's long run brought in gross receipts of $317,000, half of which he kept himself. The quotations are from Lawrence, *Strong on Music*, 417, and the rest of the information is from *Amerigrove* 1:440.

36. *Amerigrove* 4:183. The Pyne and Harrison English Opera Company, another such outfit, performed in 1854 in New York, Philadelphia, and Boston, then launched a six-month tour that took them to Baltimore, Pittsburgh, Cincinnati, Louisville, New Orleans, Mobile, St. Louis, Indianapolis, Washington, D.C., and Richmond, according to Levine, *Highbrow*, 89, which draws on research by Katherine Preston. "After a brief return to New York" in 1855, Levine continues, "the company took off again on tours to Chicago, Detroit, Madison, Wisconsin, and other interior cities and towns. During the three years the Pyne and Harrison Company spent in America, it performed complete operas more than 500 times and gave over 100 operatic concerts."

37. Lott, "Bernard Ullman," 174–75.

38. *Amerigrove* 4:7.

39. *Amerigrove* 2:445.

40. Cockrell, *Excelsior*, 33–43. John Hutchinson's journal entry notes about the Ballston concert: "Tickets 25 cts single. Admitting a Lady and gentleman 37½ cts." Cockrell notes the family's apparent policy "of adjusting their ticket prices to the relative affluence of the audience. When in rural areas at this time, tickets would typically be half or less than charged in urban or well-to-do places like Ballston Spa" (43). John also notes the family's attempt to devise new ways of appealing to the audience. "Dear Jud. & others are a trying to rake up something new. They are a playing on one anothers fiddles." Apparently it worked well enough to be continued. Cockrell quotes a Boston review of 20 September: "The way all three of the brothers play on two instruments—the violin and violoncello—at the same time, is a caution to the fraternity of fiddlers. No 1 holds and fingers the violoncello, while No 2 bows it, No 2 also holding and fingering a violin for No 3 to bow" (43n.).

41. Cockrell, *Excelsior*, 140, 150–51.

42. Cockrell, *Excelsior*, 141. Nathan, *Dan Emmett*, 158, posits a connection between blackface minstrelsy and the four-part harmonized performances of singing families—first the Rainers and later the Hutchinsons. "It is noteworthy," he writes, that in 1842–43, the very moment when "American 'singing families,'" usually quartets, sprang into existence . . . blackface comedians, too, banded together in groups of four." Nathan doubts that the two events were "mere coincidence." Most blackface groups "styled themselves 'minstrels'—'Ethiopian Minstrels,' to be exact—replacing the former designation, 'Ethiopian delinea-

tors.' " The new name, Nathan believes, was "clearly suggested by the Rainers who also appeared as 'Tyrolese Minstrels.' " The Rainers' and Hutchinsons' success, Nathan believes, "encouraged the introduction of part singing into minstrel performances, as revealed by the following playbill of the Congo Minstrels of 1844: 'Their songs are sung in Harmony in the style of the Hutchinson Family.' " Cockrell, *Excelsior,* 297–300, supports Nathan's connection with further evidence.

43. Cockrell, *Excelsior,* 149. A correspondent who heard the Hutchinsons sing at the New England Anti-Slavery Convention (Boston, May 1844) gave a remarkable account of the group's performance of "Get Off the Track," sung to the tune of "Old Dan Tucker." In this writer's words, when the Hutchinsons reached the chorus,

> When they cried to the heedless pro-slavery multitude that were stupidly lingering on the track, and the engine 'Liberator' coming hard upon them, under full steam and all speed, the Liberty Bell loud ringing, and they standing like deaf men right in its whirlwind path, the way [the Hutchinsons] cried "Get off the track," in defiance of all time and rule, was magnificent and sublime. They forgot their harmony, and shouted one after another, or all in confused outcry, like an alarmed multitude of spectators, about to witness a terrible catastrophe. But I am trying to *describe* it, I should only say it was indescribable. It was life—it was nature—transcending the musical staff—and the gamut—the minim and the semi-breve, and the ledger lines. It was the cry of the people, into which their over-wrought and illimitable music had *degenerated,*—and it was glorious to witness them alighting down again from their wild flight into the current of song, like so many swans upon the river from which they had soared, a moment, wildly, into the air. The multitude who heard them will bear me witness, that they transcended the very province of mere music. (*Herald of Freedom,* 14 June 1844, quoted in Cockrell, *Excelsior,* 254)

44. Cockrell, *Excelsior,* 160–61. Cockrell writes: "Figures like this may have been commonplace for the Hutchinsons during this time. Early in their New York stay, the Albany *Knickerbocker* (2 October 1843) reported" earnings of $750 for one concert, a figure that, according to the paper, "exceeded the revenue for Henry Russell's concert the night before by '260 dollars 75 cents.' "

45. Cockrell, *Excelsior,* 167n.

46. W. Porter Ware and Thaddeus C. Lockard, Jr., *P. T. Barnum Presents Jenny Lind: The American Tour of the Swedish Nightingale* (Baton Rouge, La., 1980), 6; see also plate [3] following 70.

47. Ware and Lockard, *Barnum and Lind,* 20, 25. Before the first concert, 11 September 1850, Barnum agreed to divide its proceeds equally with the singer, estimating her share as $10,000. After consulting with local officials, Lind distributed that sum among twelve New York charities: the Fire Department Fund ($3,000); the Musical Fund Society ($2,000); the Dramatic Fund Association ($500); several orphan asylums ($500 each); a lying-in asylum ($500); and two homes for the aged ($500 each). Proceeds from ticket sales came to $17,864.05,

less than the $20,000 Barnum had predicted. Barnum then agreed to split the proceeds of the second concert (13 September) on the same basis as the first. That event brought in $14,203.03. The "regular" concerts that followed were governed by the tour contract, under which Lind received $1,000 plus expenses for each, and Barnum took $5,500 per night, "for expenses and my services," as he put it. Proceeds exceeding that amount were split equally between Lind and Barnum (14).

48. Ware and Lockard, *Barnum and Lind*, prints complete programs of Lind's concerts in Boston (32–33), Washington, D.C. (54), and Nashville (80–81).

49. Quoted from Ware and Lockard, *Barnum and Lind*, the first from the New York *Commercial Advertiser*, 21 September 1850 (28), the second from the New York *Home Journal*, 22 February 1851 (57), and the third from the Nashville *Daily American*, 1 April 1851 (81). In a comic case of mistaken identity, Barnum's daughter Caroline was taken for Lind by members of a church congregation in Baltimore. As Ware and Lockard tell it: "When Caroline rose to sing as one of the choir, every ear was strained to catch her voice. 'What an exquisite singer!' 'Heavenly sounds!' 'I never heard the like!' " When the service was over, Caroline had to fight to reach her carriage as the congregation surged forward to catch a glimpse of her. Barnum noted afterward that his daughter "had never been known to have any 'extraordinary claims as a vocalist' " (50–51).

However much purple prose Lind inspired, many found being a part of her audience a deeply affecting experience. The Nashville review just quoted groped for language to describe the impact of her soft singing:

> If music ever becomes divine in its utterance it is in the moment when on her lips it sinks almost into a whisper, when the delicate melody is heard in every corner of the theatre. While the breath which a bare whisper would at once destroy the effect is finding its way through every portion of the house, nothing can be more thrillingly poetical. The murmur that is shed by the first faint moving of the evening breeze over some lovely bed of roses, or the distant voice of some fountain amidst rocks as yet untrodden, are but faint similitudes. It can literally be compared to nothing of which we have previously any experience in the beauties and capabilities of sound. (82)

50. Ware and Lockard, *Barnum and Lind*, 9–11, 53–54, and plate [4] following 70; *Amerigrove* 3:88. Barnum's reckoning, as noted by Ware and Lockard, *Barnum and Lind*, 98, is that Lind's net share of the proceeds of her tour under his management was $176,675 "exclusive of her very large charitable contributions." Barnum's gross receipts came to $535,486, of which it has been estimated that "something more than $200,000" was profit. It should also be noted why, when information on the financing of music in this period is so hard to come by, the details of Lind's tour are so easily accessible. We know about them because Barnum, by far the most famous entrepreneur of the age, set them down for the public to read. His autobiography, *Struggles and Triumphs, or Forty Years' Recollections* (Buffalo, 1875) contains a complete financial breakdown of Lind's concerts, reprinted in Ware and Lockard, *Barnum and Lind*,

184–85. The latter also contains the "Contract Between Jenny Lind and P. T. Barnum" (179–81).

It should be noted that Barnum did not work alone. Ware and Lockard note that "at one time he had no less than twenty-six private newspaper reporters in his employ" (12). For Lind's tour, Barnum employed LeGrand Smith, "who traveled ahead of the group to smooth out the arrangements" (29). When the party moved to a new city, e.g., Baltimore in December, Barnum's agents would telegraph ahead the time and place of Lind's train's arrival, guaranteeing that the singer would be met by a noisy crowd hoping to catch a glimpse of her (50).

51. W. S. B. Mathews, ed., *A Hundred Years of Music in America* (Chicago, 1889; reprint, New York, 1970), devotes whole chapters to "Piano Playing and Pianists" and "Concert and Operatic Singers." And in another chapter, he covers organists, violinists, and other virtuosi. Mathews writes about performers who appeared before the American public, thereby including many foreign-born musicians. But the contributions of such notable American-born pianists as Louis Moreau Gottschalk and William Mason are mentioned (114), and Julie Rivé-King (122–26), Carlyle Petersilea (134–37), and Amy Fay (137–41) receive extended biographical sketches. After complaining a bit about the dearth of good voice teachers in this country, Mathews profiles, among others, singers Clara Louise Kellogg (172–74), Annie Louise Cary (184–86), Minnie Hauk (186–88), Myron W. Whitney (214–16), and Emma Abbott (230–32).

52. Southern, *Music of Black Americans,* ranks James Bland, Sam Lucas, Billy Kersands, and Horace Weston as the outstanding black minstrel performers of the years following the Civil War (234–38). Prominent singers on the concert stage included the Hyers sisters and Sissieretta Jones, the "Black Patti" (240–45). Thomas "Blind Tom" Bethune had a long career as a concert pianist (246–47). And a number of other professional performers, including those in professional jubilee singing groups and traveling road shows, are also mentioned (228–52). See also Eileen Southern, "An Early Black Concert Company: The Hyers Sisters Combination," in *Celebration of American Music,* edited by Crawford et al., which offers some information and hypotheses on the management of the Hyers' touring (31–32).

53. Late in the century, circuits were established at which "vaudeville"— variety entertainment suitable for families—was being presented for reasonable prices. Sanjek, *American Popular Music,* vol. 2, *From 1790 to 1909,* 337–45, traces the founding of vaudeville circuits, and vol. 3, *From 1900 to 1984,* 16–17, 57–61, chronicles their sudden decline in favor of radio and moving pictures. Between 1893 and 1900, Sanjek writes, "vaudeville became a big business, with its own monopolistic apparatus, two interlocking coast-to-coast circuits—controlled by [B. F.] Keith in the east and by Martin Beck's Orpheum from Chicago to the Pacific" (Sanjek, *American Popular Music,* vol. 3, *From 1900 to 1984,* 17). To give an idea of the extent of the business, 104,000 vaudeville contracts were approved in 1911 by New York's commission of licenses. These contracts, Sanjek reports, "gave an average salary of $80 for vocal performers, $115 for teams,

and $250 for acts with four or more members." In that year there were some 1,000 "big-time" theaters putting on two shows a day and about 4,000 more "small-time" houses, many of them showing movies too, offering from three to six shows a day (Sanjek, *American Popular Music*, vol. 3, *From 1900 to 1984*, 16, 18). The owners of the big theatrical circuits were millionaires many times over. Sanjek writes that by around 1910 Keith was "so wealthy he was leaving most management decisions" to his assistant, E. F. Albee. S. Z. Poli, the leading owner of New England variety houses, had an estate valued at $30 million at his death. Other impresarios were "the Californian Martin Beck, former German waiter, builder of the Palace Theater on Broadway, who introduced fifteen-piece orchestras in 1909 and handed out printed programs; and Percy G. Williams, who began with a medicine show after the Civil War . . . and sold his theaters to Albee in 1912 for around six million dollars" (Sanjek, *American Popular Music*, vol. 2, *From 1790 to 1909*, 342).

54. An unpretentious saga of chamber music being made to pay for itself is told by Irish-born clarinetist and violist Thomas Ryan (1827–1903), who in 1849 joined with several colleagues to form the Mendelssohn Quintet Club of Boston. After a decade of local activity, the group performed in Philadelphia, Baltimore, and Washington in 1859, "practically our first playing outside of New England," Ryan writes. Urged to play in "the West," the club made a successful concert trip of about a month—Ryan doesn't give the year, but it was around 1860— with operatic singer Adelaide Phillips and violinist Camille Urso, under the management of Harry McClennen, "the well-known advertising manager, so long at the Boston Theater." "After that trial-trip," Ryan recalled, the group decided on a season-long tour. They also decided "that we did not need 'stars' to attract audiences. Individual star singers and players had been heard every-where in the West; *ensemble* playing was the novelty." On their first western tour, the group took along "one of our charming home singers . . . Miss Addie S. Ryan," who "had a rich and very sympathetic voice, was a good all-round singer, and very 'taking' in ballads." Ryan reported: "The financial result of the long season of travel was good, and for many years we made similar trips, and (which will surprise many persons) without the help of any advance agent. All details and arrangements for our appearance in towns and cities were made by correspondence." As Ryan tells it, at first the Mendelssohn Quintet Club had "the West" pretty much to itself. "There were no other musical people travelling. There were very many minstrel companies (which did not injure us), and a few dramatic troupes. We were in demand everywhere." Competition began to appear "either in '63 or '64." By 1868 the Mendelssohn Quintet Club, which continued to tour until 1872, had hired an advance agent. See Thomas Ryan, *Recollections of an Old Musician* (New York, 1899), 162–68.

55. Michael Broyles has shown that the beginnings of this development— the creation of a sphere for secular performance not obliged to support itself financially—lie in Boston during the 1830s and 1840s. In a new book, consulted in manuscript through the author's kindness, Broyles traces the

discovery of instrumental music as an artistic realm different from vocal music, bringing to the fore a broadened idea of the sacred, centered upon symphonic masterworks. That idea, as will be noted below, came to be the basis for a structure of support for music-making that relied neither on commercial entrepreneurs nor churchly sponsors. See Broyles, *"Music of the Highest Class": Elitism and Populism in Antebellum Boston* (New Haven, Conn., 1992), 13–14 and elsewhere.

56. "In those days," Thomas wrote late in life, "the only resource open to an instrumentalist was to join a brass band, and play for parades or dancing" (Theodore Thomas, *A Musical Autobiography*, ed. George P. Upton [Chicago, 1905; reprint, New York, 1964], 20).

57. The orchestra's organizational prospectus states: "The chief object will be, to elevate the Art, improve musical taste, and gratify those already acquainted with classic musical compositions, by performing the Grand Symphonies and Overtures of Beethoven, Mozart, Haydn, Spohr, Mendelssohn, and other great Masters, with a strength and precision hitherto unknown in this country" (Howard Shanet, *Philharmonic: A History of New York's Orchestra* [Garden City, N.Y., 1975], 85). *The American Musical Directory* (New York, 1861; reprint, New York, 1980) summarizes the society's object as "the cultivation and performance of Instrumental Music" (251).

58. According to *The American Musical Directory*, four categories of members—Actual, Professional, Associate, and Subscribing—supported the society. Each Actual member was "required to be a professor of music, and an efficient performer on some instrument, and to pay, when elected, an initiation fee of $10, and an annual tax of $8." Professional members, also "professors of music," were "entitled to admission to the public rehearsals and regular concerts of the Society, on the payment of $3 a year." Associate members had "the same privileges as the Professional members, on the payment of $5 a year." And Subscribing members were "entitled to three tickets to each regular concert, on the payment of $10 a year" (251). A membership list from 1861 shows that most, but not all, of the Actual members were performing members (251–53).

59. Thomas, *Autobiography*, tells how Karl Eckert, conductor of soprano Henriette Sontag's orchestra, chose him as leader of the second violins (30). He doesn't give the year, but Mathews, *A Hundred Years*, 61, notes that in March 1853, Sontag, "under direction of Carl Eckert, appeared at Niblo's in *La Fille du Régiment*." Waldo Selden Pratt, ed., *The New Encyclopedia of Music and Musicians* (New York, 1924), 329, reports that, after his American trip with Sontag in 1852, Eckert "from 1853 was director of the Court Opera in Vienna." Lott, "Bernard Ullman," 177, identifies Ullman as manager of Sontag's North American tour of 1852–54. As Thomas remembered it (*Autobiography*, 31), he was named concertmaster of the opera orchestra the year after becoming leader of the second violins. Opera orchestras, Thomas wrote, were "generally engaged and formed by some man . . . who was supposed to know the better musicians, and had some business capacity. This man would receive, besides his salary from

the manager, a percentage from every man in the orchestra. . . . As concert-meister, I had both power and responsibility, and I dispensed with this middle man, and began by making all engagements with the members of the orchestra myself" (32–33). He describes the late 1850s as his years of " 'apprenticeship' as a practical musician and conductor" (48–49). According to Upton, who edited his autobiography, in 1861 Thomas "gave up all connection with the theatre. He became animated by his great purpose of educating the public to an appreciation of music" (48n.).

60. Ezra Schabas, *Theodore Thomas: America's Conductor and Builder of Orchestras, 1835–1905* (Urbana, Ill., 1989), 16. In Thomas, *Autobiography,* 51, the conductor writes that he "called a meeting of the foremost orchestra musicians of New York, told them of my plans to popularize instrumental music, and asked their cooperation." He dates the first of the Irving Hall concerts in 1864.

61. Thomas, *Autobiography,* notes: "When I began to conduct the Brooklyn Philharmonic concerts, the conductor's fee, which was the same as Eisfeld and Bergmann had had, was not much more than that of any member of the orchestra" (37). The letter appointing Thomas conductor of the Brooklyn orchestra was written on 28 June 1866 and specified a salary of $500 for the 1866–67 season (53). But "afterwards," Thomas reports, "with the growing success of [the Brooklyn] concerts, my salary was increased until it reached several thousand dollars for the season" (37).

62. Joseph Mussulman, *Music in the Cultured Generation: A Social History of Music in America, 1870–1900* (Evanston, Ill., 1971), 110, suggests how that attitude crystallized toward the end of the century. At the death of Stephen Foster in 1864, George William Curtis wrote that "the air is full of his melodies" and that "their simple pathos touches every heart." Curtis concluded: "They are our national music" (*Harper's* 28 [1864]: 567). By 1881, however, Frederick Nast was writing in the same journal that "plantation melodies and minstrel ballads" came from "the lowest strata of society" (*Harper's* 62 [1881]: 818). "Cankerous commercialism had rendered the genre sterile," Mussulman comments. In 1904, Emma Bell Miles complained that "the commercial spirit of the age," in fact, had killed the development of folk music (*Harper's* 99 [1904]: 118; quoted in Mussulman, *Music in the Cultured Generation,* 116–17). Oscar G. Sonneck, writing in the 1910s, found "commercialism"—defined as "the creed of those who prostitute commerce, deliberately turn the temple of art into a bucket-shop of art and let every stroke of their pen be governed by the desire to do profitable work instead of good work"—still rampant, calling it "that hideous curse of our age" ("The History of Music in America: Some Suggestions," in Sonneck, *Miscellaneous Studies in the History of Music* [New York, 1921; reprint, New York, 1970], 328). In the 1960s, Irving Lowens identified the postbellum years as a period in which "American intellectual life [was dominated] by a powerful small group, the big-business class." "Crass materialism" ruled the age, according to Lowens, and "the 'almighty dollar' became the standard of value, infecting the country with contempt for things of the spirit" ("American Democracy and

Music [1830–1914]," in Lowens, *Music and Musicians in Early America* [New York, 1964], 269–70).

63. Sonneck's article, *"Deutscher Einfluss auf das Musikleben Amerikas,"* in *Das Buch der Deutschen in Amerika,* edited by Max Heinrici (Philadelphia, 1909), 355–67, is translated by the editor as "German Influence on the Musical Life of America," in *Oscar Sonneck and American Music,* edited by William Lichtenwanger (Urbana, Ill., 1983), 60–75. Sonneck finds the performance of German orchestral music by German-born musicians in America one of the most important phenomena in this country's musical life (69–70). "Since about 1850," he notes, such performances have proceeded "almost exclusively" through the efforts of "German conductors and German orchestra musicians" (71). About Thomas himself, Sonneck comments: "We younger people, who perhaps heard Theodore Thomas at the end, at the extremity of his career, can scarcely appreciate the legacy he bequeathed us. Only when the memory of him loosens the tongues of our musical veterans shall we be able to measure what America gratefully owes this great prophet of German art" (72). Sonneck also slips into his article a message for American politicians. "That the Germans are a people dedicated to music they well know," he writes, adding: "What they do not understand is that the Germans would not have become such a people without governmental subvention of music" (75).

64. Schabas, *Theodore Thomas,* 17.

65. Hart, *Orpheus in the New World,* 21. The inscription at the front of Hart's book reads: " 'I would go to hell if they gave me a permanent orchestra.' Theodore Thomas."

66. Quoted from Hart, *Orpheus in the New World,* 30.

67. Hart, *Orpheus in the New World,* 21.

68. Quoted from Hart, *Orpheus in the New World,* 22.

69. Quoted from Schabas, *Theodore Thomas,* 244.

70. Thomas also believed that "only the most cultivated persons are able to understand" the best symphonic music. "How, then, can we expect the ignorant or immature mind to grasp its subtleties? The kind of music suitable for them is that which has very clearly defined melody and well-marked rhythms, such, for instance, as is played by the best bands" (quoted from Hart, *Orpheus in the New World,* 30). The Boston critic John Sullivan Dwight, who played a key role in the establishment of instrumental music in America, wrote in 1862: "We never have believed that it was possible to educate the whole mass of society up to the love of what is classical and great in Art: we know that all the great loves, the fine perceptions and appreciations belong to the few" (*Dwight's Journal of Music* 12 [1862]: 271; quoted from Broyles, *"Music of the Highest Class,"* 264).

71. Schabas writes, "In effect, the Central Park Garden *made* the Thomas Orchestra, providing, for a third of the year, a setting in which it could hone its skills and broaden its repertoire. Thanks to these concerts, New York became the English-speaking capital (if not *the* capital) of the symphonic world" (*Theodore Thomas,* 38).

72. "Both the Brooklyn Philharmonic and my New York Symphony Concerts were successful," Thomas wrote in his *Autobiography*, but "the travelling had to be continued to fill out the rest of the time of the orchestra, for I had no subsidy from others to help to meet the expenses of the organization, but was personally responsible for the salaries of my musicians, and my only source of income was the box-office" (65).

73. *Amerigrove* 4:380–81.

74. Not the least of the hardships for Thomas was the financial risk that touring entailed. In the late 1870s, for example, the orchestra "made a week's tour to Buffalo and return. A storm came up on the way out, and we were snowbound, with the result that when we returned to New York for the Symphony Concert, we had spent most of the time in the ordinary day cars, had given but two concerts on the trip, instead of six or seven, and I had become indebted for salaries, etc., about three thousand dollars. I confess I felt that I ought to be relieved of this financial responsibility" (Thomas, *Autobiography*, 75).

75. Thomas, *Autobiography*, 58, notes with relish that "during the seventies" he received a visit from a man who proposed that Thomas " 'star' around the country under his management." "Can anybody blame me," Thomas asked with tongue in cheek, "for feeling properly elated that the greatest manager of the greatest menagerie on earth considered me worthy of his imperial guidance?" The visitor was P. T. Barnum.

76. Quoted from Schabas, *Theodore Thomas*, 52.

77. As Broyles, *"Music of the Highest Class,"* notes, as early as 1838, John Sullivan Dwight was comparing Handel, Mozart, and Beethoven to Socrates, Shakespeare, and Newton (247).

78. The context for this development is sketched out in two articles by Paul DiMaggio, "Cultural Entrepreneurship in Nineteenth-Century Boston: The Creation of an Organizational Base for High Culture in America," and "Cultural Entrepreneurship in Nineteenth-Century Boston, Part II: The Classification and Framing of American Art," *Media, Culture, and Society* 4 (1982): 33–50; 303–22.

79. The dress as well as the behavior of both performers and audience members at an orchestral concert are calculated to foster an atmosphere of respect and seriousness. Much of the occasion's aura is produced by a consciousness that a large throng can make so little sound. ("You could hear a pin drop.") Both performers and audience assume that a work performed in a symphonic concert deserves such care and attention. If it turns out not to measure up, at least it has been accorded the respect due its station, which is that of an aspirant to be heard alongside the music of Beethoven and Co. See also Mussulman, *Music in the Cultured Generation*, 135–36, however, in which opera audiences are chided for noisy, inattentive deportment at performances.

80. Charles Edward Russell, *The American Orchestra and Theodore Thomas* (Garden City, N.Y., 1927), 3; quoted in Levine, *Highbrow*, 112.

81. H. Wiley Hitchcock, *Music in the United States: A Historical Introduction,*
3d ed. (Englewood Cliffs, N.J., 1988), 54.

82. Of earlier general histories of American music, Frédéric Louis Ritter's
Music in America (New York, 1883; 1890; reprint, New York, 1970) pays the most
attention to opera performance. In the second edition, chapter 8 deals with
English opera in New York and French opera in New Orleans before 1825.
Chapter 10 covers opera in New York from 1825 to 1842, the year of the Philharmonic Society's founding. Chapter 15 picks up the same story in 1843 and
carries it to 1861, adding a few pages on French opera in New Orleans. Chapter
18 tells of opera in New York during and shortly after the Civil War. And Chapter
23 is entitled "Opera in New York: Italian, German, American; French Opera
in New Orleans." It covers New York from the early 1870s through the founding
and early years of the Metropolitan Opera Company (1883). In all, approximately
one-fifth of Ritter's book is devoted to opera performance. Mathews, *A Hundred
Years,* devotes Chapter 5 to the "Career of Opera to 1840," and most of Chapter
7, "Two Decades Preceding the War," also deals with opera. Thereafter, however, the book's focus is biographical. Chapter 12, "Concert and Operatic Singers," does not cover opera performance. In fact, only eleven of Mathews's 701
pages of text deal with the performance of opera on American shores. Louis
C. Elson's *The History of American Music* (New York, 1904), gives a good-sized
chapter to "Opera in America." In keeping with his interest in American composers, they are emphasized in his account, while Ritter and Mathews barely
mention them. Hubbard's *History of American Music* (1908) includes a substantial
chapter with the same title that treats developments outside New York City as
well as inside it. Arthur Farwell and W. Dermot Darby's *Music in America* (New
York, 1915), treats the subject more generously than anyone since Ritter, with
three consecutive chapters by Darby—"The Beginnings of Opera," "Opera in
the United States, Part I: New York," and "Opera in the United States, Part
II"—filling approximately one-sixth of the book. Farwell and Darby are the last
general historians of American music to include whole chapters on opera. With
Howard's *Our American Music: Three Hundred Years of It* (New York, 1931), musical
genres disappear as an organizing device. In his book, as well as in Chase's,
Mellers's, Hitchcock's, and Hamm's, opera performance, when discussed at all,
is subsumed into chapters focused on other issues. Hamm's Chapter 4, however,
is entitled "Concert and Operatic Music in Colonial and Federal America" (in
Music in the New World [New York, 1983]), a reflection of the work of Sonneck,
which focuses on performance rather than on composition.

83. In today's musical culture, the word "authenticity" is most often used
in connection with the performance of early music. Advocates of so-called authenticity insist on using instruments from the composer's own time, and,
through research and experiment, they strive to recover the era's performing
habits. It should be noted that, at this writing, musicians who take this approach
seldom refer to their goal as "authenticity" but rather describe it as "historically
informed performance." Faithfulness to the work's original spirit is a high prior-

ity. One performer has written that she would hope to play a piece so that the composer would recognize it, "at worst, without bewilderment, and at best, with pleasure" (Harry Haskell, *The Early Music Revival: A History* [New York, 1988], 175; the musician quoted is Marie Leonhardt). Chapter 9 in Haskell's book explores various ways in which advocates and critics of early music have pursued the ideal of "authenticity." A recent symposium on the subject, Nicholas Kenyon, ed., *Authenticity and Early Music* (London, 1989), carries debate on the issue further.

84. Broyles, *"Music of the Highest Class,"* 255, shows that in an "Address, Delivered before the Harvard Musical Association, August 25, 1841," and printed in *The Musical Magazine* 3 (August 28, 1841): 257–72, Dwight separated "sacred Music" from churches and public worship. In his new definition, music meriting the label of sacred was "elevating, purifying, love and faith-inspiring." Broyles writes that for Dwight, "absolute instrumental music represented the highest type of sacred music, because it existed purely on its own terms, uncorrupted by language."

85. John H. Mueller, *The American Symphony Orchestra: A Social History of Musical Taste* (Bloomington, Ind., 1951), 80, describes the founder's motives in economic terms. "Higginson, who had been a music student in Vienna, was well aware what a paternalistic government could accomplish. However, in this country, according to his creed, this function should devolve upon paternalistic capitalism, through the efforts of those who had been financially successful." Boston Symphony Orchestra members, Mueller notes, were Higginson's full-time employees, hired to make music "which would then be resold to the public, of course at considerable loss, by the philanthropically-minded employer." In 1881, Higginson's public proposal for founding an orchestra called for players and a conductor, paid by the year "to give in Boston as many concerts of serious music as are wanted . . . to keep prices low always . . . 50 cents and 25 cents being the measure of prices." He estimated his costs: "sixty men at $1500 = $90,000 + $3000 for the conductor and + 7000 for other men = $100,000. Of this sum, it seemed possible that one-half should be earned, leaving a deficit of $50,000, for which $1,000,000 is needed as principal." In 1914, after thirty-three years, Higginson's total deficit stood at "about $900,000" (Hart, *Orpheus in the New World*, 49, 55). Levine, *Highbrow*, analyzing Higginson's "complex agenda" (see 119–27), finds him less "a proselytizer to the masses than . . . a preserver of the faith: a builder of the temple and a keeper of the flame" (126).

86. Fay, a businessman, was the brother of pianist Amy Fay and of Rose Fay, who married Theodore Thomas after his first wife died in 1889. Mueller notes that through its first eleven seasons the Chicago Symphony Orchestra ran a deficit that averaged $33,000 per year. The trustees' solution, which Mueller calls "truly farsighted," was "to endow the orchestra by building a permanent home which would be a source of income and security." A public campaign was mounted, and the city's Orchestra Hall opened in December 1904 (Mueller, *American Symphony*, 102–5). Hart, *Orpheus in the New World*, 43, notes that rental

of Orchestra Hall and its office space made only a partial dent in the orchestra's yearly deficit. Nevertheless, he believes, thanks to the new hall's "more limited capacity and to the stimulation of interest in the orchestra by the campaign for construction funds, the Chicago Symphony secured a much stronger base of audience support, which it needed . . . to survive the death of Thomas."

87. The one told in the greatest detail, and with ample attention to economics, is that of symphony orchestras in New York. See Shanet, *Philharmonic.*

88. Howard Shanet's history of the New York Philharmonic attributes that attitude chiefly to German influence and the absence in America of effective opposition to it. For Shanet, the ultimate irony is that the United States' powerful commercial sector, which, he believes, could have helped to steer musical life, never entered the arena of the symphony orchestra at all, leaving foreign values to shape the orchestra's American history. (In a chapter called "Loss of the Native Heritage," Shanet especially deplores the Philharmonic's treatment of American composers. See Shanet, *Philharmonic,* 139–45.) Lawrence Levine leaves no doubt that he considers the mid-nineteenth century, with its volatile, heterogeneous audience, a healthier time than the more self-conscious end of the century. Levine's key pejorative words are "hierarchy"—he argues that the existence of a clear cultural one is a late nineteenth-century development—and "sacralization of culture." The latter is adapted from Paul DiMaggio's phrase "sacralization of art," used in his articles on "Cultural Entrepreneurship in Nineteenth-Century Boston," cited above. Levine's terms are clearly intended as a criticism of people who naively put art on a pedestal as a sacred object. (Levine, *Highbrow,* 85–146, centers on music. See especially pages 132–34 on the "divinity" of some compositions.) And Theodore Thomas's biographer, Ezra Schabas, is harsh on the "museum" atmosphere that came to the fore in Thomas's later years, fragmenting audiences (*Theodore Thomas,* 257). All three of these writers detect snobbishness and exclusivity at work in the later nineteenth century, and they deplore its results. In the *New York Times* of 9 June 1991, Joseph Horowitz cites Levine's analysis approvingly in a diagnosis asserting that, in 1991, "classical music is in decline—and its troubles are artistic, not just financial. The audience is old and dwindling. Piano and song recitals are disappearing. New music has no certain role. Concerts, and the canonized repertory they recycle, are rituals of familiarity, marketed and consumed according to the overpriced celebrity performers they showcase" ("Immortal Masterpieces to Snooze By," Arts and Leisure section, 1).

89. George Martin, *The Damrosch Dynasty: America's First Family of Music* (Boston, 1983), 231.

90. Martin, *Damrosch Dynasty,* 260. The implication here is that some patrons of music are more interested in the social prestige their money brings than in music itself. According to Hart, that was not true of Higginson, whose "sincere dedication to music" stands behind his heavy financial investment (see *Orpheus in the New World,* 70). Nor, apparently, was it true of financier Otto Kahn, himself a proficient amateur musician, who gave at least $2 million to the Met-

ropolitan Opera over three decades and is said to have spent "several" nights a week attending its performances (see Mary Jane Matz, *The Many Lives of Otto Kahn: A Biography* [New York, 1963], 19, 65, 98, and elsewhere).

Samuel Lipman, *The House of Music: Art in an Era of Institutions* (Boston, 1984), believes that attitude is in decline. Lipman describes himself as a critic "who now finds musical power increasingly shifting from music makers to those who are either not musicians or who are not acting for solely musical purposes" (xi). The separation "of patronage and consumption" in American musical life especially disturbs Lipman. He cites as "participant support" the patronage of past Europeans—the Esterházys, Archduke Rudolph, Ludwig of Bavaria—who "savored what they supported." In the United States of the 1980s, however,

> Our numerous governing cadres have neither historical nor present attachments to . . . high musical culture. For reasons of political convenience our leaders are willing to arrange for the transfer of public monies for artistic purposes. That they have up to this point done so with a surprising amount of disinterest is perhaps no more than a sign of their basic uninterest. It is this uninterest that makes them so eclectic in their practical decisions. Thus freed from any burden of their own tastes, they are able to preside smilingly over the gradual vulgarization of what was once a civilized glory. (310–11)

91. Luther Noss, *Paul Hindemith in the United States* (Urbana, Ill., 1989), 174.

92. Gertrude Hindemith wrote an American friend: "We feel this letter is a document of impoliteness and almost insulting hostility. As there is still a year between now and the proposed date it is at least a lack of courtesy not to have added 'I will do my best to get more dates,' or something like that" (Noss, *Paul Hindemith*, 174). Noss adds: "Needless to say, there were no further negotiations with Judson" (175).

93. Hart, *Orpheus in the New World*, Chap. 4, "Arthur Judson—Manager," confirms that Judson's view of his own position was not exaggerated. After discussions with both Judson's admirers and his detractors, Hart writes: "All agree that from 1915 to 1956, at least, Arthur Judson exercised a power and influence in the symphony and concert affairs of this country without equal then or at any other time" (71).

94. As shown by Craig H. Roell, *The Piano in America, 1890–1940* (Chapel Hill, N.C., 1989), the player piano, able to reproduce mechanically the sound of musical performances, played a key role in the transformation of music from a participant's to a consumer's activity. See especially the preface and Chapter 1.

95. Sanjek, *American Popular Music*, vol. 3, *From 1900 to 1984*, 507–17, is devoted to a chapter on the years 1967–70 called "Big Money Invades the Music Business." See also Jeremy Tunstall, *The Media Are American* (New York, 1979), and Armand Mattelart, *Multinational Corporations and the Control of Culture* (Atlantic Highlands, N.J., 1979).

96. Ted Fox, *Showtime at the Apollo* (New York, 1983), 296–97, for example, explains how recordings brought about the decline of Harlem's Apollo Theater.

Earlier in the century, Fox writes, black artists "had made most of their money from personal appearances, and the record companies kept the bulk of the profits from their recordings. . . . Most acts toured constantly, as the best way to increase their income. But as performers grew into superstars, they began to demand a larger slice of the pie from recordings. Then they could afford to relax their touring schedules." By the mid-1970s, Fox notes, "even new and untried acts could demand star salaries—if they had a hit record." Apollo manager Bobby Schiffman noted that well-known acts "could make more money in one night in a bigger and better location than they could make in the Apollo in a whole week." Consequently, the 1,683-seat Apollo "got priced out of the market."

97. Jacques Attali, *Noise: The Political Economy of Music,* translated by Brian Massumi (Minneapolis, 1985), characterizes recent musical culture as one of "repeating." "Repeating," in fact, is the title of his Chapter 4. Attali contends that "by the middle of the twentieth century, representation, which created music as an autonomous art, independent of its religious and political usage, was no longer sufficient either to meet the demands of the new solvent consumers of the middle classes or to fulfill the economic requirements of accumulation" (88). Recording, he points out, "makes the stockpiling of time possible." Hence, "people must devote their time to producing the means to buy recordings of other people's time," and "people buy more records than they can listen to. They stockpile what they want to find the time to hear" (101). In Attali's view, since "the economy of music . . . constituted itself as an industry, directly after the Second World War," its political economy has concentrated on "the *production of demand,* not the *production of supply*" (103).

98. Lawrence Bergreen, *As Thousands Cheer: The Life of Irving Berlin* (New York, 1990), is a detailed portrait of one of the most intense and successful of these competitors. As Bergreen shows, Berlin grew up writing for stage performers like Al Jolson, Eddie Cantor, and Harry Richman, all "frantic crowd pleasers" who performed "for the folks in the back of the highest balcony at the Palace." But by 1930, the new singing star was Bing Crosby, whose style was totally different. "When Crosby and the next generation of singers (crooners, they would be called—no more belting out the songs) stood before a microphone," Bergreen writes, "their careful underplaying sufficed to put the tune across." And Berlin, "the constant student of performing styles," eventually taught himself "to write a new kind of song—subtle and nuanced—for this new type of performer" (292).

99. The library of my wife, a fortepianist and harpsichordist, is full of books confirming that investment. Almost literally at random, for example, I can pull out Sandra P. Rosenblum, *Performance Practices in Classic Piano Music: Their Principles and Applications* (Bloomington, Ind., 1988), a scholarly volume of over 500 pages, with chapters on "The Fortepiano circa 1780–1820," "Dynamics and Accentuation," "Use of the Pedals," "Articulation and Touch," "Historical

Technique and Fingering," "Ornaments," "Choice of Tempo," and "Flexibility of Rhythm and Tempo."

100. To take one example among many, Bud Freeman, *Crazeology: The Autobiography of a Chicago Jazzman,* as told to Robert Wolf (Urbana, Ill., 1989), chronicles the difficulty of making a living as a jazz musician. Freeman thought that in some periods whites had it tougher than blacks. Around 1930, he writes, "there were some good-paying jobs on the North Side but they didn't last as long as the South Side jobs did. Some South Side players, such as Jimmie Noone, stayed with jobs that lasted years; we whites counted the length of ours by weeks, sometimes days. The upshot was that we often had to piece odd jobs together to make ends meet." Freeman recalls that he ran into a drummer friend around that time "and saw he was carrying a gun. I said, 'Why are you carrying that?' and he said, 'Jeez, Freeman, I can't make no money playing jazz' " (33). Freeman, however, always admired black artistry. He recalls having played in a Broadway show, *Swingin' the Dream* (1939), that combined Shakespeare's *A Midsummer Night's Dream* with black vaudeville. Despite having a cast with "the finest talent you could get," the show failed. Freeman believed that if the producer "had known the greatness of the black people he could have had a revue that would still be running" (49).

101. Jack V. Buerkle and Danny Barker, *Bourbon Street Black: The New Orleans Black Jazzman* (New York, 1973), a sociological study, centers on musicians' working lives. In a summary statement, the authors write:

> At the beginning of the twentieth century, the music business as the jazzmen know it today really had not yet begun. The Negro musician's employment status as a professional in New Orleans was not well organized. Gigs were played whenever he could get them. There was no Local [union] to act as a clearinghouse. With some exceptions, they were just unable to earn enough money to be full-time musicians. Most of the time the musician had a day job (often menial) which allowed him to do music moonlighting. In our interviews, a number of the jazzmen described their musically trained fathers as longshoremen, mattress makers, and draymen—not as musicians. After the Local was founded in the early twenties, the music scene gradually became more formal, secure, and professionalized. In time, more of the men came to describe themselves as musicians. More became full-time because the market was beginning to open up somewhat for blacks in New Orleans and elsewhere. (155)

102. Tom Davin's interview with Johnson in 1953, first published in *The Jazz Review* (1959–60), is reprinted as "Conversations with James P. Johnson" in John Edward Hasse, ed., *Ragtime: Its History, Composers, and Music* (New York, 1985). See especially pages 171–74 for information about professional life in New York City in the years 1911–14.

103. Samuel B. Charters and Leonard Kunstadt, *Jazz: A History of the New York Scene* (Garden City, N.Y., 1962; reprint, New York, 1981), 23–41, centers on James Reese Europe and the Castles. It also discusses Europe's organization of the Clef Club, a professional organization for black musicians, which from its

founding in 1909 into the early 1920s served as a booking agency and sponsored concerts. See also Eileen Southern, *Biographical Dictionary of Afro-American and African Musicians* (Westport, Conn., 1982), 73 (the Clef Club), and 128–29 (Europe), and Southern, *Music of Black Americans,* 344–45.

104. John Chilton's assessment of this group reflects present-day opinion among most writers on jazz. Because they made the first jazz recordings, Chilton writes, "the musicians achieved a degree of eminence that was out of proportion to their musical skills." He adds, however, that the ODJB's "collective vigor had an infectious spirit" (*Jazzgrove* 2:450). All sources acknowledge that the group was perceived as something new and exciting from the beginning of its New York engagement in January 1917. See, e.g., David Jasen, *Tin Pan Alley— The Composers, the Songs, the Performers and their Times: The Golden Age of American Popular Music from 1886 to 1956* (New York, 1988), 94–96, and Sanjek, *American Popular Music,* vol. 3, *From 1900 to 1984,* 29–30.

H. O. Brunn, *The Story of the Original Dixieland Jazz Band* (Baton Rouge, La., 1960; reprint, New York, 1977), flies in the face of historical consensus by claiming the ODJB as the real "creators of jazz" (v) and denying black musicians any leading role in the music's historical development. However, Brunn's treatment of commercial aspects of the ODJB's career is detailed and apparently reliable. He notes that after the successes of early 1917, Max Hart, the group's manager, "was deluged with a hundred offers for the Original Dixieland Jazz Band— dances, Broadway musicals, vaudeville tours, conventions—more jobs than the band could handle in a single lifetime" (61).

105. Southern, *Music of Black Americans,* 365, notes that "the earliest documented recording of a black female singer" was Mamie Smith's record date for OKeh on 14 February 1920. Smith sang two songs by Bradford, her manager: "You Can't Keep a Good Man Down" and "This Thing Called Love." Record producer Fred Hager "had intended" to use well-known white singer Sophie Tucker on the date, but Bradford "eventually persuaded him" to record Smith instead. According to Robert M. W. Dixon and John Godrich, *Recording the Blues* (New York, 1970), 9–10, when the recording was released in July 1920, OKeh "made no attempt to draw special attention to it. But the black press proclaimed 'Mamie made a recording' and sales were unexpectedly high." In August, Smith and her Jazz Hounds made two more recordings, including "Crazy Blues." "This time," Dixon and Godrich write, "OKeh advertised widely in black communities and when the disc was issued in November it was an instantaneous success." *Joel Whitburn's Pop Memories 1890–1954: The History of American Popular Music* (Menomonee Falls, Wis., 1986), 398, shows that beginning in the week of 11 December 1920, "Crazy Blues" ranked as one of the hottest-selling recordings and that it remained on the charts for eleven weeks, reaching a peak position of number 3. Sanjek, *American Popular Music,* vol. 3, *From 1900 to 1984,* 31, notes: "within a month, 75,000 copies were sold, mostly to black buyers." According to *Jazzgrove* 2:343, beginning in 1921, Ralph Peer of OKeh began listing recordings made chiefly for black buyers as "race rec-

ords." The term was used by the industry until 1942. See also W. C. Handy, *Father of the Blues: An Autobiography* (New York, 1941; reprint, New York, 1970), 207–8, for Handy's account of Bradford's recording, whose popularity confirmed his long-time conviction that "our people were lovers of music and . . . they were great buyers." Charters and Kunstadt, *Jazz*, 82–92, deals with Mamie Smith and her epoch-making recordings.

106. Trumpeter Joe Smith was heard prominently in Sissle and Blake's *Chocolate Dandies* of 1924. See Charters and Kunstadt, *Jazz*, 116, and Walter C. Allen, *Hendersonia: The Music of Fletcher Henderson and His Musicians: A Bio-Discography* (Highland Park, N.J., 1973), 130. Of Fats Waller's show *Hot Chocolates* (1929), Gary Giddins writes that Louis Armstrong's "rendition of 'Ain't Misbehavin',' performed at first from the pit and later onstage," was "one of the highlights." One night, Giddins reports, "the leading white musicians came uptown to Connie's [a Harlem club] and threw a party for Louis. Bandleader Ben Pollack presented him with a gold watch inscribed, 'Good luck always to Louis Armstrong from The Musicians on Broadway' " (*Satchmo* [New York, 1988], 107). On 2 July 1929, less than two weeks after *Hot Chocolates* began its Broadway run, producer Florenz Ziegfeld opened *Show Girl*, with music by George Gershwin. Duke Ellington and His Orchestra played in the pit (see Bordman, *American Musical Theater*, 452). In the same year, composer Vincent Youmans planned to use Fletcher Henderson and his orchestra in his new show, *Great Day*, but those plans were eventually abandoned. See Allen, *Hendersonia*, 228–32, for details. Rex Stewart, *Boy Meets Horn*, edited by Claire P. Gordon (Ann Arbor, Mich., 1991), 118, however, documents that some of Henderson's men, including Stewart himself, did play in the pit band of *Great Day*.

107. These developments are well documented in standard histories of American music. One perceptive early account of the concert hall's response to jazz is Roger Pryor Dodge, "Consider the Critics," in *Jazzmen*, edited by Frederic Ramsey, Jr., and Charles Edward Smith (New York, 1939), especially 301–28.

108. *Joel Whitburn's Pop Memories*, chart of "The Top 10 Artists by Decade" (625), shows that during the 1920s Whiteman's orchestra sold far more recordings than his nearest competitor, Ben Selvin and His Orchestra. The other leaders, in order of sales, were Ted Lewis and His Band, Jolson, Gene Austin, Isham Jones and His Orchestra, Nat Shilkret and the Victor Orchestra, Fred Waring's Pennsylvanians, Ruth Etting, and Marion Harris. In the same period, Bessie Smith placed fifteen recordings in the top twenty, with "The St. Louis Blues" reaching number 3 (1925), and "Gulf Coast Blues" (1923) and "Lost Your Head Blues" (1926) both reaching number 5. Louis Armstrong made eleven recordings whose sales reached the top twenty, with "Ain't Misbehavin'," which ranked number 7 in 1929, as his biggest hit. Beiderbecke was featured on six Frank Trumbauer Orchestra recordings that made the top twenty, including "I'm Coming, Virginia" (no. 5, 1927); "Changes," with Paul Whiteman and His Orchestra (no. 4, 1928), "I'm Gonna Meet My Sweetie Now," with Jean Goldkette and His Orchestra (no. 20, 1927), and two sides made under his own name,

including "At the Jazz Band Ball" (no. 15, 1928), for a total of ten top twenty sides in all. Of the nine recordings by the Fletcher Henderson Orchestra that made the top twenty in the same period, "Charleston Crazy" (1924) and "Sugar Foot Stomp" (1925) both reached number 8. Five of Oliver's recordings reached the top twenty in those years, with "Dipper Mouth Blues" achieving number 9 (1924). Four ensemble recordings of Morton made the list, with "Black Bottom Stomp" reaching number 13 (1927). Earl Hines appeared on three of Armstrong's recordings that made the top twenty in the same period, including "West End Blues" (no. 8, 1928). Bechet played on two top twenty recordings by Clarence Williams's Blue Five, including "'Tain't Nobody's Bus'ness If I Do" (no. 9, 1924). Johnson's lone appearance was with his piano performance of "Carolina Shout" (no. 10, 1922). During the same period, Paul Whiteman and His Orchestra placed 159 recordings in the top twenty, including twenty-eight number 1 hits (total compiled from *Joel Whitburn's Pop Memories*). As for the Original Dixieland Jazz Band, it placed fourteen recordings on the charts between 1917 and 1923. In 1917, "Darktown Strutters' Ball" reached number 2, "Livery Stable Blues" number 4, and "Indiana" number 8. "Tiger Rag" held the number 1 spot for two weeks in 1918, and "At the Jazz Band Ball" reached number 8. In 1921, the ODJB achieved seven top-selling records: "Home Again Blues" was ranked number 2 for a week, "St. Louis Blues," "Palesteena," and "Royal Garden Blues" all reached the number 3 spot, "Margie" and "Jazz Me Blues" were ranked number 9, and "Sweet Mama (Papa's Gettin' Mad)" went as high as number 12. The ODJB's best seller in 1922, "Bow Wow Blues (My Mama Treats Me Like a Dog)," achieved a number 9 ranking for just one week. Their last record to make the charts was "Some of These Days," which went as high as number 5 in 1923. This information is all found in *Joel Whitburn's Pop Memories*. Sanjek, *American Popular Music*, vol. 3, *From 1900 to 1984*, 29, seems to contradict Whitburn's tallies by claiming "The Livery Stable Blues" as one of the Victor recording company's "earliest million-seller Black Label records."

Paul Whiteman's fees in the mid-1920s confirm his band's preeminence. Mark Tucker, *Ellington: The Early Years* (Urbana, Ill., 1991), 192, quotes a *Boston Post* reporter in August 1926 who wrote that Whiteman commanded $2,000 per night, as compared with $1,000 for Vincent Lopez, "less than $500" for the California Ramblers and Mal Hallett, and $200 for the Memphis Five. Tucker estimates that "Ellington's fee for a one-night stand was probably between $200 and $500" at this time.

109. James Lincoln Collier, *Benny Goodman and the Swing Era* (New York, 1989), 33–38, traces the development of "modern dance-band arrangements" (33), which he attributes largely to Ferdie Grofé, Whiteman's arranger, perhaps in collaboration with West Coast bandleader Art Hickman. According to Collier, the evolution took place chiefly in the late 'teens. Its principles were: "1) the division of the orchestra into sections, at first brass, reed and rhythm, and later with brass sometimes further split into trumpet and trombone sections; 2) the playing off of the sections contrapuntally or in call-and-answer fashion; 3) the

intermixing throughout of shorter or longer solos, mostly improvised jazz, but occasionally straight renditions of a melody; and 4) the playing of ensemble passages with the jazzlike feel of an improvised solo." Collier writes: "All of these principles were at work in the early Whiteman band" (37).

110. Martin Williams, *The Jazz Tradition*, new and rev. ed. (New York, 1983), 64, writes of Armstrong that even "well into his sixties" he could "play on some evenings in an astonishing way—astonishing not so much because of what he played as that he played it with such power, sureness, firmness, authority, such commanding presence as to be beyond category, almost (as they say of Beethoven's late quartets) to be beyond music. When he played this way, matters of style, other jazzmen, and most other musicians simply drop away as we hear his eloquence. . . . [We] hear a surpassing artist create for us, each of us, a surpassing art."

111. Early responses to jazz have been described and analyzed, among other places in Neil Leonard, *Jazz and the White Americans: The Acceptance of a New Art Form* (Chicago, 1962), which is rich in bibliographical references. It is a well-known fact of jazz historiography that European authors published the first books on jazz to take the music seriously: especially Hughes Panassié, *Le jazz hot* (Paris, 1934; English translation, London and New York, 1936), and Charles Delaunay, *Hot Discography* (Paris, 1936). That fact, plus the continuing interest of English and French writers in jazz and blues, together with the knowledge that some American jazz musicians have settled overseas to escape racial discrimination, have led to a belief that Europeans have appreciated jazz more than Americans. James Lincoln Collier, *The Reception of Jazz: A New View*, I.S.A.M. Monographs no. 27 (Brooklyn, 1988), considers that belief a "myth" that has "badly distorted both the nature of American culture and the process by which jazz evolved from a local New Orleans music into a national—indeed international—phenomenon" ([1]). Collier's revisionist work has itself been criticized in a review by Lawrence Gushee in *Ethnomusicology* 33 (1989): 352–54.

112. Collier, *Reception of Jazz*, 34.

113. Roger Pryor Dodge, "Jazz in the Twenties," *Jazz* 1 (July 1942): 6. I am grateful to Lawrence Gushee for calling my attention to this article.

114. Dodge, "Jazz in the Twenties," 6.

115. "Maudlin New York eulogy," Dodge recalled, "led me to essay an exposition of jazz, which I titled 'Jazz Contra Whiteman' " in the fall of 1925. "I peddled it about to a few magazines," he noted, "with no success. The subject was too light for the serious magazines" (7). Dodge's article was eventually published in the London *Dancing Times* (October 1929) under the title "Negro Jazz." See also Dodge, "Consider the Critics," a critical survey of early jazz writing less well known than it deserves to be. Here Dodge notes: "As soon as jazz became disturbingly identifiable as something more than 'our popular music,' countless uninformed commentators sprang up with something to say about it." Most music critics, he writes, shared three mistaken assumptions: (1) jazz's "significant development is dependent upon immediate separation from the

untutored musician"; (2) so-called symphonic jazz was "a progressive advance upon primitive improvisation"; and (3) jazz would "blossom" as "an art form" only when "divorced from the dance" and allowed to develop in a way "comparable to nineteenth century concert music" (301).

116. Dodge, "Jazz in the Twenties," 7.

117. "The occasions when I managed to hear Bessie Smith in Harlem Vaudeville," Dodge wrote, "were for the most part disappointing. In show business she generally sang quick-fast popular numbers. In these her voice hardly ever took on its fine quality." Dodge found Smith at her best "singing the blues with simple piano accompaniment. Such moments would intensify all the beauty that is to be found on her best records." Dodge continued: "Constant playing of Bessie Smith records . . . deepens ordinary enjoyment [and] sustains the seriousness of her music." In his view,

> The significance of the surpassing art of Bessie Smith has been overlooked by her own race to a much greater extent than the significance of the outstanding instrumentalists. Never theatrically pointed up by good stage management, Bessie Smith missed the mass acclaim of, say, a Louis Armstrong. Amongst white people the significance of her art has been shamefully overlooked in favor of Negro choirs and their dilute spiritual music. Bessie was part of a period that could manifest art straight and clean, but those who were supposedly trained to see gave no more than a superficial look. Once more one of the best examples of period art has slipped in and out unnoticed by the mature critics of the period. ("Jazz in the Twenties," 7)

118. Dodge's article is a reminder that Armstrong's fame was a product of a later period. "While in Chicago in 1927," he wrote, "I went to the Sunset Inn to hear the redoubtable Louis Armstrong. He was very slightly known then. He was delighted that someone had come simply to hear him" ("Jazz in the Twenties," 7).

119. Dodge, "Jazz in the Twenties," 8. In Dodge's view, Miley "was the greatest trumpeter in jazz history—in fact, the greatest musician of them all." Dodge wrote in some detail about his interaction with Miley.

> Bubber rehearsed many numbers. Among other things he played the "King of the Zulus" by Louis Armstrong and did from notation his own forgotten improvisations on the "Yellow Dog Blues." When I first showed him notations of his solos taken off records, he was quite confused—doubted he even created them! But we soon discovered that when *reading* notes he used the correct valve, whereas when improvising he reached for them with his lip—sometimes reaching as much as a whole tone. I found through rehearsing with him that he was very conscious of what was important to jazz. He never had to warm up to play hot; he could play with immediate hot emphasis—even when his lips were still cold. He also *thought* in terms of musical invention and was never blandly satisfied with 'weird jungle' notes. When he improvised a melodic turn that was inventive, he tried to remember it. Often in the dressing room before going on stage, he thought of new complicated little breaks to introduce. He was a musician packed

with half-formed ideas for composition, but he was very slow in fully materializing them. Unless he was supervised by a Duke Ellington [he] would leave it [a musical idea] hanging in his mind or just play about with it in the dressing room. (8; 15)

120. Dodge was convinced that "from 1920 on . . . fragments of jazz appear which are in spite of their brevity, the exact counterpart of 'swing' solo choruses in 1939" (Dodge, "Jazz in the Twenties," 29).

121. See, e.g., Williams, *Jazz Tradition*, 252: "To a jazz musician, thought and feeling, reflection and emotion, come together uniquely, and resolve in the art of doing."

122. That, he believed, was responsible for "the more florid, rippling solo [that] came into existence" in 1927–28, replacing the earlier "rhythmic" approach (Dodge, "Jazz in the Twenties," 29).

123. Dodge, "Jazz in the Twenties," 29.

124. Few musical labels have been more widely reviled than the designation of Whiteman as "the King of Jazz." Whiteman's appropriation of that title, jazz writers since the 1930s have widely agreed, violates truth both by denying the contributions of black musicians, who originated jazz and developed it as an art form, and by applying the label to styles less adventurous artistically than Armstrong's brand of jazz in the same period. In Duke Ellington's view, however, Whiteman carried his title with "certainty and dignity." Despite his classical background, Ellington wrote, Whiteman "didn't have a snooty bone in his body." He continued: "Now there have been those who have come on the scene, grabbed the money, and run off to a plush life of boredom, but nobody held on to his band like Paul Whiteman did. He was always adding interesting musicians to the payroll, without regard to their behavior. All he wanted was to have those giant cats blow, and they blew up a storm" (Edward Kennedy Ellington, *Music Is My Mistress* [Garden City, N.Y., 1973], 103).

Gunther Schuller, *Early Jazz: Its Roots and Development* (New York, 1968), 192n., treats Whiteman even-handedly. "Hard-core jazz critics dismiss Whiteman summarily as a destructive influence," he writes, while "apologists for popular mass culture have seen in Whiteman the great arbiter between jazz and symphonic music. . . . On purely musical terms," however, "the Whiteman orchestra achieved much that was admirable, and there is no question that it was admired (and envied) by many musicians, both black and white." The orchestra "was overflowing with excellent musicians and virtuoso instrumentalists." Lennie Hayton, Ferde Grofé, and Bill Challis wrote arrangements that "were marvels of orchestrational ingenuity" for these men, and Whiteman's performances featured "excellent intonation, perfect balances, and clean attacks." On the other hand, according to Schuller, Whiteman's music was "not based on a jazz conception." That it was considered jazz, he believes, is a "sociological phenomenon . . . the analysis of which go[es] beyond the purview of this book."

125. See, e.g., Williams, *The Jazz Tradition*, which is built on that idea.

126. *Jazzgrove* 2:176.

127. A unique, useful feature of *Jazzgrove* is a geographically arranged directory of "Nightclubs and other venues" for jazz performance (2: 176–247), including bibliographical references for clubs and theaters that have been written about—e.g., in New York City: the Apollo Theater, Eddie Condon's, the Hickory House, Nick's Tavern, the Onyx, Three Deuces, and the Village Vanguard. For the latter see Max Gordon, *Live at the Village Vanguard* (New York, 1980). See also John Hammond, *John Hammond on Record: An Autobiography*, with Irving Townsend (New York, 1977), 206–10, for a vignette of Barney Josephson, owner of New York's Café Society, which opened in 1938 as an unusual enterprise: an "integrated night club with mixed entertainment and mixed audiences." Whitney Balliett, *Goodbyes and Other Messages: A Journal of Jazz 1981–1990* (New York, 1991), 245, comments on this part of *Jazzgrove*, however: "The New York night-club settings are far from complete. (See the priceless glossary of Harlem clubs in the booklet prepared in the early sixties by George Hoefer for the Columbia boxed set called 'The Sound of Harlem'—a booklet nowhere mentioned in the bibliography. And where in the New York listings are such places as Pookie's Pub, Bourbon St., Buddy's Place, the Back Porch, Frank's Place, the Royal Box, Plaza 9, Hopper's, the Composer, the Limelight, the Roosevelt Grill, the Rainbow Grill, Shepheard's, and the Guitar?)."

Music business figures like club owners receive widely varying treatment from different authors. For example, Morris Levy, founder of Roulette Records and owner of Birdland, which opened in 1949 as a bebop club, is treated sympathetically by Count Basie and Dizzy Gillespie, but Frederic Dannen, *Hit Men: Power Brokers and Fast Money Inside the Music Business* (New York, 1990), 31–57, depicts him as a rich, colorful crook. "By the eighties," Dannen reports, "Morris Levy was worth no less than $75 million" (32). In 1988 Levy "was convicted on two counts of conspiracy to commit extortion" (53). In *Good Morning Blues: The Autobiography of Count Basie*, as told to Albert Murray (New York, 1985), 322, Levy is called "our old friend." And Dizzy Gillespie, *To Be, or Not . . . to Bop*, with Al Fraser (Garden City, N.Y., 1979), 345–46, tells how, "in a shoebox full of money," Levy lent the trumpeter and his wife the downpayment on their apartment house, interest free. "Morris Levy was a nice man," Gillespie writes. "Morris Levy was very kind. If we only could have collected like that from others whose commercial success was due largely to our music."

128. Not much writing has centered specifically on jazz musicians and their management, but a good deal may be pieced together from biographies and other sources. To cite just one better-known case, under the management of Tom Rockwell, a record producer for the OKeh label, Louis Armstrong appeared in the Broadway show *Hot Chocolates* (1929). According to James Lincoln Collier, *Louis Armstrong: An American Genius* (New York, 1983), 213, the latter proved "a turning point" in Armstrong's career, making him "known to the more sophisticated New York theatergoers" as well as opening up opportunities with club owners. With Johnny Collins as manager (1931–33), Armstrong traveled to England (253), where he fired Collins for avaricious incompetence (263). Joe

Glaser served as Armstrong's manager from 1935 until he died in 1969. Collier argues that, since whites controlled the infrastructure of the entertainment business—theaters, film companies, ballrooms, record companies—a successful black artist needed a competent white manager (274). Under Glaser's guidance, Armstrong landed a new recording contract with Decca (276), began in 1936 to appear in Hollywood films, and was regularly heard on radio from 1937 on (276; 278). "By the end of the 1930s," Collier writes, "Armstrong was a star. He had good management, finally, his financial problems were being solved, he was working as frequently as he cared to, making movies, broadcasting regularly" (278). Gordon, *Village Vanguard,* devotes an affectionate chapter to Glaser, "the most obscene, the most outrageous, and the toughest agent I've ever bought an act from" (79–83). Giddins, *Satchmo,* 129–36, probes the human and business sides of the Armstrong-Glaser relationship, within which Armstrong came to be not just a jazz musician but a major force in American show business. From all reports, Glaser took at least 50 percent of Armstrong's earnings, in return for managing his career and personal financial affairs.

129. Russell Sanjek, *From Print to Plastic: Publishing and Promoting America's Popular Music 1900–1980,* I.S.A.M. Monographs no. 20 (Brooklyn, 1983), tells briefly what he covers at greater length in *American Popular Music,* vol. 3, *From 1900 to 1984,* in several chapters: "Popular Songs and the Movie Business" (47–56), "The Decline and Fall of the House of Albee" (57–61), "The Mechanical Music Business" (62–73), "A Simple Radio Music Box" (74–90), and "A Glut of Movie Music" (91–114).

130. Sanjek, *American Popular Music,* vol. 3, *From 1900 to 1984,* 123.

131. Tucker, *Ellington,* 195–98, sorts out conflicting stories, notes that Mills recruited Ellington for a Vocalion recording session on 29 November 1926, and "began to manage the Ellington band some time after the November Vocalion date, either in late 1926 or early 1927." Terms of the first agreement are not known, but Tucker reports that later, Ellington received "45 percent of his earnings, with 45 percent going to Mills and 10 percent to Mills's lawyer" (198).

132. Sanjek, *American Popular Music,* vol. 3, *From 1900 to 1984,* 124. Tucker, *Ellington,* 208, notes also that Jimmy McHugh, in charge of planning a new review for the Cotton Club in 1927, was a "former associate of Irving Mills at Mills Music."

133. Mercer Ellington, with Stanley Dance, *Duke Ellington in Person: An Intimate Memoir* (Boston, 1978), 33–42, presents details of Mills's and Ellington's relationship.

134. Sanjek, *American Popular Music,* vol. 3, *From 1900 to 1984,* 472. The buyers were Utilities and Industries Management Corp. of New York City, which Sanjek describes as "a $42-million public-utilities holding company that had been doing business for seventy-five years" (471).

135. The Mills stable also included several publishing firms: Jack Mills, Inc., the American Academy, Inc., the Gotham Music Service, and Milsons Music Publishing Corp. See Allen, *Hendersonia,* 541.

136. The years 1938 and 1939 saw the publication of three major works on jazz: Winthrop Sargeant, *Jazz: Hot and Hybrid* (New York, 1938), Wilder Hobson, *American Jazz Music* (New York, 1939), and Ramsey and Smith's *Jazzmen*, cited above. Delaunay's *Hot Discography*, also previously cited, was reissued by the Commodore Music Shop (New York, 1940). As for periodicals dealing with jazz, two foreign journals predate American counterparts: Panassié's *Jazz Hot* (Paris, 1935–39) and the older *Melody Maker* (London, 1936–), which included jazz in its purview. Charles Edward Smith, with Frederic Ramsey, Jr., Charles Payne Rogers, and William Russell, *The Jazz Record Book* (New York, 1944), 510, recommended three American periodicals, *Down Beat* (Chicago, 1934–), whose interest in jazz begins after 1936, *Metronome* (New York, 1885–1961), and *Music and Rhythm* (Chicago, 1940–42). These journals, the authors wrote, deal "with the popular music field in general, carrying articles, bibliographies of records, and so forth, on hot music insofar as space will allow. They also carry news and feature articles pertaining to the music world."

Smith et al., *Jazz Record Book*, is a canon-making endeavor. The authors write: "More and more of the record companies are looking towards standard catalogs of such music, both in their contemporary output and in the issuance of old masters. The commercial term for such items almost always is qualified by the word *classic*" (vii). They go on to say that "only from an extremely selective choice of artists and recordings" can a listener get a true "idea of the variety and greatness" of jazz. For example, "there are probably upwards of two hundred blues pianists who play boogie woogie, but out of these twenty or so might be worth listening to as exponents of style, and perhaps a dozen would find their way into the record catalogs and, hence, into the blues and boogie woogie section of this book." With the book's help, the authors believed, "the listener will be able to find his way through record catalogs and remainder piles alike, . . . reasonably confident that what he buys will be worth listening to far in the future" (viii–ix).

137. Collier, *Reception of Jazz*, 67–77, however, makes the case that many writers on jazz during the 1930s were political leftists who *were* writing within an edifying social framework: namely, the belief that jazz is the music of disenfranchised, exploited blacks.

138. Collier's article on jazz history in *Jazzgrove* says about this development that in the 1970s "schools and colleges . . . began to institute courses in jazz studies; in fact such courses became so numerous that, according to *Down Beat*, in the late 1970s a quarter of a million people were studying jazz formally. The US government and state and local governments began to offer grants totaling millions of dollars to jazz musicians and students" (1:605). Symptomatic of the institutionalization of jazz are the large numbers of organizations listed in *Jazzgrove*: Jazz and People's Movement (Roland Kirk, 1970s), Jazz Artists Guild (Max Roach, Charles Mingus, Jo Jones, 1960), Jazz Composers Guild (Bill Dixon, 1964), Jazz Composer's Orchestra Association (Carla Bley and Mike Mantler, 1966), Jazz Institute of Chicago (Don DeMicheal and others, 1969), Jazzmobile

(Billy Taylor, 1964), National Association of Jazz Educators (Music Educators National Conference, 1968), and the National Jazz Service Organization (David Baker and others, 1984), which in 1985 received "a grant from the NEA [National Endowment for the Arts, allowing] it fully to establish its operations."

139. Stanley Crouch, *Notes of a Hanging Judge: Essays and Reviews, 1979–1989* (New York, 1990), 5.

140. Among many examples, one that might be cited is Bob Dylan's appearance at the Newport Folk Festival (25 July 1965) with an electric guitar. R. Serge Denisoff, *Great Day Coming: Folk Music and the American Left* (Urbana, Ill., 1971; reprint, Baltimore, 1973), writes that the audience's reaction was "hostile." According to a report of the time: "The sight of the instrument infuriated the crowd. It was to them the hated emblem of rock 'n' roll, the tool of performers whose only aim was to take big money from dumb kids. In the hands of the man who had been their god, it was the symbol of the sell-out." "Dylan was driven from the stage," Denisoff notes. "Reportedly, Pete Seeger stood backstage with tears in his eyes" (182–83).

141. A recent compact disc recording of George and Ira Gershwin's *Girl Crazy* (Elektra Nonesuch 9 79250-2, 1990) bears its pedigree proudly. The program booklet carries statements by Lenore (Mrs. Ira) Gershwin and James H. Billington, Librarian of Congress, co-sponsors of a larger Gershwin recording project. Also included is an essay by "musical theater historian" Tommy Krasker, providing details on how the original score was constructed for this recording (39–43). One member of the orchestra told me that conductor John Mauceri had players listen to recordings from the period (1930) so that they would perform with the original concept of sound and rhythm in mind.

142. As Charles Hamm has shown, Tin Pan Alley and Broadway popular song, though sometimes touched in their rhythm and harmony by ragtime and jazz, still carried a heavy European influence. Hamm demonstrates how American songwriters from the 1920s and 1930s showed particular ingenuity and sophistication in using the harmonic vocabulary of Romanticism. See Hamm, *Yesterdays*, 361–72. "The mature style of Tin Pan Alley," he concludes, "drew its formal structures from earlier generations of popular song writers in America and its harmonic and melodic language from Western European classical music, particularly the German, Russian, and French composers of the second half of the nineteenth century and the very first years of the twentieth" (372). In sharp contrast, the roots of rock lie in rhythm-and-blues, which was black in origin, aesthetically distant from the world of Jerome Kern, and carried on chiefly by independent record companies and producers outside popular music's commercial mainstream. According to Robert Witmer and Anthony Marks, the term " 'rhythm-and-blues' (or 'R & B') came into use in 1949, when the music-trade paper *Billboard* proposed it as a replacement for 'race music;' it was in turn superseded by 'soul' in 1969, and 'black music' in 1982" (see *Amerigrove* 4:36).

143. Nelson George, *The Death of Rhythm and Blues* (New York, 1988), argues

for the authenticity of rhythm and blues on the basis of the music's close connection to black expression and black audiences. George makes his case on
economic as well as cultural grounds, stressing R & B's relationship to radio,
its chief means of dissemination. Radio, he writes, "has historically been so
intimately connected with the consciousness of blacks that it remained their
primary source of entertainment and information well into the age of television"
(xiii). Moreover, "one of the things that defined the R & B world, one that
separated it from most other American businesses, was the ability of blacks to
form businesses and profit from a product their own people created" (31). Albert
Murray, *Stomping the Blues* (New York, 1976), is excellent in explaining the
function of blues, jazz, and other styles of black music in African-American
communities. For comments that include R & B, soul, and gospel, see pages
36–42. George seeks to show that Booker T. Washington's view of how blacks
should deal with racism—seize economic control of their own destiny—has vir-
tues when compared to that of W. E. B. DuBois, who saw black involvement in
high culture as the path to social equality.

Dannen, *Hit Men*, 87, presents what he claims to be an industry view of the
difference between "pop" and "R & B." "Pop in the record industry," he writes,
"is a euphemism for white; R & B means black. Until 1949 *Billboard* listed music
by black artists as 'race' records, but then a staffer named Jerry Wexler coined
the term rhythm and blues. This is about all that has changed (though the
industry has found other euphemisms, including 'soul' and 'urban'). A rock
record by a black act is automatically R & B—regardless of its *sound*—unless
white radio plays it and white people buy it, at which point it is said to 'cross
over' to the pop charts."

144. In the late 1970s composer Milton Babbitt, a faculty member at Princeton University, complained: "We receive brilliant, privileged freshmen at
Princeton, who in their first year of college are likely to take a philosophy of
science course with Carl Hempel, and then return to their dormitories to play
the same records that the least literate members of our society embrace as
the only relevant music" (see Deena Rosenberg and Bernard Rosenberg, *The
Music Makers* [New York, 1979], 57). While those listeners would most likely
have objected that the pop music they listened to was not the music heard on
top forty radio, Babbitt's more general point—that even highly educated young
Americans have shown almost no interest in the kind of music he and other
advanced, research-oriented composers are writing—is hard to dispute. It
would probably be fair to say that for many Americans—especially those who
have come of age since the mid-1960s—music that lacks an explicit political
message, or that lends itself readily to the imposition of no such message,
lacks relevance to "real life."

145. For a start in that direction see Simon Frith, " 'The Magic That Can
Set You Free': The Ideology of Folk and the Myth of the Rock Community,"
in *Popular Music I: Folk or Popular? Distinctions, Influences, Continuities,* edited
by Richard Middleton and David Horn (Cambridge, 1981), 159–68.

CHAPTER 4

1. *The Complete Works of William Billings,* edited by Karl Kroeger and Hans Nathan, 4 vols. (Charlottesville, Va., 1977–90) was undertaken with the sponsorship of the American Musicological Society and the Colonial Society of Massachusetts as a project to commemorate the Bicentennial of the American Revolution. See also Karl Kroeger, *Catalog of the Musical Works of William Billings,* Music Reference Collection, no. 32 (Westport, Conn., 1991). The basic studies of Billings's life and music are J. Murray Barbour, *The Church Music of William Billings* (East Lansing, Mich., 1960), David P. McKay and Richard Crawford, *William Billings of Boston: Eighteenth-Century Composer* (Princeton, 1975), and Hans Nathan, *William Billings: Data and Documents,* Bibliographies in American Music, no. 2 (Detroit, 1976).

2. Both quotations are from William Billings, *The Continental Harmony* (Boston, 1794), xxviii n.; reprinted in *Complete Works* 4:29n.

3. McKay and Crawford, *William Billings,* 98–102; also *Complete Works* 3: xviii–xix.

4. Billings's *The New-England Psalm-Singer* (Boston, 1770), a collection composed entirely by Billings himself, was first advertised for sale on 10 December 1770, some two months after the composer's twenty-fourth birthday. See Allen Perdue Britton, Irving Lowens, and completed by Richard Crawford, *American Sacred Music Imprints, 1698–1810: A Bibliography* (Worcester, Mass., 1990), 176.

5. Frédéric Louis Ritter, *Music in America,* 2d ed. (New York, 1890; reprint, New York, 1970), 58, writes: "To Boston will belong most of the honor of having opened a new era for musical development in the New World. It was one of her sons who, first among Americans, stepped forward with the publication of a number of pieces of church-music composed by himself; and this first Yankee composer was *William Billings.*"

6. See Richard Crawford, ed., *The Core Repertory of Early American Psalmody,* Recent Researches in American Music, vols. 11 and 12 (Madison, Wis., 1984), an edition of the 101 sacred compositions most often printed in America before 1811. Billings composed eight core repertory pieces—besides "An Anthem for Easter," Amherst, Brookfield, Chester, Jordan, Lebanon, Majesty, and Maryland—a total exceeded only by Daniel Read, who composed nine.

7. As one example, the anonymous compiler of a Philadelphia tunebook wrote in 1790:

> On perusing the foregoing pages the Psalmodist will find a very considerable number of the most pleasing tunes, are by our ingenious countryman, Mr. *Billings.* Every lover of music will, I am persuaded, thank the Editor for inserting so great a proportion of tunes, from an author of such distinguished merit. By mere force of nature, he has excelled all his cotemporaries [*sic*], and equalled any, perhaps, who have gone before him, in composing for the voice. (*A Selection of Sacred Harmony,* 3d ed. [Philadelphia, 1790], Appendix, quoted in Britton et al., *American Sacred Music Imprints,* 548)

8. See chap. 2 above, 49–50.

9. The first section of John Tasker Howard, *Our American Music* (New York, 1931), bears that title. See chap. 1 above, 248–49n.98.

10. Billings, *New-England Psalm-Singer,* 20. Quoted in Britton et al., *American Sacred Music Imprints,* 177.

11. Gilbert Chase, *America's Music: From the Pilgrims to the Present* (New York, 1955), was the first general history to tell that story. See especially Chap. 7, "Native Pioneers" (which includes a section on "Billings of Boston," 139–45), and Chap. 8, "Progress and Profit," in which Lowell Mason plays a leading role.

12. See Britton et al., *American Sacred Music Imprints,* Appendix I, for a chronological list of tunebooks.

13. See Kroeger, *Catalog.*

14. Josiah Flagg, *A Collection of the Best Psalm Tunes* (Boston, 1764), fol. 2v, quoted in Britton et al., *American Sacred Music Imprints,* 272.

15. See Crawford, *Core Repertory,* xxiii, 3–4.

16. Both passages are from William Billings, *The Singing Master's Assistant* (Boston, 1778), [2], quoted in Britton et al., *American Sacred Music Imprints,* 181.

17. Richard Crawford, *Andrew Law, American Psalmodist* (Evanston, Ill., 1968), 16.

18. The passage is from Stowe's story "Poganuc People." Quoted in Chase, *America's Music,* 142; also in Crawford, *Core Repertory,* xliii.

19. Alan Lomax, *Folk Song Style and Culture* (Washington, D.C., 1968), 15, quoted in Crawford, "A Historian's Introduction to Early American Music," *Proceedings of the American Antiquarian Society* 89 (1979): 293.

20. Crawford, *Core Repertory,* xi–xvi, sorts out and describes the different kinds of declamatory motion.

21. Crawford, *Core Repertory,* xiv–xvi.

22. The tunes with four printings were published only in *The Singing Master's Assistant,* which appeared in four editions, all printed from the same engraved plates. The numbers are taken from an unpublished index of the entire repertory (1698–1810), made while I was working on Britton et al., *American Sacred Music Imprints,* and Crawford, *Core Repertory.*

23. Printings referred to here are in the following collections: Andrew Law, *Select Harmony* ([Cheshire, Conn.], 1779); Daniel Bayley, *Select Harmony* ([Newburyport, Mass., 1784]); *The Worcester Collection of Sacred Harmony* (Worcester, Mass., 1786); *A Selection of Sacred Harmony* (Philadelphia, 1788); *Amphion or the Chorister's Delight* (New York, ca. 1789); E. Sandford and J. Rhea, *Columbian Harmony* (Baltimore, 1793; compiled in Alexandria, Virginia); Thomas H. Atwill, *The New-York Collection of Sacred Harmony* (Lansingburg, N.Y., 1795); *The Village Harmony* (Exeter, N.H., 1795); Amos Pilsbury, *The United States' Sacred Harmony* (Boston, 1799; compiled in Charleston, S.C.); and *Wyeth's Repository of Sacred Music* (Harrisburg, 1810). See Crawford, *Core Repertory,* xxviii.

24. Nicholas Brady and Nahum Tate, *A New Version of the Psalms of David* (London, 1696). Isaac Watts, *The Psalms of David Imitated in the Language of the*

New Testament (London, 1719). Isaac Watts, *Hymns and Spiritual Songs in Three Books* (London, 1707–9). All of these works were often reprinted in America through the eighteenth and early nineteenth centuries.

25. For more on patriotic elements in Billings's texts see McKay and Crawford, *William Billings*, 63–65, 97–98.

26. See Britton et al., *American Sacred Music Imprints*, 2–8, for a description of tunebook types.

27. CHESTER was first published in *The New-England Psalm-Singer*, set to Billings's own "Let tyrants shake their iron rod," to which he added four more patriotic stanzas when he reprinted the tune in *The Singing Master's Assistant*. That text hardly survived the war, however. In later years, CHESTER appeared most often as a setting of Philip Doddridge's hymn, "Let the high heav'ns your songs unite." The original words were still sometimes sung on patriotic occasions. See Crawford, *Core Repertory*, xxx–xxxi.

28. Crawford, *Core Repertory*, li.

29. George Hood, *A History of Music in New England: With Biographical Sketches of Reformers and Psalmists* (Boston, 1846; reprint, New York, 1970), documents the custom in some congregations during the seventeenth and early eighteenth centuries of singing the whole psalter. The Salem, Mass., First Church records for 1667 complain of Ainsworth's collection of tunes that "we had not the liberty of singing all the Scripture Psalm's according to Col. 3.16" (53). Church records in Plymouth, Mass., from 1692 record that on 19 June the congregation resolved to "consider of some way of accommodation, that we might sing all the psalms," and on 14 August, "began to sing the psalms in course" (54). According to Hood, in Massachusetts in the early eighteenth century, "in pious families two [psalms] were sung every day in the week, and on the Lord's day not less than eight, thus repeating each psalm not less than six times a year" (78). Moreover, in congregations at this time, Hood writes, "the psalms were not selected to suit the preacher's subject, but were sung in order; at least this was the custom for one part of the day, and in many congregations it was their constant rule" (79; see also page 81 for Cotton Mather's documentation of that premise). I have found no evidence that congregations of Billings's time continued the earlier custom of singing the whole psalter, nor that they gave it up. Thanks to Nym Cooke for calling my attention to these references.

30. See McKay and Crawford, *William Billings*, 221–30, on Billings's attempts to copyright his music.

31. McKay and Crawford, *William Billings*, 228.

32. Of the fifty-one compositions in *The Continental Harmony*, only four—ST. THOMAS, SUDBURY, THOMAS TOWN, and WEST SUDBURY—or 8 percent, were printed in American tunebooks in the succeeding fifteen years (1795–1810). In the other four tunebooks Billings devoted to his own music, the proportion of compositions borrowed by other compilers is higher: *The New-England Psalm-Singer* (1770), 20 percent; *The Singing Master's Assistant* (1778), 72 percent; *The*

Psalm-Singer's Amusement (1781), 50 percent; and *The Suffolk Harmony* (1786), 44 percent.

33. Cf. Britton et al., *American Sacred Music Imprints*, 643–44 with 644–46.

34. Karl D. Kroeger, *"The Worcester Collection of Sacred Harmony* and Sacred Music in America 1786–1803," 2 vols., Ph.D. diss., Brown University, 1976, is the standard work on Thomas and his tunebook.

35. Britton et al., *American Sacred Music Imprints*, 6–8, documents *The Worcester Collection*'s impact as a model for other tunebooks.

36. See Britton et al., *American Sacred Music Imprints*, 7, for the figures.

37. Simeon Jocelin, *The Chorister's Companion* (New Haven, 1782–83) carries no compiler's name. However, its title page reports that it was "printed for and sold by Simeon Jocelin and Amos Doolittle." Doolittle signed the work as engraver. The preface, which is unsigned, uses the plural "we," indicating that Jocelin and Doolittle were co-compilers as well as copublishers. A second edition (1788), also without compiler's name, was "published and sold by Simeon Jocelin," and the preface is written in the singular. The preface of *The Chorister's Companion*'s first edition is dated 16 December 1782; it was advertised for sale as early as 19 December. It also contains a forty-eight-page supplement, "Part Third" with a separate title page but no separate date. Because it is not known whether Part Third was issued with the rest or later, I have treated it here as a part of the first edition. See Britton et al., *American Sacred Music Imprints*, 366–70, for bibliographical details.

38. Other spondaic tunes in *The Singing Master's Assistant* are BALTIMORE (six printings), HOLLIS STREET (five), and ROXBURY (five).

39. See *Playford's English Dancing Master 1651. A facsimile Reprint, with an Introduction, Bibliography, and Notes*, edited by Margaret Dean-Smith (London, 1957). The rhythm of "Saraband" (18) is almost identical to JUDEA from start to finish, though its melodic contour is different. And the melody to Playford's "Tom Tinker" (74) begins with a similar gesture, though it soon goes a different way.

40. *The Chorister's Companion* (New Haven, 1782), 1, quoted in Britton et al., *American Sacred Music Imprints*, 368.

41. Irving Lowens, *Music and Musicians in Early America* (New York, 1964), 72–77, illuminates relationships between Law's and Thomas's tunebooks.

42. *Worcester Collection* (1786), fol. 2v, proclaims:

For the progress of Psalmody in this country the Publick are in a great measure indebted to the musical abilities of Mr. *William Billings*, of Boston: It is but doing him justice here to observe, that he was the first person we know of that attempted to compose Church Musick, in the New-England States; his music has met with great approbation. Many tunes of his composing are inserted in this work, and are extracted from the Chorister's Companion, printed in Connecticut, from Copper-plates. (Quoted in Britton et al., *American Sacred Music Imprints*, 621)

43. *The Columbian Magazine or Monthly Miscellany* (April 1788): 212–13, quoted in McKay and Crawford, *William Billings*, 155–56. According to the author of

this piece, Billings's style "upon the whole bears a strong resemblance to that of Handel, and nature seems to have made him just such a musician, as she made Shakespeare a poet."

44. See above, chap. 1, p. 25 and n. 83.

CHAPTER 5

1. George F. Root, *The Story of a Musical Life: An Autobiography* (Cincinnati, 1891; reprint, New York, 1973), 112. The autobiography is the basic source on Root's life and career. See also Polly H. Carder, "George Frederick Root, Pioneer Music Educator: His Contributions to Mass Instruction in Music," Ed.D. diss., University of Maryland, 1971, and the article in *Amerigrove* 4: 85–87, by Dena J. Epstein and H. Wiley Hitchcock.

2. Of his life at Willow Farm in Massachusetts in the late 1850s, for example, Root wrote: "These were ideal days—writing until noon, and then driving to a neighboring town, or fishing in some of the pretty ponds that were all about us. The favorite fishing ground was a little lake in North Andover, about eight miles away, and many a time have we spent until dark, after our return, distributing to the neighbors the surplus fish of our afternoon's catch" (Root, *Story,* 122).

3. The work-list by Carder in *Amerigrove* 4: 86–87 names all of Root's collections, cantatas, and method books, plus the most popular of the more than 200 songs he composed.

4. Root, *Story,* 46–48.

5. Root, *Story,* 3.

6. William W. Austin, *"Susanna," "Jeanie," and "The Old Folks at Home": The Songs of Stephen C. Foster from His Time to Ours* (New York, 1975), 262.

7. Root, *Story,* 9.

8. Root, *Story,* 7.

9. Root, *Story,* 18.

10. W. S. B. Mathews, ed., *A Hundred Years of Music in America* (Chicago, 1889; reprint, New York, 1970), 68.

11. At the first meeting of the Music Teachers' National Association (Delaware, Ohio, December 1876), George W. Chadwick, then a twenty-two-year-old instructor at Olivet College in Michigan, delivered a paper, "Popular Music—Wherein Reform Is Necessary." In Chadwick's view, popular music lacked truth and suffered from an "utter lack of originality." As a result, he believed, "music has been and still continues to be dragged through the mire. Our own business-like, avaricious, Yankee natures have caused us to forget, in this headlong race after money, that music as an art is a very different thing from music as a business." Root, who attended the meeting, rose to defend his own popular songs when Chadwick had finished his denunciation. Although "they are simple

in character," he argued, "I have no reason to be ashamed of them" (quoted in Victor Fell Yellin, *Chadwick: Yankee Composer* [Washington, D.C., 1990], 23–25).

12. In the early 1850s, for example, Nathan Richardson entered the music publishing business in Boston. As Root tells it, Richardson

> had lived some years in Germany, and had come home filled with a strong desire to improve the musical tastes of the benighted people of his native land. This sounds like laughing at my old friend. Well, it is so; but not so much as I have done to his face many a time. . . . He determined that he would publish nothing but high-class music. I doubt if there was an American then whose compositions he would have taken as a gift. He had an elegant store on Washington street, fitted and furnished in an expensive manner through the generosity of an older brother, who had plenty of money. . . . All went well for a few months. Musicians met there and greatly enjoyed a chat amid the luxurious surroundings, and they occasionally bought a piece of music when they found what their pupils could use. . . . But it did not pay. At length both Nathan and the rich brother became convinced that they could not make people buy music, however fine, that they could not understand nor perform, and they found that calling the music that the common people liked, "trash," did not help the matter at all.

Eventually (see below), Richardson asked Root to write some songs for his publishing house "that the people would buy" (*Story*, 110–11).

In Root's judgment, musical societies in America had been blighted by the same misconception.

> The history of musical societies is pretty uniform. A few insist in the outset upon practicing music beyond the ability of the chorus to perform, and of the audience to enjoy, and both drop off. Then come debt and appeals to the consciences of the chorus, and the purses of the patrons, to sustain a worthy (?) enterprise. Then follows a lingering death—and all because a few leading members will not give up the difficult music they like best, for the simple music that can be well sung and so enjoyed. (*Story*, 204)

As for Root's own autonomous leanings, he cites with pride the formation, shortly after his move to New York City (1844), of a vocal quintet (Root, his wife, his sister, his brother, and a bass singer) that he rehearsed to near-perfection. "I could carry out every conception I had in the way of expression," he wrote: "increasing, diminishing, accelerating or retarding, sudden attack or delicate shading, with the utmost freedom, being sure that all would go exactly with me." When the quintet sang Mendelssohn's "Hunting Song" for Theodore Eisfeld, conductor of the New York Philharmonic Society, Eisfeld was impressed enough to invite them to sing on the Philharmonic's next concert. "The papers," Root recalled, "said only pleasant things of our performances," and "from that time on I had the good will and friendship of the best musicians in New York" (*Story*, 42–43). Within a few years Root was being urged by such colleagues as William Bradbury and Isaac Woodbury to compile instructional tunebooks. "We are doing well in that line," they told him. Root confides: "I am ashamed to say it, but I looked then with some contempt upon their grade of work. My ladies' classes and choirs were singing higher music and my blind pupils were exciting the admiration of the best musical people of the city by their performances of a still higher order of compositions." Still captivated by pride in his own students' accomplishments, Root compiled his first tunebook, George F. Root and Joseph E. Sweetser, eds., *A Collection of Church Music . . . with New and Original Sentences, Motetts, Anthems &c.* (New York, 1849). Root describes it as containing "an elementary department which, for scientific but uninteresting exercises, could not be excelled." The book proved ill-adapted "for popular use." See Root, *Story*, 52–54.

13. Root, *Story*, 97, asserts that only "two or three" genius composers—composers "who invent and give to the world new forms and harmonies *that live*"—appear in a century. He rates Mendelssohn, though a "great composer," a lesser figure than Beethoven and Wagner. Visiting London in 1851, Root heard performances of *Messiah* and *Elijah* that he considered "authentic and authoritative, both for tempos and style," and that served him as touchstones in later years (*Story*, 76). See also *Story*, 67–68, for evidence of his interest in performing traditions. As Root saw it,

> The first English tenor of this generation is Edward Lloyd. In the last generation Sims Reeves was the acknowledged best, and in the generation before, [John] Braham. When, therefore, at a recent Musical Festival in Cincinnati (May, 1888), I heard Lloyd, I had heard the three great tenors of the three generations, and what greatly increased the interest of this fact was, that I heard Braham sing Handel's "Sound an alarm," Sims Reeves the "Cujus animam" [from Rossini's *Stabat Mater*], and Edward Lloyd both of those songs.

14. Root, *Story*, 54–55. On page 54 he explains the failure of his first tunebook by confessing: "I did not then realize what people in elementary musical states needed."

15. Root, *Story*, 98.

16. Root, *Story*, 101. Much in demand for "conventions," Root writes that he "could easily have occupied every week of the year" in that work, William Bradbury and he "being almost the only prominent people in it for a while." Yet he also felt "a constant pressure for a book, or a cantata, or songs, so I spent about half the time at my desk" (*Story*, 121).

17. Root, *Story*, 8.

18. Root, *Story*, 9, describes the state in which the psalmody of Billings and his contemporaries had survived in his own youth.

> A singing-school had been held in the old red school-house, where "faw, sol, law, faw, sol, law, me, faw," were the syllables for the scale—where one must find the "*me* note" (seven) to ascertain what key he was singing in, and where some of the old "fuguing tunes," as they were called, were still sung. I well remember how, shortly after, we heard that a new system of teaching music had been introduced into Boston, in which they used a blackboard and sang "do, re, mi," etc., to the scale. But how silly "do"

sounded. We thought it smart to say that the man who invented that was a *dough*-head.

19. Root, *Story*, 26–27.

20. In Root's *Story*, Lowell Mason is a dominating figure: Root's respected mentor, model, and, eventually, colleague. From the time of Root's successful audition for Mason's Boston Academy Chorus in 1838 (14), to his teaching as Mason's deputy in the Boston Public Schools in 1840 (26), to his teaching in one of Mason's conventions in 1841 (28–29), to his carrying Mason's teaching methods to New York in 1844 (37), to his enlisting Mason himself to teach at the first three-month normal institute in New York City in 1853 (85), Root linked his professional destiny to Mason and his work.

21. Root, *Story*, 95.

22. Root, *Story*, 82–83.

23. Root, *Story*, 49.

24. Root, *Story*, 81.

25. After he began composing, however, Root did take "a course of lessons . . . from an excellent harmonist and teacher" in New York: "a Frenchman by the name of Girac" (*Story*, 98).

26. Root, *Story*, 81–82.

27. Root, *Story*, 82.

28. In Root, *Story*, 201, he writes: "It is interesting to note the popularity of the idea of 'cantatas for the people.' We know at once what is meant when we say 'songs for the people.' In that sense I use the term 'cantatas for the people.'" And he claims credit for inventing the genre: "They began with 'The Flower Queen,' 'Daniel,' and 'The Haymakers,' as representatives of the three kinds—juvenile, scriptural, and secular. They have multiplied greatly of late years, especially in England."

29. "The Hazel Dell," Root's "first successful song," won him a contract with New York publishing house William Hall and Son to bring out all his "sheet music publications for three years" (1852–55; *Story*, 91). At the end of that period, Nathan Richardson, who was struggling to survive in the music publishing business, asked Root to write him songs "that the people would buy." Among the half dozen that Root produced was "Rosalie, the Prairie Flower." As Root told the story:

> When I took the songs to my friend he said he would prefer to buy them outright. What would I take for the "lot"? There was a bit of sarcasm in the last word. "Well," I replied, "as you propose a wholesale instead of a retail transaction, you shall have the 'lot' at wholesale prices, which will be one hundred dollars apiece—six hundred dollars for all." He laughed at the idea. His splendid foreign reprints had cost him nothing. The idea of paying such a sum for these little things could not be thought of. "Very well," I said, "Give me the usual royalty; that will suit me quite as well." This was agreed to, and when he had paid me in royalties nearly three thousand dollars for "Rosalie" alone, he concluded that six hundred for

the "lot" would not have been an unreasonable price, especially as all the songs of the set had a fair sale, for which he had to pay in addition.

Root concludes this anecdote with a reaffirmation of his belief in the "wisdom" of musicians who understand "what people in elementary states must have" (*Story*, 111).

30. The copy is in the William L. Clements Library, University of Michigan. The added fermata is on page 5.

31. The cover reads: "Christy's Old Folks Are Gone as Sung by E. P. Christy at Christy's Opera House, N. Y." For more on Christy see above, chap. 3, 76.

32. Austin, *"Susanna," "Jeanie," and "The Old Folks At Home,"* 264.

33. Root, *Story*, 89.

34. Root, *Story*, 96–97.

35. Root, *Story*, 132.

36. Root, *Story*, 54.

37. Root, *Story*, 138.

38. Austin, *"Susanna," "Jeanie," and "The Old Folks At Home,"* 131–34, discusses Moore's influence on Foster's songs.

39. Charles Hamm, *Yesterdays: Popular Song in America* (New York, 1979), 139. "There is not a black face in this collection of lovely and beloved ladies," Hamm writes. "But their tales and tunes would have been unimaginable without the plantation song of the minstrel stage."

40. Austin, *"Susanna," "Jeanie," and "The Old Folks At Home,"* 264, also notes that Fanny Crosby wrote the words of "The Hazel Dell," as she did for "about half" the "nearly a hundred songs" that Root published in his early years (266). In *Amerigrove* 1:547, Mel R. Wilhoit also attributes to Crosby the words to "There's Music in the Air" and "Rosalie, the Prairie Flower." It was not until 1864, Wilhoit says, that Crosby "turned her poetic talents to hymnwriting," the work for which she is most often remembered today.

41. Austin, *"Susanna," "Jeanie," and "The Old Folks At Home,"* 264.

42. Quoted in Root, *Story*, 122.

43. With keen rhetorical relish, Gilbert Chase, *America's Music: From the Pilgrims to the Present* (New York, 1955), denounces "the genteel tradition" in nineteenth-century American music, linking it with "the cult of the fashionable, the worship of the conventional, the emulation of the elegant, the cultivation of the trite and artificial, the indulgence of sentimentality, and the predominance of superficiality." Admitting that "we cannot afford to neglect these songs," for "some of them continue to appeal to the sentimental streak that is in all of us," Chase still claims that nineteenth-century Americans "as a whole" lived in a "state of aesthetic immaturity. Hence the success," he explains, "of any music that made a blatant appeal to the feelings of the listeners. . . . Aesthetic appreciation—that is, the quality that permits an artistic experience to be received and enjoyed as such—was almost entirely lacking. People were continually crossing the line that separates art from reality; indeed, most of them were not aware that such a dividing line existed" (165–

66). Neither this passage nor the point it makes appears in Chase's third revised edition (1987).

44. The copy is found in the William L. Clements Library, University of Michigan.

45. Russell Sanjek, *American Popular Music and Its Business: The First Four Hundred Years*, vol. 2, *From 1790 to 1909* (New York, 1988), 137–38, prints D. W. Krummel's estimates of American sheet-music production. According to Krummel, in the half-decade 1841–45, the trade issued roughly 1,600 titles, which increased to 3,000 in the years 1846–50 and to 5,000 in 1851–55, the time of Root's own entry into the market.

46. In *Amerigrove* 3:560, Cynthia Adams Hoover writes that in 1840 Boston piano maker Jonas Chickering "patented a metal frame with a cast-iron bridge for a square piano" of the kind found in many American parlors. Hoover adds that Chickering "was the first to devise a successful method of manufacturing and selling pianos with metal frames."

47. H. Wiley Hitchcock, *Music in the United States: A Historical Introduction*, 3d ed. (Englewood Cliffs, N.J., 1988), 77, writes: "Having decided to try for some of the popular household-song market occupied by Foster but taking a patronizing attitude toward it, Root sought a pseudonym; in view of the adulation of German musicians at the time, a German translation of his own name was his choice."

48. Root, *Story*, 63, relates this incident with more than a hint of embarrassment. Guido Alary, Root's voice teacher in Paris, invited him at the end of a lesson to attend "the last rehearsal" of an opera Alary had composed. "I was in trouble," Root admitted.

> I knew I could not make him conceive how there could be any conscientious scruples against accepting his invitation, but at that time, in the church to which I belonged, it was thought wrong to go to opera or theatrical representations, and I determined when I left home that I would do nothing in Paris that I would not do in New York. So I explained as well as I could why I could not go. He did not understand it at all, as I knew he could not, and evidently regarded me as a kind of fanatic—an opinion in which I coincided a few years later.

49. Root's own explanation of his verbal disguise harks back to the conflict between whether a musician should serve music or the public. When he began to compose, he perceived at once that he was best suited for "the 'people's song.'" Yet he admitted that at that time, "I am ashamed to say, I shared the feeling that was around me in regard to that grade of music. When Stephen C. Foster's wonderful melodies (as I now see them) began to appear, and the famous Christy's Minstrels began to make them known, I 'took a hand in' and wrote a few, but put 'G. Friedrich Wurzel' . . . to them instead of my own name. 'Hazel Dell' and 'Rosalie, the Prairie Flower' were the best known of those so written" (*Story*, 83). Root adds that friends "who knew who 'Wurzel' was, used to say: 'Aim high; he who aims at the sun will reach farther than he will who has a

lower object for a mark.' But I saw so many failures on the part of those who were 'aiming high,' " he explains, "that I had no temptation in that direction, but preferred to shoot at something I could hit" (*Story*, 95).

Root was not the only song composer of the time to affect a pseudonym. He recalled an "eminent musician in New York" who boasted that he "could write a dozen" so-called people's songs "in a day. . . . Thinking there might be money in it, he did try under a *nom de plume*. But his dozen or less of 'simple songs' slumbered quietly on the shelves of a credulous publisher until they went to the paper mill" (*Story*, 97).

Chase, *America's Music*, 3d ed., 155, wrongly ascribes to "the Lowell Mason circle" Root's initial reluctance to admit publicly his composition of "people's songs." As Root says, "it was not until I imbibed more of Dr. Mason's spirit, and went more among the people of the country, that I saw these things in a truer light, and respected myself, and was thankful when I could write something that all the people would sing" (*Story*, 83). Mason's "circle," in other words, supported rather than disapproved of the spirit of Root's new venture.

50. The separation of the two personas, however, is not entirely clear-cut. While "Wurzel" compiled no tunebooks, "Root" did publish some songs. Perhaps more bibliographical work will reveal patterns that are not now discernible—Wurzel's fondness for the minstrel stage, for example, and Root's absence from it. The earliest published song by Root that I have seen dates from 1852. All the songs discovered so far from the years 1852–54 were published by William Hall of New York, to whom Root, for a time, was under contract (cf. n. 29 above). Of more than a dozen songs Hall published in those years, only "The Old Folks Are Gone," "The Hazel Dell," and "Old Josey" were attributed to Wurzel. The rest were attributed to Root, including "Early Lost, Early Saved," "Mary of the Glen," "The Reaper on the Plain," and "The Time of the Heart" (all 1852), and "Look on the Bright Side" and "The World as It Is" (1853), plus "Pity, O Saviour" (1854; arranged from Stradella by G.F.R.). In 1855, ten new secular songs came out, all attributed to Wurzel, and the single songs from 1856 and 1858 carried Wurzel's name as well. The Wurzel songs of 1855–56 were issued in Boston and New York. By 1858, Root and Cady of Chicago had become Root's song publisher, and a dozen new songs came out in 1859–60, half by Root and half by Wurzel. From 1861 on, Wurzel listings decline sharply: two of fifteen songs in 1861, two of nine in 1862, one of fifteen in 1863–64, and one of fourteen in 1865. The last Wurzel song I have found, "Banner of the Fatherland," was published in 1870.

51. George F. Root and W. B. Bradbury, *Daniel: Or the Captivity and Restoration, a Sacred Cantata in Three Parts* (Boston, 1853), was written to a text by C. M. Cady and Fanny Crosby. Of this work Root explained:

About the time the cantata was completed I was approached with reference to making a church-music book with [William] Bradbury. This I was very glad to do, and "The Shawm" was the result. All interested thought it would be a good plan to print the new cantata at the end of the book—

that many of its choruses could be used as anthems, and that some of its solos and quartets might also find a place in church service. So that was done; but in order that Mr. Bradbury's name might rightfully appear as joint author, I took out two of my numbers from the cantata, and he filled their places. "The Shawm" was a success, but the cantata was so much called for, separate from the book, that it was not bound up with it after the first or second edition. . . . "Daniel" has been printed as a book by itself ever since. (*Story*, 89)

In addition, Root published *The Pilgrim Fathers: A Cantata in Two Parts* (New York, 1854), with words by Fanny Crosby.

52. Root, *Story*, 113. From the time of the firm's founding in 1853 until 1864, Mason Brothers of New York City published Root's instructional books and cantatas, and he describes himself as being "in constant communication" with them. Root credits Lowell Mason, Jr., the house's senior partner, with a key role in *The Haymakers*. First, Mason "suggested that I should write a cantata for mixed voices, but on some secular subject." Then, "to a great extent," Mason "planned it, not only as to characters and action, but as to what, in a general way, each number should be about. Taking his plan," Root reports, "I wrote both words and music."

53. George F. Root, *The Haymakers*, edited by Dennis R. Martin, Recent Researches in American Music, vols. 9 and 10 (Madison, Wis., 1984), 197–98.

54. *Dwight's Journal of Music*, March 1859, quoted in Root, *Haymakers*, ed. D. Martin, ix. Note that the accompaniment to this work is for piano, ad lib; only a partially realized piano part is given in the published score.

55. Root's autobiography traces his involvement with the firm.

In 1858 [while he was still living at Willow Farm], my brother, E. T. Root, and Mr. C. M. Cady started a music business in Chicago . . . under the firm name of Root & Cady. My convention work brought me occasionally to their neighborhood, and it was an odd and very pleasant sensation to find in this new section a kind of business home. This was not so much on account of the small pecuniary interest I had in the enterprise as the great interest I took in everything my brother did. . . . Whatever applications for conventions I declined, none from the West were refused, and I appeared more and more frequently at the little store. It was very pleasant to see the new business grow, and it was not long before the partners said: "Come, put in some more capital, and join us; we need the capital, and your name will help us." I was delighted with the idea, not that I thought of giving up my professional work—I did not dream of that, nor of living in Chicago; but to have this connection with my brother, and this business for a kind of recreation, was extremely attractive. So it was soon brought about, and I became a partner in the house of Root & Cady. (*Story*, 122–23)

Within a few years, "the little business was improving," and Root "enjoyed more and more being in the neighborhood of its small whirl" (130).

56. Root, *Story*, 130.

57. Root, *Story*, 136.

58. Dena J. Epstein, *Music Publishing in Chicago before 1871: The Firm of Root & Cady, 1858–1871*, Detroit Studies in Music Bibliography, no. 14 (Detroit, 1969), 48.

59. Root, *Story*, 133. Facsimile reprints of "The Battle Cry of Freedom," "Who'll Save the Left?," "Tramp! Tramp! Tramp! (or The Prisoner's Hope)," "Just Before the Battle, Mother," "O Come You from the Battle-Field?," "The Vacant Chair (or We Shall Meet but We Shall Miss Him)," and "Glory! Glory! (or The Little Octoroon)" may be found in Richard Crawford, ed., *The Civil War Songbook: Complete Original Sheet Music for Thirty-seven Songs* (New York, 1977).

60. The title phrase is still firmly identified with the period. James M. McPherson's prize-winning history of the Civil War is entitled *Battle Cry of Freedom: The Civil War Era*, Oxford History of the United States (New York, 1988); and McPherson goes so far as to print the words and tune of Root's song—including a Confederate version—on the page facing his preface. A column by Mike Royko printed in my local newspaper, *The Ann Arbor News*, on Flag Day (14 June) 1990 criticized members of the United States Congress for "rallying round the flag" (i.e., trying to make political hay from a constitutional amendment against flag-burning) when more pressing issues remained to be solved.

61. Root, *Story*, 132–33, describes the song's genesis.

I heard of President Lincoln's second call for troops one afternoon while reclining on a lounge in my brother's house. Immediately a song started in my mind, words and music together: "Yes, we'll rally round the flag, boys, we'll rally once again, / Shouting the battle-cry of freedom!" I thought it out that afternoon, and wrote it the next morning at the store. The ink was hardly dry when the Lumbard brothers—the great singers of the war—came in for something to sing at a war meeting that was to be holden immediately in the court-house square just opposite. They went through the new song once, and then hastened to the steps of the court-house, followed by a crowd that had gathered while the practice was going on. Then Jule's magnificent voice gave out the song, and Frank's trumpet tones led the refrain—"The Union forever, hurrah, boys, hurrah!" and at the fourth verse a thousand voices were joining in the chorus. From there the song went into the army.

62. Mathews, *One Hundred Years*, 98.

63. *The Story of a Musical Life* makes it clear that war songs contributed greatly to Root and Cady's financial success in the early 1860s. Root's last hit, "Tramp, Tramp, Tramp," though not published until 1864, reaped a profit of $10,000 in "less than a year." But when the war ended, Root recalled, "the war songs stopped as if they had been shot," for "everybody had had enough of war" (*Story*, 151–52). As the years passed, however, public memory of the war's horrors began to fade. Root explained: "Time has changed the terrible realism of the march and the battle-field into tender and hallowed memories" (202). See also Gerald F. Linderman, *Embattled Courage: The Experience of Combat in the American Civil War* (New York, 1987), "Epilogue." By the late 1880s, the war had gained

a foothold in patriotic lore, veterans' organizations were being formed, and war songs were starting to play an important part in the new celebratory atmosphere, for these songs were still remembered by millions of Americans, and they preserved much of the emotional climate of that perilous time. Root writes of the new fashion of "war-song" concerts, of his being elected to membership in the exclusive Loyal Legion for the inspiring songs he had written, of the many anecdotes that grew up around the songs, of the letters he received from veterans and their families relating details of his songs' performances and their efficacy, and of the honors that came his way for them (*Story*, 202–4, 210–15). Root's impact on American musical life, as this chapter has sought to show, was considerable. But through his war songs, his influence reached much further. They made him a player in this country's greatest national drama as it was taking place, and, long after the sounds of battle had died away, songs like his could still kindle the war's emotion-charged memories as perhaps nothing else was able to do.

Further verifying Root's enduring place in American culture are the parodies of some of his war songs that found their way into the labor movement. Philip S. Foner, *American Labor Songs of the Nineteenth Century* (Urbana, Ill., 1975), cites "The Battle Cry of Freedom" (264, 270, 276, 279, 304), "Just Before the Battle, Mother" (163), "The Little Octoroon" (268), and "Tramp, Tramp, Tramp" (112, 114, 141, 157, 164, 217, 232, 280, and 314) as examples that have appeared over the years in labor songsters—e.g., "Shouting the Battle-Cry of Labor" in Vincent's *Alliance and Labor Songster* (270). Moreover, Irwin Silber, comp. and ed., *Songs America Voted By with the Words and Music That Won and Lost Elections and Influenced the Democratic Process* (Harrisburg, Pa., 1971), shows how "The Battle Cry of Freedom" (92, 93, 99, 135, 155, 174), "Just Before the Battle, Mother" (96, 206), and "Tramp, Tramp, Tramp" (98, 137, 142, 268) were used as rallying songs in later presidential election campaigns.

64. Root, *Story*, 193–94.

65. Root, *Story*, 174, invokes his ideal of service and duty to explain why "the English people have been using our American music for so many years." It is not, he contends, "that we are better composers than the English, but that we are nearer and more in sympathy with those for whom we write."

66. Root, *Story*, 192.

67. Austin, *"Susanna," "Jeanie," and "The Old Folks At Home,"* devotes Chapter 11 to " 'People's Song' Writers Following Foster." The chapter concludes with these words:

> The comprehensive tradition that Root called "people's song" embraced many distinguishable subdivisions, not merely a spectrum of types from simplest to most complicated, but a network: patriotic songs, hymns, parodies, cantatas; solo songs, performances with and without instruments, performances by close-knit groups and by crowds of thousands; exclusively white groups, separate Black groups, groups segregated within one bigger group, and occasionally mixed groups integrated, especially in Britain or

Canada. The Foster songs were adaptable throughout this range. They helped to unify it. It reinforced their popularity. (280–81)

68. Sanjek, *American Popular Music,* vol. 2, *From 1790 to 1909,* 66.

69. Greil Marcus, *Mystery Train: Images of America in Rock 'n' Roll Music* (New York, 1975), 113, quotes Chandler.

70. Root, *Story,* 97.

71. Root, *Story,* 99. Esther Heidi Rothenbusch, "The Role of *Gospel Hymns Nos. 1 to 6* (1875–1894) in American Revivalism," Ph.D. diss., University of Michigan, 1991, 304, notes the pentatonic melody of "The Shining Shore" and calls it a "gospel spiritual . . . bridging the gap between the end of the Second Awakening [and the campmeeting spiritual of the early nineteenth century] and the advent of gospel hymnody."

CHAPTER 6

1. Edward Kennedy Ellington, *Music Is My Mistress* (Garden City, N.Y., 1973), x. Mercer Ellington with Stanley Dance, *Duke Ellington in Person: An Intimate Memoir* (Boston, 1978), 171–72, describes the commissioning and writing of *Music Is My Mistress.* Mercer notes that Stanley Dance, Ellington's collaborator,

> had expected that it would be done with a tape recorder, following the same method they had used for articles, so he was surprised to find that Pop intended to write it himself. The manuscript that eventually materialized was undoubtedly unique. It was written on hotel stationery, table napkins, and menus from all over the world. Stanley became so familiar with the handwriting that he could often decipher it when Pop could not. That is the meaning of the minuscule credit at the beginning of the book, which they mutually agreed upon.

In the credit—part of the "Acknowledgements" printed on the verso of the title page—Ellington hails Dance as "Monarch Miracolissimo for extrasensory perception revealed in his amazing ability to decipher my handwriting." Mark Tucker, *Ellington: The Early Years* (Urbana, Ill., 1991), 310, reports about *Music Is My Mistress* that "large sections of the manuscript . . . written in longhand on hotel stationery from around the world—are now in the Smithsonian's Duke Ellington Collection." Tucker finds the work "invaluable for providing Ellington's own view of his career and development—often filtered through layers of protective coating, diplomatic tact, and historical self-consciousness." And he considers it "especially rich in information about the early years." James Lincoln Collier, *Duke Ellington* (New York, 1987), in an opinion that suggests a less-than-careful reading, treats the autobiography as evidence "that Duke Ellington was a dreadful writer. . . . There is nothing in the interviews he gave," Collier contends, nor "in his book *Music Is My Mistress* . . . to suggest that Ellington was in any way the wise and ultimately sophisticated man he actually was" (295).

2. Ellington, *Music,* 468.

3. In "Homage to Duke Ellington on His Birthday," written for the Washington *Sunday Star,* 27 April 1969, Ralph Ellison highlights the "aura of mockery" surrounding Ellington and his persona, hinting also at its complexity.

> Mockery speaks through his work and through his bearing. . . . He is one of the most handsome of men, and to many his stage manners are so suave and gracious as to appear a put-on—which quite often they are. And his manner, like his work, serves to remind us of the inadequacies of our myths, our legends, our conduct, and our standards. . . . For many years he has been telling us how marvelous, mad, violent, hopeful, nostalgic, and (perhaps) decent we are. He is one of the musical fathers of our country, and throughout all these years he has, as he tells us so mockingly, loved us madly. (See Ralph Ellison, *Going to the Territory* [New York, 1986], 225–26)

4. Tucker, *Ellington,* 24. Ellington dedicated his autobiography: "To my mother and father, Daisy Kennedy Ellington and James Edward Ellington."

5. In writing about musical associates, Ellington, who attributed much of his own success to his upbringing, lost few chances to praise the families in which these men were raised. Of Otto Hardwick he wrote: "His father and mother were wonderful people . . . Toby's background was solid and he never felt insecure, a wonderful feeling for any human being" (Ellington, *Music,* 50–51). Sonny Greer grew up "in a fine home, . . . wonderfully warm" (51). Jenny Carney, Harry's mother, was "a lovely lady, and a good cook known for her warm hospitality" (111). The family of Ray Nance, who lived in Chicago, were "wonderful" and "hospitable" (162). As for Paul Gonsalves, Ellington says that he came "from a beautiful family in New Bedford, Rhode Island. His mother is beautiful, his sisters and brothers are beautiful, and all of his children are beautiful" (221).

6. Ellington, *Music,* 457.

7. Rex Stewart, who played with Ellington from 1934 to 1945, wrote in his autobiographical *Boy Meets Horn,* edited by Claire P. Gordon (Ann Arbor, Mich., 1991):

> Ellington is the most complex and paradoxical individual that I've ever known. He is completely unpredictable, a combination of Sir Galahad, Scrooge, Don Quixote and God knows what other saints and sinners that were apt to pop out of his ever-changing personality. The above are the facets which he permits to be observed. Deep down under this facade there is the devout man, the one who reads his Bible every day and the caring family man who never forgets for a minute the ones he loves. And, at the same time, rarely did he forget or forgive anything. I could go on and on trying to describe this indescribable man. (156)

Stanley Dance, who delivered the eulogy at Ellington's funeral, noted on that occasion what a "complex human being" Ellington was,

> at once sophisticated, primitive, humorous, tolerant, positive, ironic, child-like (not childish), lionlike, shepherdlike, Christian. . . . I certainly would never pretend that I wholly knew this wonderful man, although I spent much time in his company and enjoyed his trust. . . . His various associates

and friends knew different aspects of him, but never, as they readily admit, the whole man. (Quoted in Mercer Ellington, *Duke Ellington,* 217)

Mercer Ellington's book devotes most of Chap. 6 to a discussion of Ellington's character traits, which, he said, included taking "pleasure in manipulating people" (149), watching his health (149–52), being a spokesman for black Americans (152–53), being superstitious (153–54), having a tendency toward paranoia (157–59), remaining alert to the musical opinions of the younger generation (160–61), having bouts of despondency (164), being a good businessman who didn't want to be bothered with business details (162–68), maintaining dominance by knowing the weaknesses of those who worked with him, and being sparing in compliments to his men ("after fifty years of dealing with musicians his theory was that to praise them was to raise the price," 168).

8. Gunther Schuller, *The Swing Era: The Development of Jazz, 1930–1945* (New York, 1989), 48, 157.

9. Tucker, *Ellington,* 259–72, is an appendix listing chronologically the "Compositions and Recordings of Duke Ellington, 1914–November 1927." According to Tucker, Ellington's output as a composer before 1923 consists of just two piano pieces and a song from the years 1914–17. A song called "Blind Man's Buff," for which Ellington wrote the music, was copyrighted in 1923 but never published. Ellington's first published song, "Choo Choo (I Gotta Hurry Home)," was issued by the Broadway Music Corp. on 5 September 1924, more than four months after his twenty-fifth birthday.

10. Edmund Anderson, a friend of Ellington's, recalled in an interview that later in life he had once suggested that the composer go to Juilliard and study theory formally. According to Anderson, Ellington replied: "Edmund, if I were to do that I think I'd lose everything else that I have. I would ruin everything" (Collier, *Duke Ellington,* 21–22). Ellington's early teacher was Henry Grant. See Tucker, *Ellington,* 59, 61–62.

11. Ken Rattenbury, *Duke Ellington: Jazz Composer* (London, 1990), 306–7, an appendix of "Ellington's Copyrighted Works," provides some statistics. He attributes 769 compositions to Ellington "as sole composer," 191 to Ellington "in collaboration with musicians in his employ," and 52 to Ellington "in collaboration with others," for a total of 1,012 works. In the second category, Ellingtonians who contributed 5 or more works are Barney Bigard (10), Johnny Hodges (23), Bubber Miley (5), Rex Stewart (8), Billy Strayhorn (102), Juan Tizol (8), and Cootie Williams (9). In a highly critical review of Rattenbury's book, Andrew Homzy questions the total of 1,012.

My rough count, from a nineteen-page ASCAP listing, yields 1,119 individual pieces. (This includes the few arrangements of public domain material, e.g., *The Nutcracker Suite,* that are more on the level of re-compositions or perhaps sets of very sophisticated variations. Still, many of these have fallen through the cracks because of sloppy business practices and the failure to register some pieces by Ellington's three major publishers. Nor is Ellington's last work, incidentally, the opera *Queenie Pie,* considered in either count.) (Andrew Homzy, Review of *Duke Ellington: Jazz Composer* by Ken Rattenbury, *Notes* 48 (1992): 1,241)

12. Paraphrased from Stewart in Derek Jewell, *Duke: A Portrait of Duke Ellington* (New York, 1977), 102; quoted from Rattenbury, *Duke Ellington*, 23.

13. Rex Stewart, *Jazz Masters of the Thirties* (New York, 1972), 97–98. A paper Mark Tucker delivered at the annual meeting of the American Musicological Society in 1989 (Austin, Texas), challenged the view that Ellington composed *only* in the way described here. By the late 1930s, if not before, Ellington was also writing out some pieces in much greater detail, including even suggestions for "improvised" solos. (Gunther Schuller confirmed Tucker's point in a talk at the Smithsonian Institution on 27 April 1990.) Tucker found evidence for this side of Ellington's composing in the Smithsonian's Duke Ellington Collection. Of that collection, he notes: "After years of inaccessibility, Ellington's personal library of music and memorabilia was acquired by the Smithsonian in 1988. This collection will form the cornerstone for much future Ellington research, containing as it does an extraordinary cache of Ellington original scores, orchestral parts, and sketches." He adds that "after spending two months in the summer of 1988 surveying the collection, I found little relating directly to Ellington's life and music before 1930" (Tucker, *Ellington*, 312).

14. Ellington used the phrase in *Music*. See, e.g., page 54, where he writes of Arthur Whetsol: "As a trumpet player, he had a tonal personality that has never really been duplicated. Sweet, but not syrupy, nor schmaltzy, nor surrealistic, it had a superiority of extrasensory dimensions." And in a eulogy written the night Johnny Hodges died, Ellington said: "Johnny Hodges and his unique tonal personality have gone to join the ever so few inimitables—those whose sounds stand unimitated, to say the least—Art Tatum, Sidney Bechet, Django Reinhardt, Billy Strayhorn" (119).

15. Ellington's reliance on others for much of his musical and sonic material has led James Lincoln Collier to contend that it is "not necessary to see Duke Ellington as a 'composer' in the narrow sense of the word." Rather, following Billy Strayhorn, Collier calls Ellington "an improvising jazz musician" whose instrument "was a whole band" (*Duke Ellington*, 306). Elsewhere, Collier tries another tack: "It does not hurt to think of Ellington not so much as a dramatist, as Beethoven was, or an architect, as was Bach, but as a planner of meals" (141).

16. Quoted in Rattenbury, *Duke Ellington*, 23. Ellington, *Music*, 214, confirms Stone's point. (Perhaps it should be noted that Ellington's sketches of individuals in this book appear under the heading "Dramatis Felidae"—"Cast of Cats.") He writes:

> The cats who come into this band are probably unique in the aural realm. When someone falls out of the band—temporarily or permanently—it naturally becomes a matter of "Whom shall we get?" or "Whom can we get?" It is not just a matter of replacing the cat who left, because we are concerned with a highly personalized kind of music. It is written to suit the character

of an instrumentalist, the man who has the responsibility of playing it, and it is almost impossible to match his character identically. Also, if the new man is sufficiently interesting tonally, why insist upon his copying or matching his predecessor's style?

17. Schuller, *The Swing Era*, 48.

18. Martin Williams, *The Jazz Tradition*, new and rev. ed. (Oxford, 1983), 107, makes the same point in different words. "Ellington was so attuned to the sounds of his men," he writes, "that the very originality of his textures and the daring of his harmonic language were determined not in the abstract but in his inquisitiveness about, let us say, how this reed player's low A-flat might sound when juxtaposed with that brassman's cup-muted G."

Schuller, *Swing Era*, 49n., pays special tribute to Ellington's piano playing, calling him "a rhythmic energizer of the orchestra" but, above all, "possessor of the most remarkable piano tone and touch." Schuller writes:

> Perhaps one needed to have stood close to Ellington's piano-playing to fully appreciate the remarkable fullness and depth of his sound. I had that privilege many times, and I can say with total conviction that, with but very few exceptions . . . I have never encountered a pianist, jazz or classical, who could command at once such purity of tone *and* range of dynamics and timbres as Ellington. He had a way of playing what I call "deep in the keys" to produce the clearest, most controlled impact of the hammer on the strings and, as a result, the fullest purest resonance of those strings. Ellington could play the most forceful piano, matching his entire orchestra at full tilt; and yet I never heard him force or bang, as so many pianists do when they venture into the *ff* range. His tone and projection were such that with one chord or a few fill-in notes he could energize the entire orchestra. And in addition he could combine his basic piano sonority with all manner of timbral sonorities; one heard trumpets, saxophones, horns, oboes, even strings in his playing.

19. The phrase, apparently coined by Billy Strayhorn, was used in an interview he gave in 1952. Schuller uses it in his analysis of Ellington's career. And Ken Rattenbury uses it as the title of his first chapter. Tucker, *Ellington*, which covers Ellington's life and work through 1927, calls the orchestra's recording session for Vocalion on 26 November 1926 "a turning point in Ellington's career." The recordings he made from that time on, Tucker explains, "differed in several fundamental ways from those that had come before." First, they were of Ellington's own music; second, they were made for labels aimed at distribution beyond the "race" market; third, rather than published songs, Ellington was beginning to record original instrumental pieces; and finally, they show how, in collaboration with key figures in the ensemble, Ellington was "coming into his own as a composer" (211–13).

20. Ellington, *Music*, 261. He also wrote, more ornately: "Billy Strayhorn said we were exponents of the aural art. Ours is the responsibility of bringing to the listener and would-be listener—as to those unwilling to be listeners—some agreeable vibration that tickles the fancy of the eardrum" (447).

21. Ellington, *Music*, 227. Ellington recalled a memorable example of rhythm taking over the whole atmosphere of a nightclub. During the 1920s, as he walked down the steps of the Capitol Palace in Harlem to hear Willie "The Lion" Smith and his group, he realized that "everything and everybody seemed to be doing whatever they were doing in the tempo The Lion's group was laying down. The walls and furniture seemed to lean understandingly—one of the strangest and greatest sensations I ever had. The waiters served in that tempo; everybody who had to walk in, out, or around the place walked with a beat" (Ellington, *Music*, 90).

22. Ellington, *Music*, 453.

23. Tucker, *Ellington*, quotes Otto Hardwick, a member of "The Duke's Serenaders," on this subject: "All of a sudden, around 1918, we began to get a lot of 'dicty' jobs. We would all pile into my Pullman automobile . . . and Duke would direct us to drive to an embassy or private mansion. Other times we would go out to Manassas, Culpepper, Warrenton, or Orange [Virginia], for fancy balls and society receptions. This was Meyer Davis territory and none of us was able to figure out how Duke was muscling in." According to Tucker, Ellington's "promotional efforts and attractive personal qualities" were partly responsible, and so was "his experience working under Louis Thomas" (56), a black bandleader who, as one musician recalled, managed to get "all the society work around Washington" in the years 1915–20 (48).

24. Mills's importance to Ellington's career is generally acknowledged, though *Music Is My Mistress* assigns him only a small role (and no place in the "Dramatis Felidae"). In an interview in *Down Beat* magazine (1952), Mills said that his strategy for Ellington was "aimed at presenting the public a great musician who was making a lasting contribution to American music" and to make Ellington's "importance as an artist the primary consideration" (quoted in Tucker, *Ellington*, 201, who adds that Ellington had begun to court a "sophisticated image" in Washington well before he went to New York or met Irving Mills). On the matter of record labels, Tucker notes that Ellington's orchestra in 1927 "appeared on two labels with race series aimed at black buyers—Vocalion and OKeh—but also recorded for three with a wider network of distribution: Brunswick (Vocalion's parent company), Columbia and Victor" (212). According to Mercer Ellington, *Duke Ellington*, the radio wire from the Cotton Club engagement brought the band and its music to national attention, which allowed Mills "to engineer the first trip to Hollywood" for the film *Check and Double Check* (1930), featuring the radio comedy team of Amos 'n' Andy (34). In 1929, while appearing at the Cotton Club, the band also performed in the Ziegfeld-produced *Show Girl* on Broadway, with music by George Gershwin. (In 1929, Fletcher Henderson and his orchestra were considered for an appearance in Vincent Youmans's *Great Day*. According to Rex Stewart, *Boy Meets Horn*, 118, Mills tried to keep Henderson out of *Great Day*. See chap. 3 above, n. 106.) Jewell, *Duke*, 47, calls the Chevalier event "a *coup*." And Mercer Ellington notes that it was "the first time" he'd seen the band play in a theater, "just

sitting there, going from one number to another. . . . I can remember becoming aware of Chevalier's importance" (45). As for the European tour, Louis Armstrong had anticipated Ellington by a year, but by all accounts the Ellington tour, sponsored in part by British bandleader Jack Hylton, was more successful. See Jewell, *Duke*, 48. Finally, Mercer Ellington, *Duke Ellington*, 33–41, is an illuminating discussion of "all the maneuvers and stratagems that helped push Pop to the top" (41). Mercer credits press agent Ned Williams with especially effective and faithful service on Ellington's behalf from 1931 until the break with Irving Mills in 1939.

Ellington, *Music*, 82, attributes the idea for "Creole Rhapsody," the first of his extended works, to Mills. As he tells it:

> When we were playing the Oriental Theater [in Chicago, in 1931?] Irving Mills came to me one day with an original idea. He was always reaching toward a higher plateau for our music. "Tomorrow is a big day," he said. "We premiere a new long work—a rhapsody." "Really?" I replied. "Okay." So I went out and wrote *Creole Rhapsody*, and I did so much music for it that we had to cut it up and do two versions. One came out on Brunswick and the other, longer one, on Victor. Irving almost blew his connection at both companies for recording a number that was not only more than three minutes long, but took both sides of the record. That was the seed from which all kinds of extended works and suites later grew.

Gunther Schuller, *Early Jazz: Its Roots and Development* (New York, 1968), 354, finds in Ellington's piece "some subtle 'borrowing' from Gershwin's *Rhapsody in Blue*."

25. Schuller, *Swing Era*, 49, describes Ellington's balancing act as "an extraordinary tightrope walk" but without bringing the audience into it. "Evidently," he writes, Ellington "had a phenomenal instinct for allowing a degree of individuality and creative freedom within the framework of his musical conception."

26. Ellington, *Music*, 460. In the self-interview near the book's end, Ellington poses the question: "Does inspiration come from sorrow, frustration, and disappointment? It has been said that great love songs have followed a broken heart or the end of an affair. Do emotions such as love, anger, loneliness, or happiness affect composition?" And he answers: "I think the artist's true position is that of an observer. Personal emotion could spoil his *pièce de résistance*."

27. Ellington, *Music*, 93, describes, for example, Ellington as a budding young pianist going to hear James P. Johnson play in Washington's Convention Hall. "I was always a terrific listener. I'm taller on one side than the other from leaning over the piano, listening. This time I listened all night long." Mercer Ellington, *Duke Ellington*, 160, reports:

> As he traveled and moved among people, he was always alert to opinions of all kinds. When he and Harry Carney pulled into a gas station to fill up, there would often be youngsters hanging around, and he'd get into conversation with them and find out what they listened to on the radio and records. . . . When they stopped for something to eat, he'd note what was

on the jukebox and what was being played. In this way he was always better informed than some may have imagined.

28. Ellington, *Music*, teems with references to his appreciation of "artistry"— as in his father's speech, for example. Ellington called his father "a wonderful wit," adding: "he knew exactly what to say to a lady," and "whatever place he was in, he had appropriate lines" (12). He found a similar flair in his mother who, as a cook, "had the knack, talent, imagination, and exciting skill of a pure artist" (390). In Frank Holliday's pool room on T Street, social center of the neighborhood where he grew up, the same quality abounded. Gamblers there skillfully manipulated the cards. "Interns used to come in, who could cure colds. And handwriting experts who would enjoy copying somebody's signature on a check, go out and *cash* it, and bring back the money to show the cats in the poolroom what *artists* they were. They didn't need the money. They did it for the kicks. There were also a couple of pickpockets around, so smooth that when they went to New York they were not allowed in the subway. At heart, they were all great artists" (23).

Ellington well understood that these manifestations of artistry applied to the theatrical vocation he had chosen. In 1923, he and other members of his Washington band performed with Wilbur Sweatman in vaudeville. "It was another world to us," he recalled. "We'd sit on the stage and keep a straight face. I began to realize that all cities had different personalities. . . . I also learned a lot about show business from Sweatman. He was a good musician, and he was in vaudeville because that was where the money was then" (*Music*, 36). The challenge of theatrical effect for Ellington lay in convincing the audience, which he called "the other side of the realm that serves the same muse I do" (465). Ellington analyzed Frank Sinatra's success in these terms: "Every song he sings is understandable and, most of all, believable, which is the ultimate in theater" (239). He saw himself as practicing a trade akin to that of actors and actresses. "The theater," he wrote, "is a place for skill. Some people say, 'I don't see how he can play that part every night without going out of his mind!' It may be a wild, dramatic part, but the actor doesn't necessarily have to throw his emotions into it, because he has studied how to make the people *believe* that he is doing all that suffering. It is one of the arts, and all the arts have similar qualities" (463).

29. Ellington, *Music*, 80.

30. Schuller, *Swing Era*, 46, comments: "The orchestra's ability to survive the wear and tear of literally thousands of one-night stands, of an endless succession of bus-, train-, and plane-trips, must be counted as one of the minor miracles of human physical endurance."

31. Stanley Dance, *The World of Duke Ellington* (New York, 1970), 61.

32. Lawrence Gushee, Notes to *Duke Ellington 1940* (Smithsonian Collection recording DPM 20351, 1978), [2].

33. Gene Lees, *Waiting for Dizzy* (New York, 1991), 10, writing about a group of compact disc reissues of recordings from the 1920s by Louis Armstrong, Bix

Beiderbecke, Ellington, Red Nichols, Jelly Roll Morton, Bessie Smith, Joe Venuti, Eddie Lang, and others, stresses another trait. Lees finds the music on these albums "almost universally joyous" and "enormous exuberant fun."

34. Gushee, Notes to *Duke Ellington 1940*, [2].

35. Oklahoma City native Ralph Ellison recalls the impression that Ellington and his men made when they visited his home town in Ellison's youth. "Where in . . . *any* white community," he asks, "could there have been found images, examples such as these? Who were so worldly, who so elegant, who so mockingly creative? Who so skilled at their given trade and who treated the social limitations placed in their paths with greater disdain?" (Ellison, *Going to the Territory*, 220). Stanley Crouch, *Notes of a Hanging Judge: Essays and Reviews, 1979–1989* (New York, 1990), 54, notes the efforts of Ellington and others to replace with "images of class, taste, and discipline" jazz's earlier "shady connections" with vice and superficiality.

36. Strayhorn's comment, appearing in an article in *Down Beat* (July 1952), is quoted in Nat Shapiro and Nat Hentoff, *Hear Me Talkin' to Ya: The Story of Jazz as Told by the Men Who Made It* (New York, 1955), 224, and in Rattenbury, *Duke Ellington*, 21.

37. Quoted in Schuller, *Early Jazz*, 350.

38. Williams, *Jazz Tradition*, 106.

39. Ellington, *Music*, 54, wrote of Arthur Whetsol that when illness forced him to retire from the band in 1937, "he left behind an echo of aural charisma that I can still hear."

40. Ellington, *Music*, 462. This was not a nostalgic comment, for in 1973 Ellington found "the caliber of musicians . . . higher today." In earlier days, he added, if a player could be identified by his tone quality, he "didn't even have to read. Nowadays, the same guys play in symphonies, dance bands, and radio and television studios."

41. Ellington, *Music*, 118.

42. Except for those in exx. 22 and 23a–b and table 4, the recordings cited in this chapter may all be heard on *The Smithsonian Collection of Classic Jazz,* revised ed. "Dusk" (ex. 22) is on *Duke Ellington 1940* (Smithsonian Collection); "Braggin' in Brass" (exx. 23a-b) on *Duke Ellington 1938* (Smithsonian Collection); and "Old Man Blues," diagrammed in table 4, is on *The Indispensable Duke Ellington*, vols. 3/4 (French RCA).

43. Mercer Ellington, *Duke Ellington*, 25, writes:

There are three basic elements in the growl: the sound of the horn, a guttural gargling in the throat, and the actual note that is hummed. The mouth has to be shaped to make the different vowel sounds, and above the singing from the throat, manipulation of the plunger adds the *wa-wa* accents that give the horn a language. . . . In the Ellington tradition a straight mute is used *in* the horn besides the plunger outside, and this results in more pressure. Some players use only the plunger, and then the sound is usually coarser, less piercing, and not as well articulated.

Mercer notes that "the chief exponents of growling in the band" were trumpeters Miley, Cootie Williams, and Ray Nance and trombonists Joe "Tricky Sam" Nanton and Tyree Glenn. Nanton, he recalled, "made such a science of distortion that he would sometimes use a soda bottle when he was playing in the dressing room, thereby changing the fundamental positions of the slide." Other trombonists like Lawrence Brown and Quentin Jackson "did very well . . . when they growled on trombone, but they moved their tuning slide, something that Tricky, Cootie, and Ray Nance never did. Where Tricky was unique was in the way he could make his sound so sheer that someone once likened it to tearing paper."

44. Ellington, *Music*, 106.

45. Gunther Schuller, in *Early Jazz*, 326–29, discusses "East St. Louis Toodle-Oo" at some length. Schuller follows Roger Pryor Dodge's lead in praising Miley not only for his inventive sound but for his "enormous contribution to pure classic melody in jazz." Miley and Ellington are listed as co-composers of "East St. Louis Toodle-Oo." Mark Tucker, *Ellington*, concludes with a longer description of the piece (248–57), tracing and comparing several different recordings and printed versions. Tucker sees Miley as a seminal figure in Ellington's development as a composer, especially through his mastery of the spirit of the blues. "Miley's hot trumpet filled a special function in Ellington's compositions," he writes. "When the tempo slowed down and the lights dimmed, it was Miley's turn to step forward and play the blues. Inspired by the soul in Miley's horn, Ellington fashioned pieces that went beyond hot jazz and made his band sound like no one else's. In the process he discovered new paths as a composer" (231).

46. Ellington, *Music*, 419–20, writes:

During one period at the Cotton Club, much attention was paid to acts with an African setting, and to accompany these we developed what was termed "jungle style" jazz. (As a student of Negro history I had, in any case, a natural inclination in this direction.) Its most striking characteristic was the use of mutes—often the plumber's everyday rubber plunger—by Bubber Miley on trumpet and Joe "Tricky Sam" Nanton on trombone. They founded a tradition we have maintained ever since. This kind of theatrical experience, and the demands it made upon us, was both educative and enriching, and it brought about a further broadening of the music's scope. We, too, began to think in terms of concert and theater.

Collier, *Duke Ellington*, 92–93, attributes so-called jungle music to Mills's and Ellington's perception "that the band had to have an identifiable and consistent style that could be promoted through clever publicity." For him, Ellington's jungle music was nothing more than "a gimmick . . . suggested by the fact that the Cotton Club was at one point using a lot of 'jungle' skits as excuses to introduce erotic dances—shake dances and shimmies performed by the club's dancers, like Freddi Washington and Bessie Dudley, wearing little besides feathers and beads, supposedly to suggest jungle attire." But Mark Tucker, in a paper delivered at the American Musicological Society's annual meeting in Cleveland

(1986), showed how, over the years, Ellington transformed jungle music from a floor-show convention (in the 1920s) to an important part of his expressive vocabulary as a composer (late 1930s and 1940s).

47. Ellington, *Music,* has only restrained praise for Williams, who, he writes, entered the band in 1929 and "soon became one of our most outstanding soloists. He began to use the plunger mute, one of our major tonal devices, and he used it very well" (121). Schuller, *Swing Era,* 53, notes that on a 1932 remake of "Creole Love Call" (1927), Williams "takes over Miley's old chorus with the plunger and growl, but towards the end of the performance he also breaks into a new role as the first of Ellington's trumpets to develop a prominently displayable high register." Later, Schuller goes on to say that, by 1935, "the increasing technical skills and musical sophistication" of players like Armstrong, Williams, Hodges, and others was making the notion of jazz "as a collectively improvised form of musical expression" outdated. From that time forward, what Schuller calls "the concerto idea" takes hold, in which composers and arrangers write pieces featuring outstanding soloists like these men (84). "Concerto for Cootie" is one of many products of that impulse.

Rattenbury, *Duke Ellington,* carries a detailed analysis of the piece, with copious musical illustrations (164–201). Along the way, he describes some of the different tone qualities Williams employs, including: "plunger-muted (closely), with a pronounced vibrato frequently developed into a lip trill and a trace of growl"; "plunger-muted (closely), with almost no vibrato and with no throat growl"; "plunger-muted, with the plunger cup . . . freely manipulated around the half-open position, and with a dramatic increase in volume, a savage growl, and exaggerated vibrato"; a "quiet, cool vibratoless delivery"; and a section "played with a superb tone on open trumpet" (187–89).

48. Ellington's autobiography says little about Carney as a "tonal personality," but Mercer Ellington, *Duke Ellington,* 65–66, makes comments that certainly apply to the opening of "Ko-Ko." Mercer notes Carney's "massive tone," which, he writes, "not only gave the saxophone section a depth and roundness no other had, but it gave the whole ensemble a rich, sonorous foundation that proved inimitable." Schuller loves Ellington's trombone section; in fact, by the fourth paragraph of his long chapter, "Duke Ellington: Master Composer," he is discussing its members, noting the Ellington band as "the first to acquire a permanent trombone trio." Lawrence Brown, Juan Tizol, and "Tricky Sam" Nanton, as Schuller notes, "were all totally different from each other in their musical conception: unique individual voices." And yet, he notes, "this trio of uniquely distinctive personalities could, when necessary, blend chameleon-like into a single sonority" (*Swing Era,* 47). That is what they do when playing the sharply articulated harmonies that begin "Ko-Ko."

The dedication of Schuller's book reads: "For Edwin and George—and Marjorie—and in memory of the incomparable Lawrence Brown."

49. Schuller, *Swing Era,* 116, comments that here the sound of Tizol's valve trombone "makes it the *non-pareil* instrument for the occasion. A saxophone

would have sounded ordinary," he explains (not noting that saxophone "calls" seem to demand responses from another section of the orchestra), "and on the slide-trombone *this* riff in *that* register and *that* tempo is virtually unplayable. It lies perfectly on the valve-trombone."

50. Ellington wrote that he composed "Mood Indigo" (1930) with an electronic effect in mind. Remembering that an earlier recording of " 'Black and Tan Fantasy' with the growl trombone and growl trumpet" had touched off "a sympathetic vibration or mike tone," he thought to himself, " 'maybe if I spread those notes over a certain distance . . . the mike tone will take a specific place or a specific interval in there.' It came off, and gave that illusion" (*Music,* 80). Schuller waxes personal on the subject of "Dusk," devoting several pages of *Swing Era* (122–26) to an analysis with transcriptions. He finds it "one of those pieces that go beyond the confining labels of jazz, dance music, and light entertainment." For Schuller, "Dusk" strikes a "plaintive[,] nostalgic mood, an image of loneliness at eventide, a night of longing about to descend." And he adds: "It is deeply affecting, gently, subtly disturbing, perfect in its utter simplicity. It is music that haunts you—it has haunted me since I first heard it some forty-five years ago, and it *never* fails to move me. Though it pleads and supplicates, it never whimpers; it is never sentimental" (122).

51. Schuller, *Swing Era,* 94.

52. See also Schuller, *Swing Era,* 95.

53. The song, with words and music by Hughie Prince and Don Raye, was published in 1941. See Roger Lax and Frederick Smith, *The Great Song Thesaurus,* 2d ed., updated and expanded (New York, 1989), 201.

54. Schuller, *Swing Era,* 104–5, describes this introduction, including a diagram of the textural buildup.

55. In an interview with Stanley Dance in the late 1960s, Ellington talked about some of the impulses that lay behind his music. "Everything" that Bubber Miley and Joe Nanton played, he recalled, "represented a mood, a person, a picture." He explained: "As a matter of fact, everything we used to do in the old days had a picture." For example, "the guys would be walking up Broadway after work and see this old man coming down the street, and there was the beginning of 'Old Man Blues.' Everything had a picture or was descriptive of something. Always" (Dance, *World of Duke Ellington,* 7). Whatever its inspiration, the main strain of "Old Man Blues" strongly suggests the harmonic progression of Jerome Kern's "Old Man River," from *Show Boat* (1927). The correspondence is especially strong in the bridge.

56. Schuller, *Early Jazz,* 351, notates the break.

57. Schuller, *Swing Era,* 128n., discusses Ellington's lifelong "difficulty with endings."

58. Gunther Schuller, the closest student of Ellington's extended works, deals with "Creole Rhapsody" (1930–31) in *Early Jazz,* 352–53, and "Reminiscing in Tempo," "Diminuendo and Crescendo in Blue," and the much longer "Black, Brown, and Beige" in *Swing Era,* 75–83, 90–92, and 141–50. Schuller acknowl-

edges that "Black, Brown, and Beige" and most of Ellington's later large compositions are not uniformly successful, and he devotes pages 149–57 to a forthright discussion of what they show about Ellington as a composer.

59. First recorded in New York City on 20 September 1937, the work began to show up on Ellington broadcasts in the mid-1940s, according to Jørgen Grunnet Jepsen, *Jazz Records, 1942–[1969]: A Discography* (Holte, 1964–68), 3:406ff. On 7 July 1945, for example, "Diminuendo in Blue" and "Crescendo in Blue" were performed in a New York City radio broadcast with "Carnegie Blues" sandwiched in between (406). In broadcasts recorded in October of the same year, the two pieces were separated by "I Got It Bad (and That Ain't Good)" (410). Jepsen lists nine recorded performances between 1945 and 1951; in six of them, the two flank a third item. ("Transblucency" is the centerpiece listed on pages 413, 414, and 416.) On 7 July 1956, at the Newport Jazz Festival, the Ellington orchestra gave its most famous performance of "Diminuendo and Crescendo in Blue." That night the two parts were separated by Paul Gonsalves's extended solo: twenty-seven choruses based on the twelve-bar blues. The performance, which drew an ecstatic audience reaction, is credited with boosting the band's fortunes and has taken its place in jazz lore. Mercer Ellington, *Duke Ellington,* 112, describes its impact succinctly.

60. Since bar 5 (17), however, was exactly what the ear expected, it could be understood as an addition only after the fact.

61. Standard blues practice puts calls at the beginnings of phrases, i.e., in bars 1, 5, and 9 of a chorus. In Chorus 3, however, after appearing in bars 1 and 5, the calls return at three-bar intervals (bars 8 and 11).

62. Dance, *World of Ellington,* 84.

63. Schuller, *Swing Era,* 90–92, is of two minds about the work. On the one hand, he admires the conception as "one of Duke's most ambitious efforts . . . remote from the world of popular tunes and 12-bar blues (even though based on blues changes)." Schuller is also impressed that "Diminuendo and Crescendo in Blue," in "its original 1937 form[,] was . . . a full-fledged written *composition* with virtually no improvisation." He finds it "relatively demanding in structure and harmonically, technically complex." On the other hand, he finds the 1937 performance lacking, especially in "the more complex full-orchestra episodes," which seem to him "beyond the performance capabilities of the 1937 Ellington band, particularly in respect to intonation." Moreover, Schuller thinks the work lacks thematic inventiveness. "The dichotomy between the innocuousness of the melodic-thematic material and the comparatively sophisticated and perhaps overly complex fragmentation of underlying component material," he writes, "constitutes a weakness of the work, although an interesting risk-taking one." Elsewhere in his book, however, he cites "Diminuendo and Crescendo in Blue" approvingly, as evidence of (1) Ellington's ambition as a composer ("the struggle, the torment, and the anguish," 93); (2) his playing with "unusual phrase structures" (118); (3) his achievement of "concerted constructive logic" (131) and progress in "structural unity" (147); and (4) his ability to do without program-

matic effects in longer works (152). Near the end of his book, moreover, Schuller cites "Diminuendo and Crescendo in Blue" as a "historic breakthrough creation" and one of "the dozen or so major stations in the development of jazz in the twenty years between 1926 and 1946." Other Ellington pieces on his list were "Mood Indigo," "Reminiscing in Tempo," and "Cotton Tail" (840).

64. Gushee, Notes to *Duke Ellington 1940*, [2].

65. Mercer Ellington, *Duke Ellington*, 94.

66. Schuller, *Swing Era*, 78, in discussing "Reminiscing in Tempo," writes that in this work, "more than ever before, [Ellington] was trying to break out beyond the narrow categorizations of the commercial world which by an accident of fate he was forced to inhabit. He was determined more than ever before, to avoid the trap into which the market place and the obsession for labeling were trying to lure him."

67. Stewart, *Jazz Masters*, 96, reminds his readers of the performers' role in this process. "In the Ellington organization," he wrote in the 1960s, "there is the combined knowledge of these gifted artists, who by virtue of years of experience are able to create, on the spot, any mood that they choose."

68. Mercer Ellington, *Duke Ellington*, 169, describes what occupied Ellington "in his later years." "He really didn't have time to go around listening to musicians. He had to keep his ear to the ground in a different sense. He was too busy checking prices and the politics of the music industry. When he could throw that stuff out of his mind, he was busy with the commissions he had accepted."

69. Ellington, *Music*, 463.

70. Ellington, *Music*, 459.

71. Ellison, recalling his days as a high-school student in Oklahoma City, describes the impact of Ellington's music on him and his musician friends. "We were studying the classics then," he remembers, "working at harmony and the forms of symphonic music. And while we affirmed the voice of jazz and the blues . . . it was not until the discovery of Ellington that we had any hint that jazz possessed possibilities of a range of expressiveness comparable to that of classical European music" (*Going to the Territory*, 220).

CHAPTER 7

1. Ira Gershwin, *Lyrics on Several Occasions: A Selection of Stage & Screen Lyrics Written for Sundry Situations; and Now Arranged in Arbitrary Categories. To which have been added many informative annotations & disquisitions on their why & wherefore, their whom-for, their how; and matters associative* (New York, 1959; reprint, New York, 1973), xi.

2. Gershwin, *Lyrics*, 342–43.

3. The book was by Guy Bolton and John McGowan, with music by George Gershwin and lyrics by Ira Gershwin. Eight songs from the show were published:

"Bidin' My Time," "Boy! What Love Has Done to Me!," "But Not For Me," "Could You Use Me?," "Embraceable You," "I Got Rhythm," "Sam and De-lilah," and "Treat Me Rough." *Girl Crazy*, produced by Alex A. Aarons and Vinton Freedley, ran for 272 performances on Broadway, closing on 6 June 1931.

4. A recording released in 1990, George and Ira Gershwin, *Girl Crazy*, (Elek-tra Nonesuch compact disc 9 79250–2), contains an informative program book. A plot synopsis appears on pages 62–64.

5. In Gershwin, *Girl Crazy* (program book), 22, Miles Kreuger writes:

Theater mythology tells us that the audience first felt the impact of Mer-man's vocal power when she sang "I Got Rhythm." Not so. That was her second song. Throughout the entire first act, never singing a note, Merman engaged in comic banter, generally with William Kent [Slick Fothergill, Kate's husband]. There was no reason for the audience even to suspect that she was a singer. It was not until the final scene of the first act, the bluesy saloon, with gambling couples sinuously dancing to Al Siegel's on-stage, upright piano, that the Merman explosion was felt. In a saucy slit skirt and a loosely draped, low-cut blouse, she slinked out and began to sing, "Dee-li-laaaah, was a flooosey . . ." with a disarming blend of pure vocal power and yet suggestive innuendo. The effect was stunning. No sooner had she finished "Sam and Delilah" than Ethel Merman, surrounded by chorus girls, tore the house down with "I Got Rhythm."

As Merman wrote in her autobiography, during her "high C" chorus "the audience went a little crazy."

6. The DeMarcos were a dance team, Antonio and Renée DeMarco. Others featured in the original cast were William Kent and Allen Kearns.

7. Merman's performance is pitched in F rather than the published key, B-flat. In the second chorus, she sustains the C above middle C (the dominant) on the syllable "Ahh" through the first six bars of each "A" section, then sings the words "Who could ask for anything more?" to Gershwin's melody.

8. The recording, numbered Decca DXB.153 (T34), was taped for me by Arnold Jacobson of Arnold's Archives, Grand Rapids, Michigan, in 1985.

9. In Gershwin, *Girl Crazy* (program book), 51–55, Richard M. Sudhalter discusses the jazz performers in the pit. Nichols, he writes, was "a shrewd and aggressive businessman . . . on good terms with Broadway contractors," but some musicians questioned his credentials as a jazz player. (Tenor saxophonist Bud Freeman called Nichols "a synthetic . . . [and] very mechanical player" who "copied every line he had ever learned in jazz from Bix" Beiderbecke—Bud Freeman, *Crazeology: The Autobiography of a Chicago Jazzman*, as told to Robert Wolf [Urbana, Ill., 1989], 20.) According to Sudhalter, Nichols's ensemble, plus trombonist Jack Teagarden but minus the *Girl Crazy* string section, "doubled at the Hotel New Yorker" in the evenings after the show was over (Gershwin, *Girl Crazy* [program book], 54). In the spring of 1931, when Benny Goodman left the ensemble, he was replaced by reedman Jimmy Dorsey (55).

Sudhalter also tells a tantalizing but inconclusive story about "I Got Rhythm" in its first incarnation. Before the show opened, Nichols and Gershwin were discussing the work of Robert Russell Bennett, who was orchestrating *Girl Crazy*. Sudhalter reports:

> Bennett, at the time riding high among Broadway orchestrators, had little feeling for (and reportedly even less interest in) jazz. But certain of the hotter numbers, notably "I Got Rhythm," seemed to cry out for an arranger who understood swing and could write comfortably in a more rhythmic vein. [Glenn] Miller, Nichols said, would be in the new band, so why not let him do some scoring as well? Gershwin's answer is lost to history. But reports persist that Miller wrote at least the rideout chorus to "I Got Rhythm" and some of the incidental music. (52–53)

Bennett's orchestrations and Miller's possible contributions to them are heard on the Elektra Nonesuch recording. One earwitness to several 1930–31 *Girl Crazy* performances recalled: "During the intermissions, they'd really turn the band loose, and you should have heard the hot stuff they played. It wasn't like a regular pit band—more like an act within an act" (54).

10. Russell Sanjek, *From Print to Plastic: Publishing and Promoting America's Popular Music (1900–1980)*, I.S.A.M. Monographs no. 20 (Brooklyn, 1983), 13, 15.

11. Craig H. Roell, *The Piano in America, 1890–1940* (Chapel Hill, N.C., 1989), documents the role of the player piano in the vast change that took place in American musical life early in the present century. See especially pages 42–46. Roell calls "the miracle of sound reproduction . . . indeed revolutionary." Before the invention of the player piano, the reproducing piano, and the phonograph, Roell writes, "the musician was human—active and creative—and the music was live. The ideology of the entire musical experience was derived from the producer culture. The revolutionary nature of the player piano changed these concepts forever, for increasingly the musician was a machine. The musical experience was becoming passive" (45).

12. Sanjek, *Print to Plastic*, 12–13.

13. Russell Sanjek, *American Popular Music and Its Business: The First Four Hundred Years*, vol. 3, *From 1900 to 1984* (New York, 1988), explains how publisher Max Dreyfus, for whom Gershwin worked beginning in 1918, conquered "the production-music field"—the publishing of Broadway show music—for his firms of T. B. Harms and Harms, Inc. (97). Dreyfus, Sanjek writes, "was known as a prodigious gambler, ready to advance up to $15,000 for the music to a show his writers were assigned to create" (98). By 1929, with talking pictures becoming a major force in the entertainment industry, film studios were buying music publishing companies. In the summer of that year, Warner Brothers film studios bought the Harms empire for $8.5 million. The publishing firms involved were those owned or backed by Dreyfus, including Harms, Inc., Chappell-Harms (its "repository for non-production music"), De Sylva, Brown, and Henderson, Remick Music, Green and Stept, Famous Music, T. B. Harms, "and George Gershwin's New World Music, publisher of all [Gershwin's] music" (109).

14. Sanjek, *American Popular Music*, vol. 3, *From 1900 to 1984*, notes Max Dreyfus's dictum about show music that, "although nobody could tell if a song might become a hit, 'it *would* become one if you worked to sell it' " (96). Producers of Dreyfus-backed shows, according to Sanjek, "expected one or two hit songs from any production with which he was connected. An average of twenty-one songs were generally written for a musical show, many of them the ensemble and chorus numbers to fill gaps in the action or carry the plot along. Most were printed and on sale in the theater lobby" (98).

15. In Gershwin, *Girl Crazy* (program book), 23–24, Miles Kreuger explains that after it closed the show made no post-Broadway tour, "in part due to a sudden drop-off of Depression theater attendance, and because both Willie Howard and Ethel Merman were wooed by George White to star in his *Scandals of 1931*." A West Coast production, however, opened in San Francisco on 29 September 1931 and another in Chicago on 8 October. RKO studios filmed *Girl Crazy* in 1932; in 1943, MGM studios brought out another version with Mickey Rooney, Judy Garland, Gil Stratton, June Allyson, Nancy Walker, and Tommy Dorsey and His Orchestra.

16. At this writing, the standard biography is Edward Jablonski, *Gershwin* (Garden City, N.Y., 1987). See also Robert Kimball and Alfred Simon, *The Gershwins* (New York, 1973), and Charles Schwartz, *Gershwin: His Life and Music* (Indianapolis, 1973) and Deena Rosenberg, *Fascinating Rhythm: The Collaboration of George and Ira Gershwin* (New York, 1991). For a shorter account and a complete worklist by Wayne Schneider, see my Gershwin article in *Amerigrove*.

17. Some of the workings of the Tin Pan Alley trade in which Gershwin got his start are shown by the facts and lore surrounding "Swanee." Gershwin and lyricist Irving Caesar wrote "Swanee" and placed it in a revue marking the opening on 24 October 1919 of the Capitol Theater, a new Broadway movie house. The song became a hit, however, only after Al Jolson, the era's chief male singing star, introduced it in his show, *Sinbad*. According to David Jasen, Caesar convinced "his friend" Jolson to sing it in that show. Herbert G. Goldman, on the other hand, writes that Jolson, hearing Gershwin play it at a party

> in late December . . . became intrigued by "Swanee" and made plans to record the song at his next session for the Columbia Gramophone Company. By the end of January, Jolson was belting "Swanee" to the rafters in performances of *Sinbad*, Al Goodman had his pit musicians play the number faster than it had been played by the Columbia Orchestra, and "Swanee," aided by a heavy advertising campaign, became one of the biggest hits of the season. (See Herbert G. Goldman, *Jolson: The Legend Comes to Life* [New York, 1988], 109–10)

Jasen reports: "With a full-page headshot of Jolson on the cover, 'Swanee' sold over a million copies of sheet music and two million copies of his disc. It became the biggest-selling song Gershwin would have in his life" (see David A. Jasen, *Tin Pan Alley—The Composers, the Songs, the Performers and Their Times: The Golden*

Age of American Popular Music from 1886 to 1956 [New York, 1988], 165). According to *Joel Whitburn's Pop Memories 1890–1954: The History of American Popular Music* (Menomonee Falls, Wisc., 1986), 233, Jolson's recording first appeared on his top-seller charts on 8 May 1920, remained there for eighteen weeks, and was the number 1 seller for nine of those weeks. Whitburn also lists successful performances by the All-Star Trio (Victor Arden, piano; F. Wheeler Wadsworth, alto sax; George Hamilton Green, xylophone; their recording made the top-seller charts in the week of 24 April 1920, when it was ranked number 11; page 22) and the Peerless Quartet (four male singers; the recording made the top-seller charts in the week of 27 November 1920, also as number 11; page 352). Jasen's claim that "Swanee" was Gershwin's largest-selling song is confirmed, insofar as recordings are concerned, by Whitburn.

18. Many accounts of this famous event have been written. One that captures its original flavor is Isaac Goldberg, *George Gershwin: A Study in American Music* (1931), supplemented by Edith Garson, with Foreword and Discography by Alan Dashiell (New York, 1958), 136–55. An archival recording, *An Experiment in Modern Music: Paul Whiteman at Aeolian Hall* (Smithsonian Collection recording, DMM 2-0518), with notes by Thornton Hagert, has been issued; see also *The Birth of "Rhapsody in Blue": Paul Whiteman's Historic Aeolian Hall Concert of 1924*, reconstructed and conducted by Maurice Peress (MusicMasters recording MMD 20113X/20114T, 1986).

19. Between 1919 and the end of 1924 Gershwin wrote the scores to twelve Broadway shows. From 1925 until the end of his life in 1938, he composed scores to fifteen more such works.

20. As early as 1922 Gershwin had been able to try his hand as an "opera" composer with the brief, one-act *Blue Monday,* presenting it as part of a revue, George White's *Scandals of 1922.* Even though *Blue Monday* was deemed a failure and withdrawn after one performance, Gershwin, twenty-three years old and with no prior experience, had found himself in a position to write such a work and have it produced on Broadway. (Will Vodery did the orchestration.) Here is ample indication that his was to be no ordinary career for an American composer. See Jablonski, *Gershwin,* 49–53. See also Goldberg, *George Gershwin,* 120–23. *Rhapsody in Blue* (1924), as noted, was commissioned by Whiteman and unveiled in a "historical" event, in the full glare of public attention. The *Rhapsody*'s success led to another commission, this one for the Concerto in F, from Walter Damrosch and the New York Symphony Society (1925). Gershwin's track record by the time he composed *An American in Paris* (1928), his next work for orchestra, had eminent figures competing to premiere it. As Jablonski notes, Walter Damrosch told Gershwin he "would love to arrange with you to do your new work at a Philharmonic symphony this winter." Meanwhile, "even as he worked," Gershwin was approached by Russian dance impresario Sergei Diaghilev, "who wanted to produce a ballet around it," and Leopold Stokowski of the Philadelphia Orchestra (Jablonski, *Gershwin,* 171). In 1929, the Metropolitan Opera commissioned Gershwin to compose a full-length opera, *The Dybbuk,* with

a libretto by Henry Ahlsberg, for performance in 1931. He never fulfilled the commission (Jablonski, *Gershwin,* 194–95).

21. I am grateful to James Dapogny for this suggestion.

22. Jablonski, *Gershwin,* 258–59. In Jablonski's opinion, "much of the wit and charm of this work is smothered in the reorchestration by William C. Schoenfeld published in 1953" (260).

23. The song was "The Real American Folk Song (Is a Rag)," written under Ira's pseudonym "Arthur Francis," with music by George. It was interpolated into the Broadway musical comedy *Ladies First,* whose music was mostly by A. B. Sloane. Its refrain begins: "The real American folk song is a rag— / A mental jag— / A rhythmic tonic for the chronic blues." See Gershwin, *Lyrics,* 180.

24. "Fascinating Rhythm" was sung by Fred Astaire in *Lady Be Good* and led into a dance number. See Jablonski, *Gershwin,* 83.

25. The line comes from the verse of "Embraceable You," written originally for "an operetta version of *East Is West*" (1928), a show that was never completed, then put into *Girl Crazy.* See Gershwin, *Lyrics,* 30–31.

26. The quotation is from "Slap That Bass," another Astaire number, seen in the film *Shall We Dance?* See Gershwin, *Lyrics,* 221.

27. William Austin to Richard Crawford, 23 February 1985. My own unsystematic but fairly extensive search through song lists confirms Austin's point. "Rhythm" became a kind of catchword in the 1930s, as "syncopation" had been earlier. But the only prominent use I found before the Gershwins' "Fascinating Rhythm" (1924) is the name of a well-known white jazz group that began recording in August 1922 under the name of the Friar's Society Orchestra, changed by March 1923 to the New Orleans Rhythm Kings. A search through Brian Rust, *Jazz Records, A–Z, 1897–1942,* rev. 5th ed. (n.p., [1983]), turned up no other groups that recorded between the NORK and three who began to record in 1925: the St. Louis Rhythm Kings (April), Paul Fried and His Rhythmicians (September), and the Blue Rhythm Orchestra (October). Rust's index yielded only one tune with the key word in its title that circulated before "Fascinating Rhythm" was published (December 1924): "The Rhythm Rag" by Willard Robison, recorded in September 1924 by Robison and his Deep River Orchestra. In October 1925 a tune called "Rhythm of the Day" received its first jazz recording in a performance by Ross Gorman and the Earl Carroll Orchestra. Roger Lax and Frederick Smith, *The Great Song Thesaurus,* 2d ed. updated and expanded (New York, 1989), list no hit with "rhythm" in its title before "Fascinating Rhythm." Other hits or "notable" songs that followed, according to the *Thesaurus,* are "Crazy Rhythm" (1928), "Futuristic Rhythm" (1929), "I Got Rhythm" and "Rockin' in Rhythm" (1930), "Rhythm Is Our Business" (1934), "Broadway Rhythm" and "Rhythm of the Rain" (1935), "All God's Chillun Got Rhythm" (1937), and "Lullaby in Rhythm" (1938).

28. *Good News,* with a score by Henderson, Brown, and DeSylva, opened in September 1927 and ran for 557 performances (Gerald Bordman, *American Musical Theatre: A Chronicle* [New York, 1978], 428).

29. Victor V22558. See Brian Rust, *The American Dance Band Discography, 1917–1942* (New Rochelle, N.Y., 1975).

30. Brian Rust and Allen G. Debus, *The Complete Entertainment Discography from 1897 to 1942*, 2d ed. (New York, 1989), 328, dates this recording (Victor 12332) 10 July 1938, New York City. It is part of a medley of "Vocal Gems" from *Girl Crazy*.

31. Decca 23310; the LP reissue on Decca is numbered DL 5412.

32. In his discographical supplement to Goldberg, *George Gershwin*, 366, Alan Dashiell criticizes the recording as evidence of "star trouble." "Miss Martin," he complains, "chose to bend the songs to her will (and style) so that there is as much Martin here as Gershwin." "I Got Rhythm" is one song said to be marred by the singer's "coy mannerisms." Jablonski, *Gershwin*, 404–5, follows suit. He writes: "*Girl Crazy* is spoiled a little (not enough to hurt) by the mannered singing of Mary Martin who, as A Star, was assigned songs that could have been better sung by others, i.e., hear Louise Carlyle do 'Sam and Delilah' and then wish she had done the other Merman songs from the show." Jablonski identifies this record as "an album in Jay Gold's 'American Musicals' series for Time-Life Records. These are the Goddard Lieberson-produced show reconstructions of *Oh, Kay!* and *Girl Crazy*, plus the out-of-print Capitol original cast recording of the 1952 revival of *Of Thee I Sing*" (Time-Life Records TL-AM09, three-record set).

33. Transcribed from original cast recording, MGM E2323.

34. To sum up public response to the song "I Got Rhythm," *Joel Whitburn's Pop Memories* shows it as a success on record but not a major hit. Red Nichols's recording made the top-seller charts for eight weeks beginning 6 December 1930, reaching a peak position of number 5 (page 336). Recordings by Ethel Waters (one week, 17 January 1931, number 17; page 440) and Louis Armstrong (two weeks, 2 April 1932, number 17; page 33) also enjoyed some success. However, Nichols's recording of "Embraceable You," also from *Girl Crazy* and made the same day, outsold "I Got Rhythm" (nine weeks, 22 November 1930, number 2; page 336).

Rust and Debus, *Complete Entertainment Discography*, besides Jane Froman's recording of "I Got Rhythm," lists ones by Kate Smith (New York, 6 November 1930), Adelaide Hall (London, 28 September 1931), Al Bowlly (London, 19 May 1932), Elizabeth Welch (London, 20 January 1938, as part of a "Gershwin Medley"), and the Merry Macs (New York, 5 September 1939). This work covers artists who are deemed neither "jazz and blues musicians" (though Hall's 1931 recording is also listed in Rust's *Jazz Records A–Z*) nor involved with "commercial dance bands, American and British." That leaves "the minstrel pioneers, the vaudevillians, the film stars and radio personalities, and the straight actors and actresses" who are either "artists of American birth, or of such status that they are as well-known in America as their own countries" (1).

Lax and Smith, *Thesaurus*, 57, lists "I Got Rhythm" as one of the "top hits" of 1930. It also lists "I Got Rhythm" and Irving Berlin's "There's No Business

Like Show Business" as Ethel Merman's two theme songs (166). And it notes that, as well as film versions of *Girl Crazy* in 1932 and 1943 and *An American in Paris* (1951), the song also appeared in the film *Rhapsody in Blue* (1945), the "biopic" of Gershwin (265).

Alec Wilder, *American Popular Song: The Great Innovators 1900–1950*, ed. James T. Maher (New York, 1972), is the richest account of the musical tradition in which Gershwin wrote his songs. In the introduction to this work James T. Maher estimates that in the United States during the first half of the century, roughly 300,000 " 'popular' songs of every variety" were deposited for copyright. Wilder, a composer of both popular songs and concert music, examined some 17,000 of these, from which he cites about 300 in his book (xxxviii). While granting its wide acceptance, Wilder is no fan of "I Got Rhythm" as a song. In discussing Irving Berlin's "Back to Back" (1939), for example, he notes that "its release slightly recalls that of 'I Got Rhythm' but is much less four-square, by which I obviously mean it's much better" (114). Later, in a somewhat dyspeptic mood, Wilder comments: "I know that 'I Got Rhythm' has been played ad nauseum by jazz groups since the time it was first heard. And if it made many players happy, I'm glad. But to be candid, my particular gratification is that, since jazz presumes improvisation, in all my hearing of the song by jazz groups, I've always heard endlessly different variations of the original. . . . As an effort by a major writer, I find it a passing fancy, enormously successful though it obviously has been" (151). Wilder also questioned the Gershwin brothers' taste in quoting themselves in the release of their song "Nice Work If You Can Get It" (1937). "I'm slightly embarrassed," he confides, by the "somewhat lordly allusion to a phrase from 'I Got Rhythm' ['Who could ask for anything more?']. No doubt the Gershwins were right: everyone *did* know the earlier song. But it does seem a bit like boasting" (159).

35. Rust, *Jazz Records A–Z*. Full discographical information can be found there. For an idea of how the recording history of "I Got Rhythm" compares with that of other tunes in the jazz repertory, see Richard Crawford and Jeffrey Magee, *Jazz Standards on Record, 1900–1942: A Core Repertory,* Center for Black Music Research Monographs, no. 4 (Chicago, 1992), especially v–vii and xx–xxi.

36. Gunther Schuller, *The Swing Era: The Development of Jazz 1930–1945* (New York, 1989), 127, outlines the "traditional way" jazz musicians harmonize "I Got Rhythm." In the A section, the harmonic progression is

Bb Gm7 | Cm7 F7 | Bb Gm7 | Cm7 F7 |

Bb Bb7 | Eb Eb | Bb F7 | Bb [F7].

37. A comment Virgil Thomson made about Aaron Copland may apply to "I Got Rhythm," though certainly not to many other Gershwin songs. In 1932, in a discussion of his colleague's "American" side, Thomson wrote that Copland, for all his fondness for displaced accents, "never understood that sensuality of sentiment which is the force of American popular music" (quoted in Minna

Lederman, *The Life and Death of a Small Magazine* [Modern Music, *1924–1946*], I.S.A.M. Monographs no. 18 [Brooklyn, 1983], 22). "Sensuality of sentiment" is not a conspicuous trait of "I Got Rhythm."

38. Jazz being a music in which the status of players and singers rests upon the judgment of their peers, the literature is full of stories of performers having to prove themselves. One tells of Charlie Parker, as a youngster of sixteen, being derided on the bandstand at a Kansas City jam session (Robert George Reisner, *Bird: The Legend of Charlie Parker* [New York, 1962], 185–86). Edward Kennedy Ellington, *Music Is My Mistress* (Garden City, N.Y., 1973), tells of challenges offered by other musicians. Ellington's drummer, Sonny Greer, for example, recalls that when Ellington was "just a yearling" filling in for the regular piano player in a Washington, D.C., night spot, "Bill Jones used to be drummin', and he'd catch him out there in those three-four, five-four switches, and scare him stiff. But he'd hang on, and as I said he had a pretty good left hand, and he'd hold the solid deuce till Bill let him off the hook" (446). In answer to the question "what does America mean to you?" Ellington replied that the music world in the United States "has been an extremely competitive scene, and that in itself incites drive. Without competition you wouldn't have it" (464). Ellington describes jam sessions as a very tough environment, a "cutting contest" in which "you defended your honor with your instrument" (466). In his judgment that was as it should be, as contrasted with a situation in which jazz is subsidized. "The minute you start subsidizing it," he warned, "you are going to get yourself a bastard product. It started as a competitive thing, and if you take away the competition, where a guy must fight to eat, it's going to become something else" (471).

By 1937, "I Got Rhythm" was standard cutting-contest fare. Frank Büchmann-Møller, *You Just Fight for Your Life: The Story of Lester Young* (New York, 1990), 71, reports Billie Holiday's taking Lester Young around New York shortly after he joined Count Basie's band in 1936. At a New York jam session early in 1937, Young "met Leon 'Chu' Berry, who was considered to be the greatest tenor saxophone player next to Coleman Hawkins. Berry did not have his saxophone with him, but when a duel between him and Lester was in the offing Benny Carter went and fetched it. Berry suggested that they start with 'I Got Rhythm,' which was grist to Lester's mill. 'He blew at least fifteen choruses, none of them the same, and each one prettier than the last,' Billie recalls. 'When the fifteenth one was down, Chu Berry was finished.' "

39. Miller's performance is reissued in *Big Band Jazz: From the Beginnings to the Fifties,* selected and annotated by Gunther Schuller and Martin Williams (Smithsonian Recordings, 1983). Cf. Merman's "high C chorus," which reduces the same six bars of the A section of "I Got Rhythm" to nothing but a high-energy single note. One wonders if hearing Merman belt her "high C" at this place, night after night in *Girl Crazy,* left its mark on Miller's idea of the tune to the point that, seven years later, he found a way to create a similar effect in his arrangement.

40. First issued on Commodore Records, Byas and Stewart's performance is included in the *Smithsonian Collection of Classic Jazz*, edited and annotated by Martin Williams, revised ed. (Smithsonian Recordings, 1987). Like the blues, "I Got Rhythm" was a tune on which jazz performers often improvised many choruses in succession, shaping musical statements that built in intensity from chorus to chorus. Tenor saxophonist Bud Freeman tells a story about a performance he gave as a member of a Special Service company of the United States armed forces stationed in Alaska during World War II. The point of Freeman's recollection was to expose commercial gimmicks that in his view pandered to the audience. But, considering the tradition of extended performance already established for Gershwin's song, it was no coincidence that "I Got Rhythm" was the piece on which he tried his clownishly satirical ploy.

> It was in Alaska that I found out an interesting thing about being commercial. I discovered that people don't listen as much as they look. We were doing a show on one of the little islands on the [Aleutian] chain. We were playing in the mess hall, and we were doing our best playing but it didn't seem to be going over so well. These were a lot of bitter men who had been stuck up there a long time and they just defied us to entertain them. Now we were dressed in heavy Arctic equipment and looked like a bunch of Eskimos. It wasn't that it was so terribly cold there, but this was our way of dressing. You could fall down and not get hurt because the clothing was so thickly padded. I used to play a solo, about ten improvised choruses, on "I Got Rhythm," and suddenly during my solo the idea came to me just to fall back and not break the motion of the play[ing], just to fall back. So I fell on my back with my feet up in the air and some of the men jumped up. They were completely out of their minds. "This is the greatest fuckin' saxophone player in the world," they were screaming. (Freeman, *Crazeology*, 59)

41. Martin Williams, *The Jazz Tradition*, new and revised ed. (Oxford, 1983), 94–95, puts it in a somewhat different way. "Art Tatum's capacities for melodic invention were limited," Williams writes. "He was basically an artist of the arabesque, true, but he also functioned in that middle ground which André Hodier has called paraphrase, where fragments of the original theme take their place beside invented phrases, to form allusive structures in variation. . . . Tatum's best harmonic and melodic adornments help us discover what is potentially beautiful in a popular song; his invented, passing phrases subdue what is not." By that standard, Tatum found little that was beautiful in the melody of "I Got Rhythm."

42. On 30 June 1932, Don Redman and His Orchestra made the first wholly instrumental recording of "I Got Rhythm"—an early example of many black musicians' tendency to omit Ira Gershwin's lyrics.

43. Williams, *Jazz Tradition*, 49, identifies Bechet's "Shag" as "the first non-thematic use on records of the 'I Got Rhythm' chord progression." "Shag" is

attributed to Bechet on the record label, but I was unable to find in the Library of Congress copyright records any evidence that it was published or even copyrighted.

44. "Yeah, Man," a song with words by Noble Sissle and music by J. Russel Robinson, was copyrighted as a published item on 27 May 1932 (entry no. 30349) and published by DeSylva, Brown, and Henderson, Inc. Joel Shaw made the first jazz recording in October of that year, just after Bechet and the New Orleans Feetwarmers recorded "Shag." "Stomp It Off," with a melody attributed to Sy Oliver and Jimmy Lunceford, was copyrighted as an unpublished piece on 1 April 1936 (entry no. 121547) by Denton and Haskins Music Co. Lunceford had recorded it in October 1934.

45. "Don't Be That Way," attributed to E. M. [Edgar] Sampson, was copyrighted as an unpublished piece on 16 May 1935 (entry no. 104261). Webb had recorded it on 19 November 1934. As table 6 indicates, it seems to have had the most active independent life of all "I Got Rhythm" contrafacts during the swing era.

46. Schuller, *Swing Era*, 24, attributes Goodman's arrangement to Edgar Sampson and calls it "one of the band's most popular successes." He also finds Webb's 1934 recording far superior to Goodman's two versions of 1938. Both use Sampson's arrangement, reworked in 1938

to accommodate lengthy solo spots for Goodman and [the] famous pre–*In The Mood* fade-away ending. Comparison of both bands' versions affords us a dramatic lesson in how interpretation is everything in jazz. The same arrangement, the same notes can be exciting or vapid, depending on their execution. The gulf here between Webb and Goodman was a wide one, the former delivering these pieces with a raw excitement, rhythmic drive (faster tempos, too) and heated sonority; the latter with a neatly packaged cooled-off sound, bouncing along in a safe inoffensive manner. (296)

47. *Good Morning Blues: The Autobiography of Count Basie,* as told to Albert Murray (New York, 1985), 239, confirms that "Blow Top," recorded by Basie and his orchestra on 31 May 1940, was composed and arranged by Tab Smith. I have not checked the Library of Congress copyright records for this item. "Apple Honey," attributed to Woody Herman, was recorded by Herman's orchestra on 10 August 1944. Its tune was copyrighted in unpublished form on 25 October 1944 (entry no. 395490) and as a published piece on 18 July 1945 (entry no. 133874) by Charling Music Corp.

48. Ellington first recorded "Cotton Tail" on 4 May 1940. On 20 July 1940, it was copyrighted as an unpublished piece (entry no. 225831) by Robbins Music Corp. A copyrighted orchestration arranged by Will Hudson was published on 21 June 1944, also by Robbins.

49. Ellington's composed variations on Gershwin's tune are striking. But Schuller, *Swing Era*, points out another distinctive property of "Cotton Tail"— one that surely can be traced to the tradition of performance already established

for "I Got Rhythm." Taking his cue from Ben Webster's two-chorus solo, Schuller writes:

> Never before had Ellington opened up a piece for out-and-out blowing on a record date as he did for Webster and "Cotton Tail." The occasional showcase pieces and "concertos" were considerably more pre-planned and determined *by* Ellington as *composer*. . . . [But] "Cotton Tail" and Webster's solo loosened, ever so slightly, the compositional harness that Ellington had been constructing for over a decade and more. "Cotton Tail," particularly in its execution, let in a gust of spontaneity, of freshness, of flexibility, which the Ellington band was never to lose again and which offered a whole new way of integrating composition and improvisation. (129–30)

50. Quoted from Dizzy Gillespie with Al Fraser, *To Be, or Not . . . to Bop: Memoirs* (Garden City, N. Y., 1979), 207. Roach expanded his discussion of the economic roots of contrafacts as follows:

> When the music moved from uptown to downtown, downtown meaning whites were now the clientele, a few more pennies were being made than when we were uptown. . . . Downtown, people wanted to hear something they were familiar with, like "How High the Moon," "What Is This Thing Called Love?" Can you play that? So in playing these things, the black musicians recognized that the royalties were going back to these people, like ASCAP, the Jerome Kerns, the Gershwins. So one revolutionary thing that happened, they began to write parodies on the harmonic structure. (209)

Roach's comments suggest that bebop musicians were the first to write new themes on old chord changes, a notion contradicted by the history of "I Got Rhythm" and, more generally, in Martin Williams, *Jazz in Its Time* (New York, 1989), 27–30.

51. Like "I Got Rhythm," tunes based on its chord changes are virtually all in B-flat. Art Pepper's "Brown Gold," written in E-flat, is an exception.

52. Note also that none of Parker's versions use the two-bar extension at the end of Gershwin's tune.

53. Gillespie, *To Be*, 143.

54. Examples include the following, whose dates are the earliest date of copyright deposit. Copyright entry numbers are designated EU for unpublished pieces and EP for published ones. All but three (Tadd Dameron, Bud Powell, and Sonny Stitt) have been verified in the Library of Congress copyright records:

> Clifford Brown, "Brownie Speaks" (27 December 1956, EU453249)
>
> Al Cohn, "The Goof and I" (26 March 1948, EU122626)
>
> Tadd Dameron, "Delirium" (copyright information not looked for)
>
> Miles Davis, "The Theme" (28 March 1966, EU918852; unattributed in some other sources)
>
> Dizzy Gillespie, "Anthropology" with C. Parker (10 December 1947, EU107329), "Dizzy Atmosphere" (10 June 1944, EU378389), "Oo Bop

Shabam" with Gil Fuller and Jay Roberts (12 May 1948, EP25545), "Ow" (18 April 1958, EU521399), "Salt Peanuts" with Kenny Clarke (13 October 1941, EU272651; published 1 September 1943, EP116206), and "Shaw 'Nuff" with C. Parker (22 November 1948, EP32267)

Hampton Hawes, "Hamp's Paws" (30 January 1956, EU424351)

Thelonious Monk, "Fifty-Second Street Theme" (29 March 1948, EP24775), and "Rhythm-A-Ning" from *Brilliant Corners Suite* (29 May 1958, EU516975)

Fats Navarro, "Eb-Pob" with Leo Parker (16 May 1947, EU75756)

Art Pepper, "Brown Gold" (19 March 1957, EU472263)

Bud Powell, "Bud's Bubble" (copyright information not looked for; recorded on Roost Records RLP 401)

Sonny Rollins, "No Moe" (31 March 1965, EU885064), and "Oleo" (13 June 1963, EU877719)

Sonny Stitt, "Sonny Side" (copyright information not looked for; attribution not established; recorded on Prestige NJLPo-103 by Stitt and Bud Powell)

George Wallington, "Lemon Drop" (25 May 1949, EP37174)

Kai Winding, "O-Go-Mo" (18 February 1947, EU63539)

55. Jørgen Grunnet Jepsen, *Jazz Records, 1942–[1969]: A Discography*, 8 vols. (Copenhagen, 1963–70), lists the following recordings of "Anthropology" (chronologically):

Dizzy Gillespie's Orchestra (22 February 1946; vol. 4a:307)

Claude Thornhill's Orchestra (4 September 1947; 8:48)

Tadd Dameron's Sextet (29 August 1948; 3:107), his septet (16 October 1948; 6 November 1948; 3:108)

Charlie Parker's All Stars (5 March 1949; 6:66), Parker and the Swedish All-Stars (22 November 1950; 6:69; and 24 November 1950; 6:70)

The Parker-Gillespie Quintet (31 March 1951; 6:71)

Poul Hindberg (28 July 1955; 4b:296)

Clifford Jordan (10 November 1957; 4c:240)

The Embers Quintet (29 August 1959; 4a:12)

The Barry Harris Quintet (28 September 1961; 4b:178)

The Vi Redd Sextet (21/22 May 1962; 6:237)

The Don Byas Quartet (14/15 July 1964; 2:214)

The Elvin Jones Quartet (23 February 1965; 4c:199)

The Bengt Hallberg Trio (14 May 1968; 4b:117)

56. There are many more "I Got Rhythm" contrafacts than the ones on which I have gathered information here. But to provide a statistical summary of the ones I've dealt with: Between 1930 and 1968, a total of 280 jazz re-

cordings of "I Got Rhythm" and 45 of its contrafacts have been traced. Of
that number, 160 (57 percent) were contrafacts. The count is based on pieces
listed in Rust and Jepson's discographies. The contrafacts, in alphabetical
order by title, are

"Allen's Alley"	"No Moe"
"Al-Leu-Cha"	"O-Go-Mo"
"Anthropology"	"Oleo"
"Apple Honey"	"An Oscar for Treadwell"
"Blow Top"	"Ow"
"Brown Gold"	"Passport"
"Bud's Bubble"	"Raid the Joint"
"Chant of the Groove"	"Red Cross"
"Chasin' the Bird"	"Rhythm-A-Ning"
"Constellation"	"Salt Peanuts"
"Cotton Tail"	"Shag"
"Dexterity"	"Shaw 'Nuff"
"Don't Be That Way"	"So What"
"Eb-Pob"	"Squatty Roo"
"Father Steps In"	"Steeplechase"
"Fifty-second Street Theme"	"Stomp It Off"
"Good Queen Bess"	"Swedish Schnapps"
"The Jeep Is Jumpin' "	"The Theme"
"Kim"	"Thriving from a Riff"
"Lemon Drop"	"Wire Brush Stomp"
"Lester Leaps In"	"XYZ"
"Little Benny"	"Yeah Man"
"Moose the Mooche"	

57. See chapter 2, p. 65.

58. Ella Fitzgerald, *The George and Ira Gershwin Songbook* (Verve recording
VE-2-2525).

59. As I hear it, a melodic quotation follows the semitone hike after bar 8.
Bars 9–10, plus the first three notes of bar 11, sound to me like a reference to
"The Parade of the Wooden Soldiers" by Léon Jessel, first published in Germany
in 1905 (James Fuld, *The Book of World-Famous Music: Classical, Popular and Folk,*
rev. ed. [New York, 1971], 421).

BIBLIOGRAPHY

GENERAL

Ahlquist, Karen Ethel. "Opera, Theatre, and Audience in Antebellum New York." Ph.D. diss., University of Michigan, 1991.

Allen, Walter C. *Hendersonia: The Music of Fletcher Henderson and His Musicians: A Bio-Discography.* Highland Park, N.J., 1973.

The American Musical Directory. New York, 1861. Reprint, New York, 1980.

Amerigrove. See Hitchcock and Sadie, eds.

Anderson, Gillian B. "Putting the Experience of the World at the Nation's Command: Music at the Library of Congress, 1800–1917." *Journal of the American Musicological Society* 42 (1989): 108–49.

———. "Elizabeth Sprague Coolidge." In *Notable American Women: The Modern Period, a Biographical Dictionary.* Edited by Barbara Sicherman and Carol Hurd Green, 160–62. Cambridge, Mass., 1980.

Attali, Jacques. *Noise: The Political Economy of Music.* Translated by Brian Massumi. Minneapolis, 1985.

Austin, William W. *"Susanna," "Jeanie," and "The Old Folks at Home": The Songs of Stephen C. Foster from His Time to Ours.* New York, 1975.

Baida, Peter. *Poor Richard's Legacy: American Business Values from Benjamin Franklin to Donald Trump.* New York, 1990.

Balliett, Whitney. *Goodbyes and Other Messages: A Journal of Jazz 1981–1990.* New York, 1991.

Barbour, J. Murray. *The Church Music of William Billings.* East Lansing, Mich., 1960. Reprint, New York, 1972.

Basie, Count [William]. *Good Morning Blues: The Autobiography of Count Basie.* As told to Albert Murray. New York, 1985.

Becker, Howard. *Art Worlds.* Berkeley, 1982.

Belfy, Jeanne. *The Louisville Orchestra New Music Project: An American Experiment in the Patronage of International Contemporary Music: Selected*

Composers' Letters to the Louisville Orchestra. University of Louisville Publications in Musicology, no. 2. Louisville, 1983.

Bentley, William. *The Diary of William Bentley, D.D., Pastor of East Church, Salem, Massachusetts.* 4 vols. Salem, Mass., 1905–14.

Bergreen, Lawrence. *As Thousands Cheer: The Life of Irving Berlin.* New York, 1990.

Birge, Edward Bailey. *History of Public School Music in the United States.* New and augmented ed. Washington, D.C., [1966].

Bledstein, Burton J. *The Culture of Professionalism: The Middle Class and the Development of Higher Education in America.* New York, 1976.

Bordman, Gerald. *American Musical Theater: A Chronicle.* New York, 1978.

Britton, Allen P. "Theoretical Introductions in American Tune-Books to 1800." Ph.D. diss., University of Michigan, 1949.

Britton, Allen Perdue, Irving Lowens, and completed by Richard Crawford. *American Sacred Music Imprints, 1698–1810: A Bibliography.* Worcester, Mass., 1990.

Brooks, Henry M. *Olden-Time Music: A Compilation from Newspapers and Books.* Boston, 1888. Reprint, New York, 1973.

Broyles, Michael. *"Music of the Highest Class": Elitism and Populism in Antebellum Boston.* New Haven, Conn., 1992.

Bruchey, Stuart. *Enterprise: The Dynamic Economy of a Free People.* Cambridge, Mass., 1990.

Brunn, H. O. *The Story of the Original Dixieland Jazz Band.* Baton Rouge, La., 1960. Reprint, New York, 1977.

Bryant, Carolyn. *And the Band Played On.* Washington, D.C., 1975.

Büchmann-Møller, Frank. *You Just Fight for Your Life: The Story of Lester Young.* Foreword by Lewis Porter. New York, 1990.

Buerkle, Jack V., and Danny Barker. *Bourbon Street Black: The New Orleans Black Jazzman.* New York, 1973.

Burkholder, J. Peter. *Charles Ives: The Ideas behind the Music.* New Haven, 1985.

———. "Charles Ives and His Fathers: A Response to Maynard Solomon." *Newsletter of the Institute for Studies in American Music* 18, no. 1 (1988).

Burton, Warren. *The District School as It Was. By One Who Went to It.* Boston, 1833.

Bushnell, Vinson. "Daniel Read of New Haven (1757–1836): The Man and His Musical Activities." Ph.D. diss., Harvard University, 1979.

Carder, Polly H. "George Frederick Root, Pioneer Music Educator: His Contributions to Mass Instruction in Music." Ed.D. diss., University of Maryland, 1971.

Carr, Edward Hallett. *What Is History?: The George Macaulay Trevelyan Lectures Delivered in the University of Cambridge, January–March 1961.* London, 1961.

Charters, Samuel B., and Leonard Kunstadt. *Jazz: A History of the New York Scene*. Garden City, N.Y., 1962. Reprint, New York, 1981.

Chase, Gilbert. *America's Music: From the Pilgrims to the Present*. New York, 1955. Rev. 3d ed., Urbana, Ill., 1987.

———, ed. *The American Composer Speaks: A Historical Anthology, 1770–1965*. Baton Rouge, La., 1966.

Cheney, Simeon Pease. *The American Singing Book*. Boston, 1879. Reprint, New York, 1980.

Clark, J. Bunker. *Music at KU: A History of the University of Kansas Music Department*. Lawrence, Kansas, 1986.

Cobb, Buell E., Jr. *The Sacred Harp: A Tradition and Its Music*. Athens, Ga., 1978.

Coburn, Frederick W. "Nathaniel Duren Gould." In *Dictionary of American Biography*, edited by Allen Johnson, 4:455. New York, 1928–36.

Cockrell, Dale, ed. and annotator. *Excelsior: Journals of the Hutchinson Family Singers, 1842–1846*. Stuyvesant, N.Y., 1989.

Collier, James Lincoln. *Benny Goodman and the Swing Era*. New York, 1989.

———. *Duke Ellington*. New York, 1987.

———. *Louis Armstrong: An American Genius*. New York, 1983.

———. *The Reception of Jazz: A New View*. Institute for the Study of American Music Monographs, no. 27. Brooklyn, 1988.

Complete Catalogue of Sheet Music and Musical Work Published by the Board of Music Trade of the United States of America: 1870. N.p., 1871. Reprint, New York, 1973.

Copland, Aaron, and Vivian Perlis. *Copland: 1900 through 1942*. New York, 1984.

Cowell, Henry, and Sidney Cowell. *Charles Ives and His Music*. New York, 1955.

Crawford, Richard. "American Music and Its Two Written Traditions." *Fontes Artis Musicae* 31 (1984): 79–84.

———. *The American Musicological Society 1934–1984: An Anniversary Essay, with Lists of Officers, Winners of Awards, Editors of the Journal, and Honorary and Corresponding Members*. Philadelphia, 1984.

———. *American Studies and American Musicology: A Point of View and a Case in Point*. Institute for the Study of American Music Monographs, no. 4. Brooklyn, 1975.

———. "Amerigrove's Pedigree." Review Essay on *The New Grove Dictionary of American Music*. College Music Society, *Symposium* 27 (1987): 172–86.

———. " 'Ancient Music' and the Europeanizing of American Psalmody, 1800–1810." In *A Celebration of American Music: Words and Music in Honor of H. Wiley Hitchcock*, edited by Richard Crawford, R. Allen Lott, and Carol J. Oja. Ann Arbor, Mich., 1990.

———. *Andrew Law, American Psalmodist*. Evanston, Ill., 1968.

———. "A Historian's Introduction to Early American Music." *Proceedings of the American Antiquarian Society* 89 (1979): 261–98.

———. Obituary Notice for Irving Lowens. *Proceedings of the American Antiquarian Society* 91 (1984): 40–44.

———. "Sonneck and American Musical Historiography." In *Essays in Musicology: A Tribute to Alvin Johnson,* edited by Lewis Lockwood and Edward Roesner. N.p., 1990.

———. *Studying American Music.* Institute for the Study of American Music, Special Publication no. 3. Brooklyn, 1985.

———. "Tracking Vernacular Music . . . across the Great Divide." In *Music Librarianship in America,* edited by Michael Ochs. *Harvard Library Bulletin,* n.s. 2 (1991): 92–99.

Crawford, Richard, and D. W. Krummel. "Early American Music Printing and Publishing." In *Printing and Society in Early America,* edited by William J. Joyce, David D. Hall, Richard D. Brown, and John B. Hench. Worcester, Mass., 1983.

Crawford, Richard, R. Allen Lott, and Carol J. Oja, eds. *A Celebration of American Music: Words and Music in Honor of H. Wiley Hitchcock.* Ann Arbor, Mich., 1990.

Crawford, Richard, and Jeffrey Magee. *Jazz Standards on Record, 1900–1942: A Core Repertory.* Center for Black Music Research Monographs, no. 4. Chicago, 1992.

Crouch, Stanley. *Notes of a Hanging Judge: Essays and Reviews, 1979–1989.* New York, 1990.

Dance, Stanley. *The World of Duke Ellington.* New York, 1970.

Dannen, Frederic. *Hit Men: Power Brokers and Fast Money inside the Music Business.* New York, 1990.

Davin, Tom. "Conversations with James P. Johnson." In *Ragtime: Its History, Composers, and Music,* edited by John Edward Hasse. New York, 1985.

Denisoff, R. Serge. *Great Day Coming: Folk Music and the American Left.* Urbana, Ill., 1971. Reprint, Baltimore, 1973.

DiMaggio, Paul. "Cultural Entrepreneurship in Nineteenth-Century Boston: The Creation of an Organizational Base for High Culture in America"; and "Cultural Entrepreneurship in Nineteenth-Century Boston, Part II: The Classification and Framing of American Art." *Media, Culture, and Society* 4 (1982): 33–50, 303–22.

Dixon, Robert M. W., and John Godrich. *Recording the Blues.* New York, 1970.

Dodge, Roger Pryor. "Consider the Critics." In *Jazzmen,* edited by Frederic Ramsey, Jr., and Charles Edward Smith. New York, 1939.

———. "Jazz in the Twenties." *Jazz* 1 (1942): 6–8, 15, 29.

Ellington, Edward Kennedy. *Music Is My Mistress.* Garden City, N.Y., 1973.

Ellington, Mercer, with Stanley Dance. *Duke Ellington in Person: An Intimate Memoir.* Boston, 1978.

Ellison, Ralph. *Going to the Territory.* New York, 1986.

Elson, Louis C. *The History of American Music.* New York, 1904.

Epstein, Dena. *Music Publishing in Chicago before 1871: The Firm of Root and Cady, 1858–1871.* Detroit Studies in Music Bibliography, no. 14. Detroit, 1969.

Farwell, Arthur, and W. Dermot Darby, eds. *Music in America. (The Art of Music,* edited by Daniel Gregory Mason, vol. 4.) New York, 1915.

Fiske, Roger. *English Theatre Music in the Eighteenth Century.* London, 1973.

Foner, Philip S. *American Labor Songs of the Nineteenth Century.* Urbana, Ill., 1975.

Ford Foundation. *Annual Reports.* New York, 1956–64.

———. *Contemporary Music for Schools: A Catalog of Works Written by Composers Participating in the Young Composers Project, 1959–1964, Sponsored by the Ford Foundation and the National Music Council.* Washington, D.C., 1966.

Fox, Ted. *Showtime at the Apollo.* New York, 1983.

Freeman, Bud. *Crazeology: The Autobiography of a Chicago Jazzman.* As told to Robert Wolf. Urbana, Ill., 1989.

Frith, Simon. " 'The Magic That Can Set You Free': The Ideology of Folk and the Myth of the Rock Community." In *Folk or Popular?: Distinctions, Influences, Continuities,* edited by Richard Middleton and David Horn. *Popular Music* I (Cambridge, 1981): 159–68.

Fuld, James. *The Book of World-Famous Music: Classical, Popular and Folk.* Rev. ed. New York, 1971.

George, Nelson. *The Death of Rhythm and Blues.* New York, 1988.

Gershwin, Ira. *Lyrics on Several Occasions: A Selection of Stage & Screen Lyrics Written for Sundry Situations; and Now Arranged in Arbitrary Categories. To which have been added many informative annotations & disquisitions on their why & wherefore, their whom-for, their how; and matters associative.* New York, 1959. Reprint, New York, 1973.

Giddins, Gary. *Satchmo.* New York, 1988.

Gillespie, Dizzy. *To Be, or Not . . . to Bop.* With Al Fraser. Garden City, N.Y., 1979.

Goldberg, Isaac. *George Gershwin: A Study in American Music.* Supplemented by Edith Garson, with Foreword and Discography by Alan Dashiell. New York, 1958. (First ed. 1931.)

Goldman, Herbert G. *Jolson: The Legend Comes to Life.* New York, 1988.

Gordon, Max. *Live at the Village Vanguard.* New York, 1980.

Gould, Nathaniel D. *Church Music in America, Comprising Its History and Peculiarities at Different Periods, with Cursory Remarks on Its Legitimate Use and Its Abuse; with Notices of the Schools, Composers, Teachers, and Societies.* Boston, 1853. Reprint, New York, 1972.

Green, Janet M., ed. *Musical Biographies. (The American History and Encyclopedia of Music,* ed. W. L. Hubbard, vol. 1.) Toledo, [1908].

Gushee, Lawrence. Review of *The Reception of Jazz in America: A New View,* by James Lincoln Collier. *Ethnomusicology* 33 (1989): 352–54.

Hamm, Charles. *Music in the New World.* New York, 1983.

——. "Some Fugitive Thoughts on the Historiography of Music." In *Essays in Musicology: A Tribute to Alvin Johnson,* edited by Lewis Lockwood and Edward Roesner. N.p., 1990.

——. *Yesterdays: Popular Song in America.* New York, 1979.

Hammond, John. *John Hammond on Record: An Autobiography.* With Irving Townsend. New York, 1977. Reprint, New York, 1981.

Handy, W. C. *Father of the Blues: An Autobiography.* New York, 1941. Reprint, New York, 1970.

Harrison, Frank Ll., Mantle Hood, and Claude V. Palisca. *Musicology.* Englewood Cliffs, N.J., 1963.

Hart, Philip. *Orpheus in the New World: The Symphony Orchestra as an American Cultural Institution.* New York, 1973.

Haskell, Harry. *The Early Music Revival: A History.* New York, 1988.

Hasse, John Edward, ed. *Ragtime: Its History, Composers, and Music.* New York, 1985.

Hitchcock, H. Wiley. *Music in the United States: A Historical Introduction.* 3d ed. Englewood Cliffs, N.J., 1988. (First ed. 1969.)

Hitchcock, H. Wiley, and Vivian Perlis, eds. *An Ives Celebration: Papers and Panels of the Charles Ives Centennial Festival-Conference.* Urbana, Ill., 1977.

Hitchcock, H. Wiley, and Stanley Sadie, eds. *The New Grove Dictionary of American Music.* 4 vols. London, 1986. (*Amerigrove.*)

Hollinger, David A. *In the American Province: Studies in the History and Historiography of Ideas.* Bloomington, Ind., 1985.

Homzy, Andrew. Review of *Duke Ellington: Jazz Composer,* by Ken Rattenbury. *Notes* 48 (1992): 1241–46.

Hood, George. *A History of Music in New England: With Biographical Sketches of Reformers and Psalmists.* Boston, 1846. Reprint, New York, 1970.

Horowitz, Joseph. "Immortal Masterpieces to Snooze By." *The New York Times,* 9 June 1991, Arts and Leisure Section, 1.

Howard, John Tasker. *Our American Music: Three Hundred Years of It.* New York, 1931. 4th ed., *Our American Music: A Comprehensive History from 1620 to the Present.* New York, 1965.

Hubbard, W. L., ed. *History of American Music.* (*The American History and Encyclopedia of Music,* vol. 4.) Toledo, 1908.

Ives, Charles E. *Memos.* Edited by John Kirkpatrick. New York, 1972.

Jablonski, Edward. *Gershwin.* Garden City, N.Y., 1987.

Jackson, Richard. *United States Music: Sources of Biography and Collective Biography.* Institute for the Study of American Music Monographs, no. 1. Brooklyn, 1973.

James, Henry. *Literary Criticism: Essays on Literature; American Writers; English Writers.* New York, 1984.

Jasen, David. *Tin Pan Alley—The Composers, the Songs, the Performers, and Their Times: The Golden Age of American Popular Music from 1886 to 1956.* New York, 1988.

Jazzgrove. See Kernfeld, ed.

Jepson, Jørgen Grunnet. *Jazz Records, 1942–[1969]: A Discography.* 8 vols. Copenhagen and Holte, 1963–70.

Jewell, Derek. *Duke: A Portrait of Duke Ellington.* New York, 1977.

John Simon Guggenheim Foundation. *Directory of Fellows 1925–1974.* New York, 1975.

Jones, F. O., ed. *A Handbook of American Music and Musicians, Containing Biographies of American Musicians and Histories of the Principal Musical Institutions, Firms, and Societies.* Canaseraga, N.Y., 1886. Reprint, New York, 1971.

Joyce, William J., David D. Hall, Richard D. Brown, and John B. Hench, eds. *Printing and Society in Early America.* Worcester, Mass., 1983.

Kaufman, Charles H. *Music in New Jersey, 1655–1860: A Study of Musical Activity and Musicians in New Jersey from Its First Settlement to the Civil War.* Rutherford, N.J., 1981.

Kenyon, Nicholas, ed. *Authenticity and Early Music.* London, 1989.

Kerman, Joseph. "A Few Canonic Variations." *Critical Inquiry* 10 (1983): 107–25.

Kernfeld, Barry, ed. *The New Grove Dictionary of Jazz.* 2 vols. London, 1988. (*Jazzgrove.*)

Kimball, Robert, and Alfred Simon. *The Gershwins.* New York, 1973.

Kingman, Daniel. *American Music: A Panorama.* 2d ed. New York, 1990. (First ed. 1979.)

Kirk, Elise K. *Music at the White House: A History of the American Spirit.* Urbana, Ill., 1986.

Kirkpatrick, John. *A Temporary Mimeographed Catalogue of the Music Manuscripts and Related Materials of Charles Edward Ives, 1874–1954.* New Haven, 1960.

Kroeger, Karl. *Catalog of the Musical Works of William Billings.* Music Reference Collection, no. 32. Westport, Conn., 1991.

———. "*The Worcester Collection of Sacred Harmony* and Sacred Music in America, 1786–1803." 2 vols. Ph.D. diss., Brown University, 1976.

Krummel, D. W. *Bibliographical Handbook of American Music.* Urbana, Ill., 1987.

Lawrence, Vera Brodsky. *Strong on Music: The New York Music Scene in the Days of George Templeton Strong, 1836–1975.* Vol. 1, *Resonances, 1836–1850.* New York, 1988.

Lax, Roger, and Frederick Smith. *The Great Song Thesaurus.* 2d ed., updated and expanded. New York, 1989.

Lederman, Minna. *The Life and Death of a Small Magazine ("Modern Music," 1924–1946)*. Institute for the Study of American Music Monographs, no. 18. Brooklyn, 1983.

Lees, Gene. *Waiting for Dizzy*. New York, 1991.

Leonard, Neil. *Jazz and the White Americans: The Acceptance of a New Art Form*. Chicago, 1962.

Levine, Lawrence. *Highbrow/Lowbrow: The Emergence of Cultural Hierarchy in America*. Cambridge, Mass., 1988.

Lichtenwanger, William, ed. *Oscar Sonneck and American Music*. Urbana, 1983.

Linderman, Gerald F. *Embattled Courage: The Experience of Combat in the American Civil War*. New York, 1987.

Lipman, Samuel. *The House of Music: Art in an Era of Institutions*. Boston, 1984.

Lockwood, Lewis, and Edward Roesner, eds. *Essays in Musicology: A Tribute to Alvin Johnson*. N.p., 1990.

Lomax, Alan. *Folk Song Style and Culture*. Washington, D.C., 1968.

Lott, R. Allen. "Bernard Ullman: Nineteenth-Century American Impresario." In *A Celebration of American Music: Words and Music in Honor of H. Wiley Hitchcock*, edited by Richard Crawford, R. Allen Lott, and Carol J. Oja. Ann Arbor, Mich., 1990.

Lowens, Irving. "Daniel Read's World: The Letters of an Early American Composer." *Notes* 9 (1951–52): 233–48.

———. *Music and Musicians in Early America*. New York, 1964.

Lowry, W. McNeil, ed. *The Performing Arts and American Society*. Englewood Cliffs, N.J., 1978.

McKay, David P., and Richard Crawford. *William Billings of Boston: Eighteenth-Century Composer*. Princeton, 1975.

McPherson, James M. *Battle Cry of Freedom: The Civil War Era*. The Oxford History of the United States. New York, 1988.

Marcus, Greil. *Mystery Train: Images of America in Rock 'n' Roll Music*. New York, 1975.

Martin, George. *The Damrosch Dynasty: America's First Family of Music*. Boston, 1983.

Mates, Julian. *The American Musical Stage before 1800*. New Brunswick, N.J., 1962.

Mathews, W. S. B., assoc. ed. *A Hundred Years of Music in America: An Account of Musical Effort in America during the Past Century, including Popular Music and Singing Schools, Church Music, Musical Conventions and Festivals, Orchestral, Operatic and Oratorio Music; Improvements in Musical Instruments; Popular and the Higher Musical Education; Creative Activity, and the Beginning of a National School of Musical Composition*. Chicago, 1889. Reprint, New York, 1970.

Matz, Mary Jane. *The Many Lives of Otto Kahn: A Biography*. New York, 1963.

Mead, Rita. *Henry Cowell's New Music, 1925–1936: The Society, the Music Editions, and the Recordings.* Studies in Musicology. Ann Arbor, Mich., 1981.

Mellers, Wilfrid. *Music in a New Found Land: Themes and Developments in the History of American Music.* New York, 1966.

Mueller, John H. *The American Symphony Orchestra: A Social History of Musical Taste.* Bloomington, Ind., 1951.

Murray, Albert. *Stomping the Blues.* New York, 1976.

Mussulman, Joseph. *Music in the Cultured Generation: A Social History of Music in America, 1870–1900.* Evanston, Ill., 1971.

Naipaul, V. S. *A Turn in the South.* New York, 1989.

Nathan, Hans. *Dan Emmett and the Rise of Early Negro Minstrelsy.* Norman, Okla., 1977. (First ed. 1962.)

———. *William Billings: Data and Documents.* Bibliographies in American Music, no. 2. Detroit, 1976.

Netzer, Dick. *The Subsidized Muse: Public Support for the Arts in the United States.* Cambridge, 1978.

New Grove. See Sadie, ed.

Noss, Luther. *Paul Hindemith in the United States.* Urbana, Ill., 1989.

Oja, Carol J. "Women Patrons and Crusaders for Modernist Music in New York: The 1920s." Typescript. Conservatory of Music, Brooklyn College.

Pavlakis, Christopher. *The American Music Handbook.* New York, 1974.

Pemberton, Carol A. *Lowell Mason: His Life and Work.* Studies in Musicology, no. 86. Ann Arbor, Mich., 1985.

Perkins, Charles C. *History of the Handel and Haydn Society, of Boston, Massachusetts.* Vol. 1. Boston, 1883–93. Reprint, New York, 1977.

Perlis, Vivian. *Charles Ives Remembered: An Oral History.* New Haven, 1974.

Pichierri, Louis. *Music in New Hampshire, 1623–1800.* New York, 1960.

Pratt, [Waldo Selden], ed. *American Music and Musicians.* [New York, 1920.] (Also issued as the *American Supplement* to *Grove's Dictionary of Music and Musicians* [New York, 1920].)

———, ed. *The New Encyclopedia of Music and Musicians.* New York, 1924.

Preston, Katherine K. "Travelling Opera Troupes in the United States, 1825–1860." Ph.D. diss., City University of New York, 1989.

Priestly, Brian. *Charlie Parker.* Jazz Masters series. Tunbridge Wells, England, 1984.

Ramsey, Frederick, Jr., and Charles Edward Smith, eds. *Jazzmen.* New York, 1939.

Rattenbury, Ken. *Duke Ellington: Jazz Composer.* London and New Haven, 1990.

Reisner, Robert George. *Bird: The Legend of Charlie Parker.* New York, 1962.

Rich, Arthur Lowndes. *Lowell Mason: "The Father of Singing among the Children."* Chapel Hill, N.C., 1946.

Risenhoover, Morris, and Robert T. Blackburn. *Artists as Professors: Conversations with Musicians, Painters, Sculptors.* Urbana, Ill., 1976.

Ritter, Frédéric Louis. *Music in America*. New York, 1883. New ed., New York, 1890. Reprint, New York, 1970.

————. *Music in England*. New York, 1883.

The Rockefeller Foundation. *President's Five-Year Review and Annual Report 1968*. New York, 1968.

Roell, Craig H. *The Piano in America, 1890–1940*. Chapel Hill, N.C., 1989.

Root, George Frederick. *The Story of a Musical Life: An Autobiography*. Cincinnati, 1891. Reprint, New York, 1973.

Rosenberg, Deena. *Fascinating Rhythm: The Collaboration of George and Ira Gershwin*. New York, 1991.

Rosenberg, Deena, and Bernard Rosenberg. *The Music Makers*. New York, 1979.

Rosenblum, Sandra P. *Performance Practices in Classic Piano Music: Their Principles and Applications*. Bloomington, Ind., 1988.

Rossiter, Frank R. *Charles Ives and His America*. New York, 1975.

Rothenbusch, Esther Heidi. "The Role of *Gospel Hymns Nos. 1 to 6* (1875–1894) in American Revivalism." Ph.D. diss., University of Michigan, 1991.

Rubin, Emmanuel. "Jeannette Meyers Thurber and the National Conservatory of Music." *American Music* 8 (1990): 294–325.

Russell, Charles Edward. *The American Orchestra and Theodore Thomas*. Garden City, N.Y., 1927.

Rust, Brian. *Jazz Records, A–Z, 1897–1942*. Rev. 5th ed. N.p., [1983].

————. *The American Dance Band Discography, 1917–1942*. New Rochelle, N.Y., 1975.

Rust, Brian, and Allen G. Debus. *The Complete Entertainment Discography from 1897 to 1942*. 2d ed. New York, 1989.

Ryan, Thomas. *Recollections of an Old Musician*. New York, 1899.

Sablosky, Irving. *American Music*. Chicago, 1969.

Sadie, Stanley, ed. *The New Grove Dictionary of Music and Musicians*. 20 vols. London, 1980. (*New Grove*.)

Sanjek, Russell. *American Popular Music and Its Business: The First Four Hundred Years*. Vol. 2: *From 1790 to 1909*. Vol. 3: *From 1900 to 1984*. New York, 1988.

————. *From Print to Plastic: Publishing and Promoting America's Popular Music, 1900–1980*. Institute for the Study of American Music Monographs, no. 20. Brooklyn, 1983.

Schabas, Ezra. *Theodore Thomas: America's Conductor and Builder of Orchestras, 1835–1905*. Urbana, Ill., 1989.

Schuller, Gunther. *Early Jazz: Its Roots and Development*. New York, 1968.

————. *The Swing Era: The Development of Jazz, 1930–1945*. New York, 1989.

Schwartz, Charles. *Gershwin: His Life and Music*. Indianapolis, 1973.

Sessions, Roger. "Music in a Business Economy." *Berkeley: A Journal of Modern Culture* (July 1948): 1–2, 7–8. Reprinted in *Roger Sessions on Music: Collected Essays*, edited by Edward T. Cone. Princeton, 1979.

————. *Roger Sessions on Music: Collected Essays.* Edited by Edward T. Cone. Princeton, 1979.

Shanet, Howard. *Philharmonic: A History of New York's Orchestra.* Garden City, N.Y., 1975.

Shapiro, Nat, and Nat Hentoff. *Hear Me Talkin' to Ya: The Story of Jazz as Told by the Men Who Made It.* New York, 1955.

Silverman, Kenneth. *A Cultural History of the American Revolution: Painting, Music, Literature, and the Theatre in the Colonies and the United States from the Treaty of Paris to the Inauguration of George Washington, 1763–1789.* New York, 1976.

Smith, Charles Edward, with Frederic Ramsey, Jr., Charles Payne Rogers, and William Russell. *The Jazz Record Book.* New York, 1944.

Solomon, Maynard. "Charles Ives: Some Questions of Veracity." *Journal of the American Musicological Society* 40 (1987): 443–70.

Sonneck, Oscar G. *Bibliography of Early Secular American Music.* Washington, D.C., 1905.

————. *A Bibliography of Early Secular American Music (18th Century).* New edition, revised and enlarged by William Treat Upton. Washington, D.C., 1945. Reprint, New York, 1964.

————. *Early Concert-Life in America (1731–1800).* Leipzig, 1907. Reprint, New York, 1978.

————. *Early Opera in America.* New York, 1915. Reprint, New York, 1963.

————. *Francis Hopkinson, the First American Poet-Composer (1737–1791), and James Lyon, Patriot, Preacher, Psalmodist (1735–1794): Two Studies in Early American Music.* Washington, D.C., 1905. Reprint, New York, 1967.

————. "German Influence on the Musical Life of America." In *Oscar Sonneck and American Music,* edited by William Lichtenwanger. Urbana, Ill., 1983.

————. "The History of Music in America: A Few Suggestions." In Oscar G. Sonneck, *Miscellaneous Studies in the History of Music.* New York, 1921. Reprint, New York, 1970.

————. *Miscellaneous Studies in the History of Music.* New York, 1921. Reprint, New York, 1970.

————. *Report on "The Star-Spangled Banner," "Hail Columbia," "America," "Yankee Doodle."* Washington, D.C., 1909. Reprint, New York, 1972.

Southern, Eileen. *Biographical Dictionary of Afro-American and African Musicians.* Westport, Conn., 1982.

————. "An Early Black Concert Company: The Hyers Sisters Combination." In *A Celebration of American Music: Words and Music in Honor of H. Wiley Hitchcock,* edited by Richard Crawford, R. Allen Lott, and Carol J. Oja. Ann Arbor, Mich., 1990.

————. *The Music of Black Americans.* 2d ed. New York, 1983.

Spalding, Walter Raymond. *Music at Harvard: A Historical Review of Men and Events.* New York, 1935. Reprint, New York, 1977.

Stevenson, Robert. "American Musical Scholarship: Parker to Thayer." *Nineteenth-Century Music* 1 (1977–78): 191–210.

———. "America's First Black Music Historian" [James Monroe Trotter.] *Journal of the American Musicological Society* 26 (1973): 383–404.

———. "English Sources for Indian Music until 1882." *Ethnomusicology* 17 (1973): 399–442.

———. *Philosophies of American Music History: A Lecture Delivered in the Whittall Pavilion of the Library of Congress, January 9, 1969*. Washington, D.C., 1970.

———. "Written Sources for Indian Music until 1882." *Ethnomusicology* 17 (1973): 1–40.

Stewart, Rex. *Boy Meets Horn*. Edited by Claire P. Gordon. Ann Arbor, Mich., 1991.

———. *Jazz Masters of the Thirties*. New York, 1972.

Stoner, Thomas. " 'The New Gospel of Music': Arthur Farwell's Vision of Democratic Music in America." *American Music* 9 (1991): 183–208.

Strunk, W. Oliver. "State and Resources of Musicology in the United States." American Council of Learned Societies, *Bulletin*, No. 19 (1932).

Temperley, Nicholas. *The Music of the English Parish Church*. Vol. 1. Cambridge, 1979.

Thomas, Theodore. *A Musical Autobiography*. Edited by George P. Upton. Chicago, 1905. Reprint, New York, 1964.

Thomson, Virgil. *The State of Music*. 2d ed., revised. New York, 1962.

———. *Virgil Thomson*. New York, 1966.

———. *A Virgil Thomson Reader*. Boston, 1981.

Toll, Robert C. *Blacking Up: The Minstrel Show in Nineteenth-Century America*. New York, 1974.

Tucker, Mark. *Ellington: The Early Years*. Urbana, Ill., 1991.

Varèse, Louise. *Varèse: A Looking-Glass Diary*. Vol. 1: *1883–1928*. New York, 1972.

Ware, W. Porter, and Thaddeus C. Lockard, Jr. *P. T. Barnum Presents Jenny Lind: The American Tour of the Swedish Nightingale*. Baton Rouge, La., 1980.

Webster's New International Dictionary of the English Language. 2d ed., unabridged. Springfield, Mass., 1953.

Whitburn, Joel. *Joel Whitburn's Pop Memories 1890–1954: The History of American Popular Music*. Menomonee Falls, Wis., 1986.

Wilder, Alec. *American Popular Song: The Great Innovators, 1900–1950*. Edited and with an introduction by James T. Maher. New York, 1972.

Williams, George W. "Early Organists at St. Philip's, Charleston." *South Carolina Historical Magazine* 54 (1953): 83–87.

Williams, Martin. *Jazz in Its Time*. New York, 1989.

———. *The Jazz Tradition*. New and revised ed. Oxford, 1983.

Wolfe, Richard J. *Early American Music Engraving and Printing: A History of Music Publishing in America from 1787 to 1825 with Commentary on Earlier and Later Practices*. Urbana, Ill., 1980.

———. *Secular Music in America, 1801–1825: A Bibliography.* 3 vols. New York, 1964.

"Worldwide Transmutations of American Popular Music." In International Musicological Society, *Report of the Twelfth Congress, Berkeley, 1977,* edited by Daniel Heartz and Bonnie Wade. Kassel, 1981.

Yellin, Victor Fell. *Chadwick: Yankee Composer.* Washington, D.C., 1990.

Zuck, Barbara. *A History of Musical Americanism.* Studies in Musicology, no. 19. Ann Arbor, Mich., 1980.

EDITIONS AND COLLECTIONS OF MUSIC

Billings, William. *The Complete Works of William Billings.* Edited by Karl Kroeger and Hans Nathan. 4 vols. Charlottesville, Va., 1977–90.

———. *The Continental Harmony.* Boston, 1794.

———. *The New-England Psalm-Singer.* Boston, [1770].

———. *The Singing Master's Assistant.* Boston, 1778.

Crawford, Richard, ed. *The Civil War Songbook: Complete Original Sheet Music for Thirty-Seven Songs.* New York, 1977.

———, ed. *The Core Repertory of Early American Psalmody.* Recent Researches in American Music, vols. 11 and 12. Madison, Wis., 1984.

Flagg, Josiah. *A Collection of the Best Psalm Tunes.* Boston, 1764.

[Jocelin, Simeon, and Amos Doolittle.] *The Chorister's Companion.* New Haven, 1782.

Playford's English Dancing Master 1651. A Facsimile Reprint, with an Introduction, Bibliography, and Notes. Edited by Margaret Dean-Smith. London, 1957.

Reinagle, Alexander. *The Philadelphia Sonatas.* Edited by Robert Hopkins. Recent Researches in American Music, vol. 5. Madison, Wis., 1978.

Root, George F. *The Haymakers.* Edited by Dennis R. Martin. Recent Researches in American Music, vols. 9 and 10. Madison, Wis., 1984.

A Selection of Sacred Harmony. 3d ed. Philadelphia, 1790.

Silber, Irwin, comp. and ed. *Songs America Voted By with the Words and Music That Won and Lost Elections and Influenced the Democratic Process.* Harrisburg, Pa., 1971.

The Worcester Collection of Sacred Harmony. Worcester, Mass., 1786.

RECORDINGS

The Birth of "The Rhapsody in Blue": Paul Whiteman's Historic Aeolian Hall Concert of 1924. Reconstructed and conducted by Maurice Peress. MusicMasters recording MMD 20113X/2011 4 T.

Duke Ellington 1940. With notes by Lawrence Gushee. Smithsonian Collection recording DPM 20351, 1978.

An Experiment in Modern Music: Paul Whiteman at Aeolian Hall. With notes by Thornton Hagert. Smithsonian Collection recording DMM 2-0518.

George and Ira Gershwin's "Girl Crazy." Elektra Nonesuch CD, 9 79250-2, 1990. Includes program booklet.

The George and Ira Gershwin Songbook. Ella Fitzgerald. Verve recording VE-2-2525.

The Smithsonian Collection of Classic Jazz. Compiled by Martin Williams. 1973. Revised, 1987.

MANUSCRIPTS

George Chadwick to W. L. Hubbard. 13 September 1907. William Lines Hubbard Papers.

Frank Damrosch to W. L. Hubbard. 29 September 1907. William Lines Hubbard Papers.

Duke Ellington, "Diminuendo in Blue" and "Crescendo in Blue." Duke Ellington Collection. Smithsonian Institution, Washington, D.C.

William Lines Hubbard Papers, Archives of the Peabody Institute of The Johns Hopkins University, Baltimore.

Oscar G. Sonneck, manuscript notes. Library of Congress, Washington, D.C.

INDEX

Except for Gershwin's "I Got Rhythm," which is indexed in two separate entries under its title, all compositions are listed alphabetically by title in the entry "Compositions" and all recordings in the entry "Recordings." For Boston, Chicago, and New York, readers will find not only a general entry for the city but also separate entries, by city, for musical institutions and venues in each. Italic page references denote musical examples.

Compositor:	Impressions, A Division of Edwards Brothers, Inc.
Music Setter:	Dennis Riley
Text:	10/13 Baskerville
Display:	Bernhard Cursive Bold, Baskerville
Printer:	Edwards Brothers, Inc.
Binder:	Edwards Brothers, Inc.